The Life of
Thomas More

PETER ACKROYD

THE LIFE OF
THOMAS
MORE

Chatto & Windus
London

First published 1998

1 3 5 7 9 10 8 6 4 2

© Peter Ackroyd 1998

Peter Ackroyd has asserted his right
under the Copyright, Designs and Patents Act 1988
to be identified as the author of this work

First published in the United Kingdom in 1998 by Chatto & Windus
Random House, 20 Vauxhall Bridge Road, London SW1V 2SA

Random House Australia (Pty) Limited
20 Alfred Street, Milsons Point, Sydney,
New South Wales 2061, Australia

Random House New Zealand Limited
18 Poland Road, Glenfield,
Auckland 10, New Zealand

Random House South Africa (Pty) Limited
Endulini, 5A Jubilee Road, Parktown 2193, South Africa

Random House UK Limited Reg. No. 954009

A CIP catalogue record for this book is available from the British Library

Papers used by Random House UK Limited are natural,
recyclable products made from wood grown in sustainable forests.
The manufacturing processes conform to the environmental
regulations of the country of origin.

ISBN 1-85619-711-5

Typeset by Deltatype Ltd, Birkenhead, Merseyside

Printed and bound in Great Britain
by Mackays of Chatham PLC

For Thomas Wright

Contents

List of Illustrations

Acknowledgements

I should like to express my obligation and gratitude to the editors of the *Complete Works of St. Thomas More*, as well as to the Yale University Press, which has published the fourteen volumes of that enterprise. Theirs is a magisterial work of scholarship, and although many of the writings are available elsewhere the Yale edition has become the indispensable companion to More studies. The other major work, in this context, is *The Correspondence of Sir Thomas More*, edited by E. F. Rogers and published by Princeton University Press. I also wish to express my thanks to the institutions and libraries that have harboured me over the last three years, in particular to the North Library of the British Library and to the London Library. I would like to thank Dr David Starkey for his suggestive advice. I must register a more private debt to my assistants, Thomas Wright and Carl Dennison.

I

This Dark World

THE infant was taken, within a week of its birth, to the
precincts of the church; the child of wrath must be reformed
into the image of God, 'the servant of the fiend' made into 'a
son of joy'.[1] At the church-door the priest asked the midwife if the
child were male or female, and then made a sign of the cross on the
infant's forehead, breast and right hand. He placed some salt in the
baby's mouth according to custom; then the priest exorcised the devil
from its body with a number of prayers, and pronounced baptism as
the sole means 'to obtain eternal grace by spiritual regeneration'.[2]
The priest spat in his left hand and touched the ears and nose of the
child with his saliva. Let the nose be open to the odour of sweetness.
It was time to enter the church itself, the priest taking the right hand
of the new-born child who had with the salt and saliva been granted
the station of a catechumen.

The litanies of the saints were pronounced over the baptismal font;
the priest then divided the water with his right hand and cast it in the
four directions of the cross. He breathed three times upon it and then
spilled wax in a cruciform pattern. He divided the holy water with a
candle, before returning the taper to the cleric beside him. Oil and
chrism were added, with a long rod or spoon, and the child could
now be baptised. Thomas More, what seekest thou? The sponsors
replied for the infant, Baptism. Dost thou wish to be baptised? I
wish. The child was given to the priest, who immersed him three
times in the water. He was then anointed with chrism and wrapped
in a chrismal robe. Thomas More, receive a white robe, holy and
unstained, which thou must bring before the tribunal of Our Lord
Jesus Christ, that thou mayest have eternal life and live for ever and
ever. The candle was lit and placed in the child's right hand, thus
inaugurating a journey through this dark world which ended when,

I

during the last rites, a candle was placed in the right hand of the dying man with the prayer, 'The Lord is my Light and my Salvation, whom shall I fear?' Whom shall this particular child fear, when it was believed by the Church that the whole truth and meaning of baptism was achieved in the act of martyrdom? 'Baptism and suffering for the sake of Christ', according to a second-century bishop, are the two acts which bring full 'remission of sins'.[3]

It was considered best to baptise the child on the same day as its birth, if such haste were practicable, since an infant unbaptised would be consigned to limbo after its death. To leave this world in a state of original sin was to take a course to that eternal dwelling, *Limbus puerorum*, suspended between heaven, hell and purgatory. There the little unbaptised souls would dwell in happy ignorance beside the more formidable and haunting *Limbus patrum*, which contained the souls of Noah, Moses and Isaiah together with (in Dante's epic) Virgil, Aristotle, Socrates and all the good men who lived on earth before the birth, death and resurrection of Jesus. Adam had already been dragged from this place at the time of Christ's crucifixion, but there was continual debate within the Church about the consequences of denying new-born children the eternal comfort of paradise. Could a child be saved by the desire, the *votum*, of its parents? Thomas More himself would eventually concede only that 'those infantes be dampned onely to the payne of losse of heauen'.[4]

In various late medieval pictures of baptism, in manuscripts and devotional manuals, the priest stands with his surplice and stole beside the font. Sometimes he seems to be balancing the infant in the palm of his hand, yet the child is so unnaturally large and alert for such an early stage in its life that we can only assume it acquired mental consciousness with its spiritual renovation. A clerk with a surplice stands behind the priest, while two sponsors and the child's father are generally seen beside the font. In some depictions of this first of the seven sacraments, an image of the dying Christ hangs behind the human scene. But the mother was rarely, if ever, present.

In the more pious households, she would have worn a girdle made out of manuscript prayer rolls in the last stages of her pregnancy, and it was customary in labour to invoke the name of St Margaret as well as the Blessed Virgin. She remained secluded after giving birth, and two or three weeks later was led out to be 'churched' or purified. When she was taken to the church, her head was covered by a handkerchief, as a veil, and she was advised not to look up at the sun or the sky. She knelt in the church while the priest blessed her and assured her, in the words of Psalm 121, that 'the sun shall not burn her by day, nor the moon by night'.[5] It was a ceremony both to celebrate the birth of the child and to give thanks for the survival of the mother. This is the late fifteenth-century world into which Thomas More was baptised.

Pretty Plays of Childhood

THOMAS More's birth was noted by his father upon a blank page at the back of a copy of Geoffrey of Monmouth's *Historia Regum Britanniae*; for a lawyer John More was remarkably inexact in his references to that natal year, and the date has been moved from 1477 to 1478 and back again. Although it is of no real consequence to the drama of More's life, the most likely day remains 7 February 1478. He was born between two and three o'clock in the early hours of Saturday morning, in the heart of London. Milk Street is in the ward of Cripplegate Within, bordering upon that of Cheap. It has been supposed that More was baptised either in the church of St Mary-le-Bow or of St Giles, but they are both in other wards; the ritual was probably performed in St Lawrence Jewry or in the parish church of Milk Street, St Mary Magdalen, now long destroyed and forgotten. If you walk down that narrow thoroughfare today, between the banks and the companies which have their home in the 'City', you will see a small statue of the Virgin lodged about thirty feet above the pavement.

Milk Street was part of a fashionable and prosperous ward: in the last quarter of the fifteenth century there were seventeen mercers, or merchants, residing in Cripplegate itself.[1] The great London chronicler and antiquarian John Stow describes the street as 'so called of milk sold there; there be many fair houses for wealthy merchants and other[s]'.[2] More was the scion of a wealthy and influential family; the churches closest to his house showed visible evidence of that urban power. St Lawrence Jewry, a few yards to the north of Milk Street, near the Guildhall, was as ornate and as sumptuous as any parish church in London. Its inventory at the time of its despoliation in the 1540s listed altar cloths of silk and velvet and sarcanet, robes and vestments of damask or linen, chalices and cups, great curtains and candlesticks. It was a church where many merchants were buried: nine are mentioned by name in Stow's *Survey*. At the other end of Milk Street, just before the corner of Cheapside, stood the little parish church of Mary Magdalen: apart from mayors and other city officials, its graves mentioned by Stow are also those of merchants. More was born within an urban tradition as closely packed and as circuitous as the streets of Cripplegate or Cheap wards. The sponsors who were his witnesses at the baptismal font were the visible tokens of his inheritance, but behind them we can see in emblematic array other figures rising up within the main body of the church – the mercers in their livery of red and violet, the members of other London guilds, the lawyers and the sheriffs, who composed the child's destiny. Beyond them, too, we will recognise the officers of the courts and of the royal Court, and then further still the circles representing the clerks and officials of the Catholic Church, all of them bound together in a complicated network of affiliations and connections, evincing a range of duties, favours, services and obligations which make up their 'affinity'. These are the true sponsors at the baptism of Thomas More.

It was customary to give a single name to the baptised child, and More's parents chose one which was as familiar to them as to every other Londoner. More's maternal grandfather had the same name, but it was also the defining name of an urban cult. Thomas Becket was still the great saint of the city, the martyr and subsequent worker of miracles. He had been born just twenty yards from More's own house in Milk Street, near the corner of Ironmonger Lane and Cheapside, and it is a striking coincidence that these two Catholic Londoners – both martyred and canonised – should have been, some centuries apart, almost nextdoor neighbours.

So the name Thomas was explicable, but the origins of More's surname cannot be so easily discovered. If such names derive from some sense of place, then the great moors or marshes around London might find an echo here. It is also a name upon which a number of puns were constructed. 'More' could be the 'Moor' or black Ethiop and Desiderius Erasmus, the Dutch humanist who became his close companion, sometimes called him 'Niger'. On More's family arms, there was the head of a 'blackamoor', and the same device appeared upon his seal when he was under-treasurer of England. On his crest, too, were 'moorcocks'. '*Morus*' was also the Latin term for the mulberry tree, and Thomas More would plant one of these 'wise' trees in his garden at Chelsea. He was aware of the power of names, therefore, to create or evoke their own set of circumstances. '*Morus*' is fool and '*Mors*' is death. Erasmus's title for his most celebrated work *Moriae encomium* – 'In Praise of Folly' – was designed also to praise More, in whose house the book was written. More himself invented puns upon his surname – *Memento Mori aeris* (Remember More's money) might become *Memento morieris* (The remembrance of death) – in a transition like that within the contemporaneous music of Lambe or Fayrfax. Yet the suggestivity of the name created effects beyond punning: *Mors* and *Morus* were the syllables of More's own destiny. Characteristically he meditated upon death and the passing shadow of the world, while also he 'played' the fool with those who were closest to him. What is in a name? For the sake of authenticity to the period as well as to the man, it ought also to be noted that there were in London eight men with the name of Thomas More in the years from 1400 to 1550.[3]

Since his death came to define him, his first biographers were happy to provide suitable anecdotes for the origin of a martyr. His mother is supposed to have dreamed of all her children, engraved upon her marriage ring, but the name and likeness of Thomas shone brighter than all the rest. Apparently More was told this by his father, which suggests familial expectations as great as filial obligations. There are more obvious examples of hagiography. He was being carried across a river by his nurse, in his early days, when her horse stumbled; the nurse threw the infant over a hedge in order to save him from falling into the water. When she reached dry ground, 'she found the babe lying unhurt and laughing'.[4] This is all in the tradition of the *Golden Legend* and the other stories of saints which would have surrounded More as a child. The real circumstances of his early life and inheritance are more interesting, if perhaps less remarkable.

More's paternal grandfather was a baker, the son-in-law of a London brewer, and his maternal grandfather, Thomas Graunger, was a tallow chandler.[5] Both grandfathers were members of their guilds – Graunger was a warden of the Tallow Chandlers' Company – as well as citizens of London. The fact that within four generations they produced judges, landed gentlemen and even a Lord Chancellor is not necessarily surprising. The greatest men in London had been merchants for three centuries; Richard Whittington had been a mercer, and William Caxton still was a member of the fraternity.

They were the 'most worshipful' of Londoners, amassing large fortunes, helping to control City government, directing the patterns of commerce, and in time often becoming associated with the king in various financial or advisory capacities. Thomas More would move easily all his life among the most powerful and wealthy citizens; he was, after all, one of them.

It might be tempting to describe him as an integral part of London's 'aristocracy', but that would be anachronistic in a hierarchical society where degree and rank were not applied in a random or metaphorical way. The world of More was one of status rather than of class, where the inheritance of feudalism and authoritarian religion pre-eminently demanded the virtues of loyalty and duty. In later life he described himself (in almost conventional terms for a London citizen) as being born of a family noted for its honour rather than its illustriousness. This is not some token phrase, however, but a true definition of what the London merchants believed to be their proper role and destiny. The most powerful citizens could attain only baronial rank, and were therefore inferior in degree to 'noblemen of the true noble blood'.[6] Yet for Londoners such as More, true virtue sprang not from high birth but from honesty and piety. In his translation of the life of Pico della Mirandola, More wrote that it was the possession of such virtues which produced honour, 'as a shadow folowith a bodi'.[7] Virtue, in other words, cannot be inherited; it is not a simple attribute of rank. The City merchants also knew that the nobility had no exclusive claim to wealth and influence.

Consider the case of Thomas More's father. John More was sixteen years old when his own father died, but he and his five siblings were not reduced to any state of orphaned wretchedness. William More was a 'baker' on the grandest scale; in his will he noted that the Earl of Northumberland still owed him the very large sum of £87 16s 2d 'for bread bought of me'.[8] And, as so often happened, William More had married well – indeed the resources of the bride or the bride's family were the most important aspects of any marriage. His wife, Johanna Joye, was the daughter of a prosperous brewer and the granddaughter of John Leycester, formerly a clerk of Chancery. Leycester was a gentleman, entitled to bear arms, and a man of some wealth with properties both in London and in Hertfordshire. So John More was from his earliest years part of a world in which the merchants and citizens of London were acquiring land and money in equal proportions.

The father of Thomas More moved easily enough, therefore, from trade to law. At the age of twenty-three or twenty-four, at about the time of his marriage, he was admitted to Lincoln's Inn. Social historians of this period have often observed that London lawyers had more opportunities of acquiring land than London merchants, but John More was a landowner by inheritance. His main business seems to have been with various City companies and guilds, and he became known as a lawyer with connections and influences which could expedite the general affairs of London merchants. This is also the milieu to which Thomas More would most easily adapt himself. In later years John More would be raised to the rank of 'serjeant', before joining, as a judge, the Court of Common Pleas and eventually the Court of the King's Bench.

It would be unhelpful to apply some nineteenth-century model of a member of the 'middle class' thrusting forward and upward. Merchants and lawyers could become gentlemen and landed gentry, but the actual nature of the society was not thereby changed. The formulae of rank and hierarchy, based like medieval architectonics upon subordination and symmetry, remained intact. In a closed system, everyone has a determined place. In the Act of Apparel 1483, for example, purple and velvet were forbidden to lawyers; in 1486 it was decreed that the hems of livery gowns were to be 'one foot above the soles' of shoes.[9] The colour and material of dress were also of paramount importance in a society which was established upon display and spectacle. Of course there were exceptions, but generally and characteristically each member of the body politic remained within the appropriate estate, or order, or degree, just as the head, eyes and limbs of the body cannot be interchanged. John More, as judge, was one of the eyes. The image of the human body was of central importance in the political and religious discourse of the period; it might be related to medieval cabbalism, but it also emerges in Thomas More's own epigrams upon the perfect kingdom.

John More married Agnes Graunger in the church of St Giles, Cripplegate; there is no name in late medieval London without its own particular resonance and, according to John Stow, Cripplegate was the site where the lame were healed when the body of St Edmund the martyr was brought into the city. They were married on 24 April 1474, the Vigil of St Mark the Evangelist, John More being described as 'Gent.'.[10] Agnes Graunger was the first of More's four wives, but it is likely that she bore all of his six children. Thomas More rarely discussed his siblings, and two of them are never mentioned by him. It is likely that they were part of that infant mortality which had provoked such concern for early baptism. At an appropriate age Thomas More's younger sister, Elizabeth, married a lawyer; his elder sister in turn married another lawyer, who later became a coroner. They had remained, in other words, within the connections of a larger official family. He had a younger brother who also survived: the young John More acted as an occasional secretary to Thomas More, but died at some time in his thirties. Agnes Graunger herself died young, although the cause and circumstances of her death are unknown. Her last child was born in the autumn of 1482, and it is possible that she died in the great epidemic of sweating sickness which visited London three years later. But, in a volume entitled *Ancient Funerall Monuments*, there is a description of a tomb in St Michael Basings Hall, in the ward of Coleman Street; the Latin epitaph upon it commemorates an Agnes More who died in 1499. This stray token of mortality is inconclusive, but it can be inferred that the mother of Thomas More died at some point in his youth or early manhood. How else would John More have been able to marry on three subsequent occasions? It might also explain one of More's early Latin epigrams, translated from the Greek, which declares that even a loving stepmother brings no good fortune to her stepson.[11] It may even be that the relatively early death of his mother engendered in More that self-protectiveness which was so marked a feature of his temperament.

Upon his own epitaph Thomas More described his father as '*Homo civilis, suavis, innocens, mitis, misericors, aequus, et integer*'; the Latin is clear enough hardly to need translation, but it is interesting to note that More emphasises his qualities of sweetness, affability and compassion. The description does not fit later accounts of apparent miserliness and strictness; but the disparity need not yet be resolved. It is typical, in any case, that Thomas More preferred to tell worldly anecdotes about his father in which the element of judgement is suspended. 'I have heard my father merrily say every man is at the choice of his wife, that ye should put your hand into a blind bag of snakes and eels together, seven snakes for one eel, yet would I ween reckon it a perilous choice to take up one at adventure though you had made your special word to speed well.'[12] It is not a sympathetic remark from a man who was married four times, but caustic comments about wives were part of the repertoire of medieval humour. A second anecdote, again retold by Thomas More, has a similar import; his father had said 'that there is but one shrewde wyfe in the worlde, but he sayth in dede that euery man weneth he hath her, & that that one is his owne'.[13] 'Shrewd' here, in one of those obliquities of meaning which render some medieval terms ambiguous, means 'shrewish' rather than perspicacious.

Yet marriage was not supposed to be a matter of 'courtly love', and there is no doubt that John More prospered. The property in Hertfordshire bequeathed to him was substantial enough for anyone who wished to think of himself as 'a landed gentleman' and who had his own coat of arms. Gobions, or Gibions, or Gubynnes, or Gubbeannes (the orthography of the period, before the full impact of the printed word, was not exact) was a 'capital messuage'[14] or main house in the parish of North Mimms, with adjoining orchards and fields as well as lands in neighbouring parishes. Little is known about the More dwelling in Milk Street itself, except that it must have been one of the 'fair houses' mentioned by John Stow. The antiquarian describes London dwellings of stone, but most were of wooden construction; others were of mixed type with stone gateways and cellars, timber-framed walls of lath and plaster, and tiled roofs.

We know of another successful merchant in the parish of St Mary Magdalen, Milk Street: James Olney, who had eight rooms 'for bedrooms and parlours'.[15] Imagine, then, a gateway on Milk Street which led into a square courtyard roughly twenty-five feet by twenty-five feet. On the left side was a single-storeyed hall, which was the principal room of the house. It was the chamber for dining and entertaining, with its long table and chairs, with its screens and tapestries and candles for both decoration and comfort; it would have been heated by a fireplace, or by a brazier, and the fire would have lit up the 'steyned cloths' hanging upon the walls. In this room, too, was placed the cupboard of plate; these were the most expensive and important items in any household, and in the hall of John More we would expect to see goblets, basins, ewers, patens and great spoons glowing in the light. Furniture was of a plain sort, with chairs and stools, small tables and chests, placed upon the rushes which acted as a covering for the floor. Here, too, would be sensed all the odours of timber and stone and smoke, of dried herbs and roasted meats.

Beyond the hall were the kitchen, pantry and butlery – even, sometimes, a parlour, where the family might dine together. But the other rooms were in the adjoining wing of the house. Earlier in the century it had been customary for families to share one bedroom, with a canopied and curtained bed for the master and the mistress, and trestle beds or mattresses for everyone else. But by the late fifteenth century two bedrooms were often used by the family (the servants slept in the attic spaces), and the surviving inventories of featherbeds, blankets, sheets, pillows and counterpanes suggest that they were designed to be as luxurious as possible; there were also various 'chambres', 'orioles' (small rooms or bays) and 'solars' (upper rooms). Such wealthy late medieval households lived in comfort. Their rooms were decorated with tapestries or stained cloths, while woodwork and wooden panelling were painted in delicate shades; halls and parlours were wainscoted, and sometimes depicted figures out of the Bible or classical legend. In the courtyard there was space for bright flowers and herbs, vines and figs and laurel trees; geese and chicken were kept here and, in one account, there is mention of 'six water potts of tyn for byrds to drynke of'.[16]

The young Thomas More, then, was raised in a prosperous and comfortable household. The prose of his maturity contains allusions to infant games and childhood ballads. Even in the anxious and bitter period of his polemical writing, he invokes a 'good chylde' playing such 'prety playes . . . as chyrystone mary bone, bokyll pyt, spurne poynt, cobnutte or quaytyng'.[17] 'Cobnutte' remains as the children's game of 'conkers', and the game of quoits or 'quaytyng' still flourishes. It is clear that little children also played with cherrystones and used marrow bones as bats or markers. In another place he writes of children shooting arrows high into the air[18] and in fact quite young boys were given bows and arrows with which to practise their skills. There are metaphors of archery throughout More's writings, with his references to 'a full shotte', the 'but' and the 'prycke'.[19] It is hard to imagine his ever being a good archer, however, let alone an enthusiastic player of 'foteball', with an inflated pig's bladder used as a ball, or of 'cokesteel' with a cock buried up to its neck in the ground and used as a target for missiles. It is easier to see him playing less ferocious games in the courtyard, 'as chyldren make castelles of tyle shardes'.[20]

There is a charming reminiscence of a late fifteenth-century childhood written by a twelve-year-old schoolboy, in which he recalls how 'I was wont to lye styll abedde tyll it was forth dais, delitynge myselfe in slepe and ease. The sone sent in his beamys at the wyndowes that gave me lyght instede of a candle.' And what did the young boy see around him, on these mornings five hundred years ago? He used 'to beholde the rofe, the beamys, and the rafters of my chambre, and loke on the clothes that the chambre was hanged with!' Then he 'callede whom me list to lay my gere redy to me' and 'my brekefaste was brought to my beddys side'.[21] This pampered childhood is enough to dispel quaint illusions about the necessary hardship of fifteenth-century life. There are other memories, too. John Colet, who became More's religious mentor, remembered the painted dolls and rocking-horses of his infancy. In John Heywood's interlude *Wytty and Wyttles*, a child remarks that 'All my pleasure is in catchynge of byrdes/And makynge of snowballys and throwyng the same';[22] he failed to mention skating, using the bones of sheep for skates, which was another popular winter pastime.

More had his own reminiscences, which are expressed by a protagonist in his *Dialogue of Comfort*: 'My mother had whan I was a litell boye, a good old woman that toke hede to her children, they callid her mother mawd.' One can imagine her in close cap and stuff gown. 'She was wont whan she sat by the fier with vs, to tell vs that were children many childish tales.'[23] He then recounts one of the fireside stories in which a fox, Father Raynard, hears the confessions of a wolf and an ass. The moral is concerned with the problems of an over-scrupulous conscience, but includes the recognisable details of city life – the pigs sleeping in 'new straw' and the goose in 'the powlters shop' with its feathers 'redy pluckyd'.[24] It is not a tale out of Aesop, since the Greek fabulist could hardly have anticipated priests or rosary beads 'almost as bigg as bolles',[25] but it is an animal narrative of the same stable. Mother Mawd was clearly devout, also, and the devotion of More's own nature may have first sprung from such close childhood influence.

During More's childhood, in 1479 and again in 1485, there was 'an hugh mortalyte & deth of people' in London; it was the 'sweating sickness' or 'English sweat', which, in the autumn of the latter year, may have claimed the lives of his mother and of two siblings. Two years later the plague visited Westminster and caused 'grete deth'.[26] Certainly his abiding and central preoccupation with death was shared by his contemporaries. The reports of these epidemics come from the London chronicles of the period, and in the pages of these long forgotten memorials the customary life of the city around the young More is also restored – men hanged and then burned for robbing a church and despoiling the blessed sacrament, bills fastened upon church doors, the gates being shut against riotous assemblies outside the walls, new towers and conduits and weathercocks being erected, a world of portents and providential signs, lavish spectacle and continual urban improvement. It was also the period that witnessed the short reign of the supposed 'crippleback', Richard III, who is presumed to have murdered the young heirs of Edward IV in Thomas More's own fifth year.

Henry Tudor was in turn the victor on Bosworth Field in 1485, More's seventh year, but those dynastic struggles or 'Wars of the Roses' did not necessarily play any formative role in City trade and politics. It has been variously estimated that the amount of actual warfare in the years between 1455 and 1487 was twelve or fourteen months, and fifteenth-century London was a relatively peaceful and increasingly prosperous city. The authorities generally ensured that they were seen to be on the 'right side' on the appropriate occasions, and supported whichever monarch emerged from the processes of fate, time and faction. John More himself is an interesting example of the alliance which might be formed between the City and the royal court; it is clear, from his will and other evidence, that he had an especial loyalty towards Edward IV, in whose reign the young lawyer rose to prominence. It was in Edward's reign, too, that the heralds bestowed on More a coat of arms. It is also clear that he had a particular connection with Archbishop Morton, who served Edward IV and, subsequently, Henry VII. The precise nature of their relationship cannot now be uncovered, and might well have resisted analysis at the time; it remained a matter of mutual services and obligations, the filaments of which over the years created a network of amity and trust. Indeed, it is much easier to chart John More's legal career in the years of Thomas More's childhood. He was involved for some years on a City body concerned with the maintenance and development of London Bridge but, while specialising in London affairs, he was also ascending the hierarchy of Lincoln's Inn. He was in turn master of the revels, butler and marshal; these posts may sound absurd or servile, but they were of paramount importance in the good administration and reputation of the Inn. The 'master of the revels', for example, was not some figure out of Rabelais but an official in charge of its most elaborate and prestigious annual ceremonies. Thomas More himself accepted the post even when he was serving as Lord Chancellor of England.

There is an account of England in this period, written by a Venetian diplomat, which is of particular interest for its depiction of London manners during Thomas More's earlier years; certainly it helps to put in context More's own distinctive and developing temperament. The English are 'handsome and well-proportioned' but are also 'great lovers of themselves ... whenever they see a handsome foreigner they say that he looks like an Englishman ... they all from time immemorial wear very fine clothes.'[27] We will find More to be lacking in personal vanity of that kind, and indeed sometimes emphasising the carelessness of his dress and deportment. 'They take great pleasure in having a quantity of excellent victuals ... when they mean to drink a great deal, they go to the tavern, and this is done not only by the men but by ladies of distinction.'[28] In later life, More was notoriously abstemious with his food and drink. But it is appropriate to end a chapter concerning More's childhood in London with the description of an encounter in a hall or street: 'they have the incredible courtesy of remaining with their heads uncovered, with an admirable grace, whilst they talk to each other'.[29] He mentions Cheapside, too, where 'there are fifty-two goldsmiths' shops, so rich and full of silver vessels'.[30] This, as we shall see, is the street down which the young Thomas More made his way to school.

III

St Anthony's Pigs

THOMAS More was enrolled at St Anthony's, in Threadneedle Street. Lessons began at six in the morning, and in winter he would have taken his own candle-light with him. He has a description of a mother telling her son also to 'take thy brede & butter with the'.[1] The schoolboy was dressed in hose and doublet, since he was considered to be a smaller version of the adult male, and he carried a leather satchel upon his back, which contained 'a pennar and an ynke horne ... a penn knyff ... a payre of tabullys';[2] the 'pennar' was a quill-holder and 'tabullys' were writing boards. While the child is being kissed upon the threshold there is the opportunity to leave the candle-lights and rush lanterns of a London winter for the brightness of a spring morning.

On his customary journey of a few hundred yards from Milk Street to Threadneedle Street the young More passed the church of St Mary Magdalen near the corner of Milk Street and Cheapside; there was a cross in its churchyard which was 'worshipped by the parishioners there as crosses be commonly worshipped in other churchyards'.[3] When he walked into Cheapside itself, or more accurately 'West Chepe', there stood in the middle of the thoroughfare a tall water fountain made of stone and known as the 'Standard'; here for two hundred years the citizens had filled their basins and pitchers with water, lately being taken from the River Tybourn. It was also a place of execution, and in More's childhood sentences of beheading and burning were exacted on this spot only a few feet from his house. Violent death was not hidden from the gaze of children. On the other side of West Chepe, beyond the Standard, stood the church of St Mary-le-Bow. The famous Bow Bell was rung each evening for curfew; this was the time for the shutting of the city gates and, to the delight of the apprentices, the closing of the shops. In More's childhood the tower was actually being rebuilt and was not completed until 1512 but still the bell tolled, according to season, at eight or nine o'clock. The tower had been brought forward to front 'West Chepe', and beside it stood a stone building with a gallery on its first floor known as the Seldam or the 'Crown slid'. It had been erected at the command of Edward III as a convenient site from which royal guests might watch the various pageants and triumphs that proceeded down Cheapside on ritual occasions. But by More's time it had been leased out as business premises and was itself surrounded by other 'slids', sheds or shops. These were owned principally by mercers and haberdashers, together with the gold-smiths mentioned by the Venetian diplomat. The old 'Chepe' had been crowded with street-stalls and street-sellers, but much of its atmosphere still survived in the late fifteenth century. With the ancient and familiar cries of 'satin!', 'silks!', 'foreign cloth!' and 'courchiefs!', it is appropriate to imagine the surroundings of an eastern bazaar or *souk*; the fifteenth-century city was closer to contemporary Marrakesh than to any version of post-Restoration London.

Thomas More turned left and walked down this relatively wide thoroughfare of mud and cobbles towards Poultry and Threadneedle Street. On his left hand he passed St Laurence Lane and Ironmonger Lane, among stone buildings with figures placed in niches, gilded and painted signs, timbers decorated with carved fruits or flowers, painted walls and gables, roofs of red tile, wrought iron poles bearing lamps, piles of dung and chips from firewood which had been chopped in the street before being taken indoors. In St Laurence Lane there was a large inn for travellers, known as Blossoms Inn, and in Ironmonger Lane there was a small church named St Martin Pomary on account of the apple trees which had grown in the vicinity. The whole quarter had once been the home of saddlers, tanners and tallow chandlers, but mercers had displaced them in one of those changes of commercial activity which are explicable only in terms of the city's own organic and instinctive growth.

There was, however, one other important former inhabitant. On the corner of Ironmonger Lane and Cheapside had stood the site of Thomas Becket's birthplace, now his church of St Thomas of Acre or Acon. So the young More passed each morning the memorial to the most famous of all London saints and martyrs. He proceeded east, past the Mitre tavern and the church of St Mary Colechurch which was 'built upon a wall above ground, so that men are forced to go to ascend up thereunto by certain steps';[4] it took its name from the coal and charcoal trades, like that of the smiths and ironmongers themselves, which had grown up around it. As he passed Old Jewry (from which the Jews had been expelled two hundred years before) he would have seen on his right hand, in the middle of Cheapside, the Great Conduit which had been erected in 1240 to provide sweet water from Paddington, carried in pipes of lead. In a contemporary map, it is possible to see the vessels of the water-carriers lying on the ground beside it.

Thomas More then took the left-hand turning towards Poultry and the Stocks Market; the poultry of Poultry are self-evident, but the 'Stocks' was actually a covered market-house for fishmongers and butchers. It took its name from a pair of stocks, for punishment, standing in the open space beside it. These were the streets and alleys among which More would spend most of his working life; he attended sessions, as under-sheriff of London, in the Compter or prison by Poultry and was also a member of Doctors' Commons, which met within the Court of Arches in the crypt of Bow Church. So the young Thomas More walked by Poultry and the 'pissing conduit' at the south end of Threadneedle or Three-needle Street, passing several more parish churches and many 'fair and large' houses,[5] until he came to a well at the meeting of Broad and Threadneedle Streets; just behind it, on the corner, stood St Anthony's School.

It was customary for boys to begin their elementary schooling at the age of seven – this was the age of the schoolboy martyr in Chaucer's *Prioress's Tale*, 'A litel clergeon, seven yeer of age', who was being taught 'to syngen and to rede'[6] – and there is every reason to believe that More's parents would have wished him to enjoy the benefits of this neighbourhood school as early as possible. St Anthony's was considered to be the finest of the four or five 'grammar schools' in London and had the distinction of being a 'free school', while others charged between eight pence and sixteen pence a week. It had been founded forty years before More's arrival, out of the revenues of the nearby church of St Benet Fink, and was attached to St Anthony's Church and Hospital. The 'hospital' was not one in any contemporary sense but, rather, an almshouse providing lodgings and sustenance for the deserving poor. The school itself stood on the corner between the church and the hospital, with a courtyard behind the school building. It is unlikely that this yard was designed for schoolboy 'play' or exercise, however, especially since it was shared by the master and chaplains as well as the almshouse. There was, in any case, little time for such activities in a school regimen as disciplined as it was prolonged. The day lasted from six in the morning until six in the evening, winter and summer, with two intermissions of an hour (sometimes two hours) for a morning breakfast and a dinner at noon. There were prayers in the morning and evening, of course, when psalms imploring God's mercy were succeeded by psalms for the dead. On his first admission to the school the seven-year-old Thomas More would have been granted some privileged status as a 'clerk' or 'cleric', since by enrolling at St Anthony's he had come within the aegis of the ecclesiastical authorities. One of the remarkable aspects of the late medieval period lies in the evidence of boys or young men becoming associated with what we might now call the Church 'establishment'.

St Anthony's was known as a grammar school for the simple reason that its primary purpose was to teach young Londoners Latin grammar, which included both language and literature. In such schools the children were required to converse in Latin with each other and certainly the young More was, as his son-in-law put it, 'brought up in the Latin tounge'.[7] But, for the youngest pupils, this was not necessarily the only form of instruction. It was important that they knew how to read and write in their native language, for example, if only because the most basic prayers and devotional manuals were in English. Early grammatical instruction was often compared to the milk which infants need to survive, and it was well known that the nurse's milk would contain various 'humours' that had to be carefully scrutinised. At a slightly later date the vernacular was treated altogether more seriously as a medium for pious or rhetorical exposition. One grammarian, Nicholas Grimald, noted that there were certain clerks 'that could also speake latine redyly, and well fauordly: who to haue done as much in our language, & to haue handled the same mater, would haue bin half blank'.[8] There was also a national and bureaucratic reason for the early study of English, since it was considered to promote 'a great aduantage to waxe vniforme'.[9] Lessons and exercises in handwriting, still to be found pressed between the leaves of old grammars, can be seen as part of that tendency towards uniformity which the printing press helped to create.

The younger scholars of St Anthony's had to apply themselves to another and, at this relatively early date, perhaps more important discipline. The 'art of song' was part of the curriculum of the grammar schools and, since the church of St Anthony's maintained a number of choristers, it was natural for the younger boys to be taught the art of plainsong and prick song in their most elementary forms. They were instructed in what one contemporary described as the art of 'sure and cleanly singing ... good and crafty descant'.[10] (The schoolboy of Chaucer's tale was murdered precisely because of his prowess as a scholar of music; he 'lerned' the 'antiphoner', or book of plainsong chants, 'And herkned ay the wordes and the noote'.)[11] Children were also taught to play such musical instruments as the viol and the lute, 'to get the use of our small ioyntes, before they be knitte'.[12] The study would have been practical in intent – *musica practica* as opposed to *musica speculativa* – and yet it was associated with the understanding of rhetoric, mathematics and philosophy. The boys of St Anthony's were taught the art of public deliberation at a later stage in their education, but there was always a formal connection between oratory and musical harmony; similarly, the examination of notational value and metrical proportion pro- vided a basic introduction to mathematics. We cannot expect these young children to have appreciated Plato's argument that the study of music marked the first stage of enlightenment, in the pursuit of ideal beauty and eternal order, but the understanding of musical harmony was part of a general education which emphasised the paramount importance of order and hierarchy.

There are only one or two accounts of Thomas More as a schoolboy – the early stages of life were not considered distinctive enough (except in the hagiographical tradition of saints' lives) to be worthy of separate examination – but we know enough of the adult More to make some well-informed guesses. He was an exceptionally intelligent, as well as clever, man; as the adult, so the child. When one contemporary, then, describes More's 'genius' at understanding the meaning of words from their position in sentences – especially in translating from the Greek – it can be assumed that the young schoolboy had little difficulty with his early lessons. He is hardly likely to have needed to study his 'ABC', set up in red and black letters on a parchment or board. 'More's intelligence,' the same contemporary wrote, 'is more than human.'[13] More's love for music is mentioned on several occasions – there is a vignette of his playing the lute with his second wife – but, according to Erasmus, he was always a poor singer. So we might assume that his study of plainsong was not without practical difficulties. No doubt he coped well enough, particularly since the descriptions of him always mention his quickness and humour.

After the preliminary studies at St Anthony's, in which More had learned to appreciate English 'congrewe',[14] or grammatical accuracy, he proceeded to the study of the Latin language. Ever since the middle of the fourteenth century this had been achieved partly by means of *vulgaria*, clauses or sentences in English which then had to be translated into Latin. Many of these useful phrases were proverbial in nature, and through such tags or apothegms it is possible to glimpse a true permanence or continuity within English culture: 'O good turne asket another'; 'When the hors is stolen, steyke the stabul dore'; 'Where is no fyre ther is no smoke'; 'Brende childe fyre dredes'; 'Many hondes maken lite werke'; 'Maner makes man'; 'The more haste, the werse spede'; 'Bettur ys late thanne never'.[15] These proverbs were old when they were collected in manuscript form, which suggests a tradition of speech enduring for almost a thousand years. It might be termed folk wisdom, but some of that wisdom has now fallen into disuse; 'It is no shame to fall, but to lye longe' and 'Thou shalt do as the preste says, but not as the preste dothe' are unfortunate casualties of time and forgetfulness.

The schoolboys also translated the classical into the vernacular and, by means of this process, came to understand the principles of syntax or accidence which they had already begun to learn. 'What shalt thou do whan thou haste an englisshe to be made in latyn?' begins one of the earliest textbooks, *Parvula*;[16] the question is answered in another grammar, 'seuen thynges must be consythered thre in casuale wordis: nomber, case, and gender and foure in verbis: mode, tens, nomber and persone'.[17]

The boys of St Anthony's were taught in the same timbered and raftered hall, divided into groups according to their ability or progress. They would sit on the floor or on stools, while the oldest of them might have wooden desks or 'forms'. It is hard to estimate the number of pupils involved – the figures for various schools range between forty and approximately one hundred and fifty. St Anthony's was a popular and prized free school, however, so that we might suggest the presence of about a hundred pupils at various stages of their education. They were taught by a principal master and probably more than one teaching assistant. In the age before the ready distribution of printed books – More was born the year after the first printed book was produced in England – the teaching was primarily of an oral kind, based upon memory and repetition. The master would dictate an example out loud, which the pupils would then in turn recite and repeat until it had been committed to memory. Some of these grammatical examples would take the form of couplets, longer rhyming verses or simple syllogisms such as that which More remembered in his later life as pertaining to 'yonge chyldren vse in grammer scholes. Asinus meus habet aures, & tu habes aures, ergo tu es asinus meus. Myne asse hath eares, and thou hast eares, ergo thou arte my asse.'[18] The pupils picked up the chant, perhaps beating time with their fingers, and the hall was filled with the voices of children enunciating one of the oldest of schoolboy jokes.

School life could be severe, however, and chastisement or the threat of chastisement was a permanent aspect of a child's education. There are rough woodcuts of the interior of schoolrooms, in some of which the master holds an open book while in others he wields a birch; in *Utopia* More writes of bad teachers who would rather beat than educate their pupils. One textbook repeats a familiar complaint: 'I played my mayster a mery pranke or playe yesterdaye and therfore he hathe thought me to synge a newe songe to daye. He hath made me to renne a case that my buttokkes doeth swette a blody sweat . . . What maketh the loke so sad? I am thus sadde for fere of the rodde.'[19] In *Piers the Plowman*, Langland translates the appropriate Latin tag *Qui parcit virge, odit filium* into his own distinctive metre: 'Who-so spareth the sprynge, spilleth his children.'[20] One of the biographers of Thomas More's greatest opponent, Martin Luther, has suggested that Luther's preoccupation with images of farting, excrement and buttocks may in part be related to the beatings he received as a child. It may also be the case that More's similar interest in the 'anal zone'[21] – his ability to find Latin terms for excrement is extraordinary – has a similar source.

But it would be mistaken to over-emphasise the pains and privations of fifteenth-century schoolchildren. There were the ordinary pleasures of childhood, with the mention and memory of schoolboys chewing 'suckets', or dried oranges, and 'marchpane', or marzipan. There was also the ordinary spiritedness of the young scholar. When one of them was late for school he explained that he had 'Milked dukkes, my moder badde'.[22] One schoolmaster complained that 'As sone as I am cum into the scole, this fellow goith to make water . . . Some after another askith licence that he may go drynke. Another calleth upon me that he may have licence to go home.'[23] Some aspects of human behaviour, like the proverbs the schoolboys chanted, seem to persist unchanged through time.

Their hours were long, but there were holidays on the 'holy days' of the many religious festivals. Shrove Tuesday was the occasion for cock-fighting, for example, when the boys would bring in their own prize birds and set them against each other; it was customary for the schoolmaster to be given all the dead animals. On the Feast of the Innocents a 'boy-bishop' was ritually enthroned in the principal churches of London; this was only tangentially an occasion of 'misrule' of a late medieval kind, and was pre-eminently a solemn church ceremony with processions as well as enthronement. As one of the statutes of the Sarum rite puts it, 'no man whatsoever, under the pain of *Anathema*, should interrupt or press upon these Children at the Procession'.[24] The child bishop, fully apparelled in ecclesiastical robes with mitre and crozier, delivered a sermon (which often touched upon the misdemeanours of the adult clergy) before walking through the streets of his district, blessing the people and collecting money for his churchwardens. This was one of the many popular festivals destroyed at the time of the Tudor Reformation. There is also a reference in one grammar book to a particular occasion when garlands of roses were made in honour of St Anthony's day, and this festival has customarily been attached to St Anthony's School itself.

More remained there for approximately five years. The pattern of his later career suggests that he must have been a quick and docile pupil; one of his early biographers, who had the benefit of a family connection, wrote that 'he had rather greedily deuoured then leasurely chewed his Grammar rules, he out stripped farre both in towardnesse of witt, and diligence of endeauors all his schoole fellowes, with whome he was matched'.[25] So he proceeded quickly from his early lessons in Donatus to more difficult textbooks such as the *Doctrinale* and the *Grecismus*. His later years at St Anthony's were also directed to the study of classical writers (Virgil and Cicero were obvious favourites) as well as to the arts of composition. He would have been expected to be able to write Latin verse and to prepare various rhetorical topics in prose. The importance of this training in rhetoric is emphasised by an account in Stow's *Survey of*

London, where the boys of St Anthony's are noted for their prowess in public disputation and deliberation. On the eve of the feast of St Bartholomew the Apostle, the scholars of the various London grammar schools met in the churchyard of St Bartholomew, a few yards from Smithfield. They set up a makeshift wooden stage upon a bank of earth and here in Latin would dispute a chosen topic; 'some one scholar hath stepped up, and there hath opposed and answered, till he were by some better scholar overcome and put down; and then the overcomer taking the place, did like as the first'.[26] The eventual winners of these oratorical contests were awarded a prize (in a time after that of Thomas More, they were presented with silver bows and arrows), and according to Stow St Anthony's 'commonly presented the best scholars'.[27]

It was no game but, rather, an important practical training for their later lives. The ability to speak and to understand Latin was the first requirement for any career in the Church, in the Inns of Court, or at the Court itself. The adult More, for example, would have conversed in Latin as often as he ever spoke in English; the majority of his extant letters are also composed in the older language. His most important prose works are written in Latin, as well, but its use has a more private aspect; he and Erasmus were for a while intimate friends but they could communicate only in that language. It was, in other words, a living tongue. But this instruction in Latin, and the deliberations of the schoolboys beside St Bartholomew's, had a more particular point. More and his contemporaries at St Anthony's were also instructed in the essential Ciceronian distinctions of *inventio*, *dispositio*, *elocutio*, *memoria* and *pronuntiatio*. When the young orators disputed on their wooden stage in the churchyard, they had been already trained to recognise and reproduce the elements of *exordium*, *narratio*, *divisio*, *confirmatio*, *refutatio* and *peroratio*. There would also be occasion to learn 'topics' and conventional formulae which could be applied as the subject required. This was not some antique discipline, equivalent to the learning of 'classics' in contemporary schools; in the late fifteenth century, the purpose of this education was to create a group of skilled lawyers and administrators. It was the perfect training for ambitious boys, or at least for the families who were ambitious on their behalf.

It ought to be remembered that, for more than two thousand years, rhetoric had been the central element in preparation for public service. In the classical world it had generally been taught as a formal alternative to philosophy; the pursuit of philosophical truth was supposed to lead to wisdom while rhetoric was concerned with a practical interpretation of, and intervention in, the world. The gifts of subtle invention and eloquent persuasion were indispensable for the right ordering of the 'commonwelth', and More himself is a fine example of that early training. His subsequent public career was essentially that of an orator, and his published works bear the unmistakable marks of a rhetorical education. He did not write, or wish to write, 'literature' in any sense we now care to think of it. He wrote polemics, refutations, confutations and dialogues in which 'the case is put' and challenged in true deliberative fashion; there have been essays written on the prevalence of rhetorical punctuation in More's prose compositions, but that is only one aspect of a style largely derived from rhetorical figures and devices. When we come to look at his open-air dialogues, of which *Utopia* is the most celebrated example, we should remember that his conduct of debate was exactly that which the schoolboys of St Anthony's practised – something to be argued outdoors and in the public domain. There was no such thing as private truth.

When the boys recited tenses and declensions by rote, when they grasped the commonplaces or topics of rhetorical discourse, when they learned by heart simple syllogisms, when they grew skilled in the memory and repetition of oral formulae, they were being made aware of the presence of external authority while at the same time becoming familiarised with implicit demands of order and stability. The same kind of lessons had been taught for several hundreds of years, and the schoolroom offered the first and perhaps best example of those virtues of permanence and continuity which the adult More was to esteem so highly. The disciplined arrangement of knowledge, evinced in the elaborate lexicographical works of the fourteenth and fifteenth centuries, impressed upon the young pupil that image of hierarchy and taxonomy which was so central to the medieval imagination. Beyond all this, too, was the image of God.

And so the boys disputed on a summer evening near Smithfield. The pupils of More's school were known as 'Anthonie pigs', because the figure of that saint was customarily accompanied by one of those animals; the pig was once a symbol of the devil, but it had now been domesticated and St Anthony himself was the patron saint of hogs as well as butchers. Little is known about London pigs in the fifteenth century, except that they were smaller than the present variety, but the connection between them and the hospital brothers of St Anthony's was well established. Those pigs which were too unhealthy or unwholesome to be fit for market were taken from the Stocks and were slit in the ear as a sign of their inedibility; it was customary for the proctor of St Anthony's to tie a bell around the necks of such animals before letting them roam among the refuse and dunghills of the London streets. John Stow reports that 'no man would hurt or take them up'.[28] Instead they were fed by hand, much as Londoners would feed the kites and ravens; they were, like the birds, consumers of noisome waste. And so the proverb was soon current, 'Such an one will follow such an one, and whine as it were an Anthony pig',[29] which duly became attached to the schoolboys themselves. There was, however, one important difference. If the pigs grew fat and healthy on their London diet, they were taken up by the authorities of St Anthony's in order to be cooked and eaten.

At the end of the day, after his release from school, it was a short journey from Threadneedle Street to Milk Street. The city surrounded More once again, and he noticed everything: his prose works are filled with brief but vivid intimations of London life, from the sight of someone squatting against a wall in order to 'ease hym selfe in the open strete'[30] to the beggars who display their cancerous or cankered legs on 'frydays aboute saynt sauyour and at ye Sauygate',[31] from the 'meretrix' and her 'leno' or procurer[32] to the wrestlers at Clerkenwell who take 'so great fallys'.[33] He made his way among the pumps and springs and water conduits, past the gardens and the markets and the almshouses, along small lanes and even smaller footways, between the stables and the carpenters' yards and the mills, past brothels and taverns and bath-houses and street privies, under archways adorned with the images of saints or coats of arms, into courtyards filled with shops, beneath tenements crammed with the families of artisans, moving from the grand houses of the rich to the thatched hovels of mud walls frequented by the poor, hearing the cries of 'God spede' and 'Good morrow!', past nunneries and priories and churches. It has been suggested that the image of God shone behind the harmonious order and authority impressed upon the schoolchildren of St Anthony's; the same image, together with that of Christ crucified upon the fallen world, rose up from the streets of London. At a distant vantage the traveller would see the towers of almost a hundred parish churches rising above the rooftops of thatch and timber; it is testimony to the piety of Londoners that no other western European city could boast so many sacred places. As the young More made his way along the lanes and thoroughfares, there was the continual sound of bells.

IV

Cough Not, Nor Spit

IT was customary for the boys of St Anthony's to move on to Eton
for the remainder of their school years, but the young More took
a more distinguished course. At the age of twelve, he became a
page in the household of John Morton, Archbishop of Canterbury
and Lord Chancellor of England. All the evidence suggests that
Archbishop Morton was John More's 'lord' and that Thomas More
joined the prelate's household as a singular mark of favour and
privilege. It had been the tradition of many centuries that children of
gentle and even noble birth should be given the station of servants in
a great household; it predates the age of chivalry and is described in
the pages of *Beowulf*, but by the late medieval period it had become
a standard practice in the quest for preferment and valuable service.
An Italian observer noted that 'every one, however rich he may be,
sends away his children into the houses of others'.[1] Although this was
an exaggeration, he touched upon an important principle of
fifteenth-century training; patronage was still more important than
formal education. With the exception of Henry VII, John Morton
was the most influential man in the kingdom, and the young More
would have entered the archbishop's service together with the sons of
earls and other noblemen. It has often been remarked how quickly
and how easily Thomas More became associated with the magnates
and rulers of England; the beginning of that invaluable connection
lies with his service at Lambeth Palace. He entered a world of
retainers and officials, clerks and councillors, through which at a
later date he would effortlessly rise.

So in 1490, after his five years of schooling, More crossed the river
to Lambeth – if he had taken the wherry, among the cockle boats and
six-oared barges, it would have cost him a penny. He came up by the
gateway of red brick which was still being finished, together with its

three-light perpendicular window above the arch itself and two great square towers of five storeys on either side. Until recent years there hung outside the arch a leaden water-pipe with Morton's *rebus*, a pictorial pun on his surname, embossed upon it. Many of the young More's most important duties were to take place in the Great Hall, which was to the right of the courtyard as he entered through the arch. The boy had already passed a winding stone staircase in the eastern tower that led to the place of imprisonment; forty-four years later he would cross the Thames again and climb that staircase as a free man for the last time in his life. It might be said that his public career began and ended on this small spot of Lambeth ground.

He had become a member of a large permanent staff which included ushers, yeomen of the chamber, grooms, butlers and others under the administration of a steward and a treasurer. More was one of the 'Children for household offices',[2] whose duties were multifarious but well defined. He lived according to a simple but not harsh regimen; the pages slept on straw mattresses or truckle beds within one chamber; cleanliness was an important consideration for those who served food in the Great Hall, and on one side of the room was a long and low stone sink with pitchers of water beside it. It is sometimes assumed that the late medieval body remained entirely unwashed (if on occasions anointed with perfume), but sweet grey soap and white soap known as 'Castell' were widely available. The apparel of the fashionable page included hose and a doublet edged with fur, and on ceremonial occasions he would don Archbishop Morton's livery.

Morton seems to have been so impressed by the cleverness and quickness of the boy, according to William Roper, More's son-in-law and earliest biographer, that it is possible he soon 'attended' the archbishop in his *sanctum* in the western tower of the palace, or in the audience chamber of polished oak adjacent to it. But his primary duties were of a more basic kind. The pages were obliged to act as 'principall servitours'[3] at the great feasts in the Hall, and as a result More became part of an elaborate ceremonial which began when the 'ewerer' brought in the table cloths upon his left shoulder and the 'panter' carried the 'principall salte' and loaves of bread (each one two inches broad and seven inches long) with a towel partly draped over his left arm. The prime duty of the page was to serve, and stand, and wait, ready to pass a pewter plate or a silver goblet; he was ready, also, to take a whispered message from one guest to another or to run an errand within the palace. The feasts were remarkable for their order and variety, with each item being served to guests according to their rank. There was a first course of beef and mutton, swan or geese, followed by a second course which might contain no less than thirty different kinds of meat, among them crane, heron and curlews; eventually came the cheese, 'scraped with sugar and sauge levis',[4] together with the various fruits of the season.

At the end of the meal More helped to place a double towel along the whole length of the tablecloth, so that after grace each guest might wash in the bowls of hot and cold water which had been put upon it. The tables and trestles were then 'voyded' of any remaining food, with the broken pieces of bread and meat collected for the 'alms vessel', and the pages escorted the guests to their chambers, where they ensured that the bed was covered 'with pylowes and hed shetys, in case they wolle rest',[5] as well as such 'neweltees' as cherries, green ginger and sweet wine. Only then were they given their own supper, together with that weak beer which was the staple beverage for children and invalids.

But if Thomas More was a 'servitour', he was also still a scholar. At Lambeth Palace there was at least one chaplain or clerk in minor orders who acted as a schoolmaster and supervised the *domestica schola* or private school for the boys within Morton's household. A contemporary of More's who had also been enrolled as a page, within the less influential household of the Bishop of Winchester, recalled how the prelate 'delighted in hearing the boys repeat to him in the evening what they had learned that day from the schoolmaster. And in this examination he who did well was nicely complimented, and given something he wanted.'[6] It is not known if Morton had time to play so benevolent a role, but such an early recognition of More's intelligence would explain his praise for the boy, 'In whose witt and towardenes' he much delighted. 'The Cardinal . . .', wrote William Roper, forgetting for the moment that Morton was given the red hat after More's departure from Lambeth, 'would often say of him [More] vnto the nobles that divers tymes dined with him: "This child here wayting at the table, whosoeuer shall liue to see it, will proue a mervailous man".'[7] How much credence can be given to this anecdote is open to question, but it exemplifies the archbishop's reputation for shrewdness as well as More's own evident cleverness.

In a household such as this, among boys of gentle and noble birth, the education would take certain prescribed forms. More soon acquired a reputation for skill in theatrical oration and disputation, and there is no reason to doubt that his formal education in rhetoric continued at Lambeth. He would by now also be instructed in the arts of *suasoriae* and *prosopopoeia*. One was concerned with the construction of convincing arguments for both sides of a debating topic, the other with the assumption of a character – fictional or real – to create a fluent and persuasive discourse.

There were more particular lessons in the Lambeth household, however. Books 'of Curteyse' or 'Books of Nurture' were texts for juvenile training in the manners of courtly and social life. These included practical, and often intricate, lessons in etiquette and general decorum. It was of primary importance, for example, that the page should know by heart the differences of estate and degree among the guests (one book lists thirty-six ranks), how to seat them and how to address them appropriately. The page must not pick his nose or teeth, 'cough not, ner spitte';[8] he must not lean against the wall, nor scratch himself. At all times he must remain mild and cheerful, replying to any remarks 'wyth softe speche',[9] and always bow to his lord when answering him. It is significant that some manuals then conclude with the need to serve the principal 'Lord' in Heaven. Questions of manners were also involved in the larger duty to 'reverence, honour and obey'[10] lawful superiors – this was the advice given by the Earl of Arundel to his son who had just entered the household of the Bishop of Norwich. Another obligation imposed upon a boy of respectable birth was for him, in the phrase of the period, to 'keep countenance'. It was his duty to preserve the dignity and demeanour proper to his rank and degree, to be civil to his inferiors and respectful to his superiors, to retain his 'temper' in every sense – the term suggesting not only moderation, calmness and a middle course, but also, according to one dictionary, the 'due mixture of contrary qualities'.[11]

Thomas More's later praise of Morton, as a man both politic and wise, indicates the extent to which he was influenced by him; from the evidence of his *Utopia* and *The History of Richard III*, Morton is one of the most imposing figures of the period. In the register of his routine episcopal business, there are reports of his threatening excommunication against various 'sons of iniquity' who had robbed a priory, and of his ordering general processions 'with chanting and mass if possible' to petition God's favour on behalf of the king and granting indulgences to those who participate in them.[12] In 1491, the year of Prince Henry's birth, the archbishop was relieved from his duty of visiting the Pope every three years, largely because of his secular business as Lord Chancellor, and a proctor took his place on these obligatory missions to the apostolic see. The affairs of the Church and of the kingdom were united in his person; Morton was the latest in a long tradition of powerful clerics who served their sovereign as well as God. There was no necessary disparity between these roles, of course, since the divine laws of order and authority were thereby being maintained. In More's later account of a conversation at Lambeth, when such matters as judicial punishment and land enclosure were discussed, the archbishop orchestrates a debate between a lawyer, idealist, friar, and fool; even in table talk there was a set of unwritten but acknowledged rules which Morton himself gently imposed upon his guests. It is not hard to imagine the admiration, even awe, which he instilled in the young page.

At the time when More first encountered him, the archbishop was the single most important example of the new unity and stability which the burgeoning Tudor dynasty had brought to the throne. Morton had managed to serve under both Yorkist and Lancastrian sovereigns, earning plaudits on both sides for his integrity, and by almost single-handedly arranging the marriage between Henry VII and Elizabeth of York he brought to an end those dynastic struggles which had threatened the peace and good government of England. During More's tenure as a page at Lambeth there were already reports of the impostor Perkin Warbeck's attempts to claim the throne, but these only heightened Morton's preoccupation with maintaining the balance and firm order of the country.

The nature of Morton's career is important in one other respect, since it may help to solve the mystery of More's later relations with Cardinal Wolsey and Henry VIII. Morton was both cleric and lawyer, spiritual and secular officer, whose capacities were rewarded with a number of lucrative ecclesiastical benefices and administrative posts. He was known by diplomats to be one of the principal architects of foreign policy, but acquired an altogether less satisfactory reputation for his conduct in domestic affairs. It was he who is said, perhaps inaccurately, to have invented the fiscal policy known as 'the fork'; it was a device for collecting new revenues for the king, and was best described as 'perswading *prodigals* to part with their money because *they did spend it most*, and the *covetous* because *they might spare it best*; so making both *extreams* to meet in one *medium*, to supply the king's necessities'.[13] As a result he seems to have been disliked and feared by many who were not always impressed by the king's 'necessities'. Francis Bacon describes him as 'a wise man and an eloquent' but 'in his nature harsh and haughty . . . envied by the nobility and hated of the people'.[14] The fact that this was the man whom Thomas More praised for his *prudentia* (judgement) and *auctoritas* (authority and prestige) raises interesting questions about More's scale of values.

It has often been suggested, for example, that Thomas More despised or distrusted Cardinal Wolsey's uses of power and displays of pomp. But in neither respect was Wolsey departing from the essential roles promulgated by Morton or his predecessors. Morton, too, loved pomp and circumstance – or, rather, he understood its importance in a culture irradiated by spectacle and display. The performance might sometimes be of a severe kind. In preparation for his installation as Bishop of Ely, he walked bare-legged and barefooted from Downham to Ely with a rosary in his hands. But when he was to be installed as Archbishop of Canterbury he rode from London with a vast retinue, 'greatly accompanyde with lordes espirituels and temporels' and with an estimated cavalcade of a thousand horse in a grand progress that took six days. On his visitations to various of his dioceses in 1490 and 1491 – on which occasions it is possible that the young More was in attendance – he insisted upon proceeding in 'great state',[15] with an imposing cross carried before him and a vast retinue behind him. This was the man whom More praised for possessing *prudentiam rerum*,[16] or one skilled in human affairs. Is it likely, then, that More would have any principled objections to Cardinal Wolsey's similar use of magnificence and power?

It is important to remember that, for most of his life, More was a lawyer and a public administrator; he was not a visionary or a scholarly humanist, however much he celebrated men such as Pico della Mirandola and Desiderius Erasmus. That is why he particularly admired in Morton his 'great experience the verye mother & maistres of wisdom';[17] he believed that experience in the practical business of the world led to prudent deliberation and good judgement. It also becomes clear from his history of Richard III, in which Morton plays a prominent part, that reason or theory does not prevail in human affairs; the wise man is Morton, who manages to guide events with diplomacy and rhetoric. More's admiration for Morton was based upon that prelate's astuteness and efficiency, which were precisely the characteristics that More was to display in all the affairs of his life.

After the meal was over in the Great Hall, there were occasions when players stepped forward to engage in dialogues and dramatic disputations, often accompanied by music and song; it was the natural entertainment for a group of people accustomed to debate and oratory. In one of those cultural transitions which can only be observed in distant retrospect, formal debate was turning into more informal drama; the theatrical world of Marlowe and Kyd is in turn connected with medieval rhetoric. The young More was present at some of these performances, and his son-in-law records that 'thoughe he was younge of yeares, yeat wold he at Christmas tyde sodenly sometimes steppe in among the players'[18] and would then improvise a part so skilfully that he excelled all the other actors. This cannot literally be true, since the decorum and propriety imposed upon a junior member of the household would prevent him from 'sodenly' doing anything, but it may be that Archbishop Morton, recognising the boy's 'witt and towardeness',[19] asked him to take on a role in the Christmas interlude. Certainly we know what kind of drama would have been prepared for the occasion. Morton's chaplain by the year of More's entry into service, Henry Medwall, was a skilful dramatist who supplied material both for professional actors (the *mimus* or the *histrio*) and occasional players. At least two of his works survive and one of them, *Fulgens and Lucrece*, has been dated with reasonable certainty to the time of More's sojourn at Lambeth Palace.

It is in many respects the direct heir to the academic and legal disputations of the period, since two characters known respectively as 'A' and 'B' begin by outlining a plot in which the rival claims of nobility and virtue are to be tested. Cornelius is a wastrel patrician and Flaminius a virtuous plebeian; they vie for the hand of the lovely Lucrece, and the drama of their contest is suitably adorned with legalistic and oratorical terms. It is not hard to imagine More, as a graduate of the St Bartholomew disputations, taking some part in these entertainments. The elevated cadences of the argument (couched in rhyme royal) are, however, in contrast to the scatological aspect of certain passages. There is, for example, a reference to one character who 'For a medsyn must ete his wyves torde' and a request that 'ye had be taken up behynde'.[20] Similar jokes will be found in the work of Thomas More. The 'frankness' of fifteenth-century people

33

about the body and its functions has often been observed; if you believe human nature to be fallen from grace, and irredeemably flawed, then there is no reason to be discreet or fastidious about its natural properties. It might be useful, even beneficial, to exploit and to parody them. But there was also a positive delight in the material world; in the sacrifice of the Mass, for example, Christ's actual body was believed to animate the bread and wine. If the natural order might act as a visible token of an invisible sign, then the sacramental and the excremental can be seen in tacit partnership. We know from the babooneries in the margins of certain sacred manuscripts that a sense of ritual and a sense of ribaldry are not unrelated; they can be seen as part of the same instinct for game and for play.

And so the young Thomas More stepped in among the players. William Roper's story has an air of authenticity for the manner in which, at the beginning of his biographical narrative, the element of theatricality in More's character is revealed. He, along with everyone else, acted his part. The discovery of the world as a stage goes back beyond Shakespeare to Lucian and other classical satirists. Yet the apothegm had a particular resonance in the religious culture of the late medieval period; in a world where the truths of divine authority were fixed and established, the fallen world of human nature could be seen in part as a game of little consequence. It is merely the antechamber of eternity. There is no abiding city, as More emphasised in all of his devotional works. So the guests in the Great Hall play their roles according to the divinely ordained hierarchy, dressing (and being addressed) in accordance with their precise degree and estate. But it soon became time for More to play another part. When Archbishop Morton 'sawe, that he could not profitt so much in his house, as he desired, where there were manie distractions of publick affairs, having great care of his bringing up, he sent him to the Universitie, and placed him in Canterbury Colledge at Oxford'.[21]

V

Set on His Book

THOMAS More entered Oxford University as a scholarship boy, most probably as one of the *collegii pueri* ('college boys') nominated by Archbishop Morton for a place at Canterbury College. At the time of his arrival, in the autumn of 1492, the university contained approximately one thousand young scholars scattered among the colleges of regular and secular clergy as well as the various halls. More was in his fourteenth year, the average age on first coming to the university. His stay at Oxford, and his reasons for being despatched there in the first place, have been the subject of endless conjecture. Since he remained only for two years before moving on to New Inn, in London, it has been suggested that he was the unfortunate object of his father's ambition; according to this theory John More insisted upon his son following a legal career like his own, thereby forsaking the academic delights of the college library and the dangerous 'new learning'.

But there are more convincing explanations for his relatively brief university career. There can be little doubt that Archbishop Morton understood the boy's potential for public service, and an education at Canterbury College in the charge of Benedictine monks would have been the ideal preparation for a successful career within the ecclesiastical establishment. Morton's connection with Oxford was a strong one; in 1494 he was elected as its chancellor. The young More would have been able to study civil as well as canon law, as Morton did, before taking holy orders and joining the professional administrative class of church and state. It is possible, on the other hand, that More's progress from an Oxford college to a London Inn was planned in advance. It was not unusual for young men to spend a year or two at the university, without taking a degree, before moving on to more serious study at an Inn of Court. Several of his contemporaries made precisely that journey; a preliminary grounding in logic and dialectic offered an ideal preparation for the intensive study of common law. It would be of a piece with More's later career to see his progress from Lambeth Palace to Oxford, from university to Inn, as a carefully managed and willingly undertaken process of advancement.

There are two extant illustrations of Canterbury College, Oxford, both of them showing it close to demolition in the middle of the eighteenth century. The college had been established in the four-teenth century for a small community of student monks from Canterbury itself – Benedictines or, as they were known, 'black monks' – but was suppressed with its parent monastery at the time of the Henrician Reformation. It was neither the largest nor the most distinguished of the monastic colleges, but by the 1490s it had already acquired an interesting history. Its warden in 1365 had been John Wycliffe, a little over a decade before he began his more widely known career as a reformer. A recent influence was William de Selling, the prior of Christ Church in Canterbury, who had fostered the teaching of Greek and increased the number of monk-fellows at Canterbury College itself. Selling had brought back Greek manu-scripts from two visits to Italy and is believed to have translated a work of St John Chrysostom; he takes his place, then, as one of the first of those pious Christian 'humanists' who were to affect More so strongly at a later date.

The college itself took the shape of a small quadrangle surrounded by hall, chapel, kitchen and chambers for scholars and fellows. The buildings were of two storeys, the ground floor constructed of Headington stone and the upper storey built with timber and 'covered with plaster impressed with fantastic designs'.[1] A library had been completed some forty years before More's arrival, and within it the books were still fastened upon chains in the old medieval style; this was an understandable precaution, since scholars had been known to remove the more attractive volumes. Surviving lists and catalogues refer to works of biblical and patristic literature, as well as to cupboards containing books of grammar and law. It is difficult to be precise about the number of collegians. There are likely to have been approximately six monk-fellows, together with a warden, and five or six secular scholars like More himself. There were also a number of *commorantes* -- lodgers or 'sojourners' who paid for their accommodation. Each chamber was generally shared by two fellows or scholars, with one end of the room partitioned into separate studies.

So More had entered a small community, organised upon a quasi-monastic pattern. His role as a secular scholar, one of Morton's *collegii pueri*, was similar to that of a monastic oblate; he was required to assist during the services in the chapel and to wait upon the fellows in the hall. He was of course accustomed to such service in Lambeth, but the Great Hall of the palace was now exchanged for a smaller room with a central hearth, a high table, a woollen tapestry picked out with images of animals as well as 'an old hanging with ostrich feathers'[2] – the feathers no doubt part of some tribute to a Prince of Wales. It was declared, however, that such menial service was not to be so arduous that it interfered with the studies of the *collegii pueri*; they would have been free, for example, to attend the college lectures or disputations in grammar and philosophy.

But this may not have been the only institution where the young More received his education. There are persistent reports that he was also a member of St Mary's Hall in Oxford. One early seventeenth-century account of the university states that he was educated 'in aula S. Mariae', and a late history proclaims More as one of the eminent men of that place.[3] There is no real contradiction here, since it was possible for More to be formally attached to Canterbury College, while residing (and even being instructed) in St Mary's Hall; the college and hostel were situated close together in the same street.

The halls were different in character from the colleges; they were not closed monastic institutions but, instead, were self-governing and for a long period self-regulatory. Each one held less than twenty students, with a central hall for meals and disputations as well as a small number of shared chambers. The image of the family, or household, had a firm hold upon most medieval institutions; the terms *aula* ('hall') or *hospicium* ('hostel') were sometimes exchanged for *domus* ('house'). The hours for any 'yonge scoler' were long, with his rising at five for divine service before the morning lecture (with perhaps a second lecture at nine) to face a day which included studies between dinner and supper followed by further studies until retiring to his hall at eight or nine in the evening. The students ate together in 'commons', with a bell or horn announcing dinner at ten or eleven in the morning and supper at five; only Latin was permitted in conversation, and of course they were expected to attend Mass each day. After their studies were over, and before they retired to bed, the community of the hall chanted the *Salve Regina* or some other antiphon to the Virgin Mary. 'To thee do we cry,' they sang together, 'poor banished children of Eve.' Such were the institutions during More's short period as an undergraduate.

His studies were not confined to the college and the hall. In his first year at the university he embarked upon the *trivium*, incorporating grammar, rhetoric and logic. These were the 'liberall artes'[4] as opposed to the study of theology, with much of the emphasis resting upon logic or dialectic. The syllabus was supposed to last for two years and, since More remained at Oxford for that length of time, it can be supposed that he completed it. The texts which he would have been required to read included the *Rhetoric* of Aristotle (to which three terms were given), Boethius's *Topics*, the *Nova Rhetorica* of Cicero, as well as selected works of Priscian and Ovid. The method of teaching was as precisely organised as the curriculum itself. Public instruction was by the traditional means of lecture and disputation; the lectures were generally held at six o'clock in the morning, at which time the master took up the set book for that part of the curriculum and expounded upon its meaning. He would be expected to provide interpretations of, and glosses upon, the text while at the same time dividing his approach into a number of *quaestiones* or investigations arising from it. Books were heard, rather than seen. Clearly the approach could be highly formalised and restricted, differing very little from the teaching by rote within the grammar schools, but there were opportunities for resourceful masters to provide more inventive glosses and interpretations. On other days were held the disputations – on a *dies disputabilis* rather than a *dies legibilis* – and once again the young Thomas More was involved in the world of formal oratory and public debate. In front of the young scholars, or sophisters, masters and bachelors were required to argue on either side of a proposition or an interpretation – there would normally be one proponent against two opposers – until a final judgment or *determinatio* on the matter was given by the presiding master.

In the Bodleian Library at Oxford there is a Latin 'commonplace book' that contains the signature 'Thomas Mor' and the initials 'T.M' on three separate folios;[5] it includes one of the books of etiquette which More studied as a page in the Morton household, *Stans puer ad mensam*, as well as a Latin dictionary and a glossary. In his later writing, there are other intimations of his Oxford studies.

His memories of morning disputation are to be found in his references to solving a question 'after an Oxforde fashyon',[6] and to a 'yonge sophyster ... at Oxforde at a peruise'.[7] More's training in logic and dialectic as well as grammar is rehearsed in his casual employment of such terms as 'thantecedent' and 'symylytude', 'profe' and 'contradyccyon'.[8] He is a little more formal in his invocation of 'preposycyon aduersatyue' and 'coniunccyon copulatyue'[9] in an attack upon an opponent's logic. So it was that in Oxford, according to his great-grandson Cresacre More, he 'profitted exceedingly in Rhetorick, Logick and Philosophie'.[10]

In the summer of 1493 there was a sudden and unwelcome interruption to this course of work when a 'sore plague',[11] one of six visitations between 1485 and 1507, came upon Oxford; More and other contemporaries retired to the village of Culnam (or Culham) five miles south of the city – 'for deth' as it was known, or prevention – and in one of his prose works he recalls the 'scholers of Oxenforde' passing the time by making riddles in the house of 'an olde wyfe of Culnam'[12] with whom they were lodged for the duration. Yet although More's studies were not necessarily continuous, his general conscientiousness and self-discipline are apparent in Cresacre More's report that 'his whole mind was set on his booke'.[13]

Erasmus sets the appropriate context when he remarks that at Cambridge, in the same period as More was a scholar at Oxford, the curriculum was dominated by Alexander and the Scotists.[14] William Tyndale was at Oxford twenty years after More, but the nature of the studies there had not changed. The scholars were corrupted with 'sophistry', 'alleging unto them texts of logic ... of metaphysic, and moral philosophy, and all manner of books of Aristotle, and of all manner doctors which they never yet saw ... What wonderful dreams have they of their predicaments, universals, second intentions, quiddities, haecceities and relatives.'[15] It is rare that More ever endorses any point made by the 'heretic' Tyndale, but he mounts much the same attack in his own prose writings. In one long and satirical letter to a lecturer in theology at the University of Louvain, he ridiculed the scholastic preoccupation with *'ampliationibus, restrictionibus, appellationibus'*,[16] which were all names for the properties or 'supposition' of terms within a formalised logical structure. He also attacked the basic training of university scholars, just as Erasmus had done, and described the learning derived from it as *'stultissima solertia'*[17] or the most foolish kind of ingenuity.

Martin Luther also scorned the fatuity and mischief of 'an unreformed university'.[18] But the fact that these four dissimilar men of learning – More and Luther, Tyndale and Erasmus – felt it necessary to launch a prolonged assault upon 'scholasticism' (to give this set of disciplines its most general name) suggests the power and authority which it still commanded. It was at the very centre of medieval education and practice; it had helped to fashion and instruct More, as well as Tyndale and Erasmus, to the extent that we cannot fully understand him without first understanding the precepts and demands of a system of learning which had already lasted for more than three hundred years.

In the late twentieth century, cosmologists and physicists have been trying to produce what has been called the 'theory of everything',[19] a 'grand unified theory' complete and self-consistent which would in particular unite 'quantum theory and general relativity'.[20] Medieval theologians and philosophers knew nothing of relativity theory (at least not under that name) but there is no doubt that they pursued the same goal with as much ardour and with more success than modern scientists. One twentieth-century physicist, Stephen Hawking, has suggested that this general theory would then in turn allow us to know 'the mind of God'.[21] No scholastic would have dared to presume so much, but his beliefs and aspirations would have been similar.

It was a question of authority – or, rather, that need for authority which encouraged the elaborate and voluminous organisation of knowledge. Scholasticism is in that sense a methodology rather than a specific discipline, an immense, powerful and persuasive form of organisation which was considered to be a token of the divine dispensation. The concern was with the arrangement of distinct parts which could be in turn divided and subdivided into discrete but interrelated elements. The ornate structures of late fifteenth-century polyphony (of which English composers provided the finest examples) have sometimes been used to suggest the nature of scholasticism, where the need for elaboration is matched only by the passion for lucidity, where clarity and complexity are not considered to be irreconcilable virtues. But all these *partes* and *quaestiones* and *distinctiones* are built upon the single sustaining belief in the presence of absolute and objective authority. It was not the duty of the philosopher or artist to 'add to' knowledge, only to reveal it. In late polyphonic music the central aspect is the delicate interplay of voices without any single one of them taking precedence. In music of a century later we find the dramatic use of a powerful individual voice, but in fifteenth-century English polyphony the emphasis rests upon the intricate melody of many voices. The character and abilities of the individual are only of consequence as an element within the harmonious organisation of parts; we do not know the names of the masons who created the bell towers and fan-vaults of the great fifteenth-century English churches. This is not the world of Luther or of what has become known as post-Reformation culture, but it remained the world of Thomas More.

It would be a misinterpretation of More to believe that he attacked the inheritance and authority of scholasticism in general. He would have found it difficult to argue with the central proposition of scholastic philosophers, lawyers and theologians that 'Truth is one and indivisible' and that their task lay 'in reconciling all existing knowledge logically with the One Truth' by means of 'laws or formulae'.[22] That truth was pre-eminently to be found in the Bible, which, along with the books of Aristotle and the texts of canon law as promulgated by Justinian, made up the core teaching of the scholastics. These represented the bounds of true knowledge beyond which it was neither necessary nor desirable to stray. All human effort must, instead, be devoted to exploring and expounding the material which they contained. For Anselm, and other great scholastics, the fundamental purpose of education lay in realigning classical learning with Christian revelation. The methods of interpreting that knowledge were of a piece with a culture established upon an intricate system of rights and duties, as well as an elaborate hierarchy and order devolving from a central authority within western Christendom. The manifold texts of the Bible were subjected to a profound and subtle exegesis, and the scholastic divines composed analogical and anagogical glosses upon each phrase, word and even syllable. For how long and in what manner did Christ lie in the womb of the Virgin Mary? Could Christ have taken on himself the likeness of a woman, or a mule? If so, could a mule be crucified? Will there be food and drink after the general Resurrection? These are some of the examples adduced by Erasmus, who took no time in denouncing them as 'Formalities, Quiddities, Ecceities',[23] but the scholastic theologians also considered the provenance of original sin, the formal substance of the Eucharist, and the nature of the Trinity. In a similar fashion the scholastics of the fourteenth and fifteenth centuries, with the universities of Europe as their home, treated the works of Aristotle and Justinian as summations of true knowledge to be elicited by syllogism, deduction, inference and all those techniques of formal and logical word play distrusted by More and Tyndale. For Francis Bacon, writing *The Advancement of Learning* in the early seventeenth century, all this was no more than a dark web of words without substance or profit; but it can also be seen as representing one of the glories of the human imagination.

The *Summulae Logicales* or *Parva Logicalia*, compiled by Peter of Spain, was the basic and essential work to be studied, repeated and recalled by the young More. It is prefaced by the statement that 'Dialectic is the art of arts and the science of sciences',[24] a declaration followed by a digest of the 'logic of the ancients', pre-eminently that of Aristotle, as well as of medieval variants known as *logica moderna*. It was to the latter which More objected, since Peter of Spain's additions to the corpus of classical logic were of a highly technical and specialised kind which did not appeal to More's sense of practicality or usefulness. Medieval logic came close to the enclosed and self-referential qualities of modern mathematics; the formal conditions of truth were established but, in that space, there was room for highly intricate and subtle elaboration. In later life More mocked the kind of questions which university scholars were supposed to debate, with examples taken from the standard textbooks. What is the difference between '*Vinum bibi bis*', 'Wine I drank twice', and '*bis uinum bibi*', 'twice wine I drank'? Is there a differently implied set of probable circumstances in the statements '*Papam uerberaui*' and '*uerberaui papam*' – 'Pope I have scourged' and 'I have scourged the Pope'?[25] And so it goes on, as More multiplies examples of supposed scholastic folly. It ought to be pointed out that certain modern theorists consider scholastic logic of this kind to be an interesting and successful discipline, close to symbolic logic of the present century, but it is easy to understand why it should seem remote and impractical to young men who, like More, were intent upon a worldly career in London. He himself realised, of course, the importance of studying the essential elements of '*dialectica*', in order to reckon the truth of propositions or the plausibility of certain arguments; such skills were essential for a lawyer. It was also the necessary training for any citizen or officer, who would need to detect specious reasoning or ordinary fallacies in public discourse. The scholasticism to which More and Erasmus acknowledged their debt, therefore, was that which was concerned with the right employment and understanding of rhetoric. That is why More employs scholastic methods in his later writings; in many respects his polemical texts take on a scholastic form, since it was the only viable kind of argument available to him and his contemporaries.

There are, of course, always contrary forces working within any advanced culture – which suggests that terms like 'humanism' and 'scholasticism', 'Renaissance' and 'Reformation', should be used with the greatest caution. But More's objections to the elaborations of medieval logic were based upon two fundamental tenets which he maintained until the end of his life. He refers on various occasions to the principles of *sensus communis* and *consuetudo*; he deployed them against the scholastics but he also used them against those who supported the supremacy of Henry VIII. *Sensus communis* may mean in its most obvious signification what we call 'common sense', able to cut through the persiflage of the dialecticians, but in More's later writings it takes on the further emphasis of common or universal understanding, which in turn implies a shared and traditional inheritance of belief. It is significant, too, that in scholastic psychology *sensus communis* was the faculty through which instinct and memory were able to make random sense-impressions cohere. It is one of the great metaphors of the age. *Consuetudo* is the Latin noun for custom or habit; it can be taken as a reproof to those scholastics who twist language beyond the range of its ordinary meaning but, again, in More's subsequent writings it acquires larger authority as the term denoting the body of inherited practice and behaviour. When at the close of his life More, faced with his accusers, declared that he would 'conforme my consciens' only to 'the generall Councell of Christendome',[26] he was reinforcing the same general principle. It is impossible to over-emphasise the authority which custom and tradition exercised upon More; he was, in that sense (as in others), one of the last great exemplars of the medieval imagination.

He made one other observation of his time at Oxford, not long before he was arrested and brought in front of his judges. After he had resigned from his office as Lord Chancellor, he is supposed to have gathered his family around him for one of those dramatic recitations at which he excelled. The domestic income was about to be reduced, and he informed them that they might fall to the level of 'Oxford fare, where many grave and ancient fathers be continually conversant; which of our power stretch not to maintain, then may we, like poor scholars of Oxford, go a-begging with our bags and wallets, and sing *Salve Regina* at rich men's doors'.[27] It is unlikely that the young More ever needed to go begging from door to door, but the general privations of Oxford life are suggested by a contemporary who recalled that dinner consisted only of a 'penye pece of byefe amongest iiii, hauying a few porage made of the brothe of the same byefe with salte and otemell'. After their evening studies were completed they had 'to walk or runne up and downe halfe an houre, to get a heate on their feet' before they retired to their chambers.[28]

It is an affecting picture, but it may in part be ironically conceived. There was a convention for complaining about the hardships and difficulties of university education – literally a convention since in the teaching of the art of letter-writing, or *ars dictamen*, there were 'model' letters which provided standard rhetorical tropes for laments on the life of the student. Among the principal complaints was lack of money, of course, which in turn meant lack of food and material for heating as well as more general discomforts. It is generally reckoned by economic historians, however, that students lived above the level of a minimum 'decent subsistence',[29] and it is likely that their cost of living actually fell in the last decades of the fifteenth century. As one of Morton's own scholars More would have received an annual sum for his maintenance, and payments by Morton range from ten to twenty shillings.[30] It is in this context that we should take a remark by one of More's early biographers that 'in his allowance his father kept him verie short, suffering him scarcelie to have so much monie in his own custodie, as would pay for the mending of his apparell'. The same stock repertoire of images, deriving in part from sermons and fabliaux, may also be glimpsed in Chaucer's description of the clerk of Oxford who was 'nat right fat, I undertake' but 'looked holwe, and therto sobrely'.[31]

A more accurate description of student life in More's days at Oxford can be gathered from diligent reading of the various statutes, codes and inventories of the period. Among the items which are taken to be normal accoutrements of the student are blankets and a 'matteresse' (if not necessarily sheets), proper clothing and a 'cofer' for storing them, knives and spoons and possibly even candlesticks. His shared chambers would have included a table, together with stools or chairs, as well as a bowl and pitcher for washing. Many students would have brought with them a musical instrument, the staple means of entertainment during the period, while others would not have left behind the bows and arrows which were the favourite form of sport. The more scholarly or wealthy students might even possess a 'presse' for their few and prized books.

It ought to be repeated here that the younger scholars of Oxford, unlike their modern counterparts, were only fourteen or fifteen years of age, and that they were entering halls or colleges which, like monasteries and guilds, considered themselves to be formal communities based on the by then traditional idea of the household. That is why elaborate codes of discipline were established to curb individual disruption or general disorder. No student, for example, was to make unkind comparisons between 'one country, or one people, or one class of the community and another' and there were heavy fines for those who struck a colleague or brought the hall into disrepute; some of the heaviest fines were levied against those who maintained 'erroneous' religious principles, or who neglected to attend High Mass at times of religious festival. They were not allowed to frequent taverns or brothels, of course, and the playing of dice and chess was expressly forbidden; chess, in particular, was considered an unsuitable pastime. They could be fined a farthing if they sang or played a musical instrument too loudly, and they were prohibited from keeping hawks, dogs or ferrets. No arms were to be carried, except on the occasions when a scholar was compelled to travel. If healthful recreation was considered necessary, then all the students of the Hall would leave together and afterwards return together. It is possible to learn something of the natural propensities of scholars, even from these strict codes of conduct, and it is hard to believe that the atmosphere of the small halls (perhaps even of the colleges) was as restrained as it was supposed to be. It is only necessary to look at the vignettes of urban and rural life depicted in the margins, or within the very letters, of sacred texts to understand how a vigorous and joyful natural life could flourish within the customs of a ceremonial and hierarchical society.

On feasts such as that of Epiphany or All Saints, entertainment was provided after the religious observances had been fulfilled. Some scholars furnished their own form of 'misrule' at the festival of the Holy Innocents, three days after Christmas, and in one Oxford college there was a *rex fabarum* or king of beans.[32] There were also occasions when minstrels and players would be introduced into the normally sober precincts of hall or college, among them the *fistulatos* and the *tubicens*. By the time that More had come to Oxford, comedies and other plays were also acceptable entertainment; there are records of the works of Plautus and Aristophanes, two of the favourites of student comedy, being performed on just such occasions. The young More had 'stepped in' among the players in the hall of Lambeth Palace, but his dramatic skills were greatly extended after his arrival at Oxford. Erasmus mentions in one letter that, while he was still an *adolescens* (a youth of fifteen years or upwards), More wrote, and performed in, short comedies or comic sketches.[33] There is confirmation of the fact in the first sentence of More's earliest extant letter, when he mentions the composition of 'partes' or a role in a comedy about Solomon.[34] Comic episodes of this kind were often employed in the teaching of grammar. Scholars were sometimes also required to compose short plays in order to furnish proof of their grammatical and rhetorical abilities. We cannot divorce More the scholar from More the dramatist, therefore, and any modern idea of 'creative literature' must give way to a proper understanding of rhetoric as the basis of all his work. His wit, his ingenuity as a writer, his skill as an actor, and his public roles, were all part of the same dispensation.

More had also begun to write poetry, of a highly accomplished kind. We must turn again to Erasmus for the information that in his youth More wrote verses – 'carmine ... exercuit'[35] is the phrase, which might mean either songs or lyric poems. Recent scholars have suggested that certain epigrams and comic English verses might be attributed to More, but the evidence is at best only conjectural. It would be inconceivable that he did not compose in verse, however, especially since it was one of the requirements of the curriculum. There is in any case no doubt about his first elaborate poem, 'Nyne pageauntes', which appeared in the English edition of his works some twenty years after his death. The publisher of his verse and prose 'in the Englysh tonge', his nephew William Rastell, states that More 'in his youth deuysed in hys Fathers house in London, a goodly hangyng of fyne paynted clothe, with nyne pageaunts', complete with verses.[36] Another story suggests that John More was so delighted by the proficiency of his son's poetry that he had cloths painted and hung upon the walls in order to display it to best advantage. Over the first image, of a boy playing with a whip and top, More has written a verse of iambic pentameters in the form of rhyme royal. It begins,

> I am called Chyldhod, in play is all my mynde
> To cast a coyte, a cokstele, and a ball.[37]

Eight other painted scenes follow, to display the passing 'pageant' of the world from youth to age, accompanied by images of death crushed under the feet of Lady Fame and of time prostrate before 'Eternitie' sitting in a great chariot like some figure out of Petrarch's *Trionfi*. It is all highly theatrical, and might even have set the stage for dramatic recitations by the More family. The powerfully assured verses of 'Nyne pageauntes' emerge from a technical mastery of grammatical and rhetorical devices which seems almost unprecedented in a young scholar. This was no doubt one of the skills which appealed to Samuel Johnson, that great classicist and composer of Latin verse, who in his *History of the English Language* devoted more than twice as much space to More's poetry as he did to Chaucer's. He praised its 'pure and elegant style',[38] and indeed all of More's English verse is characterised by great purity of diction and simplicity of cadence. It represents in the very finest form what was known as 'discrecion' in the apt arrangement of parts. That is why 'Nyne pageauntes' should be read and understood in terms of its use of metonymy and metaphor, asyndeton and metathesis, peristasis and paralepsis. It is necessary to expel any notion of poetry as self-expression and to consider it instead as a particularly affecting form of grammar.

But it should not therefore be assumed that it was some theoretical exercise; grammar was the companion of rhetoric and oratory, which in turn are implicated in drama. More might equally well step among the pageants as among the players, since the very scheme and cadence of the poem associate it with the guild pageant plays and the mysteries which he saw performed on the streets of London. It has been suggested that More owes his central debt to the verse of Petrarch, but we may find his inspiration closer to home. In Clerkenwell or in Cheapside, figures from classical and biblical legend would be displayed upon chariots, or would step down and address the crowd in the same spirit as More's emblems of time and fatality. On the afternoon of Corpus Christi thirty-six painted pageants passed through the streets of London with these verses of explanation hung among them:

47

With theos figures shewed in youre presence,
By diuers likenesses you to doo plesaunce.[39]

The pageant wagons for the procession of the Midsummer Watch
were constructed and stored in Leadenhall; they were painted, gilded,
and carried in procession upon the shoulders of porters. In the
morality plays performed at Skinners' Well, and elsewhere, the rise
and fall of humankind were plotted in much the same terms as
More's rendition of youth and age. 'I gynne to waxyn hory and olde,'
declares Mankind in one such play, 'My bake gynnyth to bowe and
bende'.[40] A pageant was literally, in the words of one contemporary,
'a house of wainscot painted and builded on a cart with four
wheels'[41] and upon these wagons allegorical figures would address
each other just like Fame and Eternity in More's own poem. When a
prominent member of the Spanish royal family entered London, she
was greeted by six pageants constructed at various points along her
route from London Bridge into the City. Painted wooden castles built
upon stone foundations, columns and statues, fountains and artificial
mountains, mechanical zodiacs and battlements, were all arranged
before her as Virtue spoke:

And therffor wyth lesse labour and payn
To myne acquayntance ye shal well attayn.[42]

The verse is not as skilful as that of More, but the general form of
address and meaning is very similar. It has been necessary to multiply
these examples of late fifteenth- and early sixteenth-century theatrical
rituals to suggest the urban tradition and inheritance from which
Thomas More drew. He might have derived inspiration, also, from
the allegorical figures of illuminated manuscripts, from the stock
types and situations to be found in sermons and fabliaux, from the
richly painted verses and pictures upon the walls of the cloister of
Paul's Pardon Churchyard close to his house in Milk Street. All these
images and words were around him since the young More was part
of a culture which was still oral, communal, spectacular and
ritualistic. His 'Nyne pageauntes' harbours a medieval voice in which
the cadences of the liturgy and the plays, of debate and disputation,
as well as a whole wealth of sounds and signs and emblems, are still
to be recognised. It was his genius, as we shall see, to put his

rhetorical and grammatical skills at the service of this popular culture; but, at this point, we may return with him to that city which, according to John Lydgate in 'London Lykpeny', 'of all the land . . . beareth the pryse'.[43]

VI

Duty is the Love of Law

HE left Oxford, without acquiring a degree, and took up his studies at New Inn. This was one of the Inns of Chancery, where More – now sixteen years of age – began a legal training which would last for the next six or seven years. The general supposition among his biographers is that he was commanded by his father to follow a legal course, against his own better wishes and instincts. It is certainly true that a few of his contemporaries at Oxford or Cambridge (most of them later became his friends) had decided to pursue a different career directed towards what was called the 'new learning'; these were the scholars who would in retrospect be given the title of 'humanists' or even the 'London humanists'. They took part in what was already a familiar pilgrimage to the sites of new classical scholarship; in Florence, Padua, Rome, Ferrara and Jerusalem, they placed themselves in the care of tutors imbued with Neoplatonism and Greek study, concerned with a purer grammar taken directly from classical sources, intent upon training the understanding as well as the memory. Thomas Linacre had gone to Padua in 1487; William Grocyn was in Florence by the following year. John Colet travelled in Italy for three years after finishing his studies in England, and More's nearest contemporary at Oxford, Cuthbert Tunstall, followed Linacre to Padua in search of further enlightenment. In the autumn of 1494, when More attended New Inn, Savonarola was preaching, with a tongue of flame, upon apocalypse and the rebirth of grace in Florence. The cities of Italy seemed, in their different ways, to be advancing the cause of *rinnovazione*. This is to say nothing of Leonardo in Milan, or of Michelangelo in Florence itself.

But the young Thomas More returned to the household in Milk Street. He seems to have had little interest in scholarship or the pursuit of classical studies for their own sake. Instead he prepared himself for what, with only a slight anachronism, can be described as the family business. Did his father force him to do so, as biographers have suggested? Erasmus intimates that John More threatened to disinherit his son if he did not enter an Inn,[1] but all the circumstances of More's life and temperament suggest that this was never the case. He had an abiding respect for the practice, and a deep admiration for the principles, of law. He knew that human justice was only the faintest reflection of divine law, but it became for him the principle and model of conduct upon the earth. Of course more practical reasons might have persuaded the young More to embark upon a legal career. In the same sentence that Erasmus talks of More being disowned or disinherited (the verb '*abdicare*' has both connotations) he goes on to admit that characteristically in England lawyers were '*magni clarique*', important and distinguished. He was certainly well informed on that point, since in the last decades of the fifteenth century lawyers were seen as a professional class of administrators who took up the key positions in various royal councils and offices. The sons of the landed gentry were now being directed towards the law, where there were growing rewards of prestige and wealth, rather than to the Church or trade. Serjeants-at-law, one of the principal ranks among common lawyers, were considered to be of equal status with knights. But they were not necessarily held in such high esteem, however, since they were often condemned as avaricious and mendacious. The possibilities of financial reward were obvious enough, and one metrical tale of the period makes the point succinctly:

> To grete worshippe hath the lawe
> Brought forth many a pouere man.[2]

And how could it not be so, in a society and culture which have been rightly called obsessed by the law and legal relationships? Every activity of life was seen within a network of duties and obligations, which in turn led to a concern for precise formulae and ordinances. It has been estimated that in each law term there were more than a thousand pleas or bills being conveyed through the various courts.[3]

More had not advanced to the later stages of an Oxford education precisely because it seemed to offer no advantage in the affairs of men. On entering the field of law, however, he was being despatched to a practical career in the public world. It was only within this sphere that he could properly deploy the lessons in rhetoric and dialectic which he had already learned. There were also more immediate advantages to be gained from his admission to New Inn. The sons of other gentlemen and of nobles were also being educated there, and at once the young More was in the company of those people who would eventually administer the affairs of the king and the nation.

Perhaps most importantly, the role of lawyer suited his own temperament. He was a resourceful actor and he became an equally skilful rhetorician; in later life he was sought by both Court and City for his gifts as an orator. (That is why he also became, according to the reports of foreign observers and others, the perfect diplomat.) His polemic texts reveal the persistence, subtlety and inventiveness of his attacks against his opponents; as a forensic orator, and judicial examiner, he is as fierce as he is persuasive, continually changing or extending his line of attack, looking for the smallest inconsistencies, finding weaknesses and deriding mistakes of terminology or presentation. More as a lawyer is the apotheosis of the clever and practical man. Yet cleverness alone is not enough. In More it was accompanied by a consistent doubleness or ambiguity of mind. He had been thoroughly trained in the art of disputation, where it was necessary to take up either side of a question, and his prose works themselves are generally couched as dialogues or debates. The most famous description of him by Erasmus as a man '*omnium horarum*',[4] because of his affability and sweetness of nature, was translated in the period as 'a man for all seasons'; but it could have additional connotations. He was always most reluctant to reveal himself as the author of his works and often used the masquerade of an assumed name. Throughout his life, in fact, he seems to have maintained a curious detachment – one example of which lies in his almost impersonal maintenance of authority both as councillor of the king and defender of the faith. He was always precise and shrewd, but there is a suspicion at times that he was playing some kind of game. His son-in-law remarked that More never showed 'of what mind himself was therein'.[5] Here, then, are the makings of a perfect lawyer – skilful yet detached, cautious as well as theatrical, persuasive and practical in equal measure.

New Inn, formerly a tavern known as Our Lady Inn, was situated at the lower end of Drury Lane (where the crescent of the Aldwych was built in the early twentieth century); it was not a pastoral spot, despite the fields and grazing cattle shown around it on an Elizabethan map, since it was essentially a legal quarter between the City and Westminster, where other Inns were to be found. There were at least ten Inns of Chancery, most of them being connected as preparatory institutions to one of the four Inns of Court – New Inn was affiliated with the Middle Temple, for example, although Thomas More followed recent family precedent by going on to Lincoln's Inn. Familial ties might well also have been responsible for his admission to New Inn. The property upon which it stood was owned by a serjeant-at-law and later chief justice, John Fineux, who is believed to have been associated with Lincoln's Inn (and therefore with John More) and who was certainly the grandfather of More's son-in-law and first biographer, William Roper. It is often difficult to discern all the lineaments of family connection or affinity, but they are almost always present beneath the surface of any important medieval transaction.

The great fifteenth-century master of jurisprudence Sir John Fortescue described the Inns of Chancery as the proper home for 'young men, learning or studying *the originals*, and as it were the elements of Lawe, who . . . as they grow to ripenesse, so are they admitted into the greater Innes of the same studie, called the Innes of Court'.[6] The history of these Inns is as mysterious as the origin of English law itself (some historians dated it to the time of Julius Caesar or even, in one case, to the beginning of the world), but it seems likely that they developed from the *hospicia* or hostels in which lawyers stayed while they pleaded at the nearby courts of Westminster; the tavern of Our Lady in Drury Lane was no doubt among them. By the time of Thomas More's admission, however, the Chancery Inns were well established. They comprised approximately one hundred students, or *apprenticii*, and were considered to furnish 'an university or schoole of all commendable qualities requisite for Noblemen'.[7] They were indeed universities but with a more special-ised curriculum; Oxford and Cambridge provided some kind of training in civil and canon law, but the Inns of Chancery taught English common law – the law of the courts – which was perhaps the single most significant achievement of medieval England.

The young More set out to acquire the basics of what had become an elaborately codified system of procedures and precedents. But first it was necessary to understand a new language, the language of the law, which was not simply a matter of terminology but also of tongue. English was used for general argument in the courts, while most of the statutes and writs were composed in Latin; but formal pleading, and the exercises known as 'moots', were conducted in a strange judicial vernacular called 'Law French'. This was an inheritance from the Norman kings, but it had developed into a hybrid form of speech suited only to judges and lawyers: 'Est un question in nos livres si ... l'opinion des touts les justices ... Amendez votre ple.'[8] Even the 'Year Books', those records of pleas and cases going back to the thirteenth century, are in that tongue. It is testimony to their faith in custom and authority that English common lawyers continued to use this hybrid form, although Latin and English were readily available. And when one of More's earliest biographers records that 'he learnt French, as being useful for diplomatic work',[9] we can note the fact but alter the reason for it.

Early training began, also, with the intensive study of particular statutes or pleas, as well as treatises of a more general nature on the role of custom and reason in the formation of law. The Year Books would have been too cumbersome and elaborate for a sixteen-year-old 'apprentice'; there was instead one of the few law books in print, the *Old Abridgment*, which contained judicious summaries of various aspects of royal prerogative. The king's 'priviledges' became one of the great concerns of More's own writings and would of course eventually decide his fate; but, as a student, he merely had to learn them by rote. Procedure, in the strictest and most formal sense, was the centre of the law; the process was of more importance than any judgment, and the formal rituals of presentation and challenge took precedence over the desire for any particular result. The young More had to learn how to classify and formalise the materials of an individual case; he was first brought to the learning of writs which were, as one parliamentary petition of the previous century had put it, 'the chiefest part of that law which is the sovereign law of king and kingdom'.[10] The oldest book of common law was the *Register of Writs*; it was not printed until 1531, but there were manuscript copies in the great households as well as the Inns. Here the writs were classified according to custom – writs of trespass and writs of liability, writs of covenant and writs of right, writs for every manner of action and occasion, all of which had to be studied and remembered. The lawyer was obliged to choose exactly the right writ before proceeding; otherwise his client's case, however apparently just, would be rendered void and inadmissible. The choice of writ determined the nature of the court, the nature of the proceedings and, of course, the nature of the judgment.

The evidence of judicial procedure could also be found at first hand. It became the custom for the *apprenticii* to attend the morning hearings of the various courts in Westminster Hall. Here they would listen to the 'pleadings' which were at the heart of the judicial process; there was no written evidence, only the oral submissions and the subsequent arguments between bench and bar. Reports of these conversations are to be found in the Year Books: 'Shame to him who pleaded this plea . . . This is not the first time we have heard a plea of this kind . . . That is a sophistry and this is a place designed for the truth.'[11] These verbatim records bring us as close to the people of the period as we are ever likely to be permitted, and for a moment we can stand with the *apprenticii* behind the bars or barriers of the court and listen to them talking. 'My client is a poor man and knows no law,' an attorney pleads, to which the judge replies, 'It is because he knows no law that he has retained you.' Another judge notes the stupidity of a plaintiff but adds, rather marvellously, 'He will have a remedy here in Chancery, for God protects the simple.' And so we hear their voices again, after five hundred years. 'Leave off your noise and deliver yourself from this account . . . It will go to the winds, as does the greatest part of that which you say . . . Are not the tallies sealed with your seal? About what would you tender and make law? For shame.'[12] There was even an occasion when a reporter noted how a judge winked at a lawyer to convey 'the best procedure for him to follow'.[13]

When they returned from Westminster to New Inn, the *apprenticii* would debate the arguments and procedures raised by the cases which they had heard. They were instructed both in theory and in practice, therefore, and learned the principles 'whereupon the lawe of England is grounded'.[14] What is the nature of equity? What is meant by the phrase *ex aequo bonoque*? What are the boundaries of judicial discretion and written statute? These were just some of the questions that exercised law students of the period, all of them being resolved or elaborated by means of oral teaching and disputation; More's education, from school and university to the Inn, was in that sense of a piece. He was learning how to plead, and in the process discovering the rules of confirmation and confutation, of dilatory pleas and pleas in bar, of special traverse and general traverse. More himself, in later work, recalled the oral and judicial exercises to which he applied himself; in the course of an elaborate legal argument with one opponent, he 'waxen me thought a yong man agayn and semed set at a vacacyon mote with hym in some Inne of the chauncery'.[15]

Each evening, at dinner in the hall of the Inn, a report on some legal topic or actual court case was placed beside the salt cellar; no one was allowed to know its contents but, after the meal was over, two junior barristers were required to argue on either side of the legal matter presented to them. This was known as 'putting the case' or 'putting case that', a phrase which More often uses in his polemical writings against heretics – writings that are the work of a lawyer rather than of a theologian. If the senior members of the Inn found the issues arising from this 'case' debatable or 'mootable', then in Law French more senior barristers would analyse the themes and questions further. This was the 'mote'. It was the single most important formal instruction in pleading and procedure that the student received, and inculcated lessons in argument which More used to the end of his life.

His advanced legal training, however, began when he left New Inn after two years and entered Lincoln's Inn. This was the Inn of which his father was a senior member, and More would have been enrolled here as a matter of familial propriety and obligation. He was admitted on 12 February 1496, just after his eighteenth birthday, and according to the register of the Inn he was excused four vacations at the instigation of John More; the 'vacations' were, paradoxically, the time of the most intensive study and it may be that Thomas More's proficiency allowed him to move rapidly and easily through the established stages of learning. It may, however, simply have been a favour to John More; on the same day he arranged the admission of another member of his extended family, a future son-in-law, with a similar dispensation.

Lincoln's Inn was across the fields from New Inn. Its history was obscure but, by the time of More's arrival, it was already prosperous; there was an excellent library, and a new hall had recently been constructed in that red and damson brick so characteristic of late fifteenth-century buildings. The Inn had more than a hundred members and, at some point, More shared chambers or *cubicula* with a student named Edward Arnold, who was acquainted with Erasmus. Nothing is known of this intriguing connection. More's earliest biographer does not allude to his contemporaries, mentioning only that he was kept at Lincoln's Inn on 'a very small allowance' from his father and remained there until he became an 'utter barrister'.[16] The term itself has now fallen out of use, but it reflects one stage of the career upon which More had now embarked. The Inn was governed by a formal hierarchy and, in order to understand it properly, it may be better to begin at the beginning of More's own life here. He had begun as an apprentice of the law, from which lowly degree he now proceeded to the rank of 'inner barrister'. He was still a student of the law and his title meant only that during his tuition he sat upon an inner row of *barrae*, the late Latin word for seats or benches. He would be obliged to sit here, for example, to be exercised in the art of 'bolting' when he was examined by his seniors on various hypothetical cases or points of law. After several years of this preparatory training – estimates range from four to eight years and it must have depended to a large extent upon individual ability – he was then eligible for the rank of utter or outer barrister. In the customary phrase he was called 'to the Bar' – he was no longer sitting 'under the Bar' with the inner barristers. More's legal education would already have lasted at least six years, but he would not have been allowed to practise law in Westminster for a further three years. Eventually he joined the 'apprentices-at-law' there, and could plead in most of the courts of the country. But it was a protracted training, lasting on any actuarial basis almost a quarter of an adult's life in the period.

From the ranks of the utter barristers were then chosen the readers, who lectured upon the law during the 'learning vacations', and the benchers who made up the governing body of the Inn. From these in turn were picked the most senior lawyers in England, the serjeants-at-law and the judges. Elaborate ceremonials, both religious and secular, attended the election of these most important officers; when Thomas More's father was appointed a serjeant in 1503, there would have been seven days of celebration culminating in a great feast. John More was given a white silk coif, like a skull-cap, which he was not permitted to remove even in the presence of the king; he wore long multi-coloured robes with vertical stripes, to distinguish his order from the diagonal stripes of the barristers. The colours of these gowns changed over the decades, but in the early sixteenth century we might surmise the stripes to be of that mulberry and blue which became standard issue by 1521. In addition, serjeants were expected to wear seasonal liveries of scarlet or violet or green. Again, the emphasis is upon display, hierarchy, precedent and ceremony.

The diurnal life of Lincoln's Inn manifested similar characteristics. It was a life in which all the members of the body ate, worshipped, disputed and celebrated together. Members of the various degrees and ranks, from clerk to bencher, lived in close proximity and thereby created a 'tight professional community'.[17] Of course it would be misleading, as well as false to any notion of common sense, to idealise or even to over-emphasise the extent of this 'community'. Not all of the law students fulfilled their course with the same punctiliousness as Thomas More; some left early and returned to less prestigious practice as country lawyers, while others must have found the prolonged period of study too exacting or demanding. Recent research has suggested a 'drop-out' rate (including early death, a factor which must always be introduced in such calculations of late fifteenth-century life) of 'nearly twenty per cent in three years'.[18] Even though the students were obliged to attend the Inn for only half of the year, between twenty-three and twenty-eight weeks, there were still fines being levied for neglecting moots or readings. Sir John Fortescue described the Inn as a *gymnasium* or academy for the noble arts; he mentioned singing and dancing among them, but there is no evidence for such diversions from any other source. It is more likely that dancing and singing schools – not unlike those of eighteenth-century London – sprang up beside these communities of young men on the borders of the city. Youthful lawyers, in such a situation, were also likely to neglect their studies from time to time; there are records of punishments for dicing, harlotting, fighting and drunkenness. A brothel in Holborn, 'John Hasylrykke's House', was known to the authorities; there was also a famous inn in the vicinity, the White Hart, where swords were drawn on more than one occasion.

Here, then, is one of the expected contraries of late medieval society – the appetite for order and hierarchy is matched only by the tendency towards disorder or violent disruption. These opposing forces were held together by bringing them both within the rituals of display and seasonal ceremony. That is why the Inns of Court, at the centre of the education of a new generation, placed so much emphasis in their internal administration upon revels and feasts of misrule. In Lincoln's Inn a lord of misrule supervised the festivities of Christmas, which included masques and plays of the kind in which

Thomas More had participated at Lambeth Palace. But there were
other revels on different occasions of the year, and we read of a 'Jack
Straw' and a 'king of Cockneys' as well as of 'splendid shews,
notable pastimes, and costly feastings'.[19] Yet there can be seasonal
misrule only within a prevailing architecture of order, just as the
debates and disputations of the late medieval period are possible only
within the context of an assured and absolute truth which governs
humankind.

During the festivities marking the election of a serjeant-at-law the
new serjeant presented rings to his colleagues, marked with a legend
and design of his own choosing. It was a sacred ritual, no doubt
deriving from the ancient rites of coronation when the monarch was
given a ring as one of the symbols of divine ordination. The religious
element of the ceremony did not go unnoticed by contemporary
theorists. Fortescue himself quoted with approval Justinian's remark
that judges were 'priests of the law',[20] and John Wycliffe compared
the white silk coif of the serjeant to the religious head-dress of the
Jewish priests. A medieval Italian jurist, Baldus, also claimed that
doctors of law 'discharge the office of priesthood'.[21] These allusions
might be taken to infer that law was seen to be part of religion, or
even religion to be part of law; but the central and important point is
that both were conceived to be visible aspects of the same spiritual
reality. The common metaphor, of the temporal and spiritual
jurisdictions as being two edges of the same sword, puts the matter
more starkly; and the implications are clear enough. Common law
was believed to be 'grounded upon the lawe of reason and the lawe
of God', and Fortescue paraphrased the words of the Old Testament
king Jehoshaphat in declaring that 'All judicial sentences are the
judgements of God.'[22] Religion and law were not to be considered
separately; they implied one another. That is why law was considered
to be perfect in itself, undamaged by the bad judgments of individual
practitioners; the same argument, on the merits of the Mass as
opposed to the virtue of the priest who offered it, was at the heart of
Catholic eucharistic belief. That is why the law was also considered
to be permanent; it was what was known to be true, withstanding
change or decay. It is possible to see how in its theoretical state it
became the image and explanatory model for all areas of human
activity: it stood upon the ground which we are now accustomed to
call politics, for example, and marked out the very nature of society
itself. There were laws of custom and the law of nature. 'If there were

no Law,' says one judge quoted in a Year Book, 'there would be no King and no inheritance.'[23] That is why it is misleading to separate 'social' from 'political', 'legal' or 'religious' matters in this period; they represent the same central concern of fallen man, which lay in understanding and organising his temporary sojourn upon the earth.

The attitude More adopted towards the primacy and authority of law governed all his subsequent actions. It is of the greatest significance in understanding his behaviour, for example, to realise that he wrote about the law in precisely the same way he described the Church. There was, for him, no essential or necessary difference. That is why he understood at once the nature of Martin Luther's heresy, when the German monk spoke of judgement 'according to love ... without any law books'. When Luther emphasised the importance of the 'free mind', as opposed to the tenets of 'the law books and jurists',[24] More recognised instinctively that he was mounting an attack upon the whole medieval polity as constituted by the Catholic Church; when Luther argued that law was written within the heart of man, and that judges should ignore matters of precedent and tradition, he was assaulting the principles by which More's life and career were guided. More defended the law, in turn, by emphasising the importance of 'consensus' and 'usus', and by invoking the common feeling and customary usage of the Christian world.[25] In his description of this general authority, he distinguishes between formal statutes or laws and the oral tradition which is handed down by generation upon generation of English judges and is embodied in the Year Books as precedent or commentary. This is perhaps not worthy of remark, except that More comes to define the Catholic Church in precisely the same language, even to the extent that he distinguishes the written scriptures from the oral tradition conveyed from the lips of the apostles down the ages. In his recognition of the identity of Church and Law, we come closer to More's general sense of life and to that particular self-awareness with which he conducted himself.

He had not entered the world fully armed with these notions of authority or tradition, of course, and we must look elsewhere for their origins. Thomas More had followed his father's steps by joining Lincoln's Inn – John More was a bencher there even as his son sat below him as an inner barrister – and in their reciprocal relations something may be revealed. There is evidence of three books owned by John More. One was the history of Britain composed by Geoffrey of Monmouth (in the pages of which he had entered the birth date of his son), and the two others were volumes of legal precedents and abridgements. There is a story of Thomas More using the arcane concept of 'withernam', a term used for a legal act of reprisal, to confound an opponent. It is in itself an uninteresting story (except so far as it provides evidence for More's occasional sarcasm) but it has one significant aspect: John More's extant book of abridgements concludes with three of his handwritten notes on the subject of 'withernam'. His own concerns were, in a real sense, Thomas More's inheritance.

VII

Most Holy Father

THOMAS More, as Lord Chancellor of England, invariably attended Westminster Hall to preside over the Court of Chancery; John More was a justice of the King's Bench in the same Hall and, whenever Thomas More passed him on his way to his duties, he knelt down among the noise and business in order to ask his father's blessing. The scene is evocative enough to have been described by all of More's biographers, suggesting, as it does, More's reverence for authority as well as his humility; he took precedence as Lord Chancellor, but maintained his obligations as a son. It also suggests in cryptic form the preoccupation with ceremony and display that More shared with his contemporaries. It was, you might say, his habit. Every morning and evening, when he was a child, he would also have knelt down in reverence before his father.

There is a drawing by Hans Holbein the Younger of John More; it shows him as judge, wearing the cap and the robe edged with miniver fur (believed to have been that of the Siberian squirrel). But it is the individual face and temperament that arouse interest. Holbein was depicting medieval men, but he was not a medieval artist; he illustrates his sitters in the light of some sudden but characteristic emotion, as if he had caught their thought on its wing. Thus they seem purposeful without being, in a fifteenth-century sense, emblematic. The drawing of John More must have been completed rapidly, in preparation for the great portrait of the More family at Chelsea, but the artist has sketched the lineaments of a full and awakened life; the thin mouth and fleshy nose are recognisable features of the More physiognomy, but the study of John More has none of the remoteness and diffidence which appear in the portrait of his son. The father's eyes are bright, almost glaring, with the set composure of the face suggesting the presence of someone who has mastered and understood his world. There is a starkness in the face, not untouched by humour but calculating and forceful nonetheless.

It would be foolish to establish an entire biographical narrative upon the basis of one sketch, even by so distinguished an artist. On this occasion it is important only to register the dependence of father and son; the whole of Thomas More's life is caught up in the maintenance of authority, and we can look for the first stirrings of it within the family of Milk Street. It might be said that More possessed genius precisely because he stood in symbolic relation to his age; he embodied the old order of hierarchy and authority at the very moment when it began to collapse all around him. He died for the sake of the order which he had first learned in his father's house.

The discipline of late medieval households was well known; one manuscript in the Ashmolean Library describes how men and women even in their thirties might not sit in their parents' presence 'without leave, but stood like mutes bare-headed among them'.[1] This may be an exaggeration, designed to impress rather than to inform, but it imparts the general tenor of household life. Manuals suggested early and strict discipline for the child – with the use of 'harsh suppositories' to encourage toilet training[2] – and More's references to his nurse rather than to his mother in turn imply a degree of separation or estrangement. His relationship to his father was, according to the later members of his own family, equally subdued. Cresacre More reports that More 'never offended nor contradicted him in anie the least worde or action'.[3] No doubt there would have been penalties for so doing, and in later life More asserted the symbolic significance of the father chastising the child – 'that father is not accompted for vnlouyng and cruell that beteth hys chyld but rather he that leueth yt vndone'[4] – as an image of divine paternalism. Yet the mature Thomas More never beat his own children except, on occasions, with peacock feathers. John More is supposed to have been economical with his son's funds; Thomas More was continually giving gifts and coins to his own children. His daughter remembers her father losing his temper only twice in the whole course of her life. Would it be too much to suggest, in similar spirit of reprisal, that More witnessed his own father losing his temper too often? It does not take a psychologist, of whatever school, to realise that such reversal of his father's habits suggests a certain innate dislike or hostility which can be expressed in no other way. Yet throughout his life he displayed nothing but a meek spirit towards John More. It was a form of piety in the strict sense – in *The City of God*, Augustine defines piousness as the attitude of duty and deference to parents – and bears the marks of the prevailing belief that it was sinful to disobey lawfully constituted authority. More also defines it as the 'naturall charitie' that 'bindeth the father and the childe'[5] and tells his own son, also named John, that he should be 'eager to delight' and 'cautious not to give offense' to his father.[6] Certainly More himself gave no offence and followed a career which delighted his father.

John More must have been an ambitious man to succeed in becoming serjeant and justice, especially since he was the first member of his family ever to train as a lawyer, and no doubt he also focused his ambition upon his son. Was More following his father's orders in becoming Lord Chancellor? There is no evidence at all that he did so unwillingly; the facts suggest the opposite, and it can be surmised that More 'internalised' his father's predilections and preoccupations without undue disquiet. He stands in marked contrast once again to his greatest opponent: Martin Luther defied his father's wish that he should become a lawyer, and it could be said that Luther's quarrel with paternal authority was eventually heard all over Europe. But More suffered from no such neurotic or ideological crisis and it was he who, against Luther, defended the old order of Christendom. It is interesting to note, when More was attacking heresy, the particular way in which he chose to remember his father; he is generally described as recounting oral tales or proverbial phrases. In *A Dialogue Concerning Heresies*, John More appears on four occasions – telling the story of a feigning beggar in the days of King Henry VI, for example, and of a 'gentlewoman' who refused to believe that 'our lady was a Iewe' but when convinced of the fact by John More affirmed 'so helpe me god and holydom I shall loue her the worse whyle I lyue'.[7] So the father is connected with earlier times and with the old faith, conveyed in stories and remarks that emphasise the common frailty of humankind. These stories can be seen as the oral equivalents of the histories, precedents and legal abridgements which were part of his library. The inheritance and meaning of the past are to inform present actions; as in the Catholic doctrine of purgatory, the dead can and must be heard among the living. The name of the father, too, can be heard throughout More's writings. In *Utopia*, the inhabitants of that ambiguous country worship an eternal unknown being called father.[8] In more theoretical contexts More always adverts to the authority of patristic sources, 'the fathers' whom he addresses as *sanctissimos* ('most holy') and *doctissimos* ('most learned').[9] But the image of the father is not simply representative of ancient wisdom; in the context of religious change it becomes of pressing contemporary significance, since the English Church could no more forsake Rome 'than might the child refuse obedience to his natural father'.[10] In this refrain of 'father' and of 'fathers', most holy and most learned, we can hear also the cry for authority and restraint.

More's single most bitter accusation against Luther and his followers, was that they incited disorder. He is the first English writer to employ the Greek term *anarchos*, and he related the whole great change of European consciousness in the sixteenth century to the 'hatred that they beare to all good order' and 'the great hunger yt they haue to brynge all out of order'.[11] He detested vain meddling and what he called 'newefangylness'; even if there were to be such a thing as a bad law, he once argued, public discussion of the matter was to be avoided at all costs. But when Luther attacked Henry VIII and the Pope he seemed to More to be also imperilling the civilisation of a thousand years. His attitude is reminiscent of Edgar Allan Poe, who wrote, three hundred years later, that 'The people have nothing to do with the laws but to obey them'.[12] It is why More had no 'ideas' as such; he had no need for them, and part of his dislike for medieval logic was its potential for creating discordancies or problems where none had previously existed. It is significant in this context that an extant copy of Euclid's *Elements*, with annotations in More's hand, shows him to have been particularly interested in theoretical geometry and altogether impressed by a closed system of knowledge which offered 'absolute certainty' and 'self-evident truths'.[13] In the words of the prophet Samuel, 'to obey is better than sacrifice'.[14]

But cannot obedience and sacrifice be intimately related? Two episodes from this period make a suggestive connection. In later life More wrote a Latin poem to a lady called 'Elisabetha', in which with much circumstantial detail he recounts his youthful infatuation for her. He says that he was sixteen at the time (and therefore about to enter New Inn), she fourteen, when he was struck by '*innocuo ... amore*',[15] or harmless love, at a dance. She seems to have returned his affection, but a '*custos*' or guardian was employed to keep them apart. The poem is possibly a poetic fiction, designed simply to display More's skills in amatory elegiacs, but it does receive some corroboration from Erasmus. He wrote a letter, at about the same time as More composed the poem, in which he describes how the youthful More was not immune to the charms of young women.[16] But he hastens to add that More preferred a union of minds rather than of bodies and that he stopped short of 'infamia' or disgrace. It is in a similar spirit that More, in his poem, emphasises more than once that his love for Elizabeth was 'sine crimine'.[17] It is an interesting little story, not least because it marks one of the few occasions when More was willing openly to discuss his private feelings, but it has an even more intriguing sequel.

According to one of More's biographers – one who had the additional advantage of talking to those who had known him – 'even as a youth, he wore a hair-shirt'[18] as a form of penance and mortification. Cresacre More repeats a similar claim: 'When he was about eighteen or twentie years olde, finding his bodie by reason of his yeares most rebellious, he sought diligently to tame his unbrideled concupiscence by wonderfull workes of mortification.'[19] One is reminded, somehow, of his large nose and rather thin lips. So he tried to chastise and tame his 'unbrideled' sexuality, even to the extent of wearing a rough and knotted hair shirt at such a young age. In his later work he evinces what is almost disgust at the body and its functions; he despised lechery and drunkenness, and there are reports that when a very young man he drank water rather than beer. The sense of order was one which had invaded his own physical being; he bore its marks in a literal sense, when he put on the hair shirt which chafed his skin. This, too, is the bitter fruit of duty and obedience.

If we reflect upon his relationship with his father, as well as on the general authority which John More embodied, we might be tempted to see his whole career in the light of that obedience. There may be no need to look for any private motive or specifically individual choice in any of his decisions (perhaps not even that concerning his death), but rather the dutiful assumption of public roles. There is, after all, an element of humility and self-abasement in the acceptance of the parts which he played – whether that of lawyer, or diplomat, or courtier.

When Thomas More knelt down with reverence before his father in Westminster Hall, his bowing was a form of humility and clarity of spirit. He was bowing to the Church and to the Law, to the authority of the past and the hierarchy of the world, to the eleven circles of the eleven heavens, to the order of the spheres which proceeds upwards to the crystalline universe, to the *primum mobile* and to that eternal 'circuite [of] enumerable angells singing'[20] around God. He is bowing with gravity and deliberation. But is he also smiling? He believed implicitly in the need for this ritual, but he was also playing a role to perfection.

VIII

We Talk of Letters

URING the reign of Edward III literate laymen had been granted the privilege of clergy and were not subject to the jurisdiction of the secular courts. But in 1489 the legislation was changed, and lay scholars became distinguished from clerks in holy orders; if they committed murder, for example, they would have the letter 'M' branded upon their heads as the punishment for a first offence. Nothing could better demonstrate the respect afforded to those who could read; they were, literally, members of a privileged class who might get away with murder. It is the most appropriate context for More's first entry into print. *Lac puerorum*, or *Milk for Children*, was published in 1497. It was a basic Latin grammar for schoolboys – a book about learning how to read. Its author, John Holt, had been a teacher of grammar at Magdalen College School in Oxford, but was at this time resident tutor for the younger members of Cardinal Morton's household at Lambeth Palace. Since the little treatise is dedicated to John Morton, and since it includes two Latin poems by an erstwhile member of that school, Thomas More, we may be inclined to see *Lac puerorum* as a production from the very centre of ecclesiastical and administrative life in the period. More refers to the lessons within it as *nostra*, 'ours', and it may be that he contributed more than poetry to its making. He was nineteen at the time of its publication – on an early page, his poems are described as the work of '*diserti adolescentuli*'[1] or eloquent young man – and the treatise bears all the marks of a youthful attempt to purge the basic curriculum of the dead matter which had grown about it. The lessons are conveyed in English, with little woodcuts of a candlestick and open hand as aids in the memorising of Latin cases and declensions. But no activity in the late fifteenth century was without possible spiritual connotation; the declension of Latin nouns was sometimes compared to the declension of the soul into the body.

John Morton died in the autumn of 1500 without, it must be said, any great evidence of public grief. By that time, however, Thomas More had clearly attracted the attention of other mentors. The evidence suggests that, even while studying at Lincoln's Inn, he found himself among a small group of scholars and clerics who had already sensed his worth. They have become known in recent years as the 'More circle', but at the time he was by no means the most eminent among them. In a letter of Erasmus's from this period More is praised for being *'mollius'*, *'dulcius'* and *'felicius'*,[2] easy-tempered and generally charming. These are hardly words of praise for his intellectual abilities, unless we take *'felicius'* in its subsidiary meaning of being fruitful of good works, but the important point of the letter is the setting in which Erasmus places More. It is a setting of erudition and classical scholarship, where the exemplary figures are John Colet, William Grocyn, Thomas Linacre and More himself. Colet is compared with Plato, while Grocyn is praised for his learning and Linacre for his good judgement. It is all the more remarkable that More should be included in this company, when it is remembered that Grocyn was thirty years, and Linacre almost twenty years, older than he was; Colet himself was born more than ten years before him. In his dialogues More tends to place an older man in conversation with a younger one, and it seems that the notion of wisdom and guidance being transmitted from age to youth was one that he established in his own life. In a letter to Colet, for example, he refers to Grocyn as the *'magister'* or director of his life and Linacre as the *'praecepter'* or instructor of his studies;[3] Colet himself acted as More's 'confessor'. In the pattern of these relationships it is possible to recognise the role which the young More frequently adopted towards those closest to him. Two salient characteristics of his friends are also relevant; they all took religious orders and all had spent some years in Italy or Greece as part of their scholarly training. So Thomas More was the exception among them; he was much younger, a student of the law and a layman apparently dedicated to a lay career. It is hard to assess the impact upon him of those who had lived or worked outside England, but it is significant that all his life he was able to combine a comprehensive understanding of what might be termed 'European' culture with a specific instinct for the life and genius of London. There was no necessary disjunction between the two. More had become attached to a group of people who, as far as Erasmus was concerned, comprised one of the finest centres of classical learning in Europe and one which was indeed superior to any in Italy.[4] The Dutch scholar was inclined to flattery, especially when it concerned prospective patrons, but there was a genuine truth to his remark. In these early days of what has become known as Christian humanism, before the Henrician reforms helped to destroy any English participation in this more general European culture, the scholars of Oxford and London and Cambridge were at the centre of intellectual enquiry and classical studies.

William Grocyn was the oldest of the group, but in a sense his career was exemplary. He had begun his studies at Oxford, where he became a fellow and later a Reader in Divinity; he was one of the few scholars there who acquired a knowledge of Greek, perhaps through one of those private tutors who, before the advent of humanism, kept alive the memory of the classical world. In 1488, in his early forties, he resigned his academic posts and travelled to Italy, part of that migration among the wealthier or more devoted English scholars towards the fount and source of good learning. There were tutors here from Athens and Jerusalem as well as Florence and Padua; there were small academies devoted to classical learning; there were manuscripts and libraries and printers. On his return to England Grocyn kept chambers in Exeter College, Oxford, where he taught and lectured in Greek studies. After some five years at Oxford Grocyn received the 'benefice' of St Lawrence Jewry through the agency of the Bishop of London – the acceptance of a 'benefice' from a patron, by those scholars who were also in holy orders, was the best way of ensuring a modest income with which they could continue their studies. St Lawrence was the church close to More's home in Milk Street, and here More himself would later lecture upon St Augustine's *City of God*; in turn Grocyn would lecture on the pseudo-Dionysius in St Paul's at John Colet's instigation.

Grocyn had perhaps become acquainted with More through More's close friend William Lily. Lily had made the customary journey from Oxford to Greece and Italy before returning to London. Here he became a tutor in Greek and Latin studies, in which capacity he assisted More in his private studies; certainly they were soon translating epigrams together. But Lily was also William Grocyn's godson and may have introduced the younger man to the older. There are other connections: Grocyn and John Colet were already acquainted, sharing an interest in the study of divinity free from scholastic accretions; and Grocyn had travelled in Italy with another of More's mentors, Thomas Linacre.

Linacre was a classical scholar with a difference. He made the familiar journey from Oxford, where he had attended More's college, to the various cities of Italy, where he is believed to have studied at the court of Lorenzo the Magnificent in Florence, as well as in Padua and Rome. But there came a moment in his Italian travels when he turned to thoughts of medicine; he began to read Aristotle and Galen, in the original Greek texts, and from that time must have harboured the ambition of translating them which eventually (if only in part) he fulfilled. He had returned to London by 1499 and, having already been awarded a degree *in medicinis* at Padua, he began to practise medicine as well as to teach Greek. In the latter position he had Thomas More as a pupil; William de Selling, the great patron of Canterbury College, had taught Greek to Linacre and now Linacre imparted it to More. He became, eventually, the most famous physician in England and his epitaph in old St Paul's declared that he had restored to life men 'who had already despaired of recovery'.[5] But his most permanent memorial must be as the expired hero of Robert Browning's 'A Grammarian's Funeral', where he is described as saying, in very mid-Victorian terms, 'What's Time? leave Now for dogs and apes! Man has For ever.' He was for a while also tutor to Prince Arthur, elder son of Henry VII and heir apparent; he translated a cosmographical treatise by the pseudo-Proclus, *De Sphaera*, but earned his place in Robert Browning's poem by composing a grammar for schoolboys that was considered as difficult as it was erudite.

More has left only one anecdote about Linacre; he describes a physician, 'the best expert, & therwith the most famouse to, & he that the greatest cures did vppon other men' who, when he himself grew sick, was so fearful of every symptom that 'his feare did hym some tyme much more harm than the siknes gave hym cause'.[6] In *Moriae encomium* Erasmus describes Linacre as a jealous and distracted man, who never could find rest in physic or in grammar. There are other reports of his being busy, no doubt over-bearing; one contemporary account describes how as the King's physician 'he might be seen striding among the nobles of the royal court, wearing a crimson gown reaching to his ankles, and a full cloak of black velvet thrown across his shoulders'.[7] This touch of extravagance will be seen among others of the 'More circle'.

It may even help us to understand the fourth of the English scholars, whom Erasmus most admired and whom More most loved. John Colet was a Londoner, from a famous and wealthy mercantile family living in Budge Row; his father had been Lord Mayor on two occasions, as well as a member of parliament for the City. Colet was one of only two of the twenty-two children of his family to survive; this would probably guarantee a curious or at least idiosyncratic attitude towards life, even in the funereal conditions of late fifteenth-century London, and there is no doubt that Colet left a definite impression upon his contemporaries for his character as much as his scholarship. He had also gone to St Anthony's School in Thread-needle Street, though before More, and had then been admitted to Cambridge University; Sir Henry Colet and John More were part of the same group of lawyers and administrators who organised the City's affairs, but it is not known for how long John Colet and Thomas More had known each other. The earliest document that brings them together is from 1502, reporting a ceremony at which More acted as a witness for Colet's resignation of an ecclesiastical preferment, a role that suggests, if nothing else, a measure of friendship. John Colet's younger brother, Richard, had entered Lincoln's Inn in the year before More was admitted to New Inn; the two families, then, had much in common. Colet left Cambridge to pursue studies in divinity at Oxford, but in his early twenties he also made the pilgrimage to Italy, where he was impressed by the fervent works of Marsilio Ficino and Pico della Mirandola, as well as by the fiery words of Savonarola. It is said that, in his academy in Florence, Ficino was accustomed to keep a votive lamp before the bust of Plato as well as the image of the Virgin; he wrote that man's whole duty lay in the aspiration towards immortality and the infinite, in the ascent of the soul to God by means of contemplation. It was in this heady atmosphere that Colet found his true faith. He has been variously described as a Christian Neoplatonist and a Catholic reformer, but really he was neither; like More, he simply found a more arresting method for fulfilling what remained essentially a late medieval piety. On his return from Italy, he took up a professorship at Oxford, where he began a series of lectures and commentaries upon the Bible and, in particular, upon the letters of St Paul.

There is an amusing description of John Colet in one of Erasmus's

Colloquies, concerning pilgrimages; they had travelled together to the shrine of St Thomas Becket in the cathedral church of Canterbury, where Colet was less than impressed by the various relics paraded before them by the pious guides. He drew back in disgust from a holy arm which still had some flesh adhering to it; he was 'of ardent temper',[8] too, and berated one priest for not distributing some of the riches of the shrine, bedecked in gold and silver and jewels, to the poor people of the area. There was one other characteristic touch when Colet, offered a piece of linen once supposedly used by Becket as a handkerchief, 'disdainfully replaced it; pouting out his lips as if imitating a whistle'.[9] The little *moue* which Colet made is entirely recognisable; he was a man of fastidious temperament, abstemious to a fault, disturbed by 'indecent or ambiguous words',[10] and a great preacher upon the horrors of the flesh. After he had become Dean of St Paul's, he ordered that signs be put on its walls and doorways proclaiming 'This is a holy place, and urinating is forbidden.' Colet also had a reputation for irascibility, contentiousness and stubbornness; as More said, he had a habit of '*disputandi*'[11] and was therefore fond of argument. His withdrawal from the finery and pleasures of the world was also emphasised by his dress; he always wore black, while his ecclesiastical rank demanded a scarlet hue. There was without doubt a certain extravagance in Colet's behaviour, which we may see as characteristic of this era in English life in which dress and gesture and deportment were considered to be indispensable elements in the creation and presentation of character.

Certainly the strident example of John Colet had a profound effect upon More, and he is described by two early biographers as the younger man's 'mentor'.[12] There seems little doubt that Colet introduced the younger man to the work of Pico della Mirandola, whose biography More subsequently translated; perhaps more importantly, Colet's sermons and arguments provided a model for reconciling More's intelligence, austerity and devotion. When Colet delivered his commentaries upon the letters of St Paul, for example, he was drawing upon the central texts of the period; the epistles, with their news of awakening and regeneration through the Holy Spirit, were soon to become of crucial importance in the theology of the Reformation; Luther would claim for his own new faith the apostle's conclusion that 'a man is justified by faith without the deeds of the law'.[13] But Colet was no reformer, at least not in that fundamental sense. In his own commentaries upon the Pauline texts, he chose to interpret the apostle's notions of grace and illumination within the context of the Neoplatonism Colet himself had imbibed at Florence. The declarations of Paul were taken as indications of the soul's thirst for the divine presence and of its ascent through the hierarchy of the universe towards the vision of godhead. It might be argued that Colet anticipates Luther in his emphasis upon individual enlightenment, but for Colet it takes place within the stable sphere of the Church upon earth. But his central point, for any understanding of More, is that the life of the spirit could be amplified by reference to classical sources.

Colet had a particular, angry dislike for the *Summa Theologica* of Thomas Aquinas, for example, and it is in this spirit that we can understand his emphasis upon love rather than knowledge in his *Lectures on Romans*. 'It is beyond doubt,' he wrote, 'more pleasing to God himself to be loved by men than to be surveyed, and to be worshipped than to be understood.'[14] Colet also talks of the need for the loving imitation of Christ, as the true model of active virtue in the world. It is possible to see here how religious devotion and the new emphasis upon classical scholarship are part of the same movement of the spirit – the return to the pristine sources of truth and the avoidance of commentary and interpretation, are part of the same great renovation of piety and learning which More and his contemporaries ardently wished for. They are a part, too, of their sense of the necessity for active involvement in the world. If Augustine learned from Paul, More in turn learned from Augustine.

These were the interests, then, that brought together Linacre the physician and Lily the grammarian, More the lawyer and Colet the preacher and educator. But there is one other person who would play a permanent and significant role in Thomas More's life. The name of John Rastell is now forgotten, yet he could lay claim to the title of 'Renaissance man' with greater plausibility than most of his more famous contemporaries. He was an 'utter barrister' of the Middle Temple, some two or three years older than More, and it is likely that they met when the younger man first entered New Inn. Rastell married More's sister, Elizabeth, while he was still a student of the law; some three years later, in 1499, he provided security for a loan together with John More and Thomas More. He and his wife returned to his birthplace of Coventry for a few years, but on his return to London he manifested all the energy which the city seemed to invest in those of a passionate nature. The details of his career can be summarised here as an indication of the range of interests associated with the 'More circle' itself. John Rastell was a play-wright, theologian and compiler of English history; he was a maker of pageants, a mathematician and a student of cosmography; he was an engineer, a legal theorist and a putative religious reformer; he constructed the first public London stage and proposed to set up a colony in the New World; he was an MP, a printer and a publisher. It was Rastell (and, later, his son) who published More's polemical works, for example, and from his press issued a number of plays, legal abridgements, 'merry tales' and musical texts which owe some of their inspiration – if not their origin – to Thomas More and his household.

So we may include John Rastell with Linacre, Lily, Colet and More himself as constituting a group which has been variously described as that of 'London humanists' or 'London reformers'. It is pertinent that they came to prominence at a time when intellectual self-conscious-ness itself was beginning to emerge from the communal spirit of medieval piety. They found their proper role, too, in a city whose mercantile power under Henry VII was at last commensurate with its status as the central focus of national life; it was this moment of confidence and prosperity that encouraged the spirit of reform. Most importantly, perhaps, the London reformers were in positions of power and authority – Linacre tutor to the Prince of Wales, John Colet soon to be Dean of St Paul's – which allowed them to exert a direct and sometimes decisive influence upon the more public aspects of London life. It would not be too much to claim that the progress of law reform and the changes in the educational curriculum, let alone the improvement in public hygiene and the conduct of general administration through various humanist courtiers, were directly attributable to the work of this group of people. There are other significant associations. John Morton had been a patron of the 'new learning' and his successor, William Warham, also played a part in promoting it. Other leaders of the English faith, such as Christopher Urswick and Richard Fox, supported it as an important means of improving the piety of the Church and renovating its teachings.

It would be wrong to apply the title of 'London humanism', however, in too narrow or exclusive a sense. As far as Thomas Linacre was concerned, for example, his interest in a revived classical scholarship was inspired and shared by the scholars of Louvain,

Antwerp, Florence and elsewhere. In particular he kept up a close and steady contact with the great Venetian printer Aldus Manutius, who had published his translation of *De Sphaera*. More importantly, Aldus had single-handedly promulgated the works of Aristotle; he had constructed a Greek typeface in 1498, and Linacre himself had already participated in the 'Aldine Academy', which was devoted to the study of the language and literature of that civilisation. Clearly Aldus was not a printer, or publisher, in any contemporary sense of those terms. He was, rather, one of a group of innovative technicians and intellectual pioneers who had found in the invention of printing access to a whole new conception of learning. Johann Amerbach, and later Froben, were responsible for the first publication of the works of St Ambrose and St Augustine in Basle; there was Plantin-Moretus of Antwerp, Badius of Paris and Theodoricus Martens of Louvain. These were the actual sources of that learning which the reformers and humanists of London were in the process of expounding. Their workshops were also libraries, with the press and the foundry as the indispensable furniture in what were literally the newest academies of learning. They hired scholars to improve the editing of texts; their premises were used for lectures and public readings.

But they were only the intellectual vanguard of a rapidly growing trade; by the end of the 1470s there were printers in all the major cities of the Low Countries, and it has been estimated that by 1500 there were altogether seventeen hundred presses in operation throughout Europe.[15] It was a world in which commerce and learning, scholarship and merchandise, came together for the first time. That is why it has been suggested that the proliferation of books and pamphlets is directly related to the success of the Reformation in parts of Europe; this, at least, was the theory of the Protestant martyrologist John Foxe, who believed that God's cause was 'advanced, not with sword or target ... but with printing, reading and writing'.[16] In fact there is every reason to believe that the expansion of the printing press led to a revival of Catholic piety in the publication of saints' lives, arts of dying and various works of a liturgical or homilectic nature. More himself encouraged his close relations, the Rastells, to publish an extensive variety of books both in Latin and in English.

There were certain colleagues of More – in particular Colet and Grocyn – who made no determined effort to launch their own work into print, however; they still relied upon the resources of the manuscript culture of their youth. This may in turn be related to Colet's continuing interest in cabbalistic learning, in the 'secrets' of such ancient writers as the pseudo-Dionysius, not to be divulged to the vulgar throng. It is certainly true that the enclosed and hierarchical nature of the medieval Church could not easily have withstood the climate of learning and opinion generated by the printing press, but this was something which the London reformers understood perfectly well. That is why their concern was with a purified faith, together with the persuasive eloquence of the classically trained grammarian or orator, as a means of renovating that Church. That is also why Thomas More used the new printing technology with an assiduity and determination worthy of any Lutheran reformer. It is at this moment, too, that another figure should enter the narrative of More's life – a Catholic scholar and rhetorician who used the art of printing to disseminate his work across all Europe. It is Desiderius Erasmus to whom we must now turn, when he visited England for the first time in 1499.

Since there is a tradition of anecdotes concerning the meeting of great personages, it is not surprising that the first encounter of More and Erasmus has been embellished with coincidence and with Latin witticisms; in one version Erasmus admits to coming '*ex inferis*', which might mean from the cellar, hell, or the Low Countries. In this particular account the two men are supposed to have met at the table of the Lord Mayor of London; this is probably the reflection of some garbled report that they were introduced at the house of John Colet's father, Sir Henry Colet, who had indeed held that office. But it is more likely that they met at the London house of Sir William Say, who was the father-in-law of Erasmus's most noble pupil and a member of Henry VII's council.

The great scholar of late medieval Europe was born in Rotterdam in 1466; he was some twelve years older than Thomas More, therefore, and was the child of very different circumstances. He was illegitimate, but was nevertheless supported by both parents; at an early age he was sent to a school at Deventer, where his youthful proficiency, quick understanding and retentive memory brought him to the attention of his elders. 'Well done, Erasmus,' one of them is supposed to have exclaimed, 'the day will come when thou wilt reach the highest summit of erudition.'[17] It is very much like the prophecy of John Morton on the future of young Thomas More and, in both cases, we may safely place the remarks within the standard repertoire of the 'golden legends' of historical figures.

Both of Erasmus's parents died of the plague fever when he was in his thirteenth year, and when at a later date he revealed that 'some secret natural impulse drove me to good literature'[18] it is possible that part of this impulse derived from grief and the need for forgetfulness. His books became his companions; they did not change, or decay, or die. 'I was just a sick and solitary child,' he once wrote;[19] such a child is likely to be drawn to reading, and to its concomitant learning, as a bulwark and defence. After the death of his parents his guardians sent him to a monastic school, or 'Brothers' House', where he came under the aegis of a group of lay brothers known as 'the Brethren of the Common Life'; these men and women practised a religious life deeply imbued by the spirit of *devotio moderna*, a form of austere and practical piety which dwelled upon the inward imitation of the life of Christ rather than upon external observances and rituals. Erasmus was not altogether impressed by their devotion, excluding, as it did, the appetite for learning and the aptitude for scholarship; but at a later stage its influence upon him, and more especially upon More, will become apparent.

Already it is possible to see how different an education this was from More's; his was a practical and administrative training, whereas that of Erasmus led ineluctably towards teaching or the Church. Under the influence of his guardians he was persuaded to enter a monastery of Augustinian canons, where he was ordained in 1492. The length of his residence there has been estimated variously between six and ten years, certainly long enough to give him a permanent distaste for monastic life. Yet it afforded him the opportunity to indulge that passion for friendship which was, according to his biographers, one of his salient characteristics; Erasmus said that 'life without a friend I think no life, but rather death'.[20] He believed himself to be ugly and when he remarks upon More's '*venustus*',[21] charm or beauty, there is a note of self-abnegation which in certain circumstances might lead towards excessive devotion to those more favoured than himself. It is no surprise, then, that his enthusiasm for companionship often led to disappointment or a sense of betrayal. His true friends, after all, were indeed his books. On several occasions he echoed Pliny's belief that time not spent in study is time wasted, and he often repeated the precept that you must 'live as if you are to die tomorrow, study as if you were to live for ever'. It was an instruction which he took to heart, as anyone who has had cause to review the extent of his work will testify, and even in this early part of his life he lost himself in manuscripts and words. He was largely self-taught and from the beginning he wrote so eagerly, effortlessly and fluently that we may say of him what he once remarked of St Jerome, that 'compared with him, the others appear able neither . . . to . . . read nor write'.[22] He composed poetry, and quoted as his authorities in that pursuit Virgil, Horace, Ovid, Juvenal, Statius, Martial, Claudian, Persius, Lucan, Tibullus and Propertius. It is a long list, but there is every indication that he knew his models very well. His reputation for eloquence and learning was such that he was taken into the service of the Bishop of Cambrai, but in 1494 he was given permission to undertake further studies at the University of Paris. He was compelled to earn his living there as a teacher of rhetoric, and for a while he was resident tutor in a boarding-house for the sons of English nobles and gentlemen; in this household he first met William Blount, Lord Mountjoy, who eventually persuaded him to travel to England.

So he arrived in the summer of 1499, with an early if still somewhat inconclusive reputation as a poet and a scholar. We might see him, on first encountering More in a London household, as unaffected and fastidious, reserved and delicate. He was a man with a great desire for the peace and security which his own early years had unhappily lacked. But it would be wrong to present too mild or bland a description of the great scholar; the man whom More was to call 'my derlynge'[23] was also possessed of a spirited and sometimes sarcastic sense of humour. The irony, sometimes light and sometimes ferocious, in *Moriae encomium* or in *Colloquies*, is evidence of a man who knew the world well enough to be able to mock it successfully. Yet he was capable of great enthusiasms – for learning, for books, for scholarship – and the secret of his swift and intimate companionship with More may be gauged from Erasmus's recollection of another friendship. 'We talk of letters,' he once wrote, 'till we fall asleep, our dreams are dreams of letters, and literature awakens us to begin the new day.'[24] So they met, conversed gaily in Latin, and within four months Erasmus was addressing More as *mellitissime Thoma* ('sweetest Thomas').[25]

One other record of their intercourse, during Erasmus's first visit to England, has survived. It comes from Erasmus himself in a *'catalogus'* written some twenty-four years later, in which he recalled an occasion during the summer of 1499 when he was staying at the country house of Lord Mountjoy in Greenwich. More arrived there with a friend from Lincoln's Inn, Edward Arnold, and he suggested to Erasmus that they all walk to the neighbouring village of Eltham. In fact they were to visit the royal palace there, where Prince Henry was in residence; More and Arnold thereupon presented the prince with some 'writings' to commemorate the occasion. Erasmus was annoyed at not having been warned to prepare verses of his own but, after a request from the young Henry, produced some suitably patriotic poetry three days later. It is an intriguing story, not least because for the first time it brings More face to face with the prince who was one day to be master of his destiny. Who could have imagined that this pretty boy of nine years would one day bring such havoc upon the Church and the civilisation which both More and Erasmus came in their different ways to represent?

But there is a more immediate interest to Erasmus's anecdote. It was surely unusual for a young law student to be allowed access to the royal family of England, and to be on terms of such familiarity that he might bring a companion apparently unannounced. Certainly it throws a distinctive light upon More's social position, at the very summit of that world of privilege and authority in which he had moved easily all his life. The evidence of his later career testifies to his self-confidence and social ease, qualities which came as much from his background of affluence and power as from his personal virtue. But if his place in that world can be described, it is difficult to know precisely how to define it, sustained as it was by a network of friendships, affinities, households and social obligations. How, for example, was it that young More was able to stroll across the new stone bridge over the moat and walk into the great hall of Eltham Palace with its music gallery, mullioned windows and panelled screen?

It has already been noticed that Erasmus was staying on the Greenwich estate of William Blount, Lord Mountjoy, at the time of the Eltham expedition. Mountjoy had been his student in Paris over a period of three years, and eventually Erasmus had come to reside with Mountjoy's household in that city. Mountjoy was the same age as More, and had already gained such a reputation for honesty and learning that Henry VII had chosen him as a companion for his younger son and, according to Erasmus, as an associate in the young Henry's studies of Latin and of history. That is also why there were members of Mountjoy's household in attendance at Eltham Palace when More, Erasmus and Arnold made their journey there. The connection between Mountjoy and Erasmus is clear, therefore, but it is not enough to explain More's familiarity with the young royal family. More and Mountjoy were contemporaries enamoured of the new learning, and Mountjoy's father-in-law, Sir William Say, was acquainted with John More; a few years later we find More himself named as a trustee for one of his estates. The executor for the will of Sir William's father was, in one of those many circuitous links characteristic of the fifteenth century, none other than Archbishop John Morton. So by means of many different paths Thomas More and William Mountjoy could have met.

But friendship might in turn become part of faction. It has often been suggested that, at a later date, More professed hostility towards the financial exactions which Henry VII tried to levy upon London. There is no evidence of any open dispute but certainly, at the time of the accession of his son, More composed a sharp attack upon the dead king. He could not have done so, had he not been absolutely sure of his ground; so it seems possible (to put it no higher) that the association of More, Mountjoy and the young prince eventually acquired a politic flavour.[26]

Mountjoy did not introduce Erasmus to More only, and through his agency the Dutchman became acquainted with those humanists whom he extolled in his subsequent letters; he met scholars such as Grocyn and patrons such as Warham, then Archbishop of Canterbury and Lord Chancellor, all adding to his impression that England was a fortunate island to have such people in it. But the most immediate impression and influence upon him derived from John Colet, the black-gowned lecturer upon the Pauline epistles. In the autumn of 1499 Erasmus determined to visit the University of Oxford; he arrived as a visitor at St Mary's College, a hostel for members of his own order, where two or three days later he received a letter of welcome from Colet. Erasmus replied in his usual fulsome manner and the two scholars were soon on good enough terms to argue over points of theology. Erasmus, styling himself 'the poet', recounted one occasion at dinner when he and Colet disagreed over the nature of Cain's first fault. The English divine was 'grave' and 'severe', but it seems that the force of his argument overcame all others. On a different occasion he and Erasmus disputed the nature of Christ's agony in Gethsemane, before his arrest and death upon the cross, and once again it seems that Colet's dogmatic and insistent arguments vanquished those of his opponent – or perhaps Erasmus was polite, or ironic, enough to retire from the unequal struggle. But if there were differences of emphasis and interpretation between the two scholars, there was still broad agreement upon certain essential principles. Here, too, we may bring in Thomas More as the silent party to that agreement. Colet moved much closer to the Neoplatonism of Florence than Erasmus ever did, and the Dutch scholar had a much broader range of learning as well as a more complex understanding of the theological tradition; but both agreed fundamentally upon the need for a spiritual reception of the gospels and the epistles of the New Testament, as part of a simplified and deepened piety free of scholastic commentary or interpretation. The early Fathers were praised by both men for their lucidity, and in the same spirit the connection between classical and Christian ideals was reaffirmed; true eloquence might lead auditors once again to true piety, and the communion of the faithful be restored. Their shared ambition was for a Church purified of the dross of observances and rituals which had accrued to it; when they eventually journeyed together to the shrine of Becket, it was in a similar spirit of detached and even sardonic enquiry. They were not reformers, only renovators; that is why their inspired efforts to restore the Church were frustrated and dissipated by the more subversive actions of Luther or of Zwingli. More himself, an admirer of Augustine, shared their practical concerns during this period. When the Church became the object of sustained and ferocious attack from the European reformers, he returned to a wholly traditionalist defence of its customs and ceremonies; but, in the early years of the sixteenth century, it was possible for him and his companions to believe that the Church itself could be made new.

Erasmus returned to France in the first month of 1500, having first been relieved of all his money by officials at Dover. His stay in England had been profitable in other senses, however, not least because it inaugurated his long friendship with Thomas More. The story of their relationship is well known, at least by its fruits in *Moriae encomium* and *Utopia*, but it may be worth rehearsing certain of its aspects which throw some light on their conduct over the next few years. Both men looked after each other's interests, 'puffing' works where necessary and providing elaborate testimonials to publishers, patrons and fellow-humanists. They shared other secular interests, too, but there were certain divergences of taste and opinion which materially affected their respective fates. It might be said that, in the end, Erasmus was not wholly convinced of More's humanism and not wholly inclined to share his friend's particular forms of piety. He did not share More's temperamental attraction towards monasticism, for example, perhaps because he had experienced it at first hand, and he never really understood the darker recesses of More's spiritual life. Certainly Erasmus was not interested in martyrdom of any kind, and his lament at what he believed to be More's unnecessary fate was part of his general aversion to dogmatic dispute and doctrinal divisiveness.

Yet their shared belief in educational reform and their mutual interest in patristic literature provided the foundation for a friendship which survived the various pressures of many difficult years. They have been enrolled in the ranks of 'humanism' but it is better to be wary of the term, not least because it was coined at the beginning of the nineteenth century. The circumstances of 'humanists' in the period when More and Erasmus shared their enthusiasms can be better described by means of a book, a seal and an anecdote.

IX

If You Want to Laugh

ON his return to Paris in February 1500, Erasmus set to work
upon the publication of his first book. *Adagiorum Collectanea* came from a small press in the rue Saint-Marceau; it was
announced as the first selection of classical adages and proverbs ever
printed, or what Erasmus described as the material for '*noui operis*'[1]
or new work. He had collected more than eight hundred maxims, in
Latin and Greek, to which he appended short commentaries of his
own. In later years Erasmus was inclined to condemn it as roughly
and hastily conceived, but this little volume of some 140 pages,
published at the very beginning of the sixteenth century, was the
harbinger of a literature which was to change the nature of European
discourse. It was published in twenty-six editions within the lifetime
of Erasmus himself, and for almost three centuries it was the
companion of the parlours and bedsides of Europe. Yet its first
impact was of a different kind; this slim book, printed in what was
the then revolutionary 'roman' typeface as a mark of its novelty,
offered for most contemporaries their first general and accessible
view of the classical past. It was part of Erasmus's aim to restore the
meaning of that past by emphasising the presence and permanence of
the truths that Greek and Latin authors had adumbrated, albeit in a
language more polished and refined than anything to which a late
medieval audience was accustomed. The *Adages* also furnished
conclusive proof that classical wisdom and scriptural revelation were
not incompatible; Erasmus's quotations from Plato or from Cicero
are amplified by biblical allusions, with the strong intimation that a
forgotten area of spiritual and intellectual endeavour was being
restored to a generation at last capable of profiting from it. In his
dedicatory letter Erasmus credited his inspiration for the work to
Lord Mountjoy and to the prior of the Oxford college where he had

stayed, and parcels of the book were sent across the Channel for the immediate perusal of More, Grocyn and others. He must have done some work of preparation and organisation in England, since it was published just six months after his departure from Dover, and there can be no doubt that he was actively encouraged by More and those other Englishmen who were also intent upon the study of Greek and Roman originals.

From Erasmus's book we may move to More's seal. It is known that in later life More acquired a collection of ancient coins; some of them he gave as presents to those who would appreciate them, while the rest have been dispersed and lost irretrievably. Perhaps his collection was confiscated, along with so much else, after his imprisonment. But one of his classical memorials survives intact; it is an impression of the private seal which he used for his correspondence. The seal had been remodelled from an antique coin bearing the head of the Emperor Titus, and takes its place with two others that More used – one seeming to bear the imprint of the goddess Fortuna and the other of a bearded Roman emperor or statesman. For More, also, the classical past did not comprise some closed library of books and manuscripts but, rather, it represented a valuable and living reality. It was a way of retrieving a lost inheritance in a world that seemed to More and his contemporaries to have grown stale and decayed in its attachment to old verities.

There is an anecdote of More told by another contemporary 'humanist' and courtier, Richard Pace. It seems that More, while still an *adolescens*, was in the company of two scholastic philosophers who informed him that King Arthur had manufactured a cloak from the beards of the giants whom, according to Geoffrey of Monmouth, he had slain in battle. More apparently received the news with his customary composure, perhaps not even remarking that in Geoffrey's account it is the giant Retho who disposes of his hirsute victims in that manner. Instead he asked them the technique which Arthur used, and was informed that the hair of the dead stretches wonderfully well. The young More asked them, in turn, if it were true that when one of them milked a he-goat the other waited with a sieve to collect the drops. This little sally, a tribute to futility and ignorance, actually comes from Lucian's *Demonax*; but there is no reason why he should not have borrowed it for the occasion. For Pace it was another example of More's sarcasm, but it can also be seen as an indication of his dislike for the vagaries of scholastic enquiry. His borrowing from Lucian was highly appropriate, too, as we shall soon discover.

Book, seal and anecdote illustrate the complexity of the term 'humanism'. If Cardinal Wolsey, Desiderius Erasmus, Marsilio Ficino and Thomas More were all humanists, then the term has such a wide applicability that it becomes for all practical purposes useless. If we stay close to the immediate context, however, we may define the humanist as a student of classical learning in the related fields of grammar, rhetoric and literature. This is *studia humanitatis*, the pursuit of *bonae litterae*, which in turn is related to educational reform and to a more disciplined training in the principles of good government. It was in one aspect, then, a civic and secular movement which directly affected developments in rhetoric, medicine and law; in retrospect, at least, it seems also to have demonstrated a certain piety and purity of intent with its return to the pristine sources of classical literature and with its aversion to medieval codes of war and chivalry.

It has of course been related to the gradual decay or dissolution of the old European medieval order, at least in those historical narratives which treat the past as a form of heroic fiction in which various protagonists fight for mastery. But it might be more fruitful to recognise in the writings of the humanists a culmination of various aspects of medieval thought which had hitherto escaped intense examination or elaboration. The pursuit of classical rhetoric, for example, had always been part of the life of the Italian city-states; the *dictatores* or public orators had followed the model of Cicero or Quintilian throughout the thirteenth and fourteenth centuries. There were 'humanists' – scholars who were interested in obtaining and reading classical texts – at both English universities throughout the fifteenth century. Manuscript copies of Cicero, Plato and Plutarch, among many others, were available in college libraries, while there was a steady trade in imported books during the last decades of the century. In addition, Greek and Italian scholars were welcomed both in the universities and in the courts of Edward IV and Richard III. It would be quite wrong, therefore, to suggest some sudden awakening or resurgence of learning in England.

The single most important patron of humanistic learning in More's lifetime was Henry VII. He was known for his partiality towards foreign scholars (sometimes to the chagrin of the indigenous variety) and throughout his reign he employed 'humanists' in various royal and ecclesiastical duties. These clerks and secretaries were patronised precisely because of their rhetorical skills, in the writing of letters as much as in the delivery of formal orations. Indeed, More's eventual entry to the court of Henry VII's successor was not some misjudgement on More's part – as has been suggested by those who wish to emphasise the saintly or scholarly aspects of the man – but the obvious and almost inevitable culmination of his career as a practising orator and trained grammarian.

Yet this affirmation of continuity, rather than change, might be questioned by those who note the scorn of More and others for the 'barbarism' of much earlier learning; it was More, after all, who is supposed to have laughed at the scholastic theologians and who on many occasions was scathing about the ignorance and triviality of those who refused to acknowledge the merits of '*graecarum . . . literarum*'[2] or '*seculares disciplinas*'.[3] There can be no doubt that there was a sense of 'new learning' in the air, together with an atmosphere of reform and renovation; but how exactly, then, does More's interest in classical literature differ from that of previous scholars? It is a matter of timing and of time itself. When Erasmus appends his commentaries to the maxims of Plato or of Terence in his *Adagiorum Collectanea*, he invokes a long temporal perspective in which the implications and connotations of those phrases have changed; he is creating a history of usage. It was also plain to his first readers that the civilisations of Rome and Athens were markedly superior to any they might see around them; as well as being a history of usage, the *Collectanea* was a history of decline (and even, sometimes, fall). Repeatedly Erasmus emphasises the dangers and inconstancies of the modern world as opposed to a classical culture erected upon 'the noble old systems of thought'.[4] This perspective – which we might describe, perhaps anachronistically, as one of historical relativism – is quite different from any that More would have known in the scriptural dramas and historical compilations of his youth. In a play where Noah or Judas would wear contemporary dress, and in a history where miracle and legend emphasised the archetypal significance of events, there is no decline and no progress, only the re-enactment of the rituals of eternity. The world was suspended in a cosmos of unchanging truths. It is all in marked contrast, therefore, to that history of change, decay and possible restoration which is at the centre of the humanist enterprise as outlined by Erasmus and More.

The idea of institutions and societies living through history lies at the very heart of the humanist's belief in civic activity and involvement within the world. Consider again More's private seal which displays the face of the Emperor Titus. Titus was not a Christian emperor, but for More he was an image of practical wisdom and civic virtue. He had conquered Judaea and wasted Jerusalem, in what was considered to be an act of divine reprisal for the death of Christ less than forty years before, but More would have read in Suetonius of his exemplary social actions during his brief reign. Titus provided an example of what might now be called 'enlightened government', and More would also have known that he had once trained as a lawyer and had a great facility in composing verses and orations. He had stamped his image upon the changing times, just as More would use that image upon the seal with which he conducted public business. This sense of usefulness in public affairs characterised the 'humanism' of the early sixteenth century and prompted More's own involvement in civic life. It is to be seen in the production of the new maps and globes, in the renewed interest in medicine and natural science, and in that belief in the efficacy of the will which was soon to be elaborated by Machiavelli in his great treatise on the uses of statecraft. For More, public duty was the natural consequence of his professional training as a rhetorician, and at no point did it ever come into conflict with his instinctive piety; indeed, it was an aspect of it.

One proviso ought to be added, however, in a life replete with ambiguity. In *The Prince* Machiavelli distinguished the ideal world of eternal verity from the actual world of human affairs; he directed his enquiry towards the lessons of history rather than the idealised concepts of a medieval polity. He also distinguished ethics from politics, thus promoting the forces of human will and the possibility of harnessing '*fortuna*' to individual ambition. In his own writing More would adopt a cautious attitude towards this new understanding of the self; he was attracted by its novelty and even welcomed it in the sphere of civic activity, but at the same time he sensed its dangers.

His early composition of verse, as of prose, was also associated with this practical instruction in rhetoric and grammar; it is impossible to separate his 'creative' activities from his scholarship and general training. From the beginning his own writing was firmly based upon classical models. In his youth, according to Erasmus, he had written a dialogue in defence of Plato's *Republic* – a suggestive preliminary to his own work in the sphere of political fantasy. His first poetical exercises were translations into Latin from the Planudean Anthology, better known as the *Greek Anthology*, and it is these Latin verses which manifest the first stirrings of his genius. They were eventually published in 1518, together with the third edition of *Utopia*, but he had been writing epigrams since the beginning of the century. That he was composing them in his early twenties, while still a student of law in Lincoln's Inn, is not unusual; the invention or translation of epigrams was a customary method among humanists for beginning a literary career. Some of the earliest were written by More in conjunction (and friendly rivalry) with William Lily, the grammarian who later became the first high master of St Paul's school in London. On publication they were given the title *Progymnasmata* ('preliminary exercises'), which suggests that they were meant to provide examples of rhetorical and grammatical correctness; these Latin versions of Greek originals are not entirely free of solecisms, but they provide skilful examples of a relatively 'pure' Latin. More employs a variety of metres, and his concern for balance, co-ordination and symmetry shows evidence of a good instructor. A line on holding fortune in contempt, '*Iam portum inueni, Spes et Fortuna ualete*' ('Now that I have found port, farewell hope and good fortune'), is not simply an exercise in syntax and metre but also a handy classical maxim to be put to use in the world; it is an example of what Erasmus meant when he declared that the best poetry was always rhetorical in nature. Some of More's most original epigrams, for example, are on the horrors of tyrannical rule and the evils of avaricious or despotic monarchs; they represent his unique contribution to the epigrammatic tradition.

Yet the general mood of these short Latin poems – there are 276 of them in the authoritative edition of his works – is one of irony and mordant wit. He could be sarcastic at the expense of a doltish philosopher with 'the brains of a donkey' or of a young woman who pretends to have been raped. He takes pleasure in repeating jokes or farcical tales – there is even one about an attendant removing flies from a drink – and the epigrams bear as much relation to a London tradition of 'merry tales' or 'quick answers' as to the *Greek Anthology* itself. It has in the past been noticed how close in spirit More remains to Geoffrey Chaucer, and we may see this as another aspect of More's native traditionalism. There are times, indeed, when his becomes the poetry of the streets, and there is a good reason for the description of him as '*Londinii gloria*'.[5] There is one verse about a fart, and another about the merits of eating '*merda*' or excrement. One short poem might be quoted in full to gauge the nature of More's humour:

> *Ergo puella uiri quis te negat esse capacem,*
> *Quam tua tam magnum circumdant crura caballum?*[6]

It is addressed to a girl riding a horse: Who denies that you can take a man, when your legs can get around even that pack-horse? It might not be the refined humour of sainthood; but by staying closer to a grossly secular level we may come nearer to More himself.

In his earliest work More was drawn to imitation and adaptation; this was, of course, the condition of all verse-writing. But in mastering the expression of so many themes and attitudes, he seems to revel in doubleness, disguise and impersonation. He wrote seven epigrams on the topic of a lame beggar carried by a blind beggar, as if he were testing his ability to describe the situation in a variety of ways. He is able to capture a character in a redolent phrase and discern a human folly in an instant of perception. He is always observant, but always able to keep his distance. Some of the stenches and the more disagreeable sights of late medieval London are embedded within the verses; his aversion to the flesh is also clearly rendered, in epigrams condemning '*coitu*' and '*libidine*'. But all these themes are carefully and formally sustained within the tight syntactical and cultural frame of the epigram itself. One of them makes a pointed allusion to '*bifrons Janus*',[7] the two-faced god who thereby saw everything. There are, similarly, two faces to More's first work. These epigrams were said by Sir John Harington to 'flie over all Europe for their wit and conceit',[8] while to another poetaster they were 'too obscene to be lookt upon, and who so rubbeth stincking weeds, shall have filthy fingers'.[9] But even if they did fly over Europe, despite their bawdiness, they were overtaken on the way by another of More's classical imitations.

His translations of Lucian became by far the most popular of his productions; estimates of the number of editions within his lifetime vary from nine to fourteen but on any count they outdistance the sales and general reputation of the now more famous *Utopia*. The truth is that, in Lucian, the young More found his perfect match. It was said of this second-century satirist that '*ridentem dicere verum*', he spoke the truth through laughter, and Erasmus noted that he treated everything '*naso*',[10] with a nose – with ridicule and with a certain dislike for the odour of old verities. Erasmus also said of himself that he had a nose; this is generally taken to represent his dislike for the smell of fish and domestic stoves, but it perhaps implies a shared distaste for the more farcical elements of orthodoxy, custom and traditional observance. Lucian was one of the ancients, therefore, who could join the ranks of the moderns. His extant works, and in particular his satirical dialogues, were some of the most widely circulated and translated of the fifteenth century; he also hit the mark for those prose writers of the early sixteenth century, such as More, who were looking for a model upon which they could establish their own satire of vain ritual and conceit.

More had started his systematic study of Greek under the aegis of Thomas Linacre and William Grocyn, putting aside his Latin for a time in order to master the new language. It is not known when he first came upon the works of Lucian – an edition emerged from the Aldine press in 1503, however, and it seems the likely spur to his interest. It is remarkable, in any event, how quickly he acquired a working knowledge of this difficult tongue. Within four or five years of beginning to learn how to read and write an entirely different set of characters, he was able to translate one of the finest exponents of the language in a proficient and reliable fashion. He worked with Erasmus upon some of Lucian's dialogues, and their Latin versions were published in the winter of 1506. More was the junior partner in the enterprise, providing four translations beside twenty-eight by Erasmus, but the influence of Lucian upon his subsequent writing was permanent and profound. When Erasmus suggested that a correspondent read *Utopia* '*si quando voles ridere*'[11] ('if you want to laugh'), we are in the same Lucianic world of '*ridentem dicere verum*'. Medieval schoolmen were generally supposed to lack humour; certainly any sense of irony might have proved fatal for their aspiration towards total and systematic knowledge. Lucian provided an antidote for the somewhat mirthless pursuit of certainty upon the uncertain earth. It was reported of More that he could make even the most solemn colleague burst into laughter; in that respect he resembles Tiresias, who, in one of the Lucianic dialogues, declares that it is not necessary to become anxious over the affairs and events of the world but, rather, to remain as cheerful as possible and pass your life in laughter.

There are formal, as well as informal, connections with Lucian. In the work of the satirist More discovered the possibilities of dialogue as a way of exploiting the dramatic possibilities of the world; most of his own prose works would eventually assume the same form. He thereby became the begetter in the English language of a tradition which stretches from the spirited dialogue of Blake's 'Island in the Moon' and Walter Savage Landor's 'Imaginary Conversations' to the particular London art of 'after-pieces' and comic dialogues. But Lucian had also been a rhetorician, and More persuaded Erasmus to extend their translations with their own 'declamations' in reply to one composed by Lucian on the theme of tyrannicide. More always excelled at the art of impersonation, and Lucian himself compared the orator to the actor and the pantomimic.

Yet every play must end, and in More's epigrams there are intimations of a greater reality; there are verses on death, on earthly vanity and on the necessary contempt for this world. One poem opens with an observation that could have been used as the epigraph for much London writing: 'Damnati ac morituri in terrae claudimus omnes/ Carcere'[12] ('all of us, condemned to death and about to die, are inmates of the prison of this world'). In Thomas à Kempis's The Imitation of Christ, More read that devout monk's paraphrase of Isaiah, 'I will open the doors of the prison and reveal unto thee hidden secrets.'[13] The doors of the contemplative Charterhouse had already opened for More, even as he was composing his epigrams and translations of Lucian. When he bent over his classical texts, he was wearing his hair shirt. It is to the site of More's spirituality that we must now turn.

X

The Wine of Angels

THOMAS More's first biographer asserts that More 'gave himselfe to devotion and prayer in the Charterhouse of London, religiously lyvinge there, without vowe, about iiii yeares'.[1] Another chronicler, Cresacre More, believed that his famous relative only lived 'nere the Charterhouse, frequenting daily their spirituall excercises without any vowe'.[2] The more general aspect of his faith is emphasised by Erasmus, who has an account of the young More applying his whole mind to the study of piety,[3] by means of vigils, fasting and prayer. Yet another narrative suggests that More also consulted a friend in holy orders, William Lily, about the possibility of being ordained as a priest. Everything at this time, then, points in the direction of the monastery.

It survives still, largely restored or rebuilt, to the north of Smithfield. In the sixteenth century it was beyond the western gates of the city, between Smithfield itself and the unhappy Pardon Churchyard where the bodies of plague victims and executed felons were indiscriminately buried. The cells of the monks had been erected upon another old burial ground, and a chapel of St Mary the Virgin had once stood upon the area in spiritual commemoration of 'above one hundred thousand bodies of Christian people'[4] who were interred there. Perhaps the vast concourse of the dead may account for the visions and miracles that occurred in the Charterhouse during More's lifetime. The Carthusian 'House of the Salutation of the Blessed Virgin Mary' was established in the 1370s by a wealthy foreign patron, Sir Walter de Mauny, who had been knighted for services to Edward III. In this combination of money, royal affinity and European connection, we can discern the more secular aspects of the Carthusian order; from its foundation by St Bruno at the end of the eleventh century, its regimen of seclusion, labour and perpetual prayer had attracted the beneficence of powerful patrons as well as the spiritual ardour of rich merchants or noblemen who desired to find a place where 'springs not fail'. Certainly the austerity of the monks formed a suggestive contrast to the lives of the regular clergy; it was said that they had never been reformed because they had never been corrupted. By the time of More's association with the London Charterhouse its twenty-four cells (with a different letter of the alphabet upon each door) had been built and financed with the aid of individual patrons, while many of the monks themselves came from rich or noble families. Nor was it unusual for 'guests' to stay in special accommodation, for an appropriate fee, and the Charterhouse was one of the two or three Carthusian foundations where young men of spiritual tendency could lodge while at the same time pursuing a secular career – in the Inns of Court, for example. Many did eventually choose the holier profession, however, and in More's lifetime there were at least three former lawyers and one royal courtier who donned the white robes and cowl.

More's own position, within or beside the Charterhouse, is not entirely clear. It is possible that he remained in its guest quarters for four years; the rules limiting the stay of these secular sojourners had not yet been enacted. Under ordinary circumstances he would have remained a resident of Lincoln's Inn, to which he was formally connected; although such a requirement was less important than his regular attendance in chapel or in hall. But it is most likely that Cresacre More has passed on a reliable item of family information – having attained the rank of 'utter barrister' at the Inn, but still unable to attend the courts at Westminster, he can be supposed to have taken temporary lodgings near the Charterhouse. It would not have been difficult to find accommodation; there were houses in Aldersgate Street, St John Street and Charterhouse Lane, while Smithfield was 'compassed about with buildings'.[5] He was also close to his chambers in Lincoln's Inn; it was no more than a five minute ride away, down Cow Lane and across Holborn Bridge, past Ely Place and through Holborn before turning left into Chancery Lane.

More, then, was an expected and familiar 'guest'. He never took vows and never entered the less exalted ranks of either the oblates or the lay-brothers, known also as 'converses' because of their choice irrevocably to turn away from the world. Yet even if More had not taken that extreme decision, the great oak doorways into the courtyard of the Charterhouse admitted him to a world of discipline and devotion that affected him profoundly. The spirit of the place was reflected in its buildings, which followed the standard plan of a Carthusian foundation. There was a *'parvum cloistrum'*, where there were guest cells on the upper floor; the monks used the arcade and quadrangle below, but the guests had a private staircase to their rooms so that they would not disturb the meditative privacy of the inmates. To the north was the 'guesten hall' or dining-room for visitors, while a 'slype' or passage on the west side led to the 'Wash House Court'. This was the area reserved for the accommodation of the lay-brothers; their cells were on the first floor, their workshops on the ground floor beneath them. Here were installed the brewery house, kitchen, buttery, larders, wine cellar and the 'wash house' itself. The cells of the monks were built individually around the great cloister, to the north-east of these smaller courts. A 'cell' comprised three wainscoted rooms on the first floor – a study, bedroom and oratory – with a work-room and wood-house on the ground floor looking out upon a small garden. There was a hatch beside each cell through which food was dispensed to the resident monk. These were austere but not penitential surroundings, appropriate enough for inmates from wealthy families. The Charterhouse itself was not entirely deprived of the more luxurious examples of religious observance; at the time of its dissolution it was stripped of much plate, gilt ornament and rich cloth. There were bay trees, ponds of carp, rose-bushes and small falcons known as merlin birds, all of them adding to that air of *sancta simplicissitas* on the edge of the city. The church was 'semi-public', with several chapels, rich alabaster tombs and more than fifteen altars complete with intricately carved statues and painted images.

Yet here also was the centre of great spiritual devotion. At eleven in the evening the monks would be woken from a short sleep and would proceed into the fathers' choir for the recitation of Matins, Lauds and the Office of the Dead; in a darkness attenuated only by the lights they carried with them, and by the gleam of the sanctuary lamp, they sang, chanted and prayed for three hours. Their robes were of undyed wool and descended to their ankles; they wore white leathern girdles around the waist, and much of the body was covered by a great white cowl and hood. They chanted slowly, as if engaged in meditation rather than song. Guests were permitted to attend these services, watching from a gallery in the smaller brothers' choir, and there are accounts of the 'night-slippers' and lights that they were given by the kitchener as they left their plain lodgings. It is a scene which Thomas More recalled in *Utopia*; the citizens of that insular community also wear white robes in their temple, while all is veiled in semi-darkness.[6] The monks returned to their cells in the early hours of the morning and, after reciting part of Our Lady's Office, retired to their narrow beds before being awoken again at five or six in order to attend Mass followed by prayers and spiritual meditation. Their hours between ten and two were devoted to intellectual or manual labour, in their cells, and then at a quarter to three they went back to church for Vespers; they remained at their devotions until half-past six or seven when once more they returned to their solitude in preparation for the 'night vigil'. In solitude, too, in those hours of the day not dedicated to work or communal devotion, the monks recited the Divine Office, the Office of the Blessed Virgin, and certain prayers for the restoration of the Holy Land. It was an echo-chamber of prayer, this small London community interceding for the living and pleading for the dead. We might see Thomas More watching from the stone gallery above, as the white-robed monks continued their perpetual chant of psalms, canticles, antiphons, responsoria, prayers and hymns.

He became thoroughly conversant, too, with a precisely regulated life of prayer and study. There was a moderate, almost paternal, discipline on such matters as the occasions for bowing in greeting or kneeling to ask pardon. Silence was generally observed, and the Carthusian diet was unique in its absolute prohibition of meat. The monks left the Charterhouse only once a week, for a Sunday afternoon walk together, known as *Spatiamentum*. Whether they chose to venture down the notorious Turnmill Lane towards Clerkenwell and the fields beside the village of Islington, or whether they walked down Ludgate and past the Black Friars towards the Thames, is not recorded. One or two members of the community needed to have more elaborate contact with the external world; the procurator, for example, was obliged to administer the estates owned by the Charterhouse in Bloomsbury and Edmonton, Tottenham, Kent, Hertfordshire and elsewhere. It is not difficult to imagine More, as a constant guest and friend, advising on the legal and financial matters attendant upon these worldly possessions.

The calling of the Carthusian, according to one history of the order, 'is far more to weep than to sing',[7] and the solitude of the monastic life did on occasions lead to emotional or even histrionic scenes. The monks were indeed particularly prone to weeping, in the exercise of what was known as 'the gift of tears'; tears were, after all, according to St Bernard, the wine of angels. There is an extravagance and intensity within late medieval life which are revealed at sudden moments of ardour, or crisis, and which cannot be separated from the general love of spectacle and display. Of course the ardour may take strange forms, and in the records of the early sixteenth-century Charterhouse there are accounts of visitations and apparitions. The crucified figure of Jesus turned its back upon one recalcitrant monk, in sight of the community, while another was always struck with blindness on entering the church. One wastrel who declared that he would rather eat toads than fish (Erasmus noted that the meat-free Carthusians generally smelled like otters) found that his cell was instantly filled with the creatures 'crawling and leaping after him'.[8] In the uncertain period before the Reformation, the brothers saw in the air 'a globe as of blood, of great size',[9] and in the same period swarms of flies covered the entire surface of the monastery, 'all which things we feared were the signs and forecasts of other events'.[10] There were more fortunate visitations, too, and among these reports of bloody omens are records of strange sweet scents and music infiltrating the church at times of prayer. Such accounts come from intelligent and well-educated contemporaries of More himself; his was still a world of marvels and apparitions.

But there was another aspect of medieval piety which led him towards the gates of Charterhouse. The Carthusians were as well known for their learning as for their devotion, and one of the monks' principal occupations lay in the copying of manuscripts; the more artistic or erudite of them were given parchment, pen and ink for the transcription of pious works. We have the names of individual monks such as William Tregoose and William Exmew who copied versions of that great mystical treatise *The Cloud of Unknowing*, and there are records of other texts being sent from the monastery to religious centres throughout the country. In 1500, for example, some thirty-two volumes were lent by the prior of the Charterhouse, Richard Roche, to a monastery in Coventry. At the time More himself frequented Charterhouse, a copy of *The Cloud of Unknowing* was being produced, but, perhaps more pertinently, in its library were to be found Walter Hilton's *Scale of Perfection* and *The Imitation of Christ* by Thomas à Kempis. Such was the significance of these works to More that he mentions them specifically as ones to 'norysshe and encrease deuocyon',[11] and alludes to them throughout his own writings. The *Imitation*, which More believed to be composed by Jean Gerson, is perhaps the finest expression of a renovated piety, based upon austere communal living and prayer. To imitate Christ is to bear all the humiliations and the indignities of the world; there are wonderfully elaborate meditations on the passion of Christ for the world, and the necessity of discipline and suffering to be worthy of his love. Each man must find his own cross and bear it willingly into what à Kempis calls 'the valley of my nothingness',[12] where it is necessary only to 'write, read, chant, mourn, keep silence, pray'.[13] More discovered in à Kempis an account of the worthlessness of this world and its rewards, together with the desire for solitude, prayer, and that longing for death as the gate to eternity. The simplicity and purity of these themes are taken up in More's writings with a fervour which suggests the intensity of his own nature, and there can be no doubt that the library of the Charterhouse helped to shape his own spiritual temperament.

The *Imitation* and Hilton's *Scale of Perfection* are generally also seen as part of the broad tradition of late medieval piety, with its emphasis upon Christ as both the victim and saviour of the world. The extravagances of this devotion have been well documented, with the measuring of Christ's wounds and the counting of the drops of his blood as part of a ritualised attention to the more visible aspects of his redemptive sacrifice; the image of the dying Christ casts its shadow over a popular piety animated by the fear of wrath and the need for forgiveness, sustained by the idea of placatory prayer, and possessed by an awareness of last things. The Dance of Death painted upon the wall of St Paul's churchyard, and the skeletons adorning the *transi* or cadaver tomb of Colet within that church, are obvious examples of a religious culture permeated by the recognition of death and decay. Yet how is this refrain upon the uses of suffering, and this emphasis upon the hollowness of the world, consistent with the life of a young lawyer in early sixteenth-century London? Kempis's injunction that man 'often uses violence to himself: and labours to bring the flesh wholly into subjection to the spirit'[14] can be connected with the discipline of More's piety and the wearing of the hair shirt. Similarly à Kempis's image of the tortured Christ is one that can be glimpsed in More's own preoccupation with the passion and the crucifixion. But these are external signs and tokens. If *The*

Imitation of Christ was More's golden book, as is often surmised, where was the spiritual profit to be found?

It lies at the centre of à Kempis's teaching, when he urges the reader to 'look on all things as passing away, and on thyself as doomed to pass away with them'.[15] It is the theme taken up in many of More's earliest epigrams and might be supposed to be his great subject; yet such a deep and permanent awareness of transience seems difficult to reconcile with More's successful life in the world. But a recognition of the hollowness of the world no more precludes ambition than it does conviviality. It simply places it within a larger context. All becomes part of the same play which, in the words of More, you must act out to the best of your ability.[16] The whole elaborate medieval edifice of spectacle and display is built upon the awareness of death. Yet within the overwhelming context of divine truth and eternity, there is also a delight to be found in the transient game and an energy to be derived from the passing spectacle. It is in this crucial area of the late medieval imagination, so open to misunderstanding and to misinterpretation, that we must place Thomas More. There is a Japanese image of the 'floating world', wonderfully constructed and designed in full knowledge of its eventual demise: there ceases to be any private motive in collaborating upon this infirm beautiful project, but rather an awareness of common inheritance and destiny. We may see More's education and career as part of the same process; that is how he could combine ambition and penitence, success and spirituality, in equal measure. He could move easily through a society permeated with religious values and images; the faith of his nation was a social and political, as well as a spiritual, reality. His sense of transience, and recognition of eternity, could only be enhanced in a city which from the southern bank of the Thames looked like an island of church steeples. More kept in fine balance these complementary vistas – of the hollowness of the world and of the delight in game. From this awareness of duality (and perhaps the duality within his own nature) springs his wit, his irony and the persistent doubleness of his vision.

That is why it is wrong to assume any struggle or crisis over the nature of his vocation; Erasmus suggests that More's prayers and meditations in the Charterhouse were in part supposed to test his capacity for the priesthood, and that he thought seriously of ordination, but that the recognition of his sexual appetites persuaded him otherwise. Certainly his preoccupation with lechery in his later polemical works and his occasional lubricious comments suggest a man whose sexuality was easily aroused; he might have become, as he feared, an impure priest,[17] in a period when the holiness of virginity was being extolled with increasing fervour. But there was also throughout More's life an almost overpowering sense of duty – although the citizens of Utopia revere celibacy, some believe that they 'owe' ('*debere*') both their country and nature itself the responsibility of propagating children. It may also be that his inherent sense of purposiveness and practicality guided him away from the cloister; he would have been aware of the Augustinian emphasis upon 'service to the earthly city'[18] among those who are not yet citizens of the eternal one. There are even occasions when More attacks the lazy acceptance of the monastic ideal of silence and isolation as a way of cultivating pleasure and as a way of avoiding the tribulations of life.[19] The London humanists around him believed themselves to be living in a time of reform and renovation; it would not have been possible for him to take part in such a revival from the interior of a cell.

It is often supposed that More's lay piety was something of an anomaly, the obsession of an aspiring and unsatisfied contemplative. But the merits and rewards of a secular vocation are described in the very books available to More in the library of the Charterhouse. The second chapter of Walter Hilton's *Scale of Perfection*, for example, is concerned with the active Christian life in the world; it is 'speedful that we know the gifts which are given us of God',[20] with St John as the image of the contemplative, and St Peter of the active, calling. Hilton also composed a volume entitled *The Mixed Life* in which the proper administration of the world is praised for its efficacy in supporting and assisting 'the uncouth and uncunning'.[21] The example of Christ is adduced, and a hasty retreat into a cell or monastery is condemned. 'Thou makest thee for to kiss his mouth by devotion and ghostly prayer' but by failing to participate in the world 'thou treadest upon his feet and defilest them'.[22]

It is appropriate, then, that, even while pursuing his legal training, More should lecture upon Augustine's *City of God* in St Lawrence Jewry. In this neighbourhood church, where two of the principal attractions were the tooth and shank-bone of a supposed giant chained up for display, More addressed what is reported to have been a large congregation; no doubt his own family, living a few yards away, also attended. He was in his early twenties, but was already considered to be an able exponent of patristic texts. He had been asked to prepare the lectures by William Grocyn, the incumbent of St Lawrence Jewry, while Grocyn himself was lecturing on the pseudo-Dionysius at St Paul's. Successive biographers of More have suggested that the congregations abandoned St Paul's and flocked to St Lawrence, but there is no evidence for this. It is likely, however, that the audiences had a similar composition. Erasmus mentions in particular the attendance of priests and elderly men at St Lawrence Jewry, in order to emphasise that More's learning was not some empty extravagance. In a letter written at the time More himself takes a less charitable attitude, at least towards Grocyn's audience; he informed a friend that the size of the congregation in St Paul's was greater than its intelligence and that it included the ignorant.[23] Some had come to learn about new things, others out of the desire to seem intelligent, and certain people had stayed away simply because they wanted to pretend that they already knew all about the subject. Yet the very existence of these lectures, on Augustine and the pseudo-Dionysius, as well as the large numbers who apparently attended them, testify to the fact that there was a genuine curiosity about the 'new learning' which both More and Grocyn represented. Their knowledge of Greek (although More was still very much the pupil of Grocyn in this respect) and of patristic sources offered a new formulation or restatement of old truths.

No record of More's lectures on *The City of God* survives, but they can be placed at the centre of his concerns during this period. He had already composed his dialogue in defence of Plato's *Republic*, and his contemporary epigrams on the dangers of a weak or avaricious monarch provide further evidence that he was thinking as seriously about civic as about religious issues. In his legal studies, too, he was concerned with matters of civil law and common law which had a direct relation to the good government of the 'common welth'. More quoted from the works of Augustine all his life, and it is easy to see why he should have been drawn towards the saint even as a young man. Augustine was a rhetorician, a master of Latin prose, but he was also a revered figure of the Church who had imbibed and mastered true classical learning; his interest in Neoplatonism as implicitly heralding Christian revelation, in particular, brought him very close to More's contemporaries. Augustine was a living authority for the time, in other words, and in expounding *The City of God* More was addressing the issues of the day.

At the centre of Augustine's work was the question that was

uniquely to concern More himself: Do we wish to live in the earthly city or in the heavenly city? It was a question posed to him at the end of his life, when he chose the latter, but in these early years it had more than private import. Was the true state a congregation of believers ruled by the intervention of grace and divine law, or was it an association of men ruled by national law and positive law? Was it essentially a *corpus mysticum* or a natural human grouping? This was the debate which More continued in his lectures at St Lawrence Jewry, but its significance is that it was precisely from these questions that *Utopia* itself would emerge. Of course we do not know what conclusions More reached in front of his learned audience, and yet certain speculations are possible.

In Augustine's work the history of the world is conceived in terms of these two cities, the city of the world and the city of God, distinct but not entirely separate, together experiencing 'the vicissitudes of time'.[24] The heavenly city exists within the earthly city, in separate individuals or in communities of believers, so that it is possible to see within the fallen city – let us say, London – 'an image of the Heavenly City'.[25] The physical presence of the churches themselves in the City, some of them of ancient date, was a token of sacred history within the walls. The city of the world could aspire, at least, to the condition of the city of God; there was a strong tradition in the fourteenth and fifteenth centuries which affirmed that human community, with the possibilities for instruction and joint worship, was the most appropriate place for the pursuit of the divine. That was partly More's experience of the Charterhouse, but as he lectured in the church by the Guildhall he may have possessed a wider vision. Could he be at the same time a citizen of London and a citizen of the heavenly city? Was it possible to live in the city of God while remaining in the city of men? It seems possible that this indeed became the lifelong project of Thomas More. He knew that London was no abiding city, and it is clear from the actions of his subsequent career that he believed himself to be part of a larger spiritual community (the living and the dead together); at this time in his life, with that combination of intelligence and piety unique to him, it might have seemed that they could be reconciled.

There is further evidence of his spiritual devotion in a short treatise which he translated from the Latin in this period. It is a biography of Pico della Mirandola, the young Italian scholar and philosopher who died of a fever in Florence, in 1494, after seeking the truths of the universe. It is likely that More was introduced to his work by John Colet; Colet had already annotated Pico's commentary upon Genesis, and he was in any case immensely attracted to the mixture of cabbalism, Neoplatonism and deep spirituality that the Italian exemplified. The formal context for More's translation was that of a traditional new year's gift; he presented what was essentially a devotional work to a friend, Joyeuce Leigh, who had been admitted to the order of the Poor Clares or Minoresses – a house of nuns situated outside the city walls, just beyond Aldgate. It is likely that she came from a wealthy London family well known to the Mores and had made the orthodox journey into relatively comfortable seclusion. More's translation was part of a hagiographical tradition, but it was not merely an exercise for a specific occasion. It is clear that he was powerfully affected by his subject; there were similarities between the two young men which could not fail to have impressed themselves upon More. Pico possessed 'an incredible wit' and 'a marvelous fast memory' but his 'besy & infatigable study' was tempered by the fact that 'He was of chere alwaye mery & of so beninge nature he was never troubled with Angre' and always evinced 'a plesaunt and a mery cotenaunce'.[26] He derived 'great substance' from reading Greek and Latin authors, but gained no profit from academic learning which 'leyned to no thing but only mere traditions & ordinaunces'. Precisely the same qualities and opinions were shared by More, and it seems likely that Cresacre More was right to believe that his great-grandfather saw in Pico a very pattern of action and belief.[27] There was much emphasis in this period on the virtues of 'imitation' – *Imitatio Christi* being the single most important example – which is the more pious aspect of that conception of the world as a stage in which each must play a part.

If we can take the *Life* of Pico as in certain respects an act of self-definition, then, More's excisions from, and alterations of, the original (written by Pico's nephew) take on a biographical relevance. More is particularly interested in explaining how Pico had for a time followed 'the croked & ragged path of voluptuouse lyving'[28] but had chastened the appetites of the flesh with prayers and self-flagellation. A later printing of the little book has on its title-page an image of the crucified Christ, along with the assorted scourges and whips of his Passion. It is clear that the need to tame the possibilities of 'delitious pleasure'[29] was one of More's early and principal concerns. The omissions within his translation are also significant, since he touches only lightly upon the more quixotic or occult reaches of Pico's knowledge in order to emphasise his devotional orthodoxy. Walter Pater in his *Studies in the History of the Renaissance* turned Pico della Mirandola into a fabulous youth whose mission was to reconcile pagan and Christian learning; certainly his interest in esoteric knowledge, and his almost Paracelsian belief in the image of the divine man within every human being, suggest his true affinities. But the young More had no interest in such matters and instead celebrates his subject's following of God, Church and 'ye faith of Chryst'.[30]

His relation to the text is also marked by his additions; he inserted an opening paragraph on the importance of true virtue rather than inherited honour, although this was becoming a commonplace in More's circle of friends and London citizens. He also versified some of Pico's spiritual precepts, and out of them created some powerful and haunting poetry. It is upon More's great theme of mutability and transience, animated by the fervent desire 'To bere his body in erth, his mynde in heven' and deepened by the knowledge that life passes 'As doth a dreme or a shadowe on the wall'.[31] This is the music that More carried with him always, even though in some of his later prose works the tone is more combative and theoretical. More's poetic powers are often undervalued, but the remarkably controlled and melodious 'rhyme royal' of these interpolated verses – a form borrowed from Chaucer, the English poet whom he most admired – suggests that he was one of the most accomplished poets of the early sixteenth century. The prose of this biographical treatise is perhaps not so successful, yet the occasional awkwardness of More's style testifies to the enthusiasm with which he treated the pious and scholarly life of the young Italian who died at the age of thirty-one and was buried in the habit of a Dominican monk. The *Life* has something of the charm and impetuousness of a first novel or, rather, a *Bildungsroman* in which More could convey an idealised image of himself. Of course, like many writers of such romances, he did not necessarily tell the whole story. 'Fashion thyself,' as Pico himself wrote, 'in what form thou likest best.'[32]

More's spiritual preoccupations did not inhibit his work in the world, and it is important to recognise that throughout these formative years he was playing an active role in the social, administrative and institutional affairs of London. In the same period that he was lecturing on *The City of God* in St Lawrence Jewry, he was also Reader in Law at Furnivall's Inn – this was an Inn affiliated to his own Lincoln's Inn and it is further evidence of his burgeoning reputation as a lawyer as well as a scholar. He lectured here for three years to an audience of clerks and young attorneys and no doubt he seasoned the instruction with the stories he took delight in telling – how one witness was so forgetful that he handed his counsel 'hys tynder boxe wyth hys flynte and hys matches'[33] rather than the box of evidence, which he had left at home; or how one conscientious juror refused to accede to a majority decision by saying 'I dare not in such a matter passe for good cumpany'.[34] More was certainly also practising as a lawyer, conducting the same kind of London business as his father, and there are brief extant records of his being nominated as a London alderman, of his being in some way associated with the guild of the Mercers, of his even renting a house owned by that guild.[35] But he was not lacking social connections of a grander kind.

The death of Prince Arthur in the spring of 1502, followed by that of his mother, Elizabeth of York, ten months later, provides a solemn context for More's direct experience of royal life. Her body was laid in state in the Tower, close to the spot where her two brothers had been secretly buried twenty years before; for the funeral procession a wax effigy of her in full royal regalia was carried on a chair above the coffin, while along the route groups of thirty-seven virgins were stationed, dressed all in white and carrying lighted tapers – their number bearing witness to Elizabeth's age at the time of her death. In a powerful memorial elegy on the death of Elizabeth, whom he had known well, Thomas More returned to his theme of human transience and the prospect of eternity around 'Ye that put your trust and confidence/ In worldly joy and frayle prosperitie.'[36]

Only months before, he had witnessed the procession of Catherine of Aragon, chosen companion to the short-lived Prince Arthur, as she made her triumphal way into the city. This provided the opportunity for one of the most gorgeous and elaborate spectacles, with pageants and tableaux greeting her on the various stages of her journey from London Bridge and Gracechurch Street, turning into Cornhill before moving along Cheapside towards St Paul's. On her route were displayed painted castles, gushing fountains and elaborate mechanisms; there were dramatic monologues and allegorical scenes, making use of a wealth of astrological and numerological symbolism as well as biblical allusions and contemporary references. More goes on to mention that the Spanish escort looked as if it were made up of 'pigmei Ethiopes'.[37] In the midst of display and magnificence, he never lost his eye for the ridiculous.

This is nowhere more evident than in a comic ballad he composed in the same period. It is entitled 'A meri iest how a sergeant would learne to play the frere', and develops the themes of disguise and false identity which are so central to the period:

> In any wyse
> I would auyse
> And counsayle euery man,
> His owne craft use,
> All newe refuse . . .[38]

The mode of address and general tenor of the verse strongly suggest that it was recited – or dramatised – at a banquet of one of the London guilds. It is delivered to 'masters all' and the injunction for each man to keep to his 'craft' was a conventional stricture in so elaborate and hierarchical a society; we can imagine the young More standing in front of his fellow Londoners and acting out all the voices in this theatrical ballad. His general high spirits, and what we know from his contemporaries of his 'deadpan' delivery of comic lines, ensured its success.

But his role in London affairs may have required a wider stage. William Roper suggests that More was 'a burgess of the Parliament' for one session during the reign of Henry VII and that his intervention was responsible for the king's financial demands being 'clean overthrown'.[39] The king was so incensed, again according to Roper, that he promptly imprisoned More's father in the Tower until John More had paid a fine of £100. More himself is supposed to have considered leaving England in order to escape Henry's vengeance. It is a perfect story to emphasise how More's conscience worked against the king's will, even in these early days, but it has the disadvantage of being less than plausible. There is no record of More in the Commons at this early date and, in any event, the king's demands were not 'overthrown'; Henry VII eventually accepted less than parliament offered him. It was the first session in seven years and the king would have shaped its deliberations carefully. It is also highly improbable that Henry would imprison one of his own serjeants, especially upon so outrageous a pretext; certainly in the chronicles of London there is no mention of any such remarkable incident. All the signs are that More and his father were prospering; in the year of the supposed parliamentary fracas, 1504, together they purchased part of an estate in Hertfordshire. Two years later More was dedicating his translations of Lucian, in fulsome terms, to the king's own secretary. Yet it would be unwise completely to dismiss biographical anecdote; it is evident from More's coronation poem to Henry VIII that he detested the old king's financial exactions and considered him to have become grasping and tyrannical. More was already associated with the London merchants upon whom, according to his own report, harsh duties had been exacted; no doubt he implicitly sided with those members of court or council who distrusted or disliked the king's policies. Here, if anywhere, lies the truth of Roper's story.

There is at least one clearer token of More's character and behaviour during this period, since it is to be found in his own words. In a letter to John Colet, he laments his friend's absence from the city and in an elaborate passage complains of the difficulties of leading a virtuous life in London among false friends and enemies, beset on every side by tradesmen ministering to greed, surrounded by tall houses so that he cannot even see the heavens. More's words should not be taken literally, since he is engaged in a self-conscious performance of *ars dictamen*, or letter-writing, and for the purpose descants upon the familiar topic of the evils of the city; he could have borrowed it from Juvenal or Seneca or St Gregory. Yet there are two points of special relevance from the young man who had lectured upon Augustine's *City of God*. He alludes to his efforts to ascend the track of virtue,[40] while at the same time confessing that by some strong force and urgent necessity[41] he is in peril of being thrust down again into darkness. It is hard not to recall here Erasmus's comment that More's sexual appetite dissuaded him from ordination, and it seems likely that More himself is here confessing his own weakness. But he knew well enough the cure for lechery. He decided to marry.

XI

Holy, Holy, Holy!

AND when More attended Mass each day, as was his custom, what were the sights and sounds which encompassed him? The church is a busy and noisy place, visited by moments of stillness and solemnity, echoing to bells, prayers and whispered gossip. All around him are wax tapers and tallow candles lit before the images of the saints and the Holy Family, together with paintings and cloths and banners and richly decorated carvings; the whole effect is of a mysterious painted chamber with the gleam of crucifixes and candlesticks, chalices and patens, against the old stone. The melody of plainsong or prick song might linger in the recesses and corners of this place, together with the odours of incense or of charcoal mingled with the human smell of the worshippers come to witness the Mass. They stand or kneel in the nave with the great picture of the rood or crucified Christ hanging before them, waiting to glimpse part of the drama which is about to take place within the chancel itself. The church of St Stephen Walbrook, which soon became More's principal place of worship, had images of the apostles and the holy doctors; there were stone tablets upon which were inscribed the commandments as well as 'the seven works of Mercy and the seven deadly sins'.[1] More heard the Mass here with his family; he heard the same Mass at St Thomas of Acon, where he worshipped with the mercers; he heard it with the monks of the Charterhouse and the students of Oxford, and would hear it with the king at Greenwich and with the judges in Holborn, with the villagers of Chelsea and with the prisoners of the Tower. It was the single most important aspect of his life, and the source from which much of his earnestness and his irony, his gravity and his playfulness, springs.

The priest enters, together with his ministers and servers, and stands before the altar step while the others take up their customary positions for the ritual; then he ascends to the altar and inclines before it while he intones the orison. After the Office and Kyries he censes the altar and then lifts up his hands to proclaim 'Gloria in Excelsis'. So the Mass begins. The worshippers in the nave are separated from these rites by the rood screen; they can see only stray gestures and hear muttered words in a language most of them could not understand. They are not expected to participate in, or even necessarily follow, the Mass; they have their own sets of prayers and devotions, with particular attention being given to the hours of the Virgin, the psalms of penitence and the Office of the Dead. The Mass was in some sense a secret ritual, all the more powerful for being partly concealed; the prayers and blessings of the Mass were known to have mysterious efficacy and its words were not translated into the vernacular for fear that they might be misused by witches or 'cunning men'. The host was a magical talisman which was reputed to heal sickness, to cure blindness and to act as a love charm. Those who saw its elevation would suffer no hunger, or thirst, or ill fortune, that day. The eucharist was displayed to some unruly Londoners in Fleet Street, as a way of quelling the disturbance. There was an inexpressible element of wonder and awfulness in a ceremony that brought the body and blood of Christ down to the earth once more; in a world of mysteries and miracles, this was the greatest mystery of all. It is what More meant when he wrote of 'the mystycall gestures and seremonyes vsed in the masse'.[2] But essentially it was a public, rather than a private, ceremony. The Mass at the high altar was conducted behind the rood screen, but in innumerable chapels and side-altars it was celebrated with the worshippers sometimes literally crowded around. The notable divine Thomas Cranmer relates how people called on their neighbours to 'stoop down before' so that they could get a better view.[3]

In ceremonial manner the priest enacted the stages of Christ's ministry, passion and death; as one spiritual writer put it, 'the process of the mass representeth the very progress of Christ to his passion'.[4] Every movement and gesture of the celebrant had dramatic significance so that, for example, when the priest holds out his arms before the altar he is an image of the crucified saviour. The most sacred truths of the faith are given full material reality, leading up to that moment when Christ himself becomes present at the altar. This was marked by the moment of elevation when the priest held up the host, become by a miracle the body of Jesus. At that instant candles and torches, made up of bundles of wood, were lit to illuminate the scene; the sacring bell was rung, and the church bells pealed so that those in the neighbouring streets or fields might be aware of the solemn moment. It was the sound which measured the hours of their day. Christ was present in their midst once more and, as the priest lifted up the thin wafer of bread, time and eternity were reconciled. The worshippers knelt down and held out their arms in adoration, since this was the sight for which they had come. There are reports of the people running from altar to altar to catch a glimpse of the consecrated host at different Masses, and one priest complained that at the sound of the sacring bell the people rushed away from his sermon to witness the elevation.

The lay congregation generally communicated once a year but, after the sacrifice of the bread and wine was complete, a holy object or 'pax' was passed among them to be kissed and handled. This was a small wooden tablet or metal amulet upon which was carved a paschal lamb, or a cross, with the legend IHS – *Iesu Hominum Salvator*. Then, at the conclusion of the Mass, bread is blessed and distributed to the congregation; it was known as 'singing bread', and, when one martyr at the moment of death in the flames is supposed to have smelled of baking bread, perhaps this was the variety implicitly meant. These were the rites of the community, affirmed and strengthened by Christ's presence within it; the parishioners were bound to their church precisely because the Mass was the centre of their lives and activities. It redeemed them from their toil and their sinfulness, from their tedium and their suffering.

But this was not simply the communion of the living; at the most sacred moments of the Mass prayers were offered up for the dead and, once a year, the names of dead parishioners were recited from the 'bede-roll'. The souls in purgatory, in particular, were anxiously watching the living, seeking their prayers and acts of charity to allay their own sufferings; the dead were in a real sense mingled with those still upon the earth. If at the moment of elevation time and eternity were reconciled, so also were the living and the dead, past and present coming together in the form of the body of Christ. His body was considered not only to be the transubstantiated host, but also the entire Catholic Church from its beginning in human history. The public drama of the Mass was enacted each day as a memorial to this historical community, Christ returned to earth in the form of the consecrated host and in the presence of the worshippers. This is what

Thomas More meant when he invoked 'thys vyne of Crystes mystycall body the knowen catholyke chyrche',[5] and when he quoted from St Paul's letter to the Corinthians, 'We many be one bread and one body'.[6] There are intimations here of Christian society making up one physical body, but we must see it more properly as a symbolic and imaginative order in which Christ, the eucharist and the Church partake of the flesh and the blood and are incarnated in the heart of the city.

On Corpus Christi, then, when the sacrament was carried in procession down the main streets 'wyth baners, copys, crosses, and sencers',[7] London is not only a physical community but also a host of angels singing 'Holy, holy, holy!' The consecrated wafer was surrounded in Cornhill and Cheapside by a hundred torches of wax and two hundred priests chanting. It is the *genius loci*, the meaning of the place where they stand. In the same spirit passion plays were performed in Clerkenwell and Skinners' Well. The presence of relics, of shrines and of holy wells, in London and elsewhere, testifies to a sense of time utterly at odds with the twentieth-century vision of the city as a quickly running mechanism or an endless flow of passing human beings. In early sixteenth-century London time was not considered to be some evenly flowing current or stream; although the comparison would not have occurred to the citizens themselves, it might be seen as resembling a lava flow from an unknown source of power. Some parts of time moved more sluggishly than others, and some parts did not move at all because they were already mingled with eternity. The sense of the sacredness of place is central here: in Rogation Week the bounds of each parish were walked in ritual procession with sacrament and cross, handbells being rung perpetually to banish demons and other evil spirits (Thomas More firmly believed in demons) from the vicinity. One foreign observer was surprised by the piety of Londoners, and remarked, with some exaggeration, that 'they all attend Mass every day, and say many Paternosters in public (the women carrying long rosaries in their hands), and any who can read taking the Office of Our Lady'.[8] Against that testimony we must place More's lamentations on the viciousness of the city, on the prostitutes and the cut-purses, but of course in such a culture the accounts of sacredness and sin are not incompatible. Who knows what might have happened in Paternoster Row, Creed Lane or Ave Maria Lane?

In St Paul's itself we read of sermons and services being drowned out by the sound of general business being conducted elsewhere in the church and of what John Fisher, the Bishop of Rochester, called 'the great noyse of the people'.[9] Forty Masses were said each day within the cavernous cathedral, while outside in the courtyard and precincts the business of the city was conducted. The rood at the north door of the cathedral was supposed to have been carved by Joseph of Arimathea, and was the site of miracles; under the weathercock had been placed a relic of the Holy Cross. On the feast day of the commemoration of St Paul, a buck was brought to the high altar; it was then killed and its head fixed upon a pole for a procession to the west door, at which time horns were blown through the city.

The festivals and holy days of the ritual year now seem inconceivably remote, so thoroughly has the work of the reformation been done. Yet they were an important part of the faith, and the city, in which More dwelled. A long pole was kept on iron hooks beneath the roofs of a row of houses in Shaft Alley, off Leadenhall, and on May Day it was set up on the south side of St Andrew the Apostle, which was given the name 'St Andrew under Shafte'; it was one of London's many maypoles, with a 'knape' or bunch of flowers on its top, so high that it towered over the steeple of the church itself. It may also be seen, perhaps, as an emblem of the paganism generally present within London rituals.

John Stow tells the story of this maypole and how it was eventually hacked to pieces as an 'idol' in 1549. He is an altogether reliable chronicler of the London ceremonials that had all but disappeared in his own lifetime. He depicts the dances, pageants and 'shows of the night' on May Day itself, the ivy and bays put out before every house at Christmas, the procession of the Skinners' Guild through the streets of London on Corpus Christi, the plays and disguisings of the Midsummer Watch when the doors of London houses were 'shadowed with green Birch, long Fennel, St John's wort, Orpin, white Lillies, and such like, garnished upon with Garlands of beautiful flowers'.[10] There were bonfires in the main thoroughfares; in New Fish Street, Thomas Street and other places hundreds of glass lamps were hung in curious display. These were the streets where More walked, and on these days of festival they created an atmosphere of play-acting and game which seems to have been close to More's own temperament. Yet the play-acting was part of customary ritual and the games an aspect of religious observance.

Holy, Holy, Holy!

That is why everything, for More and his fellow citizens, has its source and origin in that single most dramatic moment of faith when the host is raised before the adoring people.

XII

Craft of the City

PICO della Mirandola had departed in the time of lilies, according to prophecy, while Thomas More still walked among the temptations of London: better to marry than to become an unchaste priest, better even to marry than to burn, and at the age of twenty-six, in the first month of 1505, he was duly wed. The little that is known about Jane Colt can soon be told; she was the daughter of a titled landowner, Sir John Colt, or Cowlt, of Essex. His household at Netherhall, in the parish of Royden, was fifteen miles from the Mores' Hertfordshire estate at North Mimms; only a gatehouse of faded red brick still remains, but it is clear that it was an impressive and even grand house. If you are to marry the daughter of neighbours, it is important that they are affluent and well connected: the tomb of Jane Colt's grandfather, in the parish church of Royden, proclaims him to have been '*Edwardi regis consul honorificus*'. Jane Colt, sixteen years of age, was the oldest daughter of the family; More's son-in-law, William Roper, records that More preferred a younger daughter but chose Jane out of a sense of propriety and 'a certain pity'.[1] The anecdote suggests the sense of duty which More carried with him everywhere, but if, as seems likely, it was told to Roper by More himself, it also confirms a slight attitude of dismissiveness or comic disparagement towards his wives. When asked why he chose short women, he is supposed to have replied 'of two evils you should choose the less'; it sounds like a remark made by his father and is perhaps not to be taken seriously except to the extent that he feared or distrusted his own sensuality and therefore felt the need to caricature the women who ministered to it.

It is not known in which church Thomas More and Jane Colt were married, although it is likely to have been the parish church of Royden where her ancestors were interred. Much of the ceremony took place outside the door of the church, the man standing to the right hand of the woman to signify that Eve was formed from one of Adam's left ribs. The banns were asked by the priest, the cause of any impediment enquired and then the bride was given in marriage – the ring placed upon her fourth finger because it was believed that a vein ran from there directly to the heart. Only after the marriage ceremony had been performed did the participants enter the church itself for Mass. At one point the husband and wife prostrated themselves upon the steps of the altar, with a pall extended over them while benediction was bestowed; that night the priest entered their bedchamber, blessed the bed itself and then sprinkled holy water over the couple.

In a Latin poem where he refers to '*mea*',[2] which might imply my wife or my betrothed, More counsels against choosing a girl for her beauty or dowry alone; she must be modest, reserved, of good parents, capable of being instructed as a true companion and educated in good letters or at least with a propensity to study them.[3] He also suggests that she becomes versed in the best of the old books. It is not known to what extent Jane Colt met these requirements but, according to Erasmus, from the start More determined to fashion her character and to educate her in all forms of music as well as '*literis*':[4] the Dutch scholar would have had the opportunity of discovering this at first hand, since he visited them soon after their marriage. More was almost ten years her senior and, although it was not a particularly unusual disparity of age in this period, it gave him the opportunity of training her in the same manner as he later trained his own daughters. It provided an opportunity for controlling the female spirit, of course, but it was also a means of exercising his dramatic imagination. It was a question of inculcating true virtue as well as learning, in the style recommended by manuals devoted to female perfection, and there is a sense in which he must have treated her as a child as well as a wife. Another friend described her as '*facillima*',[5] most good natured or tractable, and there is no reason to doubt that she responded eventually to her husband's guidance. Since More was just as determined and methodical, if more gentle, with the members of his family as he was with himself, there may have been some early disagreements. In a story from one of Erasmus's *Colloquies* a young girl from the country is married to a man who wished to instruct her in literature, music and other accomplishments; she was not accustomed to such a regimen at home and seems violently to have objected until she was persuaded by her father to behave like a good and docile wife. The anecdote may have no connection with Thomas More and Jane Colt but it is suggestive. Certainly his wife was compliant in another sense: she bore at least four children in the remaining six years of her short life.

After their marriage they moved to a house in Bucklersbury, off Cheapside, which More leased from the Mercers. Some confusion exists about what he leased, and where he leased it, in this early period; there is also a record of 'Thomas More' renting from the Mercers a 'messuage' – a site of land with a dwelling erected upon it – called the White Hart, beside the church of St Thomas of Acon in Cheapside, in the April of this year. But it may be another Thomas More, or it may be that he leased it for members of what had become an even more extended family. Or perhaps, since it was just around the corner from Bucklersbury, he and Jane Colt stayed here while their new chambers were being prepared. The two significant aspects of this transition are that More was already associated with the Mercers, and particularly with the House of St Thomas of Acon where the guild met, and that for the first time his sixteen-year-old wife, brought up and educated in the country, was plunged into the bewildering and noisy life of London.

Yet Bucklersbury was not as unsavoury as other quarters of the city. It was a rather grand street, only recently repaved, and was the locality for the shops of herbalists and apothecaries who sold spices and preserves, 'dragon-water' and 'treacle'. Falstaff speaks of young gallants who 'smell like Bucklersbury in simple time',[6] or midsummer, and in a sermon one preacher commented that 'they that be used to stinking savours can not live in Bucklesbury or in the poticaries shoppe'.[7] More and his wife inhabited part of a large house here, known as the Old Barge, and eight years later he leased the whole of it. It was the last house on the south side of the street, by the corner of Walbrook, and was described by Stow as a 'great stone building . . . manor or great house';[8] one map depicts gardens behind the row of houses of which it is a part. It was called the Old Barge because the adjacent Walbrook, before it was paved over, had been used by vessels coming up from the Thames. It may not have been as sweet-smelling as the sources suggest, however, since the 'pissing conduit' and the Stocks Market were only a few yards to the north.

By a stroke of good fortune it is still possible to enter the house, in imagination, and view some of its contents. An inventory survives from the time of the tenants to whom More in turn leased the house; they were his adopted daughter and the tutor to his children, so they were in a real sense members of the household. We can assume, then, that we are in the presence of family items – a 'gret cage fir birds', a 'gret crucyfyx and dyvers images in the chapell', 'a gret mapp of all the world', 'a table of Sir Thomas More's face', by which a picture is meant, and more than three hundred books. We read of more homely items in the Old Barge, also, with 'two lomes to work gyrdells and rybandes', 'a myll to grynd corne' and 'a payer of balans to waye medycyns'.[9] We can reconstruct a grand and commodious house of studies, chambers and parlours, a chapel and a gallery, stables and servants' quarters, great hall and courtyard. It was the London house where More was to spend the larger part of his adult life.

The parish church, of which he was also to become a part, was across the road. St Stephen Walbrook was of ancient foundation, but had been rebuilt less than a hundred years before More moved to the parish: it was here that he worshipped, served at the altar, sang (albeit not very well) and went in procession. It was filled with pictures and statues – in the lady chapel alone, there were seven wooden images – and in its accounts there are references to the amount spent on the singers 'at the alehouse after the last evyn song'.[10] It was a typical, if perhaps more than usually wealthy, London church.

When Erasmus visited London in the spring of 1505, he found More as cheerful and as witty as ever; More's mind was so extraordinarily sharp and subtle that he made the perfect advocate.[11] Since Erasmus had no very high opinion of lawyers, this is true praise. They were working together on the translations of Lucian, and More, in his high spirits, had persuaded his reticent friend to declaim in Latin. From the evidence of Erasmus's letters, it is possible to sketch out the atmosphere and society of which the brilliant lawyer was a part. It was essentially a world of power and privilege: Lord Mountjoy, now a member of the king's council, had invited the Dutchman to England in the first place. Erasmus had been promised a benefice by the king, and renewed his acquaintance with the young Prince Henry; he had rowed over the Thames to Lambeth to see the Archbishop of Canterbury, William Warham, and had stayed with John Fisher. He was in his own words mingling with the greatest and most learned of the kingdom;[12] these were also the people with whom Thomas More was associated. Of course the names of More's closest friends also appear in Erasmus's correspondence: he knew Grocyn well by now, for example, and Thomas Linacre acted as his doctor in London. John Colet had also returned to the city, having been appointed Dean of St Paul's in May of that year, and shortly after he began to outline to his friends and acquaintance a wonderful project; his father died that autumn, leaving a great inheritance, and with that sum Colet decided to establish a school in the precincts of St Paul's to be known as St Paul of the School of Child Jesus. If he could enlist the help of men such as Erasmus and More, it might be a new school for a new age.

It was almost certainly at Erasmus's urging that More made his first journey out of England; in particular he visited two great centres of learning, Paris and Louvain. Erasmus had been attached to the universities in both cities, and had recently spent two years at Louvain: his various contacts with printers and scholars would also have been useful for the Englishman. We do not know the names of the scholars and humanists whom More met on this journey, but in his only surviving recollection he makes it clear that one of his principal aims was to study the curricula and the methods of teaching currently available. It is possible that he was conducting legal business on behalf of the London merchants, but in his capacity as a trained grammarian and orator he was also taking stock of the progress of the 'new learning'; in these early years of the sixteenth century, More clearly saw himself as part of a European community of scholarship.

Another journey at this time was more provincial in nature. At some point after his marriage, More decided to visit his sister Elizabeth in Coventry. She had married the lawyer John Rastell, who succeeded his father as coroner of that city in 1506. Since he also presided over the Court of Statute Merchant, and since many citizens of Coventry were merchants of the Staple of Calais, it is possible that More was involved in business as well as family reunion. Coventry was a city of 'fayre stretes' and 'fayre towers', their stone a 'darkshe depe redde'.[13] It was also noted for its devotion. The Cathedral Church, Trinity Church, the Church of Grey Friars and the Churches of St John and St Michael were the five most eminent places of worship; there was a Charterhouse of Carthusians and a famous Hall of St Mary which was filled with tapestries emblazoned with the Virgin's heavenly splendour. At the time of More's visit the city was seized by a particularly severe fit of Mariolatry, with a Franciscan monk preaching the good news that whoever recited '*psalterium beatae virginis*'[14] (by which he meant the rosary) each day could never be damned.

More took horse and began his three-day journey, along well-kept country roads and across the many stone bridges, through Barnet and Dunstable and Daventry. Almost as soon as he arrived, as he himself told the story, he was asked if he believed the Franciscan's precept. He laughed off the whole matter as '*ridiculum*'[15] – '*Contempsi*', I scorned it. Here again we have a brief vision of More's manner in the world, at least when confronted by the excesses of popular devotion. But then, at dinner, he was interrogated by the monk himself, who had brought with him several books containing accounts of miracles and other divine interventions in the affairs of men; More tried to treat the matter lightly, but eventually made the reasonable response that it was unlikely anyone could purchase heaven at so little cost. Whereupon he was laughed at for being foolish.[16] The new humanism was no match against the credulity of the people.

Another possible reason for More's visit to Coventry, also connected with his extended family, was that the city had become the single most important site for the staging of the Corpus Christi play. The annual event attracted people from all over the kingdom; in 1492 Henry VII watched the pageants at Jordan Well and Broadgate. It would have been natural for More to have made the journey with this other purpose in mind, if only because John Rastell was involved in the ritual celebration. He was known to be an ingenious maker of pageants and spectacles; as a boy in Coventry he had been admitted to the Guild of Corpus Christi, which played a prominent part in the annual cycle of plays, and it can be assumed that he first acquired his skills as a pageant-maker while preparing for the Coventry cycle of plays.

These guild plays were performed in at least twelve different cities, providing a national dramatic repertoire which has few parallels in other periods or other cultures. They celebrated the entire history of the world, from the Creation and Fall to the eventual Day of Doom; the theatrical rituals were presented on Corpus Christi since the world was, in a real sense, the suffering body of Christ. Christ's passion and crucifixion were of course central, but there were other biblical scenes which became a standard part of the performances, among them Cain and Abel, Noah and his wife, Abraham and Isaac. Individual guilds were responsible for each specific scene or pageant, and were chosen appropriately – 'The Last Supper' was assigned to the bakers, for example, and 'The Shepherds' Play' to the shearmen – but the plays were given a unity and coherence not only through their themes but also through the nature of their staging in the streets of the city. There is the story of the Warwickshire curate who, after expounding the beliefs of the Church, informed his parishioners, 'If you believe not me then for a more sure and sufficient authority, go your way to Coventry, and there ye shall see them all played in Corpus Christi play.'[17]

The pageant wagons were approximately eighteen feet in height; they were stored in sheds, and then wheeled out into the streets of Coventry for the play. It is not clear whether each pageant wagon had one stationary site, or whether they were wheeled to different positions for various performances; common sense suggests that, in a city of six thousand people, increased by curious visitors, the latter was the case. The inventories of some pageants still survive: 'A brandreth of Iren that god sall sitte vppon when he sall sty vppe to heuuen . . . ii peces of rede cloudes & sternes of gold langing to heuuen . . . vii grete Aungels halding the passion of god . . . A grete coster of rede damaske payntid for the bakke side of the pagent . . . helle mouthe.'[18] Hell mouth was characteristically a painted set of gaping jaws, perhaps on a separate smaller wagon wheeled in front of the main pageant; the unfortunate victim could then be seen to be devoured alive to the sound of pipes, drums and gitterns. The 'brandreth' of iron was a small tripod which was winched up on pulleys so that Christ or the Virgin might ascend from the pageant stage into an upper region of heaven decorated with angels and painted clouds. It was a highly embellished dramatic art, with certain scenes played out in the street with noise and bustle, while others were presented in the solemn stillness of a holy picture. Adam and Eve wore white leather costumes to symbolise their nakedness, the prophets wore golden wigs while Judas was conventionally adorned with one of flaming red; yet, on the whole, the actors wore contemporary dress. The Corpus Christi play was not an historical entertainment, but a restatement of the eternal truths and episodes of the faith.

Its significance lies in the living moment of its conception, when a whole community was caught up in the rituals of a common faith.

When Herod grows wrathful, 'I stampe! I stare! I loke all abowtt!',[19] he is not an allegorical, but a living, figure. He is the parish clerk who, in Chaucer's *Miller's Tale*, 'pleyeth Herodas upon a scaffold hye'. When the shearmen and tailors of Coventry presented their nativity pageant it was as if the images upon the church wall had come alive and were being revived by the people themselves. There was also live animals (foreshadowing Shakespeare's use of the bear in *The Winter's Tale*), flying machines, burning fires as an accompaniment to the gaping jaws of hell; the sacred scenes were interspersed with episodes of sometimes ribald comedy, such as the famous one in which Noah tries to persuade his foul-mouthed wife to enter the Ark. Once again the spiritual and the secular need not be separate, since they were aspects of the same reality. Comedy and irony came not from ambiguity or disbelief; in many respects they emerged from an excess of belief in a world where sacred truths need not be questioned. Even the hierarchy of the guilds who staged the pageants was a reflection of the hierarchy of the heavens. All his life More referred to human affairs as a spectacle upon a stage or wooden scaffold; and when on the last day of his life he advanced among the crowd to a more solemn scaffold, he might have been enacting his own mystery play.

He is not known to have visited Coventry again, and indeed there could have been few occasions when he had the opportunity to break from legal work and London business. In Lincoln's Inn, for example, he was being promoted to positions of more responsibility: he became pensioner, or financial administrator, before becoming in succession butler, marshal and autumn reader. These were the stages of the *cursus honorum* which the successful lawyer was obliged to follow, moving forward according to the principle of 'anciety'. The roles of butler and marshal were administrative or disciplinary, while as the autumn reader he was engaged only in instruction. At eight o'clock in the morning, in front of the assembled Inn, More lectured for four mornings of four weeks in Law French; it was the practice of the reader to interpret aspects of statute law in that strange *argot*, and his exposition was followed by responses from the more senior members of the Inn. There were also formal reader's dinners, and throughout the term of his appointment he was granted special privileges. He was in a literal sense following the path of his father, who had also been butler and marshal of the Inn.

We must see More as submitting to a hierarchy of needs and

obligations. That is why, like his father before him, he was made a 'freeman' of the Mercers. In March 1509, 'Maister Thomas More, gentilman, desired to be fre of this felishipp, which was graunted hym by the holle compeney to haue it franke & fre'.[20] Part of the oath which More then read counselled mutual obligation and dependence, 'the secrets whereof to you shewed you shall keep secret',[21] as well as piety and obedience. It was the policy of the Mercers to bring influential Londoners within their ranks; John Colet, for example, had been made a freeman only the year before. And it is likely that More was recruited as a freeman precisely because of his legal acumen. The Mercers were at the time engaged in a protracted struggle with Henry VII, who had determined to curtail the powers of the established City companies; the king had been actively promoting the interests of a new guild, the Merchant Taylors, and had directly interfered in City elections. Equally importantly, four months before More's entry into the fellowship, he had threatened to levy a new tax upon cloth exports. It was in the interest of the Mercers, therefore, to have as members the best lawyers in London in order to protect their interests. The advantages for More, in turn, were obvious. He was joining the richest and most powerful of the City companies, highly influential in London administration, with a network of contacts throughout England and Europe.

There were more than sixty guilds or fraternities within the city at this date, but the Mercers were at the forefront of affairs. London had been a mercantile city since its earliest foundation; it had been built upon commerce and the profits of trade. It was perhaps inevitable, then, that the fellowship of the 'merchant adventurers' would be paramount. Trade guilds have existed for almost as long as trade itself, of course; in second-century Italy, workers 'associated by a common trade' would partake together of meals and divine worship.[22] But the growth of the London guilds was peculiarly elaborate and complex. The first surviving records of an association of Mercers come from the late twelfth century, but its origins are earlier. It was known variously as 'Compeny', 'the Mystere of Mercers', 'craft of the city', guild or fellowship. By the time of More's association it included the Company of Merchant Adventurers, the Merchants of the Staple and other interested parties variously engaged in the export of cloth and wool. Its headquarters, Mercers' Hall, lay by Cheapside and Ironmonger Lane – the area in which

More had dwelled all his life – beside the church of St Thomas of Acon to which it was affiliated.

John Colet said that he trusted this body of London citizens more than any other estate or degree and, in order to understand More's role among them, it is important to remember that the company was established upon community and religion as well as commerce. One early ordinance requires 'the cherishing of unity and good love' among them,[23] and we must see it as part craft, part fraternity and part religious society. More would have been obliged to wear the 'livery' on formal occasions; this included hood and robe of red or scarlet, although the precise colour seems to have been changed every two years. He would have engaged in the feasts on holy days, contributed to the funds for 'decayed' mercers, and walked in the procession of the festive pageants. The pageant image of the Mercers was that of the Blessed Virgin, and for the celebrations of the Midsummer Watch a 'Maiden Chariot' was drawn through the streets in honour of Our Lady and various allegorical personages who shared the stage with her. By the beginning of the sixteenth century, the religious aspects of the Company were not the most important; yet the mercers prayed together in the church of St Thomas of Acon 'the better to their great worship and profit in this world, but also to the great merit both to their bodies and souls after the departing out of this present life'.[24]

More's particular role in the Mercers was as negotiator and orator, and documents survive which show how he conducted himself in such business. Only six months after being 'made free' of the company, he was involved in complicated bargaining with the 'Pensonary' or chief magistrate of Antwerp over the precise streets and houses which the English merchants would be allowed to use in that city. The records demonstrate just how prominent a part he played. At eight o'clock, on a Thursday morning in September, they all assembled in the Mercers' Hall on the appropriate benches, 'euery man in his degre', and the Pensonary of Antwerp was summoned from the church below. More sat opposite him 'ende next the wyndowe' and, after politely desiring him 'to Couer his hedd', he 'tolde a longe and goodly proposicion in Latin' on the business to be transacted. In fact the magistrate from Antwerp was already known to him: Jacob de Wocht, known in humanist circles as Jacobus Tutor, was an intimate friend of Erasmus. The Dutch scholar had once lived with him for three months, and had also dedicated his edition of Cicero's *De Officiis* to him; this treatise is concerned with the conflict between justice and expediency, which might be thought to have some bearing upon the negotiations of the Mercers. Certainly, in the colloquies of More and Tutor, we have a vivid and practical example of the way in which learned European humanists were also at the heart of commercial and social affairs in this period. After More had finished his initial peroration, Tutor 'tolde his tale in Latyne and first he commended Maister More greatly for makyng of his Oracion'. And so it continued, with More translating Tutor's remarks for the Englishmen assembled and then replying in Latin.

The negotiations continued for several days, until a final settlement was reached. 'Than when that he had declared as is a forsaid all in Laten, Maister More dyd enterpret the same in Englisshe to the compeny, and than they arose and euery man went his waye.'[25] The agreement was satisfactory to the Mercers, principally because they obtained everything they wanted; More was a skilful lawyer who, as Erasmus once said, could defend cases which were not the best.[26] There is an intimation here that Erasmus did not necessarily approve of all More's public activities, and thought he was somehow betraying his gifts by working as a lawyer, but he could not have foreseen then the full tragedy of his friend's public career. That career might even be said to have begun in these months of 1509, for something had happened between More's entry into the Mercers and his conduct of the autumn negotiations. In the spring of the same year the old king had died, and Henry VIII ascended the throne.

XIII

Milk and Honey

HENRY VII had reigned for twenty-four years; the eight-year-old boy living in Milk Street witnessed the victor of Bosworth's triumphal progress along Cheapside, in the early autumn of 1485, surrounded by the dignitaries of London 'all clothed in Violet',[1] and during the course of his reign More had grown to adulthood. His notions of order and authority might in part be derived from his experience of that monarch's personal rule; certainly More died a sacrifice to the principle of kingship which Henry VII helped to establish. He was the victim of the older, no less than the younger, Tudor. More's family, however, had flourished under Henry's rule. His policy of reforming administration had meant that lawyers as well as clerics were now at the centre of affairs; his role as a patron of continental scholars had also created the climate in which men such as Colet and Linacre could flourish. Equally importantly, Henry had restored peace and stability within the realm. Two kings of England had suffered violent deaths during More's early childhood; through a judicious mixture of military expertise, financial exaction and political acumen the new king created a secure regime which would last more than a hundred years. The fact that he came between two monsters, at least of historical legend – Richard III and Henry VIII – has meant that his actual stature and achievement have been eclipsed. Yet if it had not been for the order which Henry maintained, the whole humanist enterprise in England, for example, would have been impossible. His close supervision of all aspects of administration, financial and political, suggested that in a real sense all authority now radiated from the monarch; he was the central symbol of the power and unity of the nation. It was a legacy that his son would exploit for quite different purposes.

The long rule of this autocratic king helps to explain More's youthful preoccupation with the nature of true kingship as opposed to tyranny. It is a theme of his Latin epigrams. Even such later works as *The History of Richard III* and *Utopia* are concerned with the contrasts of just and vicious government. In a Latin poem celebrating the coronation of Henry VIII, which was transcribed in a highly embellished presentation copy, More invokes the atmosphere of fear, suspicion and rapacity that the dead monarch's avarice had created. It was an opinion shared by other contemporaries and, although modern historians have tended to regard his exactions less as evidence of greed than as an instrument of royal supremacy, it is not lightly to be disregarded. There is also the story of the delight of the English Court when Henry VII's pet monkey destroyed the papers in which he had set down his observations and criticisms of those around him.

Yet the old king had died muttering words of contrition, a crucifix held before his face. His body was carried from Richmond Palace through the streets of London, surrounded by priests and bishops, followed by six hundred of his household bearing lighted tapers; a large effigy of him, in royal state, had been placed upon the hearse. During his funeral oration in St Paul's, John Fisher emphasised Henry VII's devotion to the crucifix and his desire always to be 'kyssynge it'.[2] Then the body was taken to Westminster Abbey, where it was interred. In his will Henry had left money for the purchase of ten thousand masses to be celebrated for the sake of his soul and, after the obsequies in the Abbey, all departed for 'a greate and a sumptuous feast'.[3]

Other celebrations were about to begin. Less than a month later, in April 1509, the seventeen-year-old Prince Henry assumed the throne as Henry VIII. The old king had been of sallow complexion, with black decayed teeth and thinning hair. The new king was as handsome as he was amiable, known both for his piety and his prowess, a young man acquainted with books as well as with jousts and hunting. In his coronation poem Thomas More described him as the glory of the era, renowned no less for learning than for virtue; truly this prince was about to inaugurate a new golden age. When he appeared on the streets of London the crowds filled the houses and rooftops along his route and thronged about him so that he was hardly able to make his way. Lord Mountjoy, in a letter to Erasmus, proclaimed that under the rule of this great prince '*Ridet aether,*

exultat terra; omnia lactis, omnia mellis' ('the heavens laugh and the
earth rejoices, all is milk and honey').[4] Baldassare Castiglione, the
courtier and diplomat from Mantua, had in more general terms
depicted the monarch as 'full of liberality, munificence, religion and
clemency . . . capable of being regarded as a demigod rather than as a
mortal man'.[5] This reverence may elucidate More's own attitude
towards the young king. On the day before the coronation, when
Henry and his new queen processed through the streets of London,
Cornhill and Cheapside were hung with cloth of gold; 'Virgins in
white, with braunches of white Waxe'[6] lined the route together with
all the guilds of London in their preordained order, as well as priests
in rich copes who censed the royal couple as they passed. Edward
Hall devotes many pages of his chronicle to the finery of this
procession as well as to the coronation itself, with its mixture of
piety, drama, politics and spectacle. He dwells upon the richness and
grandness of the apparel of the various guests, with damask gold
and cloth of silver, green silk and blue velvet, all 'poudered' and
embroidered. There are ritual challenges and elaborately staged
feasts, carefully ordered manifestations of rank and authority,
displays of wealth and power, all contributing to a picture of the
world in this lower sphere where we may mimic the magnificence and
splendour of heaven.

More was already close to members of the young king's household; he was also on good terms with some of the clerics who were
part of the council, in particular with William Warham and Thomas
Ruthall, Bishop of Durham. His immediate political hope, as an
influential Londoner, was that the new king was about to lift taxes
and reform the conduct of policy; Henry was expected to renew the
arts of ruling.[7] This is the principal theme of More's coronation
verses, with his celebration that unjust laws and unfairly imposed
debts are to be repealed. He speaks here as a representative of the
merchant class. But there is another aspect of his encomium. The
young Henry had already been instructed in noble arts,[8] and in
'Philosophia'.[9] More's own humanist interests here become paramount. Not much older than the century itself, Henry might be
considered to be the king for a new age of restored piety and
scholarship. There seemed every reason to believe he would patronise
the new learning and, more importantly, maintain the peace and
stability in which such learning could flourish. It is hard to think of

any other century, or reign, in England which opened with such hopes.

Mountjoy's enthusiastic letter to Erasmus, then residing in Rome, summoned his old teacher to the brave new world which seemed about to open. William Warham had promised the Dutch scholar a benefice on his return to England, and Mountjoy sent him five pounds for the expenses of his journey. Erasmus left almost at once and, on his arrival in London, lodged with More and his wife at their house in Bucklersbury. The strain of travel and the sea-crossing had brought on a pain in his kidney and he was forced to spend several days indoors. His library of books had not yet arrived and, in order to occupy his time, he wrote a little treatise. By this time the More family had substantially increased. Four children had been born since the marriage; Margaret, now four, was the eldest and was succeeded by Elizabeth, Cicely and John. It was not a quiet household, therefore, and yet within the space of seven days Erasmus completed the work which more than any other is now associated with his name and fame. The title itself suggests its origin in the More household, *Moriae encomium*, 'In Praise of Folly', but also, with a subtle shift of language, 'In Praise of More'. However, More is connected to the book by more than a pun. Erasmus describes him as its '*auctor*', or its inspiration, and he also refers to the jokes[10] that he and More shared. But these were not necessarily of a frivolous nature. The vivid and acerbic tone of *Moriae encomium* represents the temperaments not only of More or Erasmus but also of what Hazlitt called 'the spirit of the age'. The Dutch scholar read it out to More's friends in Bucklersbury, who were delighted by it. On its eventual publication, it sold rapidly and widely. It became the most famous secular work of the century, affecting writers as diverse as Rabelais and Cervantes, and can almost be read as a general compendium of Northern humanism. It was prefaced by a letter from Erasmus to More, in which he describes his friend as the Democritus of a new age; by which he meant that More was constantly amused by the follies all around him, but managed to blend his sense of the ridiculous with manners at once 'so friendly and pleasant'.[11] The main text is an oration by Folly herself, in which she exposes those of her adherents who pretend to be wise men and announces her courtiers as flattery and self-love, sophistry and delusion. Folly soon proves herself to be the true deity of this world, with all of its people as her followers. In many respects *Moriae encomium* is the forerunner to More's *Utopia*;

both books use irony and ventriloquy in order to reveal contemporary society within a wider and clearer perspective. The great success of the book suggests that there was an appetite for the kind of writing which pricked the follies and abuses of the period, with attacks upon lazy mendicant friars as well as greedy princes of the church, lawyers as well as scholastic theologians. It is as if the whole structure of the late medieval world was being shaken.

In this spirit, too, we must understand More's enthusiasm at the accession of the young king. Now anything seemed possible. More's life of Pico della Mirandola was published by his brother-in-law John Rastell and was soon pirated by Wynkyn de Worde. The renovated spirituality of that treatise perfectly complements the close of *Moriae encomium*, in which Erasmus extols the life of simple piety. In the same spirit, too, John Colet was discussing with his friends the constitution and the syllabus of his new school. Colet wrote that 'My entent is by thys scole specially to incresse knowlege and worshipping of god and oure lorde Christ Jesu.'[12] The new learning was not incompatible with a deep piety; indeed, for Colet, it was an aspect of faith. Neither was it incompatible with secular business. John Colet asked the Mercers' Company to maintain the school, for which purpose he gave them estates in Middlesex, Buckinghamshire and elsewhere. So this group of London merchants became the trustees and governors of a school devoted to 'Christ Jesu'; once again it emphasises the extent to which spiritual and secular concerns were part of the same pattern and texture of living. Land was granted for the school in 1509, but actual building began more than a year later; the school, complete with master's house and chapel, was finished in 1512. It was situated in the east part of St Paul's churchyard, beside the great stone bell-house containing the four 'Jesus bells', which were reputed to be the loudest in the kingdom. Some ground was leased where the children might urinate, the rent being a red rose every ninety-nine years.[13] Late medieval ecclesiastics did not necessarily lack a sense of humour.

More himself was vitally concerned with the manner and methods of education; he would later set up a flourishing 'school' within his own household. But other friends became involved in Colet's enterprise, pre-eminently Erasmus and Thomas Linacre; as More put it in a letter to Colet, St Paul's was designed to banish ignorance[14] and he made a pointed allusion to the Greeks who subverted '*barbaram Troiam*'.[15] He envisaged the school, in other words, as a preserve of the new learning. One other, more exotic, scholar might also have been an adviser: the hermeticist and exponent of angel-magic Cornelius Agrippa stayed with Colet in 1510. This was the year in which he had completed *De occulta philosophia*, a subject in which Colet was deeply interested; in fact there is a strong tradition of magical theory and practice in the work of the humanists whom Colet most admired, Ficino and Pico and Reuchlin, concerning such matters as the cabbala and the summoning of angels. This was magic performed in an atmosphere of piety and prayer, which Agrippa himself described in language close to Colet's own meditations and to the spirit of Thomas à Kempis and *devotio moderna*: 'Faithe and Praier: not the studie of longe time, but humblenes of Spirite and cleannesse of Hart'.[16]

It may have been Agrippa who suggested to Colet that the number of boys at his new school should be limited to 153, a powerful piece of number symbolism related to the Trinity. The school was one large chamber divided into four apartments by means of curtains, and even the interior reflected the advice of More and his friends. At the suggestion of Erasmus, for example, an image of the boy Jesus 'in the attitude of teaching' was placed above the master's chair, with an image of God the Father saying '*Ipsum audite*'.[17] Erasmus's influence on the school was profound and particular. He composed a textbook for the boys, *De Copia* ('Of Abundance') which proved popular for more than a hundred years, as well as some prayers and sermons; he translated a little catechism by Colet into Latin hexameters, and went to some trouble to find a suitable under-master for the school. It is likely that he also helped to draw up the syllabus. Colet also enlisted Thomas Linacre, to compose a Latin grammar; Linacre entitled it *Rudimenta*, but it was not rudimentary enough for the young scholars of St Paul's. Colet eventually rejected it on the grounds that it was too abstruse. This provoked some bad feeling between the two men, as always fuelled by spiteful gossip, but Erasmus acted as placator and mediator. As a result Colet asked another member of this London group, William Lily – whom he had already chosen as high master of the school – to help in the preparation of an easier textbook.

So they all worked together on Colet's educational project. That More, and his colleagues, were markedly different from other groups in London is well established. Erasmus tells the story of how a scholastic philosopher scorned his concern in the teaching of the

London children; the more orthodox scholars were not interested in the training of the juvenile mind, precisely because they were not interested in the possibilities of a new age of piety and learning. Another assault upon 'the Greeks' came from the quondam and perhaps even self-styled poet laureate John Skelton, some seven years after the establishment of the school. Skelton attacked a new Latin grammar which Lily had adopted for his pupils, and the ensuing exchange of pamphlets and poems became known as 'the grammarians' war'. In particular Skelton believed that the young pupils were being introduced to classical texts before they had mastered the elements of syntax and vocabulary; it is an old and perhaps permanent argument between educational theorists but Skelton's extraordinary poem, 'Speke, Parrot', brings its sixteenth-century manifestation vividly to life:

> Plautus in his comedies a chyld shall now reherse
> And medyll with Quintylyan in his Declamacyons.[18]

Thus the new humanists – More, Erasmus, Linacre and Lily – 'go about to amende, and ye mare all'.[19] The irony is that the curriculum which Colet eventually organised was highly conservative and orthodox in intent. He wished to educate the children with 'Cristyn auctours',[20] preferring those from the fourth century rather than the classical writers themselves. It seems likely that this instruction was quietly broken by William Lily – there was no substitute for Cicero or Quintilian – but it emphasises that, in this London circle, piety was often considered more important than learning. Some of Colet's injunctions to the pupils may also help us to comprehend the life of the period – 'Lose no tyme', 'Wasshe cleane', 'Awake quykly', 'Reuerence thyne elders', 'Enrich thee with vertue'. At the end of his introduction to grammar, he introduces a note which brings us closer to the man than a thousand precepts: 'And lyfte vp your lytel whyte handes for me, which prayeth for you to god.'[21]

The cause of restored piety was not confined to the schoolroom. Colet shared his contemporaries' concern with education as part of the humanist endeavour but, like them, he was equally convinced of the need for reform within the Church. In a speech to convocation which he made in the year after Henry's accession to the throne, he declared that the 'Church is become foul and deformed'[22] with abuses. He condemned 'the secular and worldly way of living on the part of the clergy',[23] in particular the search for benefices as well as the inclination towards sensuality and hypocrisy. He recognised that the Church was troubled by heretics, but said that the greater heresy lay 'in the vicious and depraved lives of the clergy'.[24] Then he spoke of the need for 'Reformation' – not as it came to be applied twenty-five years later but, rather, a reformation of mind and spirit. It was a carefully worded attack, at all times adverting to scriptural authority, and was part of the concerted attempt to revive and restore the Church at this fortunate moment in English history. Of course the substance of Colet's sermon was not new. There had been attacks on Church abuses almost from the moment of the Church's foundation; fourteenth- and fifteenth-century sermons, for example, are filled with attacks upon priests who are 'fornicators ... gluttons ... plunderes in the church of God'.[25] A previous Bishop of Rochester, Thomas Brunton, spoke of other prelates as 'Dumb dogs',[26] and the vices of the clergy provoked his early sixteenth-century successor, John Fisher, into believing that God was 'in a maner in a deed slepe'.[27] Yet the Church was even then in the midst of one of its periodical fits of reform. Many of the bishops whom Colet addressed in convocation were both active and virtuous; the problem of the non-residency of hired clergy was in that period being addressed, and it is clear from the written evidence that the educational standards of clerics had been improving. Smaller monasteries were being dissolved – sometimes to make way for collegiate foundations – and the records of Archbishop Morton's 'visitations', in the late 1480s and 1490s, reveal a surprisingly low record of abuses. In fact most of the complaints about the clergy came from the clergy themselves. The record of lay benefice, the provisions of wills and the level of bequests confirm what religious historians have already established: the piety of the people was actually increasing in the last decades of the fifteenth, and early decades of the sixteenth, centuries. It was the great age for the building, and rebuilding, of churches. But, more importantly, the inner faith and private spirituality, encouraged both by Colet and More, addressed the very needs and preoccupations of the time.

That is why it is impossible to separate More's theoretical interests from his practical pursuits; the immediate point of his humanism was social reform and, after the accession of Henry VIII, he played an increasing part in the affairs of London and neighbouring counties. John More and 'yong More', as he was called in a chronicle for this year, were part of a royal commission concerned with the legacy of a dead viscount; father and son were also part of a larger royal commission for Middlesex. A few months later More was member of a party 'to see and viewe the comen grounde whereuppon the Master of seint bartholomus hath bilded'.[28] This was the area where he had disputed as a schoolboy; now he was one of London's guardians. It is also likely that he played some part, at the end of 1509, in negotiations to create 'an unity' between the Merchant Adventurers and the Merchants of the Staple. It was the kind of task which he had been trained all his life to fulfil.

In that same month of December a more singular honour was afforded him: 'Thomas More, mercerus' was elected as a burgess for London at the next meeting of 'the parlement'. He was one of four representatives of the city at Westminster, and had been chosen to replace another mercer. He did not have to suffer the indignity of a free vote; his election was theoretically based upon the suffrage of the freemen of London, but in practice it was arranged by the mayor, aldermen and senior councillors. More was now part of the hierarchy which promoted him, of course, and the role of 'burges' was becoming increasingly important. The accounts of the chamberlain of London show that 'extraordinary' expenses and clothing allowances were liberal; when the London MPs met in a parliament at Cambridge, for example, their staff included 'a steward, butler, cook and kitchen boys'.[29] More's experience in civic and mercantile matters, as well as his reputation as a lawyer, would have given him authority in the 'Common House', where matters of taxation and subsidy were pre-eminent. But 'yong More' may also have been chosen because of his amicable relations with king and council.

He was one of some three hundred members of the Commons, who generally assembled in the chapter house of Westminster Abbey. Parliament met only irregularly over the years – it had last been summoned six years before – and the duties of its members were not arduous. They convened between eight and eleven in the morning, over a period of approximately four weeks. The chapter house was filled with merchants, knights of the shire, citizens, burgesses, lawyers and landowners; anyone who wished to speak walked to a lectern in the middle of the room and addressed his colleagues. At the end of each session, the Speaker summarised the various arguments and proffered his own advice about how best to proceed. He might then crave audience with the lords temporal and spiritual, sitting in

Westminster, where he would present the arguments of their inferiors. There might be supplications, or petitions, or the rehearsal of grievances, or remonstrances about taxation. But if it was still in theory a petitionary rather than a legislative body, the Commons was now also originating bills to be amended or passed. There survives a drawing of the parliament chamber itself, with the bishops, abbots, archbishops and lords seated in due order in a rectangular-shaped area; the judges sit on woolsacks in the centre, while two clerks are seen kneeling with pen and parchment in hand. The Speaker of the Commons stands behind a barrier and addresses them.

The parliament of 1510, which More attended, had been called by Henry VIII just a few months after his accession to the throne; it met on 21 January, and continued until the last week of February. The most important consideration was, as always, finance. There were various other bills, on the limits of prosecution and against justices of assize as well as technical matters of 'escheat' and 'traverse', but the main business lay in the granting of customs duties to the king; money was also given to his Household and Wardrobe. As a representative of the London merchants Thomas More must have been urged to speak out against some of the sums involved, and it seems that there was some overt opposition to the king's demands from the London burgesses, but by the end of the year Henry had prevailed. It was an early lesson for More in power, perhaps, but he was not averse to royal authority; the next time he returned to parliament, thirteen years later, it was as Henry's appointee as Speaker.

Other official posts followed his entry to parliament. In the autumn of 1510, for example, he was appointed as one of the two under-sheriffs of London, the judicial representative of the sheriff who presided over the Sheriffs' Court. It was convened at the Guildhall on Thursday mornings, on a raised stage at the east end of the Hall. (More was also in charge of the 'Poultry Compter', a common gaol situated to the north of Bucklersbury and only a few yards from his own house.) In the Guildhall itself More dealt with the cases involving 'foreigners', an unhappy term for those Londoners who were not freemen as well as people from the rest of the kingdom. He held the post for eight years and during that period he had to deal with every kind of crime and offence – robbery, rape, assault, vagabondage and arson among them. He was in the middle of London's 'low life' and encountered a noisome and pestilential environment. He wrote once, with some conviction, of the taverns and bathhouses, the public toilets and barbers' shops, used by servants, pimps, whores, bath-keepers, porters and carters, all of them swarming among the streets. There was an epidemic of what seems to have been influenza in the year that More began his duties, and plague was always in the air; certainly the diet of poverty, disease and violence which he endured each week must have considerably hardened his character. It is sometimes surmised that his obscene vocabulary and bawdy humour are derived from Chaucer or the balladeers, but he could have found them closer to home. He left only brief allusions to his time among the condemned men and women of London. There was a thief who, sentenced to death, stole a purse at the very bar of the court. When asked the reason, since he was due to be hanged the next morning, he replied that 'it didde hys heart good to be lorde of that purse one nyght yet'.[30] In a long attack upon Luther, More ruefully compares the German reformer to the whores who, when accused of some offence, reply '*impudenter*'[31] ('You're a liar!'). These were Londoners whom he knew at first hand.

In a description of More's post Erasmus noted that he had a reputation for quick and fair decisions; it seems that no one promoted London justice more effectively and, in addition, More often remitted the fees which litigants were generally obliged to pay. As a result he was held in the highest affection by the City.[32] This might simply be regarded as friendly flattery, but the evidence of More's later career as judge and Lord Chancellor corroborates Erasmus's testimony. Erasmus believed that More's responsibilities were not particularly onerous, largely because the Sheriffs' Court met only once a week. But as under-sheriff More played several different roles. He acted as legal adviser on various city bodies – perhaps the most important being concerned with the maintenance and administration of that great urban thoroughfare, London Bridge – and he acted as the representative for London at the Westminster courts of justice. It also seems likely that he played some part in the court of the Lord Mayor, where he would be asked to consider matters of maritime law and Roman law. His son-in-law wrote, with some truth, that 'there was at that tyme in none of the princes courtes of the lawes of this realme, any matter of importans in controversie wherein he was not with the one parte of Councell'.[33] Of course More was following familial precedent and so the duties were not unknown to him; his maternal grandfather, Thomas Graunger, had been a sheriff of London, and his father had been a member of the same City bodies as More himself. There was one other, less happy, precedent. Sir Edward Dudley, member of the old king's council, had also once served as under-sheriff of London. In the month before More himself took up that office, Dudley was beheaded on Tower Hill. Such was the way of this world, as More had already come to know it.

XIV

A Jolly Master-woman

DESPITE More's increasing public duties the Old Barge had developed into a scholarly household in the spirit of, if not upon the same scale as, the academies of Italy. One of its members was congenitally restless, however, and in the spring of 1511 Erasmus travelled to Paris in order to arrange the publication of *Moriae encomium*. He was on occasions also absent-minded and eventually recalled that he had left some books, borrowed from John Colet, in his '*cubiculum*' or study in Bucklersbury. So he quickly wrote to another scholar living with the More family, Andrew Ammonius. Ammonius was an Italian, who earned his living first as Latin secretary to Lord Mountjoy and then to the king. He and the Dutchman traded complaints about English houses and English manners; they grumbled about draughts, bad wine and offensive smells. But they had not refused More's hospitality, and now Erasmus asked Ammonius to remind their host that the books had to be returned to their owner. It is a measure of More's own relation to the household that Erasmus did not write to him directly: he knew that he was too busy.

In reply to this letter from his colleague and companion, Ammonius sent the greetings of More and his household to Erasmus. Jane More was affable and the whole family in good health. But then something happened. Three months later Jane More, at the age of twenty-two, was dead. The cause of her death is not certainly known. It might have been the plague, or the sweating sickness, or influenza, or any of the other feverish disorders which visited London; an allusion in the letters of Erasmus, however, suggests that she died in childbirth together with the new-born child. This seems likely, since her pregnancies were frequent and regular. She was buried in St Stephen Walbrook by the parish priest, John Bouge, who took up the story: 'within a month after, he came to me on a Sunday at late night and there he brought me a dispensation to be married the next Monday without any banns asking'.[1] More had been given especial permission by a friendly churchman to marry quickly, but there is no reason to interpret his rapid action in an unfavourable light. This was not an age of individual romance and it was not uncommon for a man to have two wives in relatively quick succession – or, indeed, for a woman to take two husbands in a similar manner. But this has not prevented More's detractors from such comments as 'he mourned her [Jane] in a wedding garment'.[2] He was an intensely practical as well as a decisive man; he had a young family to care for as well as a household to maintain, and really had no choice but to find a helpful partner.

Alice More, or 'Dame Alice' as she has come to be known, has always been a stock figure of fun for More's biographers. The family version of their courtship introduces her in a characteristic light. More is supposed to have approached her on a friend's behalf, but she replied: 'Your wooing will speed better if you do it on your own account, Mr More. Go tell your friend what I have said.'[3] It is highly improbable, but it reflects the familiar image of Dame Alice as a plain-speaking and perhaps imperious lady who might have 'caught' innocent More unawares. Certainly he himself seems to have encouraged the impression that he had married a woman whose temperament lay somewhere between the Wife of Bath and Noah's Wife in the guild pageants. He repeats anecdotes of his unsuccessful attempts to tutor her in the more abstruse disciplines: she pretended to listen to his account of the lack of motion at the centre of the planetary sphere, for example, but 'she nothyng wente about to consyder hys wordes but as she was wont in all other thynges, studyed all the whyle nothynge ellys, but what she myghte saye to the contrary'.[4] She later borrowed her maid's spinning-wheel and declared that any stone thrown through it 'wolde gyue you a patte vpon the pate that it wolde make you clawe your hed'.[5] On another occasion More was attempting to teach his children the properties of a straight line, but Dame Alice called them into the hall and pointed to a wooden beam. 'Here,' she said, 'is a line.'[6] As More told her himself, 'I neuer found you willyng to be rulid yet.'[7] According to Cresacre More, he called her 'a iollie Maister-woman',[8] all bedecked in finery 'with strayt bracyng in her body to make her mydle small'.[9] In More's anecdote he tells her, 'Forsoth madame if god give you not hell, he shall do you greate wronge.'[10] Yet 'somewhat in dede he stode in awe of her' and at one example of her somewhat strident manner 'he durst not laugh a lowde nor say nothing to her'.[11] All the evidence suggests, however, that they did make each other laugh and the testimony of one of More's own stories may have a homely application. A wife came back from confession and said: 'I purpose now therfor to leve of all myn old shrewdnes & begyn evyn a fresh.' Yet her undertaking is succeeded by a remark that 'she said yt in sport to make her husband laugh'.[12]

More knew Alice Middleton long before he decided to marry her; it is likely that he was acquainted with her even before he met his first wife.[13] Her first husband, John Middleton, had been a wealthy silk merchant who was part of the Merchant of the Staple; he was a member of the Mercers' Company, therefore, of which More himself was also a freeman. It is inconceivable that they did not know each other, especially since More would already have been well aware of Alice. Her family owned a manor and estates in Essex, where their neighbours were the Colts – when Jane Colt was three, Alice was twenty-one. Alice was a member of the Arden family and was related to Owen Tudor, great-grandfather of Henry VIII. Her own grandfather had been a serjeant-at-law, just like John More, and such connections ensured that Thomas More knew of Alice's character before he married; it is precisely why he did marry her.

Alice Middleton was, in other words, a good prospect for any man rising in the world. On the death of her merchant husband, she had become a considerable heiress with estates in Essex, Yorkshire and elsewhere. It is often suggested that this apparent termagant was also much older than the innocent and victimised More; in fact she was eight years senior to her new husband, who was already in his thirty-third year. But no doubt she offered a sharp contrast to the young and apparently docile ('*facillima*') Jane More; she was of a grand family, technically an heraldic heiress, and she was of independent means. She was forceful, witty, practical and efficient; more significantly, she was faithful to her bewildering husband even to the end. She was one of those women of the fifteenth and early sixteenth centuries who defy categorisation; far from being oppressed by what we might now term a male-dominated and hierarchical society, their strong characters were recognised and appreciated. Andrew Ammonius and Erasmus seem to have delighted in mocking her, but only behind her back. Ammonius, in cautious Greek, called her 'a hook-nosed harpy'.[14] Erasmus described her as unyielding and, even more insultingly, after only eight years of marriage, as approaching old age.[15] No doubt she suffered the whims or demands of her husband's guests with less compliance than the much younger Jane; she had been brought up among gentry and businessmen and may not have been impressed by wandering scholars. It is unlikely that she could converse in Latin, either, or bother to understand it. More is supposed to have described her as neither pretty nor young;[16] once again one must assume that he wished to minimise any intimacy, sexual or otherwise, which he shared with her. The business of running a household seems to have been conceived as a duty and obligation rather than a pleasure but it is also likely that, in the case of Alice More, he did not wish to reveal how large and forceful a role she came to play in his life and later career.

They were married in the early autumn of 1511 in the parish church of St Stephen Walbrook. The service was similar to that of More's first wedding but, since both partners had been married before, there was no blessing of union. The marriage seems to have been happy enough, even according to Erasmus; he speaks of the Mores' domestic peace, and remarks that More had persuaded his wife to practise upon the lute, the lyre and the recorder.[17] The contemporary humanist Richard Pace recalls that More learned to play the lute with his wife. It is a pleasant picture of familial harmony. Alice More participated not just in music-lessons, however, and More relates how she enthusiastically entered discussions on church matters – to the extent that she would let a meal wait rather than miss an argument.[18] On one occasion she took the trouble of checking a heretic's apparent quotation from the gospels and discovered that it was not there.[19] So she was shrewd, as well as interested. The surviving portrait of her, after Hans Holbein, shows a middle-aged woman expensively dressed and ornamented in the fashion of the day. She holds a devotional manual, but seems to be entertaining some private and amusing thought; her nose is large, even slightly protuberant, but she has the broad forehead which was a Renaissance token of female beauty. More alludes to the 'payne she toke in strayte byndyng vpp her here to make her a fayre large forhed'[20] and in another place refers to a woman who prides herself upon 'her brode forehead' but is better known for 'her crooked nose'.[21] He was an ironical, if not sarcastic, husband.

There are also hints of quarrels; More writes of the desire to enter a monastery 'when our wyues are angry'[22] and in a letter to a friend he remarks that, if you have a wife, you will never be free of trouble.[23] But there must have been a large element of playfulness here, at least as much as is exhibited in the last phrase of a letter from More to Erasmus. The Dutch scholar had wished Dame Alice a long life – for which, More says, my wife thanks you since it will give her more time to be '*molesta*'[24] or vexatious. Yet even here there is a suggestion of the old tale of the wife as shrew, and he seems unwilling to describe his private affairs in terms other than those of convention. The sermons and tales of the period are filled with images of garrulous or disobedient wives; 'over much spekynge'[25] and quarrelling were constantly cited as the characteristics of women. There was also the stock figure of the widow who takes care to dress in the fashions of the day. And of course 'Dame Alice', as More's wife was known, is also the name of the Wife of Bath, who displays all these female propensities to their utmost extent. That is why Alice More has been generally treated as if she were a literary character, with the salient addition that More himself initiated and encouraged the process both in his letters and in his printed works.

The family in Bucklersbury had been quickly and securely reconstructed; it was indeed one of the most important aspects of More's life. Erasmus depicted the household as one of peace and amity, with More himself as the benign agent of harmony. His eldest daughter, Margaret, said that she had seen her father angry only twice – they must have been striking occasions to be so firmly retained in her memory. More might not have wished to accept all the praise for such a well-tempered and well-ordered family, however, since on one occasion he wrote of the spirit which maintained household peace.[26] It might be noted that '*familia*' described the residents of a monastery as well as of more secular households. Certainly he created his own family as if it were a pious community of souls, regularised by method and ordered by discipline. There were prayers each morning and evening in which the entire household joined; at table, passages of sacred scripture and biblical commentary were read aloud for the edification of family and guests. No games of dice or cards, or any form of gambling, were permitted among servants or children. The sexes were also kept segregated; male and female servants slept in different quarters of the house and More ensured that they were fully occupied at all times. On holy days everyone was awoken, in the middle of the night, for the appropriate Office. He might be said to have organised the household as a form of lay monastery following the liturgical cycle. He was also obeying the precepts of those who taught the rules of the 'mixed life'; Walter Hilton, for example, considered it a divine commandment to keep 'a good household in good Christian order and fashion'.[27] In *The City of God* Augustine had extolled the 'ordered peace' and 'domestic harmony' of a true Christian household, and in particular emphasised that 'a man has a responsibility for his own household'.[28] But there is no doubt that, even by sixteenth-century standards, the family at Bucklersbury was carefully and consciously controlled. Family life and public life were not to be separated; both were suffused with the same spirit of duty.

It was predominantly a household of females. Alice More brought one daughter with her from her marriage to the silk merchant (a second had died two or three years previously) and of course More had three daughters of his own. A few months after his second marriage he obtained the wardship of another young girl, Anne Cresacre; she had inherited estates as well as income, and was therefore a suitable candidate for More's affluent and increasingly well-connected family. More, as guardian, was in sole charge of her property until she came of age; shortly after that climacteric she would marry More's only son.

More was deeply interested in women; clearly there was some sexual component to his attachment, but his concerns were more profound and persistent than that lust which he tried to slake with prayer and penitence. It could fairly be said, for example, that he was the first Englishman seriously to consider the education of women, whom he considered not a jot less intelligent or scholarly than men. But his opinion, and practice, should be set in context. As well as the stock image of the woman as the source of sin (the 'Queanes' and 'Kits' of the Southwark brothels testified to that) there was an equally strong tradition of female virtue and holiness. The extensive cult of Mariolatry encouraged attention to the female role in the life of piety, but female saints were also venerated; there were holy nuns and female recluses who completed this picture of sanctity. It has sometimes been suggested that the central role of women in the worship of the Church meant that, in Catholic England, women were treated with more respect and seriousness than they ever were after the Reformation. There were certainly some powerful women in late medieval society; Lady Margaret Beaufort, the mother of Henry VII, was perhaps the single greatest benefactress of education in the period. The wives of merchants were allowed to continue with their husbands' trade and could also become officers of their guild. But the status of a few women should not be misinterpreted. The legislation against 'scolds' and the proclamation at one time of crisis that husbands should prevent their wives from 'babble and talk' together,[29] suggests that they were the oppressed sex. It was also taken for granted that a man was allowed to beat his wife, as long as he used a stick 'no thicker than his thumb'.[30]

In a letter to his children's tutor, some years later, More remarked that erudition in women was a new development,[31] but that there was no reason why women should not acquire learning as well as men. We will find proof of this in the life of his eldest daughter: Margaret translated Erasmus and Eusebius, was complimented for her emendation of a corrupt passage in St Cyprian, composed in both Latin and Greek, wrote a treatise on 'The Four Last Things' and an oration after Quintilian. She was undoubtedly the most learned woman of her day, at least in England, and once engaged in a philosophical disputation before the king. When More's household is being portrayed, therefore, it must be seen as the setting for what he called '*mea schola*'.[32] This was almost a school in a literal sense and, in subsequent years, there were between eleven and thirteen wards or grandchildren attending it.

It had been established around the time of his second marriage, when Margaret was six years old. More was responsible for the curriculum and there is one indication of his early method; he made use of the fact that children enjoyed archery, and had the letters of the Latin and Greek alphabets put up in place of the standard target. His young family would learn them by shooting at them. He might have taken advice from Erasmus when instituting this game, since the Dutchman wrote frequently of the need to educate children from the earliest possible age by combining instruction with pleasure. In that sense it might be said that More was the first Englishman to employ humanist methods of learning. The studies were equally innovative, at least for young girls, and over subsequent years they included logic, geometry, astronomy and philosophy as well as Latin and Greek. One daughter would be asked to translate a Latin epistle written by her father into English, while another would then turn it once again into Latin. The young family were also taught to memorise and interpret the sermons that they heard, whether they were delivered in Latin or in English. Indeed More was as concerned with the vernacular as with the classical tongues; two of his children eventually translated Latin works into English, while Margaret completed an original composition in her native language. She was, as one contemporary put it, 'erudite and elegant in eyther tong'.[33] Music was not neglected, of course, in a household where husband and wife were accustomed to practise the lute together; it can be assumed that Alice More played some part in that training, and her role in the school should not be underestimated. Erasmus describes her as the director or overseer of the '*collegium*',[34] who kept everyone at their studies; she may not have been learned, but she was pragmatic and sensible. She also maintained the children in good health, at a time when mortality rates were high, and in a letter to a subsequent tutor More praised her maternal tenderness[35] in the training of her adopted children.

He had other assistance, too. Erasmus wrote brief commentaries on the *Nux* of Ovid for the school and played a formative enough role to be described by Margaret as her '*praeceptor*' or tutor. This may have been an honorific title, although his work with John Colet on the curriculum of St Paul's school has already suggested the extent of his interest in early education. Cuthbert Tunstall's *On the Art of Calculation* had a dedication for More with the instruction that the treatise should 'be passed on to your children'.[36] More's contemporaries were aware of the significance of his experiment, and his educational example was followed by one or two more advanced households – the Elyots and the Parrs among them. Erasmus believed, with some exaggeration, that as a result of More's practice there were now very few noblemen who did not wish their children to be skilled '*bonis literis*'.[37] He also gave an indication of one of his friend's other educational methods: More pretended to be unhappy with his children's orthographic skills but, when they had copied out once more their own Latin essays, he sent them to Erasmus for comment. The Dutch scholar confessed himself amazed both by their style and their subject. He had once taken no interest in the education of women, but the example of Margaret More and the other girls changed his opinion.

Yet testimony does not come from outsiders only. More, when away from home, sent several letters to his young scholars which manifest the nature of his interest; he composed them in Latin, as a model of style, and expected his children to reply in the same spirit. Each of them was supposed to write to him once a day, preparing their letters in advance so that they would be ready for the messenger. He urged them to continue their practice of verse composition and of disputation; he expected them to make constant progress in their essays and in their reading, at one point particularly recommending Sallust; he advised them to write in English and then translate their sentiments in Latin, remaining alert to solecisms and faulty constructions. On one occasion he sent his '*schola*' a Latin poem. It was again meant as an exercise, in part, but also it is a charming expression of his deep and tender love for them;[38] he recalls how he often took them in his arms, how he fed them cake and pears, how he dressed them in silken garments. Now, he said, they combined learning and eloquence with all their childhood charms. He was particularly interested in the skills of his eldest daughter, Margaret. He continually praised her virtue and her erudition; when he showed her letters to various dignitaries, they were uniformly surprised by the purity and dignity of her Latin style (one of them even insisted on presenting her with a gold coin). He wanted her to pursue her studies in philosophy and classical literature, but urged her to concentrate her attention at some point upon medical learning and sacred scripture. This might seem an odd combination of subjects but it was a sensible division of skills and scholarship: other members of More's household were to become known for their medical ability as well as for their piety, at a time when practical learning was considered to be an aspect of Christian revelation.

There are also in the letters various allusions to the tutors whom More employed for his children; they tended to be young men who went from More's famous household, where they had in a sense been trained, to administrative service or university teaching. The first of them, John Clement, had been educated at St Paul's School and may well have entered More's household on the recommendation of John Colet. After his service to More, he was taken into the employment of Cardinal Wolsey and eventually lectured on rhetoric at the newly created Cardinal College in Oxford. His is a perfect example of a late medieval career based upon preferment as well as scholarship, on households as well as books, and it is charmingly embellished by the fact that Clement married one of More's wards. There were at least four other tutors after his departure – two of whom had been known by Erasmus before they entered the More household. No doubt he suggested them, and their presence suggests the scholar's continuing interest in the education of the young family. More's own interest, of course, was profound and permanent. He had turned his household into a form of the community with which he was most comfortable, part monastery and part school, but it is impossible not to notice the amount of deliberation and control which entered his choice. In certain respects he resembles the inhabitants of his imaginary island, who are convinced of the efficacy of what in a later time would be called social engineering. In Utopia the priests are responsible for the training of children, applying to their still unformed minds the principles of order and good government as well as the precepts of learning. But once he had created his school of love and duty, More in a sense remained apart. There were few occasions when he divulged his true feelings and beliefs; it was only by accident, for example, that one of his children realised that he wore a hair shirt. There would also soon come a time when he was weeks, even months, away from home.

XV

Kings' Games

NOW, in his early thirties, More was always occupied. He professed himself to be a bad correspondent because of his work and his duties in the city; the impression he gave was of one thoroughly absorbed in the business of the world. Andrew Ammonius reported, for example, that More was with the Archbishop of Canterbury '*quotidie*' ('every day');[1] the nature of their transactions is not known, but they must have been of some importance, in a city where the Church was the most powerful landowner and employer. More himself was steadily gathering wealth and property; he decided to take the whole of the Old Barge on a lease from the Mercers and he also purchased some land in Essex. His more formal City business can be partly reconstructed. In the early months of 1512, for example, he was one of a deputation going 'to the Kynges counsell to knowe their pleasure for Bysket etc. for the Kynge'.[2] From the affairs of bakers he went on to those of the fishmongers, whom he assisted in negotiations, and in the same year 'yong More' appeared before the House of Lords with the wardens of 'all craftes'; they went on a barge to Westminster, where More was one of the principal parties 'to speke and make aunswere' for the London guilds.[3] He was also involved in negotiations with the Duke of Buckingham and the Bishop of Norwich over the right of certain tradesmen to participate in City government. Nor had his work for the Mercers noticeably decreased; he was one of eight negotiators 'whiche the compeny of the Stapull have electe & chosen to haue Communicacion with the merchauntes adventerers'.[4] More's role would have been that of an arbitrator or legal representative trying to conclude an agreement in complex negotiations. It was said of his practice as a lawyer that he always attempted to persuade opposing parties to agree in advance, thereby avoiding a lawsuit, and he seems to have been preoccupied with the maintenance of harmony and good order. He was also made a commissioner for sewers, covering the long stretch of Thames bank between East Greenwich and Lambeth. His responsibilities comprised such matters as routine maintenance and the avoidance of flooding, but the riverside area included the noisome Long Southwark and Short Southwark (better known today as Tooley Street) as well as the Hospital of St Thomas the Martyr, and there were also real questions of public health to be considered. More, with his connection to Linacre and his deep interest in medical scholarship, was perhaps the first commissioner to deal with such matters in a practical and orderly way.

His legal business was, in the meantime, flourishing. In 1515 he was appointed the senior 'Lent' reader of Lincoln's Inn, where, beginning on the first Monday of that season, he would once again lecture in Law French on legal statutes. He had been made a 'Double Reader', an appointment that usually preceded the elevation to serjeant-at-law. It was an honour 'to which few but rare and singular Lawyers doe euer attaine',[5] and with it More's legal career was assured: there was every reason to suppose that he would eventually become a 'Judge of the Lawe'.[6] His own practice was eminently successful; as well as being involved in most major cases, he also engaged in the general law business of the day. The case of *Broughton* v. *Thorneton* (1511) includes a record of '*Thomam More eruditem in lege*' being retained in a dispute over maintenance.[7] In his prefatory letter to *Utopia*, More humbly excused the weaknesses of the book on the grounds that he was always involved in legal business, as arbitrator, or counsel, or under-sheriff.[8]

He had a chamber in Lincoln's Inn and, such was his name and fame, he had no need to resort like many of his colleagues to the pillars of St Paul's where new business was to be found. No record of his pleadings has survived, but he has left evidence of his style in certain published disputations. We may imagine him in one of the courts of Westminster Hall, on a floor spread with rushes mixed with cloves and crushed herbs; all around him was the noise of argument and debate, with the rustling of papers and the mending of pens, the hurried consultations and the sporadic abuse from prisoners who were sometimes brought in cages to the Hall itself. More would have worn the 'party coloured' gown of the barrister with stripes of light blue, or green, or brown. He stood at the bar before the judges, or beside a table covered with papers, writs, seals and subpoenas.

Tho: Moor Ld Chancelour

Sir Thomas More: while authority remained intact More
was 'merry', to use one of his own favourite words, but if it was
challenged he turned savage and unforgiving.

FAMILIA THOMÆ MORI ANGL. CANCELL:

Thomas Morus Æt. 50. Alicia Thomæ Mori uxor. Ætat. 57. Ioannes Morus pater Æt. 76. Ioannes Morus filius Æt. 19. Anna Grisacra Ioannis Mori Sponsa Æt. Margareta Roperia Thomæ Mori filia Æt. Elisabetha Danea Thomæ Mori filia Æt. 21. Cecilia Heronia Thomæ Mori filia Æt. 20. Margareta Giga Clementis uxor Alicis filia Æt. Henricus Patensoni Thomæ Morari morio Æt.

Holbein's
drawing of the
More household at
Chelsea; this
study of intimate
relations is also a
portrait of the last
age of Catholic
England.

Judge More Sᵗ Tho: Mores Father.

Sir John More, the father of Thomas More, who dominated his son's life and career.

William Roper, More's son-in-law and first biographer, who helped to fashion the saintly legend.

Margaret Roper, More's eldest daughter, who was reputed to be the cleverest woman in England.

The Lady Barkley.

Elizabeth Dauncey, More's second daughter; her fashionable and expensive dress emphasises the fact that the entire family was rich, privileged and influential.

Cicely Heron, youngest daughter of Thomas More; like all of his daughters, she materially assisted the family fortunes by marrying a man of wealth and power.

Anne Cresacre, the wealthy young woman who became one of More's wards; she completed her association with the household by marrying More's son.

John More, the son of Thomas More; the large nose and thin lips are also characteristic of the father in whose shadow he always lived.

Henry VII: the astute, if autocratic, founder of the Tudor dynasty in whose long reign More established a lucrative and successful career.

Richard III: Thomas More was five years old when this 'malicious, wrathfull, enuious ... euer frowarde' king began his short reign.

Elizabeth of York, wife of Henry VII, upon whose death More wrote a lament eschewing 'worldly joy and frayle prosperitie'.

ELIZABETHA · VXOR
HENRICI · VII ·

The young Henry VIII, whose princely virtues encouraged More to enter public service for the benefit of 'the comon welthe'.

Catherine of Aragon, the first wife of Henry VIII, who at the time of their separation asked him, 'Wherein have I offended you?' She considered that More, of all the royal councillors, 'alone was worthy of the position and the name'.

Anne Boleyn, the king's mistress and second queen, who had woven into her livery the motto which, translated from the French, reads: 'It will happen, whoever grudges it'.

'*Quaeso iudices diligenter attendite*':[9] I ask you, judges, to listen carefully . . . Who would have believed it . . . Let us imagine . . . Who would have thought? . . . I request you again and again to be as attentive as possible . . . Let us look into the matter more carefully . . . I will provide you with very clear and sound arguments. And then, at the close, '*Dixi*'. I have finished.

But his legal associations were not simply with Westminster Hall and his interests were wider than those of a common lawyer. At the end of 1514, for example, he was admitted as a member of Doctors' Commons in Paternoster Row; this was a loose association of canon lawyers and civil lawyers involved in international and maritime affairs. It has been suggested that he joined this body, later known more formally as the College of Advocates, in order to prepare himself for the diplomatic and commercial ambassadorial career which soon followed. But Doctors' Commons was also a convivial society that offered an opportunity to discuss affairs away from the press of business. Among those who met in that narrow street north of St Paul's were John Colet, Andrew Ammonius and William Grocyn, any one of whom could have persuaded – or invited – him to join them. At precisely the point More was admitted, however, there were tokens and intimations of significant change in the application of canon law. One case, in particular, was an object of intense speculation among More's colleagues.

The affair of Richard Hunne remained a source of polemic and controversy for more than thirty years. A convenient if not exact analogy might be with the Dreyfus scandal in France – not exact because it can plausibly be claimed that the Hunne imbroglio was the first indication of that great transformation in England which was to occur at the Reformation. Richard Hunne was a wealthy London tailor. His infant child, Stephen, died at the age of five weeks; the rector of the parish in Whitechapel where he was buried, Thomas Dryffeld, asked in traditional fashion for the dead baby's christening robe as a 'mortuary' gift, but Hunne refused to make this customary offering. A year later he was summoned to Lambeth Palace, where Cuthbert Tunstall – the chancellor of the diocese – declared him to be at fault. Still Hunne refused to pay the 'mortuary'. Two significant events followed. At the end of that year, when he entered his parish church of St Margaret in Bridge Street for Vespers, the priest formally excommunicated him with the words 'Hunne, thowe arte accursed and thow stondist accursed';[10] not only was Hunne exiled from the life of the community, but he was also in peril of losing his own soul within the perpetual flames of hell. But Hunne struck back. He accused the priest of slander and then issued a writ of praemunire against Dryffeld and his assistants. Praemunire was a late fourteenth-century provision which maintained the rights of the king and the common law courts against the Pope and the clerical courts; in essence by involving praemunire Hunne was claiming that the ecclesiastical authorities had no right to claim his property, the christening robe, with perhaps the further claim that by being tried in Lambeth Palace he had been brought before 'a foreign and illegal bar'.[11] The king and his judges, not the Pope and his representatives, should be the final arbiter of English rights.

This was a vivid anticipation of later struggles, of course, but the Hunne case had its own sensational outcome. Hunne was next accused of heresy – both of protecting a known heretic and of possessing heretical books in English. On the face of it this might seem a fabricated charge to discredit Hunne's resort to praemunire, but evidence exists that he was one of those London merchants who supported (and even espoused) Lollardy. His wife's father had been a proselytiser of that radical cause, so close in many respects to early Protestantism, and it seems likely that Hunne had originally challenged the right of 'mortuary' precisely because of his Lollard or Wycliffite sympathies. He was arrested and imprisoned within the Lollards' Tower in the west churchyard of St Paul's. But before any conclusion had been reached, on the matters of slander or praemunire, he was found dead in his cell. Although the church authorities declared that he had hanged himself, rumours spread that, in the words of John Foxe, 'his neck was broken with an iron chain, and he was wounded in other parts of his body, and then knit up in his own girdle'.[12] A coroner's inquest was held, which concluded that Hunne had been murdered by the Bishop of London's chancellor, Dr Horsey, as well as by the sumner and bell-ringer of St Paul's.

Huge consternation and uproar followed as a result of this verdict. The furore was deepened when the Bishop of London declared Hunne to be a heretic, posthumously, and ordered that his corpse be taken to Smithfield and ceremonially burned. The ramifications went much deeper than the death of one man. After numerous disputes in parliament and convocation, it became clear that the death of Hunne raised questions about the privilege of clerics to be tried only by the spiritual courts. Could Dr Horsey escape secular justice? The details of the statutes and precedents were so intricate that the king himself initiated a series of great debates, in the newly improved Baynard's Castle by the Thames, on the Hunne case and its consequences. The lords temporal and spiritual, as well as the judges of the realm and other interested parties, listened to conflicting arguments and testimony. Yet it was the king's silence which prevailed. He refused to respond to a request that the whole matter should be laid before the Pope in Rome and, by insisting that his own traditional powers should in no manner be abridged, he dismissed any suggestion that praemunire should be lifted; the minor clerical orders were, therefore, still in peril of being surrendered to the secular courts. But the decisions had this further consequence. If papal jurisdiction could be exercised only after royal licence, then essentially the Church could be reformed only by consent of king or parliament. The young king had in the plainest fashion asserted his own authority and had thereby threatened the powers of Pope and Church.

More never forgot the Hunne affair, and at a much later date provided an elaborate defence of the Church's role. He was also involved with the matter in a more immediate context. He had been present at one of the conferences called by the king in Baynard's Castle, where the question of Hunne's death had been discussed; he had also been present at the ecclesiastical judgment given in St Paul's by the Bishop of London, where Hunne's books and body were ordered to be burned in Smithfield. Indeed, he was so engaged in the case that, as he wrote later, 'I knowe it frome toppe to too that I suppose there be not very many men that knoweth it moche better'.[13] He provides a colourful account of the proceedings in Baynard's Castle, for example, which evince a mixture of formality and comedy possible only in a culture where ceremonial order is so much taken for granted that it can be breached without offence. The lords temporal and spiritual had been told that there was one man who claimed that 'he coulde go take hym by the sleue that kylled Hunne';[14] but, as it transpired, each witness claimed to have been told this story by a neighbour. Eventually the supposed infallible claimant turned out to be 'an Egypcyan' – a gypsy woman – who had been lodged in Lambeth but had now gone overseas. As More writes in the colloquial speech of which he was a master, 'here was a grete post well thwyted [whittled] to a puddynge prycke'.[15] A second witness claimed to be able to tell, on sight, if a hanged man had committed suicide; but his testimony collapsed under questioning when it was discovered that he had only ever seen one such sight in his life, and 'that was an Irysshe fellowe called croke shanke whome he had sene hangynge in an olde barne'.[16] And, as More reports, 'the lordys laughed well'.[17]

But More is also at pains to make light work of it. His principal concern is to defend the Church authorities against any and every attack, so he suggests that Hunne did indeed hang himself when he realised that his praemunire suit was about to fail and that he was also to be convicted of heresy. His vice, More believed, was 'pryde',[18] which shrank back from publicly bearing a bundle of sticks as a mark of the heretic and symbol of the Smithfield fire. On Horsey and the other supposed conspirators to murder, More rightly points out that they were proven not guilty; but the circumstances of the acquittal were somewhat obscure and Horsey was quickly removed from London. There is no reason to believe that More was deliberately misrepresenting the truth; he was only doing what was natural to him, in putting a lawyer's gloss upon ambiguous circumstances.

It is hard to strip this employment of its modern connotations; lawyers are not necessarily supposed to be devout or principled, except in the minutiae of legislation, but for More the law was a central image of natural reason and authority. It furnished the principles which governed his behaviour in the world, established upon order in all its forms. It should come as no surprise, for example, that in this period he was also enrolled as a teacher of grammar at Oxford University; he was required to lecture upon Sallust and write an epigram in praise of the university which could be affixed to the doors of St Mary the Virgin. This was another formal investigation into precedent and order. To 'inform in' grammar, as the phrase went, was primarily to teach Latin language and literature, but in More's words *grammaticus* meant the same thing as *litteratus*;[19] the grammarian was a man of letters. His extant remarks upon the use of the definite or indefinite article, as well as of periphrasis and hyperbole, suggest that he was well versed in the technicalities of the subject; but, as an exponent of the new learning, he was most concerned with practice and usage. Order and experience had to be harmoniously combined. He was, therefore, like Erasmus, convinced of the need to restore texts to their original purity; only then could the true usage of the classical authors be ascertained. It is a happy coincidence that More should be licensed for the teaching of grammar in the same period that Erasmus was Professor of Greek at Cambridge. But the circumstances were not necessarily propitious for humane learning.

From the autumn of 1511 Erasmus had been making anxious enquiries about the condition of Europe where the various principalities and powers – Spain, France, Venice and the Pope among them – had been engaged in consistent but sporadic warfare. At the time these conflicts were blamed upon the greed and vainglory of princes, but in retrospect we might attribute some of the animosity to the assertiveness of burgeoning nation-states. The collapse of European Christendom was only two decades away. Erasmus placed much of the responsibility for the warfare upon Pope Julius II, known as '*Il Terribile*', who in full armour led his troops against Perugia and Bologna; he was a man of silent thoughtfulness and violent temper, reputed to have the body and soul of a giant with the will of a Titan. He commissioned Michelangelo to sculpt a fourteen-foot statue of him in bronze, and patronised the young Raphael. He fathered three children, in his earlier days as a cardinal, and the citizens of Rome adored him.

Yet Julius II was not the only ruler who wished to stalk the fields of Europe with fire and sword. It was rapidly becoming clear to More and his contemporaries that their young and pious king, in whom all their hopes resided, was not necessarily a prince of peace. He yearned for battle, even if his martial longings took a knightly and courtly form. His examples of history were set, not by impersonal forces or causes, but by myth and glorious precedent. Just as piety was sustained by saints' lives and popular legend, so good and noble governance was guided by patterns of virtuous kingship. The young king was in particular affected by the exploits of Henry V, whose successes in France were directly to inspire his own attacks upon that country. *Gesta Henrici Quinti*, or *Deeds of Henry V*, was to be found in two manuscripts, and no doubt had been required reading for the heir apparent; significantly, they were published as a volume in 1513. But the single most important lesson of these '*gesta*' was of piety rather than valour. The historian of Henry V was likely to have been a cleric, and throughout his narrative he suggests that Henry's conduct and combat were part of God's providence; he was the Lord's anointed, tested and proved by divine dispensation, whose devotion gave him a private and intercessionary relationship with the spirit of God. The victory at Agincourt was the single most important token of divine favour and blessing. All the actions of Henry VIII's reign suggest that he believed himself – or wished to believe himself – to be similarly blessed. His predecessor had been 'the floure of chivalrie', according to John Lydgate's *Troy Book*, illustrious both for his commitment to just governance and for his courageous pursuit of glory in battle. The new king wished to follow the same course; to go to war against France with papal approval was the first stage of proving himself a worthy successor of a most holy king.

Henry had in fact been promoting the conflict ever since his accession to the throne, against the inclinations of some of his council, and within three years the pageants and spectacles of court took on ever more ardent forms. On the new year's night of 1512 there appeared in the great hall of Greenwich Palace 'a Castle, gates, towers, and dungeon, garnished with artillery, and weapon after the most warlike fashion';[20] on a banner before the castle was inscribed *'le Fortresse dangerus'*, and it was ritually taken by the king himself with five other knights in richly apparelled coats of fine gold. These were true war games, since three months before Henry had joined with the Pope and Spain in a Holy League against France. It is not coincidental that, at this time, the men who espoused learning and piety condemned war as the greatest of all social evils; Colet and Warham delivered sermons in praise of the pleasures of peace, while Erasmus's lamentations could also be heard in *Moriae encomium*. But the twenty-one-year-old king was more enamoured of conquest than of learning; in the space of two or three years, he had disappointed the extravagant hopes that the humanists had placed in him. There is no need here to chronicle the tides of war; one year was squandered in futile and self-defeating activity, while the second brought small successes hailed as triumphant victory. The principal military action of the period, that of the defeat of the Scots on Flodden Field in 1513, was undertaken while Henry was in France.

More's response was to compose Latin epigrams in celebration of his monarch's exploits. Many of his friends had gone over to France with the king – Ruthall, Mountjoy and Andrew Ammonius among them – and his own attitude to these first manifestations of war was characteristically more ambiguous than that of Erasmus. In a sermon against war preached before Henry himself at Greenwich, John Colet had declared it more fitting to follow Christ rather than Caesar; but More, in a verse celebrating the capture of Tournai, declared that the king was *'maior Caesare'* ('greater than Caesar').[21] When a French poet wrote an epic poem in praise of his country's supposed success in a sea-battle off Brest, More retaliated with some furiously sarcastic epigrams against him as the exponent of *'falsa'*.[22] Of course much of his enthusiasm came from his loyalty to the king and established authorities of his country, yet it is also susceptible of a wider interpretation. More believed, or professed to believe, that Henry had engaged in war on behalf of, and at the behest of, the Pope. Julius II had formed the Holy League in the face of French attempts to promote schism within the Church; this had at least become the respectable formal cause of the war, and there is reason to suppose that More accepted it. The fact that he died for that concept, of the unity of the Catholic Church, suggests that it was of some importance to him. So in his encomia he praised Henry's participation in war at the request of the Pope[23] and his conquests on behalf of *'Rhomano pontifici'*.[24] The belligerent character of Julius II was well known to him but, according to Catholic doctrine, a wicked priest could still perform the miracle of the Mass. The frail human was less important than the institution that he represented.

Throughout this period More was well aware of human frailty; he was engaged on the 'history' of Richard III, the usurper of evil countenance through whose brief reign More himself had lived. It is a 'history' in the loosest possible sense, even by the historiographical standards of the early sixteenth century, and has variously been described as drama, biography or propaganda. Since it is the primary source of Shakespeare's play on the same subject, which fixed for ever the image of the malevolent hunchbacked king, it might also now qualify as myth. Its origins and purpose are wholly obscure. No original texts survive and editors have relied upon manuscript copies of some supposed first source. There are versions in both Latin and English, at various stages of completion, and it has to be presumed that More composed in both languages. They are not straight translations of each other but, rather, original works displaying the particular merits of each language. In both versions the story remains approximately the same; it is the tale of the 'croke backed' usurper who came from his mother's womb 'feete forwarde' and was for the rest of his life 'malicious, wrathfull, enuious . . . euer frowarde',[25] 'not letting [averse] to kisse whome hee thoughte to kyll'.[26] On the death of his brother, Edward IV, he welcomed the king's sons under the guise of avuncular responsibility only to remove those closest to them; he obtained the crown by a mixture of guile and hypocrisy, and of course killed the lawful king and his brother in the Tower. It is a satisfactory and theatrical version of evil-minded dynastic politics.

Thomas More, according to one of his earliest biographers, was an eager reader of historical works who took up any treatise he could find; he would have known the London chronicles and the monkish annals, the lives of the saints and the moralised histories of the world since Creation. But his own account of Richard III bears little relation to any of these except, perhaps, by a form of ironic reversal in which the usual accoutrements of the saint's life are turned upside down. But More also knew the work of contemporary historians (sometimes, even, the historians themselves), such as *Gesta Henrici Quinti* and Andrae's life of Henry VII. It is also likely that he saw, in manuscript form, the *Anglica Historia* upon which Polydore Vergil was engaged. They were both members of Doctors' Commons. But it is not likely that he saw his own work in a similar light; there are coincidences of phrasing which suggest echoes or borrowings from Polydore Vergil, for example, but More's work is too badly structured to meet the requirements of serious historical narrative; more importantly, it is incomplete and shows no signs of being intended for publication of any kind. It is also replete with errors and omissions, the most noticeable occurring in the first sentence, where the age of Edward IV is overstated by thirteen years. More relied upon his own invention on certain occasions; many of the long speeches which fill the narrative seem to have been composed by him rather than the actual participants in the events.

But the history is also heavily dependent upon oral sources and, in particular, upon the anecdotal memories of those who witnessed the rise and fall of Richard III at close hand. It was recent history, after all, and instinctively More was careful not to offend the sensibilities of anyone still living who might have participated in Richard's supposedly tyrannical reign. Even if the text was not to be published, it would still have circulated in manuscript form. He was evoking a period crucial to any understanding of the new Tudor order which had succeeded the instability of Richard's short rule, and More has written a kind of morality drama in which fate, fortune and evil are the players. Certainly he had little interest in those ideas of causation, or evidence, which exercised other historians. But with his use of dramatic irony, and with that gift for vivid characterisation first seen in his epigrams, he revives the past in the manner of a pageant staged in the London streets. That is why his account is filled with sounds, with speeches, with 'muttering amonge the people'.[27] There was a tradition of literature on the subject of tyranny; Plato and Aristotle had speculated on the subject but, in More's own lifetime, Erasmus and Machiavelli and Castiglione (not to mention a host of lesser theorists) all considered the conditions for good or bad government. William Caxton had also written of that instruction in 'governance of empires' which might 'withdrawe emperors and kynges from vycious tyranny'.[28] But More's narrative is far more sensational and, at this late date, more appealing. Richard himself was 'close and secrete, a deepe dissimuler, lowlye of counteynaunce, arrogant of heart'.[29] And then there were moral lessons to be drawn for the benefit of the reader. 'O good god,' More wrote of one fallen nobleman, 'the blindnes of our mortall nature, when he most feared, he was in good suerty: when he rekened him self surest, he lost his life, & that w[ith]in two howres after.'[30]

If he did not look to recent histories for inspiration, More may have turned to the texts of the classical historians, among them Sallust, Tacitus and Suetonius. With its mixture of highly charged narrative and long dramatically placed oration, *The History of Richard III* bears more than a passing resemblance to Sallust's *Bellum Iugurthinum* and the *Annalium libri* of Tacitus. Erasmus had been praising this form of history since 1495.

This curious document has baffled many commentators; the fact that its English version breaks off inconclusively, for example, has been explained either by More's loss of interest or by his susceptibility to current political issues. But it is possible that his life of Richard III was designed to be a rhetorical and grammatical exercise. Although More began composing the work at the time he had been given permission to teach grammar at Oxford, it may have been the basis of exercises given to his own school or even to the boys of St Paul's: there is a sudden reference to a 'scole master of Poules'[31] for no good reason. It was composed in both Latin and English, and thus complies with the methods of composition and translation which he impressed upon his own children – one of the surviving Latin manuscripts of the work is prefaced by the explanation that it was written '*exercitationis gratia*' ('for the sake of practice'). One of the models of its form is clearly Sallust, and More had been instructed particularly to teach Sallust at Oxford. He had also recommended that author for his children's reading. And what could be a better way of studying classical rhetoric and vocabulary than to apply them to the description of more recent events? Sallust then became a living author, and a living influence, in the way that the humanists preferred. More did not need to look far for precedents; Augustine's most accomplished biographer has explained how the saint adapted Sallust's 'moral history'[32] for his own account of the decline of Rome. More adapted Sallust, also, to depict the corruption and hypocrisy of Richard's brief rule.

It is significant, too, that the most elaborate passages of More's narrative are conceived as speeches; the merits of sanctuary for the royal children are the subject of long debate, for example, while the right of Richard to be king is explained in a number of orations. *The History of Richard III* can be understood, then, as a lesson in the arts of disputation and rhetorical debate similar to those in which More engaged as a schoolboy and a scholar. But it is not a simple exercise for the school or university; More was always interested in practice and usage, rather than theory, and he has the humanist's concern for persuasion and proper government. It would be absurd to claim that the Hunne case involving praemunire, and the military ambitions of the young Henry, prompted More to consider the life of an evil king; yet they were part of the unsettled conditions in which he chose to allude to the perils of false rhetoric and faulty statecraft. It was generally believed by contemporary historians that monarchs such as Richard III could at least display, by contrast, 'the Wisdom, Goodness, Prudence and Verity of their Predecessors'.[33] In his grammatical work More was instructing those who might well be chosen to administer the government of the state: grammar was part of rhetoric, and rhetoric was part of public duty.

There are of course touches peculiar to More himself. He emphasises the role of London and London government in a manner not shared by other chroniclers of Richard III and, perhaps as a result, he deepens that vision of the world as stage which he had first gained from Lucian. He describes the 'aldermenne in scarlette with fiue hundred horse of the citezens in violette'; he depicts 'theues' and 'murtherers' dwelling 'in the verye bowelles'[34] of the city. He knew, also, of the political rituals played out in the streets around him. When Richard pretends to take up the crown reluctantly, many of the people wondered at the guile but 'they said that these matters bee Kynges games, as it were stage playes, and for the more part plaied vpon scafoldes. In which pore men be but ye lokers on. And thei yt wise be, wil medle no farther. For they that sometyme step vp and play w[ith] them, when they cannot play their partes, they disorder the play & do themself no good.'[35] There is an irony here which cannot escape any observer of More's career.

There is also a long divagation on the life of Mistress Shore, the concubine of Edward IV, not suitable in a history but useful in an exercise perhaps partly composed for his daughters. It may vaguely be based upon Sallust's portrait of Sempronia in *Bellum Catilinae* – both are called '*docta*' – but More's is a far more charming and affectionate portrait of a woman of great grace and affability, able both to read and to write, the favourite of the king (and others besides) who 'neuer abused to any mans hurt, but to many a mans comfort & relief'.[36] She had once been considered one of the most beautiful and influential women in the kingdom: she was still living when More wrote his narrative, a creature 'old lene, withered, & dried vp' who had been reduced to beggary.[37] Since Mistress Shore was the heiress of a wealthy merchant, this impoverished fate seems most unlikely;[38] but it would provide a fitting conclusion to an educational homily. In any case it is a fine and moving character study, which inspired many writers and artists to portray her in subsequent centuries.

There are other episodes and events in More's account which have been equally influential, even if they have no claim to historical accuracy. There is a scene when Richard, about to embark upon one of his more murderous courses, charmingly asks the Bishop of Ely, 'My lord you haue very good strawberies at your gardayne in Holberne, I require you let vs haue a messe of them.'[39] The Bishop of Ely had at this time been John Morton, More's earliest patron and benefactor. It is likely that Morton told him this story, although it is possible that More himself had admired the strawberries in that Holborn garden and had introduced them for light relief before a scene of butchery. It is the sort of detail that lingers in the memory, and Shakespeare borrows it for his more formal drama, when Richard once again asks: 'My Lord of Ely, when I was last in Holborn,/ I saw good strawberries in your garden there./ I do beseech you send for some of them.'[40] This illustrates, if nothing else, the curious and often eccentric process of cultural inheritance, when an exercise in rhetoric can become a constituent of great drama eighty years later.

And then, even as More was composing *The History of Richard III*, the winter of military planning and diplomatic plotting was made glorious summer by the peace of August 1514 agreed between England and France. Julius II had died, not a moment too soon, and the emollient figure of Leo X had assumed the papacy. The old king of France had also died but his young successor, Francis I, renewed the treaty of peace. All seemed to be set fair. The city authorities asked More to deliver a Latin oration in welcome of the Venetian ambassador, Giustinian, and both men engaged in an elaborate rhetorical game of compliments. More's stepdaughter made a very good marriage and his brother-in-law, John Rastell, moved down from Coventry and took a house near John More's estate in Hertfordshire. And it was May-time. The parishes of London had their maypoles and dances in the day, stage plays and bonfires in the evening. On May Day itself the king and queen rode out from Greenwich Palace, and on their way were met by 'Robin Hood' with two hundred archers dressed in green garments; the royal pair were invited to dine in a wood near Shooters Hill where, to the sound of flutes and singing birds, organs and lutes, they feasted on venison and wine. So did Henry and Catherine 'fetch in May'. There was less appetising fare to come.

XVI

The Best Condition of a Society

THOMAS More's journey to Utopia was by way of the Netherlands. In the spring of 1515, at the urgent request of the king's council as well as the Merchant Adventurers, he was asked to join an English mission which was being despatched to Flanders in order to renegotiate commercial and diplomatic treaties. More's presence was needed because this was not a simple matter of renewal – 'weightye matters and of greate importance'[1] were involved at a time when the trade in wool between England and the Low Countries was being seriously threatened by disagreements over tolls, taxes and ports. Commerce was also affected by the games of rulers. The young regent of the Netherlands, Charles, had recently entered an 'alliance and amity' with the French and the merchants of London feared that if no new 'intercourse' was agreed their ships would be seized and their goods impounded. It can only be assumed that More had become a master of the intricacies of commercial law, of the 'Sewestoll' and 'toll of the Hound', since he was summoned by the council at 'short warnyng'.[2] The day after he was given his commission for 'the kinges ambasset in to Flaunders', the City authorities allowed a deputy to take over the 'Rowme & office' of under-sheriff in his absence. Indeed, he and his colleagues on the mission, Cuthbert Tunstall and Richard Sampson, received such short notice that 'our tyme was very lityll and skarse to prepayr our self'[3] for what turned out to be a long stay in a foreign country.

They began their journey on 12 May, riding down to the coast and there taking ship across the North Sea. We may assume that they boarded one of the small English merchant ships of the period with a single square sail or perhaps, if they were in luck, the larger three-mast variety. The pilot knew the stars, the coastline, the phases of the moon, and used his 'lead and line' to measure the depths of the water; the master had his rolled manuscript of 'Routes from Silley and England into Flaunders'[4] as well as his 'compus' and his 'dyall'. More and his colleagues would have travelled together with a cargo of cloth or wool or animal hides (even, perhaps, live animals). It was customary for the traveller to take his own bed and chest with him, together with rations of bread, meat, salt and beer. He was also advised to travel with a servant, though More took one of the members of his household, John Clement, who had studied at St Paul's. More rarely mentioned his travels in foreign lands – he was not a private writer in any sense – but there is perhaps the slightest token of his voyage in his account of a sea 'sore wrought, & the waves rose very high' while the traveller 'lay tossid hether & thether'.[5]

The party arrived in Bruges six days later and prepared to enter the business of negotiations. Behind the image of the Christ child in Van Eyck's *The Virgin of the Chancellor Rolin*, the Flemish painter has depicted a fifteenth-century city. There has been speculation about its original, from Lyon to Liège, but it can best be seen as the image of a city such as Bruges itself, where the artist lived for ten years – with its churches, and guildhalls, and towers, spiralling into the air. It represents all the splendour and monumentality of a great mercantile centre. When More stayed in Bruges he was in a city of wide streets and grand houses, of market halls and mansions, of canals and great ramparts, of richly decorated shrines and elaborate churches; yet all of them were already touched by intimations of decline or decay. Bruges was a city whose time had gone; by the late fifteenth century its river had silted up and no large ship could reach it. He and his colleagues were formally met and greeted by the '*princeps*' of the city as well as some of the regent's negotiators – chief among whom was Georges de Themsecke, a lawyer and orator who was known to Erasmus as a learned scholar. The affairs of men were being conducted by humanists, even as their princes squabbled, and More was thoroughly at ease with such professional administrators.

For the first two weeks there was nothing to be done at all; some of Charles's commissioners had not yet arrived in Bruges and the city authorities themselves were proving particularly recalcitrant. When the full council for the negotiations had assembled, the business was woefully protracted and desultory; according to the English contingent the Netherlanders deliberately misinterpreted earlier treaties and refused to specify their exact demands. More remained self-possessed and, according to one participant, demolished certain arguments 'in measured tones and with a calm countenance'.[6] But it was clear that his opponents were delaying for tactical reasons and it was feared that they were waiting for the formal opportunity to seize English ships and cargoes. More, for once in his life, was not wholly pressed by business: so it was that this unwelcome but salutary departure from the daily routine of his London life created the conditions from which his most famous and inventive book sprang. He always wished to be busily engaged and if there were a hiatus in his activities he would simply set to work on something else. Why not a treatise, like the *Moriae encomium* of his friend?

But there were distractions. Erasmus visited him at the end of May, en route from London to Basle, and as usual their conversations were a mixture of scholarship and business. Erasmus had just completed his *Education of a Christian Prince*, in which he recorded the virtues of certain pagan princes of history, with the refrain of 'How much more should a Christian prince . . .'[7] It is in large measure a study of statecraft; the prince is urged to seek a true understanding of human affairs, since only then can he rule by principle rather than by expediency. Under his guidance, a virtuous society might be created. The book was addressed to Charles, who was even then proving so difficult in the commercial negotiations, but its discussions of proper statecraft might have provoked similar reflections in More – at a slightly later date More informed Erasmus that he had dreamed of reigning as king of the island called Utopia.

Yet, in Bruges, practical matters had also to be resolved. Erasmus was in need of funds, as always, and discussed with More the possibility of accepting the canonry of Tournai, which had recently been captured from the French. Thomas Wolsey had received the bishopric, although even then the resident French bishop was resisting the change. For various reasons Erasmus was reluctant to accept the post and a few days later More himself rode the forty miles to Tournai, where he was told that Wolsey had conferred the canonry upon another claimant without realising that Erasmus had been considered for it. At this, More suggested that a letter be written to Wolsey explaining that the post had previously been conferred upon Erasmus and that, in recompense for the Dutchman withdrawing from it, a greater and better provision should be made for him. None of this was true, of course, but More's wiliness suggests how difficult and tricky he could be; as he admitted himself, on occasions he did not shrink from *'mendaciolum'*[8] or a small lie.

More returned from Tournai at the beginning of June, only to face further protracted and inconclusive negotiations. By the second week of July, when More had anticipated that the embassy would have completed its work, the English commissioners were compelled to write to the king's council 'that wee may haue by the mean of your good lordshippis more money sent vnto vs'.[9] More himself, on a stipend of 13s 4d a day, was particularly embarrassed; Cuthbert Tunstall told Wolsey that 'Master More, at this time, at being at a low ebb, desires by your grace to be set on float again'.[10] There is also an indication, again from Tunstall, that he and More had been swindled by moneychangers in the city. Certainly More was not happy. He complained later to Erasmus that he had been compelled to support a household both in Bruges and in London, with the result, as he said ironically, that his wife and children did not have enough to eat in his absence. But the exaggeration can be excused; he was receiving less than a quarter of the income he earned in London, while having to maintain himself in the state customary to ambassadors of his country. He was also plainly missing his family; even when absent for a short time, he explained to Erasmus, he longed to see them again.

At the end of July, however, he made one other, and more significant, journey away from Bruges. Taking advantage of the fact that the Netherlands commissioners had returned to Brussels for further instructions, he rode to Antwerp. More already had amicable relationships with its city government, since he had once supervised the successful negotiations over the status of London merchants in the Antwerp market, and he may have wanted to enlist the help of the trading authorities there with the apparently fruitless negotiations at Bruges. Antwerp was now the most energetic and busy of all the ports in that region. It was also the site of new banking, and the elaborate market or bourse in the centre of the city testified to its commercial success. On the first page of *Utopia* More refers to its cathedral of Notre Dame, but at the time of his visit the church was still being built. He could see a new city rising before him.

He stayed for a time with a close friend of Erasmus, Peter Gillis; Gillis had been Chief Secretary to Antwerp for five years, but he had, more particularly, helped to see Erasmus's works through the

Antwerp press of Theodoricus Martens. Here was another contemporary, a man whom he called '*dulcissime*' ('the sweetest'),[11] with whom More formed a unique attachment – unique in the sense that he immortalised Gillis by making him a protagonist of *Utopia*. This was no formal tribute. More remained in Antwerp for approximately six or seven weeks and during that period, in the company or even in the house of Gillis, he conceived the idea of his famous commonwealth. In fact Peter Gillis played such a large part in preparing and circulating the finished treatise – he was also its main patron and its overseer through the press – that he felt a personal share in it. Both men were concerned with the nature of equity and civic duty and both were involved in the economic and political travails of the time; they had witnessed the perfidiousness of leagues and the abrogation of treaties.

So their colloquies on humanist values, and *Utopia* itself, did not arise in some sphere removed from the politics of the day. More was involved in the duties of an ambassador, with all the follies and futilities which such a role entailed. It was said that envoys 'wore' their words as they wore their clothes, for adornment or display, within a game of power and deception, limitation and improvisation. But, significantly, even as More sat with Peter Gillis in Antwerp the conduct of European affairs was being generally and violently disrupted. The new French king invaded northern Italy and, in a battle in the middle of September, defeated a force of Swiss mercenaries who had been deployed against him; he regained control of Milan and Pope Leo was forced to come to terms with this young man who had become the leading monarch of Europe. This was not at all to the liking of Henry, as More would have known only too well, and fresh instability entered international affairs. These were the circumstances in which the island of Utopia floated into the view of the world.

He began to write it after his return to Bruges at the end of September, at a time when his own role in the negotiations had become much less significant; at the beginning of October it even seemed possible that affairs would be concluded within a week or so. More wrote to Richard Pace, Wolsey's secretary, asking him to ensure that he was called home before any fresh complications arose.[12] Even while he was writing *Utopia* in Bruges, however, he found time to compose a long and elegant letter defending Erasmus and humanist scholarship in general; it was addressed to Martin

Dorp, a theologian at Louvain who had criticised Erasmus's *Moriae encomium* as well as his project of comparing the Vulgate version of the New Testament with the original Greek. Surrounded by the Christian humanists of the Netherlands, who played such an important part in the affairs of state, More felt certain of his position in attacking scholastic dialectic and reaffirming the importance of rhetoric and grammar for the progress of human understanding. The letter is couched in familiar rhetorical form – it might even be seen as a prime example of the kind of forensic oratory More employed in the courts of law – but it is marked by passages of heavy irony and light sarcasm that are never far from the surface of his prose. He was engaged, however, in more than a personal dispute; if a theological faculty decided to condemn the pioneering work of Erasmus, elements of the new learning might effectively be suppressed. Certainly Erasmus had formidable enemies – the inquisitional Dominicans among them – and the path of true scholarship was by no means assured. But More's sharp letter had the appropriate effect: eventually Dorp withdrew his criticisms, and the letter itself was never published.

More's appeal to be allowed to return home had been successful, and his letter of recall came just as he was finishing his epistle to Dorp. He seems to have left for England as quickly as possible, and just three days later met Richard Pace at Gravelines, 'in the highe waye'[13] a few miles north-east of Calais. It was, in one sense, an inauspicious meeting; the author of *Utopia*, at least in its early stages, encountered the man who had been sent by Henry to purchase Swiss mercenaries to fight against France. Peace met, and kissed with, war.

At a later date More professed himself delighted by the result of the Bruges negotiations, however protracted and laborious they had become, but he had greater cause to be pleased by a success of his own – a treatise that was first entitled not *Utopia* but *De Optimo Reipublicae Statu* or 'The Best Condition of a Society'. The evidence suggests that he originally wrote the second book, with its description of the island of Utopia, and then at a later stage added a first section which acts as a contemporary introduction to his fantastic society of equal citizens. Erasmus states that he had written this second book at his leisure; since the only leisure he enjoyed was during his enforced stay in Bruges and Antwerp and, since More thanks Peter Gillis for providing him with the opportunity for preparing the book, we can safely assume that the mission to the Low Countries had indeed produced immortal fruit.

It begins in Antwerp itself, outside the cathedral church of Notre Dame where Thomas More has just attended Mass. In the square outside he sees Peter Gillis talking to a sunburnt stranger with a long beard, dressed in a cloak which hangs casually from his shoulders. Gillis introduces him to More as Raphael Hythlodaeus, a Portuguese traveller who has journeyed with Amerigo Vespucci and who has visited many regions of the earth. More promptly invites him to his house where, on a turf-covered bench, Hythlodaeus converses with him on the many unknown countries which exist '*sub aequatoris linea*'.[14] And then, on this morning of late summer or early autumn, he tells More of the Utopians. He has lived among them for more than five years and is eager to extol their institutions, which are established upon the common ownership of all property and goods.[15] He invokes Plato's imaginary commonwealth as an apt analogy, and More asks him to give a full account of Utopian laws and customs.

After dinner, Raphael Hythlodaeus begins to describe Utopia itself. Here was the first marvel: the dimensions of this island are the same as those of England and the number of its city-states equals the number of English counties together with London. It is also approximately the same distance from the equator as England. Its principal city, Amaurotum, is itself like some reversed image of London; it has the same expanse as the city (if you include the urban areas beyond the city walls) and is situated below gentle hills from which a river flows as does the river Fleet. The principal river, however, runs through the city; it has its own tides and is the same distance from the sea as the Thames at London. This river is also spanned by one magnificent stone bridge, while Amaurotum itself is protected by great walls. It is London redrawn by visionary imagination, a pristine city in which, according to Hythlodaeus, there is no greed or pride or disorder – these vices have been altogether banished from the commonwealth of Utopia. The streets and houses of the city are laid out in uniform geometrical pattern, with pleasant houses and gardens which are exchanged between the citizens every ten years; members of the commonwealth learn the craft to which they are most suited, and all wear the same clothes of undyed wool with distinctions only for sex or marital status. Six hours of the day are devoted to work, while the rest of the time is spent in learning or healthful recreation. Meals are eaten in communal dining-halls, with the supervisor of each hall taking free food from the common stock of a central market. The Utopians do not value gold or silver, but use them to manufacture fetters and chamber pots. They have a population of slaves, generally comprising criminals or prisoners of war, which is treated with paternal rather than tyrannical severity. And so Hythlodaeus continues to amplify this catalogue of benevolence.

Much ingenuity and scholarship have been employed to trace the literary sources of this fabulous island of equality and happiness; among them may be mentioned Macrobius, Aristotle, Seneca, Lucian and Cicero. There is room for the Bible, too, with especial reference to Acts of the Apostles, where 'they had all things common'.[16] But since Plato is mentioned seven times within the treatise, and four times in its accompanying letters, it seems plausible that *The Republic* also furnished a model for More's own commonwealth. At the conclusion of Plato's ninth book, Socrates describes his ideal society as perhaps only a '*paradeigma*'[17] residing in heaven; *Utopia* is an attempt to bring it down to earth. Of course there are many dissimilarities between the two books and the states which they describe. More's work is less profound, more hastily written and altogether less satisfying than Plato's great discourse; nor does More address those philosophical questions on the nature of happiness or the principles of harmony that are at the centre of the earlier work. Yet clearly More has taken certain aspects of *The Republic* – in particular the obligation upon the 'guardians' to share everything in common and to own no private property – and proceeded to examine how they might work in practice. Plato insisted that only a philosopher can properly administer his republic, and at the beginning of *Utopia* More refers to the founder of the state – Utopus – who trained his people to the highest level of '*cultus*' and '*humanitas*'.[18] The conditions, then, are similar to the point where some resemblance is manifestly being suggested.

And so More devises a republic like that of Plato. In *The City of God* Plato is extolled as the greatest of pagan philosophers, who can be seen to anticipate Christianity and Christian revelation. But Plato was never vouchsafed that revelation, at least according to Augustine, and his insights were achieved through 'natural reason'.[19] This is also the condition of the Utopians, who throughout their history of 1760 years have been denied the truths of divine law. That is why

they encourage euthanasia, condone divorce and harbour a multi-
plicity of religious beliefs – all of which actions were considered
dreadful by More himself and by Catholic Europe. This may be no
ideal commonwealth, after all, but a model of natural law and
natural reason taken to their unnatural extreme.

More was joining an argument which for many years had been
conducted by schoolmen and rhetoricians, but was now of greater
import to the Northern humanists with whom he was acquainted.
The debate between reason and revelation had particular civic and
juridical consequences, after all, since it affected the very nature of
society. Was the state a product of revelation, and therefore of law
descending from God and king, or was it the result of natural
agreement and association between human beings? In the latter case
power ascended from the citizens to their government. *Utopia*
provides a paradigm for this, too, with an electoral process which
begins with the suffrage of individual families. *Utopia* was not some
isolated exercise in fantasy, but a spirited and elegant contribution to
a European discussion; that is why More composed it in Latin and
why it was eventually published by printers in France and the
Netherlands.

Yet the ramifications, for More, were religious rather than social.
When the Utopians curiously maintain that there were cities in their
world before men appeared in Christendom, it might be taken as an
argument for urban democracy on the model of the Greek *polis*; but,
for More, it is evidence that the Utopians have no notion of the
origin of humankind and therefore no knowledge of original sin.
They have no sense of an imperfect world, or of human corruptibil-
ity; in that respect, as far as More is concerned, the joke is on them.
Utopia has often been treated as a sympathetic piece of narration
which does indeed exemplify More's ideal commonwealth – and
that, in particular, he supported what has become known as the
'communism' of the Utopians. But, as he himself put it, you can
cogently make a case for that which is 'false and impossyble': 'For be
the thynge neuer so false and impossyble to, yet may it be putte and
admytted, to consyder therby what wold folow or not folow ther-
uppon.'[20] What we may expect to find in this treatise, therefore,
is a subtle rhetorical and dramatic performance. The extent to which
it has confused critics and commentators is an indication of the
extent to which they have forgotten the rules of demonstrative
oratory.

In an oratorical exercise of this kind, where a case is being made, it was customary for formal arguments to be advanced on the opposite side. Raphael Hythlodaeus seems, however, to have been given the opportunity to extol the virtue of the Utopians without any challenge. But herein lies the achievement of *Utopia* – an achievement that has a great deal to do with More's command of rhetoric but also, as in all works of art, with the forces of More's own temperament and personality. *Utopia* is an ambivalent and ambiguous work in which various absurdities, for example, are paraded in the most apparently innocent and unsatirical manner. But it also harbours various contradictions which render the account of Hythlodaeus very suspect indeed. The counter-argument, the case against *Utopia* in effect, is internalised within the narrative itself.

Consider the role and status of Raphael Hythlodaeus, this sunburnt voyager from another land. Raphael is the name of the guiding angel in the Book of Tobit, but Hythlodaeus, derived from the Greek, means one who is cunning in nonsense or idle gossip. His connection with the journeys of Amerigo Vespucci has always been taken as the token of a real traveller; by the time *Utopia* was being composed, however, the voyages of Vespucci to the New World were dismissed as fabrication or as mendacious attempts to acquire glory. It is now generally accepted that the *Mundus Novus* and *Four Voyages* of Vespucci were indeed forgeries, but that the Portuguese pilot had nothing to do with them;[21] in the first and second decades of the sixteenth century, however, the manifold inconsistencies and incoherencies in Vespucci's supposed account led most people to suppose that he was a boastful liar. (Ralph Waldo Emerson, some centuries later, described him as 'a thief' and a 'pickle dealer' who had managed to 'baptise half of the earth with his own dishonest name'.) So for Hythlodaeus to be described as the constant companion on his travels[22] was in no sense a compliment. It might even imply that the island of Utopia was his own invention; it is, perhaps, significant that in those spurious accounts of the New World by 'Vespucci' it is revealed that the natives have no concept of private property. One of the marginal annotations, composed by Peter Gillis (or perhaps Erasmus), even addresses Hythlodaeus as '*O artificem*' ('You artful man')[23] when he claims once more that he has witnessed all the things which he describes. More distrusted pure or abstract philosophising and yet *Utopia* is an island governed entirely by theoretical principles. Hythlodaeus claims to have located a Platonic society in the real world but, with his elaborate and perhaps crazed monologue, he himself is turned into a caricature of the philosopher. With his long beard, and face burned by the sun, he might almost have provided a model for Coleridge's ancient mariner, who has 'strange power of speech' and who is mistaken for the 'Devil'.[24]

It is hard to believe that Hythlodaeus ever saw the island upon which he reports in such detail. The dimensions which he gives it form an impossible shape and there are problems of size as well as distance. Utopia itself means literally 'no-place'; the principal river, Anydros, is again literally 'river without water'; the name of the city of Amaurotum is derived from the Greek for dark or dimly seen; the governor of the island is called Ademus, or one who has no people. Kierkegaard remarked of Socratic irony that it cannot fashion a picture of the absolute except as a form of nothingness; the same consideration applies here. There are also more practical contradictions. The Utopians are praised as a peaceful race but they engage in savage warfare; they are said to despise gold and silver, yet they hoard it to pay others. One of More's favourite grammatical manoeuvres in *Utopia* is that of litotes when (to quote from the *Oxford English Dictionary*) 'an affirmative is expressed by the negative of the contrary'; it is not inconceivable that such a device contributes to the spell of ambivalence and confusion which the entire narrative seems to cast. Many of the Utopian customs extolled by Hythlodaeus are impractical; no doubt following Plato's suggestion in *The Republic* that both men and women should be recruited as combatants on the battlefield, for example, Hythlodaeus describes how in Utopian warfare each citizen-soldier is accompanied by his entire family and blood relations. No greater opportunity for confusion and mass slaughter can be conceived. Even the map of Utopia, which acts as the book's frontispiece, is woefully inconsistent with the succeeding narrative; Hythlodaeus insisted that the buildings were all alike, where the map shows a variety of majestic edifices not unlike those depicted by Van Eyck. The prefatory material to this treatise, complete with letters of commendation and celebratory verses, is an elaborate parody of the learned volumes of the late fifteenth century; even More's Latin narrative, with its divisions and subdivisions, has been characterised as a satire upon scholastic prose.

One further ambiguity must be mentioned here. More's subsequent works, which were generally polemical in intent, also display signs of highly formalised constraint and an almost scholastic sense of method. His own life of discipline, and his devotion to the Catholic Church, suggest that he was naturally inclined to the imposed order of authority. That is why *Utopia*, despite More's own ironic negations and reservations, remains a powerful vision of existence; it radiates from the centre of More's being and there are aspects of Utopian worship and custom, for example, which are strongly evocative of his own experience in the Charterhouse. In his dream of being appointed king of Utopia, as he told Erasmus, he was arrayed in the habit of a Franciscan. There is perhaps even some intimation that he would like to be subjugated and controlled within such a state. It is significant that both the treatment of the sick and the slaughtering of animals are described as taking place beyond the city walls: all forms of threatening disorder and decay have to be expelled from the ordered centre.

This may, at least in part, explain why *Utopia* has frequently been interpreted as a serious attempt to construct an ideal republic; no wonder John Ruskin described it as 'perhaps the most really mischievous book ever written'.[25] Certainly it is one of the most elaborate and successful exercises in satire ever to have been composed and it confirms More's contemporary reputation as a master of humour. That humour was inevitably also directed against his own day, and in *Utopia* he takes advantage of the freedom of fable to mock some of the abuses and follies which he saw around him. In particular he berates the current practices of diplomacy and treaty-making, at the precise time when he himself was involved in just such activities. He also rids Utopia of lawyers, with a marginal annotation from Gillis that they are all 'useless'.[26]

The central fact is clear. It is very difficult in *Utopia* to gauge or determine More's own opinion upon any particular matter. Irony was the most powerful and complicated literary tone in a society where formal appearances were becoming less and less appropriate to the actual realities of power, and where traditional beliefs and authoritative customs were beginning to decay. It is the tone of Erasmus, and of Rabelais, as the cultures of the Middle Ages were gradually being displaced. It may also help to account for the popularity of dialogues in the period, where ambiguity can be sustained indefinitely. More himself remained a master of ambivalence; his written texts seem to offer both public and private meanings and study of his style demonstrates how he establishes parallels and contrasts while simultaneously trying to resolve thematic oppositions. He will often jot down two alternative phrases to express the same meaning, and moves from legal nicety to rhetorical amplification. Cresacre More has reported how he would make a quick or funny remark while remaining apparently serious, and how he 'spoke alwaies so sadly that few could see by his looke whether he spoke in earnest or in jeaste'.[27] This is the author of *Utopia*.

More completed the second book, the description of 'no-place', while still in the Low Countries and then on his return, according to Erasmus, worked on a section of preparatory dialogue '*ex tempore*'[28] in odd moments of leisure. It shows signs of being hastily written and was conceived and composed at a time when More was indirectly involved in great changes within the affairs of state. Thomas Wolsey was rising to pre-eminence in the months *Utopia* was being finished, and by the time it was completed he had attained a position of settled superiority. It might even be said that Wolsey helped to inspire the first book of *Utopia*, concerned as it is with the condition of England, and there are indications that More originally intended to dedicate the work to him.

More introduces himself as a character within this first section, which is couched as a debate or argument between himself and Hythlodaeus; and, since it takes the form of a dialogue, he is able to make specific points without necessarily affirming any opinion of his own. The cloak of invisibility was useful at the time, since in this introduction to an ideal commonwealth he dramatises the objections of Raphael Hythlodaeus to the current state of English life. In particular Hythlodaeus objects to the penalty of death meted out to convicted thieves, when some form of restitution or public service would be preferable as a punishment, and launches a wholesale attack upon the policy of land enclosure for the rearing of sheep, which had led to the removal of fields for cultivation, the destruction of houses and the eviction of tenants. The central point here is that Wolsey was known to More as a reforming chancellor – and that More had every reason to suppose that Wolsey was about to act upon the problem of enclosure. The arguments of *Utopia*, then, might easily find a willing and receptive audience. More also includes an encomium upon the sagacity and statesmanship of his old patron John Morton, one of Wolsey's predecessors as an ecclesiastical dignitary and Lord Chancellor, which might plausibly be seen as another sign of tacit approval or even flattery. By attacking foreign monarchs for their policy of war and previous monarchs for their habits of taxation, More is also able (through the voice of Hythlodaeus) to suggest the standards of polity which the new king of England might reasonably adopt.

So there are two distinct, and distinctive, narratives within the same book; one remains practical and conversational, while the other is wholly abstract and theoretical. We may again call upon More's knowledge of Plato, and his commentators, to elucidate this Janus-like form. There seems little doubt that he had read that philosopher's *Parmenides* as well as his *Republic* if only because it uncannily anticipates the method of *Utopia* itself. Plato composed the first section of his now lesser-known dialogue in the manner of a debate between Socrates and Parmenides; there then follows a second section, in which Parmenides launches into a long theoretical argument which seems to be riddled with incoherence and inconsistency.

The two great interpreters of the *Parmenides* were Marsilio Ficino, whom Colet reverenced, and Pico della Mirandola, whose biography More had translated. Ficino celebrated *Parmenides* as a holy work, to be approached with devotion; Pico della Mirandola, however, considered it to be a theoretical exercise in dialectics where the dangers of unintelligibility are continually emphasised. It was 'a treatise in logic' rather than a philosophical hymn.[29] As a late twentieth-century commentator has put it, *Parmenides* is filled with deliberate mistakes and 'multiple contradictions'; the challenge for the reader is 'not simply to notice errors but to diagnose them'.[30] This is precisely the challenge which More established in *Utopia*.

So we may place More's treatise firmly in the context of Plato and his Renaissance interpreters – within, that is, the context of humanist discourse. The very form of *Utopia* may have been modelled upon *Parmenides*. In a sense More always needed the safety of an inherited model. Just as his history of Richard III had been in part based upon Sallust, so this more accomplished production seems to rest upon Plato. The very nature of More's genius can be glimpsed here, in his ability to reformulate the classical tradition on his own terms while at the same time employing all the ironies and ambiguities of his own nature.

This in turn heralds the most interesting and significant aspect of his imaginary dialogue with Hythlodaeus, when the two men argue over the merits of royal service. Hythlodaeus rejects any suggestion that he might advise a king, on the grounds that only flattery and hypocrisy succeed in such councils; a good man is either scorned or betrayed, with his virtues acting as a cover for the activities of more vicious men. The character of More, presented in the dialogue, disagrees with this analysis and argues instead for the necessity of practical philosophy and pragmatic guidance as an arbiter of public good. This was a matter of pressing import to More, since in this period he was actually considering whether to join the king's council. Yet it is a measure of his innate caution and distance that he is able to play with the arguments on both sides as if indeed it were a drama of which he is the spectator. But Hythlodaeus is in many respects portrayed as a blusterer, mixing specious argument with impractical fantasy, and the plain fact that the traveller opposes royal service may be the single most important reason for entering it. That is, exactly, what More now proceeded to do.

XVII

Wholly a Courtier

AT the beginning of the following year, 1516, More was said
to be frequenting the smoky courts of Westminster,[1] where he
was always most punctilious in greeting Thomas Wolsey each
morning. He had returned from his mission in the Low Countries in
the previous autumn, and such was his success that Henry offered
him an annual pension; More told Erasmus that he was inclined to
refuse it, on the grounds that too close an association with royal
administration might compromise his activities on behalf of the City.
But he had not entirely waived the possibility of accepting it and was
writing on the subject to Erasmus in the same period that he was
cultivating the attention of the new cardinal. Wolsey, having become
Archbishop of York, cardinal and chancellor, was the most powerful
man in the kingdom, apart from the king himself, and More seems
genuinely to have believed that he represented the best hope of
reformation in Church and state. He praised his skills as chancellor
in the highest terms and wrote two Latin poems to him as 'pater
alme'[2] or bountiful father.

So it was More's custom to greet him in Westminster Hall. The
cardinal wore the rich crimson apparel of his rank, with a sable scarf
and a scarlet hat; he held an orange in his hand, hollowed out and
filled with a sponge soaked with vinegar and various herbs, which he
held up to his nose while in a crowd of suitors or claimants. From
York Place (his London residence, situated at what is now the top of
Whitehall) to Westminster Hall, he rode upon a mule; it was a sign of
humility to travel in such a manner, since Our Lord Himself had
entered Jerusalem upon an ass, though the animal was nevertheless
decked out in velvet cloths and gilt spurs. Before him, on horses, rode
two cross-bearers with two great crucifixes of silver, and a member
of his household bearing a pillar of silver as a token of his possession

of York; he was also accompanied by four footmen carrying gilt pole-axes, with other members of his retinue and household following close behind. On his arrival at Westminster Hall his ushers parted the throng with 'On my lords and masters, make way for my lord's grace!'[3] He walked forward, with the orange in his hand.

In popular legend he is always depicted as portly, not to say fat, but the surviving pictures show a large, strong man with a handsome profile; he was only five years older than More himself, but had already made the journey from royal chaplain and almoner to an eminence where the greatest of the land deferred to him. The progressive historians of the nineteenth and twentieth centuries have taken pleasure in depicting this last of the great pre-Reformation English cardinals as a devious and cunning prelate who wrapped himself in houses and in jewels. He was in fact an inexhaustible administrator and loyal servant of the king; certainly he was a brilliant, witty and fluent man who impressed all those with whom he dealt. Of course he made enemies, notably John Skelton, who in 'Why Come Ye Not to Court' mocked his 'magnificence' and wished 'The devil kiss his arse!';[4] the poet terribly berates him for his pride and temper, but these apparent vices can be interpreted as skilful attempts to impress upon ambassadors and other dignitaries the authority of his king and of his country. A wonderful insight into the personality of Wolsey is given by the Venetian ambassador Sebastian Giustinian, who wrote a series of despatches to his own court between 1515 and 1519 – the years in which More first entered royal service. Giustinian believed Wolsey already 'to have the management of the whole of this kingdom',[5] and chronicled his occasional anger as well as what he described as his 'very warm language'.[6] He spoke of contemporary affairs 'with extreme vehemence and mental excitement' and, on one matter of concern, declared: 'I, who am at least a cardinal, do not deserve an "*if indeed*". '[7] The ambassador had to pass through eight sumptuously tapestried rooms before coming to the audience chamber where the prelate was arrayed in pomp, with cardinal's robes that seemed to be dipped in the colours of heaven. Wolsey could also be humorous or learned, according to mood, and at all times evinced a command of address and fluency of language that rendered him a great master of diplomacy; he listened attentively, although he was prone to interrupt and ask questions; he employed biblical allusions and parallels when he wished to make a point; he was a master of decorum, but could feign temper when it was required.

There also survive records of his domestic as well as foreign authority. When certain merchants were summoned to the court of Chancery 'theye came up and kneled dowen byfor hys Grace',[8] and Wolsey addressed them with 'Ye wardens of the Mercers, what is the mynde of your Company?' and, to one of the plaintiffs, 'Woman, ye be gretely beholden to the wardens of the Mercers.'[9] The general air is one of swiftness and authority, assisted by a magisterial bearing and a quickness of wit. This was the man to whom More deferred in the courts of Westminster, bidding him good morning when he appeared with his escort and entourage. More would later say of Wolsey, 'gloriouse was he very far above all measure & that was greate pitie for it did harm, and made hym abuse many greate giftes that god had givyn hym. Neuer was he saciate of heryng his own prayse.'[10] Yet at this stage their relations were entirely cordial.

By the autumn of 1516 More had joined the king's council or, more precisely, the Council of the Star Chamber, which was controlled and administered by Cardinal Wolsey. Even if he were a reluctant servant of the Crown, which seems unlikely, there were others who would have persuaded him. His father, John More, had become a member of the council in the spring; John Colet was also there and, according to Erasmus, was '*intimus*' with the king.[11] The influence of his wife cannot be neglected, either, in his decision to accept such an influential position. Alice More knew the nature of power in her society, since she had been close to it all her life. The Council of the Star Chamber met in a building of Westminster Hall, by the side of New Palace Yard closest to the river and just south of the landing known as Westminster Stairs; there was the chamber itself, given its name because 'the roof thereof is decked with the likeness of stars gilt',[12] behind which was an inner chamber used for private consultation and for dining, with various other rooms beyond.[13] It has been estimated that between eleven and twenty councillors met in the Star Chamber on four days a week, although two other days were reserved for 'reformacion of misorders and other enormityes'.[14] Only on Sundays did they rest from their judicial labours. They met during term-times, six months of the year, and sat in the mornings. The majority of cases brought before the council concerned disputes over property and title, the real bedrock of Tudor economic transactions, but it was also involved in administrative and executive matters. In questions of law, long depositions from the parties in dispute were presented to the councillors, who might then examine witnesses before reaching their decision. Among its members were the judges and serjeants-at-law, but the central figure was Wolsey himself, who helped to promote its judicial work and thereby reserve more sensitive or secret matters to himself.

It is not difficult to understand why More was chosen for such a post; he was a common lawyer of established reputation who had already proved himself adept in negotiations. It is not in the least surprising, either, that he accepted his new role; the path from legal work to royal service was a traditional one. More's earlier biographers, wishing to emphasise his spirituality and maintain his role as defender of the old faith, have often presented him as a man torn between his duties to king and Church; but, in a period when royal power was considered to be enacted through divine agency, there was no such contrast. Nor was royal service in the least incompatible with More's humanism since members of the court and council included Richard Pace, Cuthbert Tunstall and Andrew Ammonius; Linacre was the king's physician and Colet the court preacher. Wolsey himself, so far as his multifarious activities allowed, also encouraged the new learning. The prospects for educational and religious reform were bright indeed; at the time More joined the council in the Star Chamber, new foundations of scholarship were being created. St John's College was founded in Cambridge, under the auspices of John Fisher, in the summer of 1516; Richard Fox established Corpus Christi, Oxford, in the spring of the following year, with public lecturers in Divinity, Latin and Greek. This provided the surest possible basis for humanist learning and, in the following year, Wolsey rode to Oxford in order to announce the creation of six new professorships.

More was also concerned with the spread of learning in a more private sense; throughout the spring and summer of 1516 he was trying to complete *Utopia*. Erasmus had visited London briefly at the end of July, and stayed with the More household in Bucklersbury. He found the presence of Alice More somewhat forbidding on this occasion, however; he confessed to Andrew Ammonius that she might have found him a pitiably decrepit guest,[15] and he left after a few days. He was preoccupied with his recension of the New Testament, which had just been published in Basle, but there was time to discuss the progress of *Utopia*. And, when Erasmus went to

Rochester, where he stayed with John Fisher for ten days before returning to the Low Countries, More rode down in order to see him again. Clearly there was an intimacy of purpose between them that goes beyond the bland formalities of many humanist friendships. But their letters throughout this period are not filled with apothegms of wisdom, whether secular or religious; they are, instead, preoccupied with money, preferment and plans for publication. More, especially, shows a practicality and efficiency which were so much part of his life in the world; he is even caught again, on two occasions, telling what he called 'small lies' in order to expedite his affairs.

More's visit to Erasmus preceded the no less welcome arrival of *Utopia*. The Dutch scholar received the manuscript just three weeks later, after his return to Antwerp. It was then entitled *Nusquama* ('Nowhere') and More said, with perhaps false modesty, it was nowhere written well. But he was genuinely anxious about its reception, and in a number of somewhat plaintive letters he urged Erasmus to discover what Tunstall and Gillis, among others, thought of it. He enclosed a letter to Peter Gillis with the original manuscript, which became the dedicatory epistle to *Utopia*. In turn Erasmus persuaded other northern European humanists to add their own letters and tributes, so that the treatise on an ideal commonwealth might have the best possible introduction to the world of humanist learning. He also supervised every stage of the book's preparation and publication. He edited it – it might even have been Erasmus, rather than More, who changed the title to *Utopia* – and may have added certain of its marginalia. He arranged the text for printing and, approximately two months after he received it, gave it to Theodoricus Martens of Louvain. The book itself emerged from the press by the end of that year, small in size but eventually large in reputation. More told Erasmus that he was awaiting its arrival with as much expectation as a mother for her son who has travelled overseas.

In many of his letters during this period, to Erasmus and others, More professed himself to be so pressed by urgent matters that he had no time to write or think;[16] he was 'distringor'[17] or distracted. His continual attendance with the council in the Star Chamber meant that, according to Erasmus, he was being carried away by the tempest of public service.[18] But he was also still under-sheriff of London, while at the same time pursuing cases for private clients. He was asked by the Mercers for his 'advice and counsel'[19] on legal matters, for example, and it is reported by his first biographer that he acted on behalf of the papal interest when one of the Pope's ships was seized at Southampton. He was also asked to adjudicate in a boundary dispute between the parishioners of St Vedast and the Saddlers' Guild, who had adjacent premises in Forsters Lane, and in the same year he was sitting on commissions variously concerned with park lands, enclosures and the maintenance of yeomen. So he wrote of the hard grind[20] of public life, and told Erasmus that he was being diverted from all learning by *'forensibus litigiis'* ('legal disputes').[21]

His work as under-sheriff, in particular, had not decreased. There was a drought in the autumn of 1516, and very little rain fell for nine months; this was a serious matter when so many used the water from the rivers and streams, from the Fleet and the upper reaches of the Walbrook, which flowed down into the City and its environs from the northern hills. Then, on 12 January 1517, a great frost descended upon London 'in suche wise that no bote might goe betwixt London and Westminster all the terme tyme'.[22] There were alterations in inner, as well as outer, weather. In the spring of 1516 a virulent form of the sweating sickness emerged and for three years lingered in the city, breaking out with particular ferocity in the summer of 1517. Colet and Wolsey both suffered from it several times, but recovered; the king anxiously moved from place to place in order to avoid the contagion. More wrote to Erasmus that everyone was in a state of grief as well as danger and that many people were dying all over the city – More's own household had been affected, although his wife and children were safe. After a fever of twenty hours, Andrew Ammonius died in that most difficult summer.[23] There are numerous and rather lurid accounts of its symptoms. It killed most on the first day, sometimes within an hour or two; it manifested itself by 'a profuse sweat which dissolves the frame'[24] and which smelt foully with 'a great and a strong sauore',[25] as well as by extreme thirst, delirium and eventually the drowsiness that led to death.

Epidemic sickness was often considered as a harbinger of disease in other parts of the body politic; Polydore Vergil notes how the first appearance of the sweating sickness had been taken as a sign that the rule of the old king, Henry VII, was to be a harsh one – although Vergil himself believed that it was a token that Henry would have to govern 'in the sweat of his brow'.[26] Certainly, at this later date, a kind of fever or delirium visited the people of London for a time. In the spring of 1516 a notice was fixed to the main doors of St Paul's and All Hallows, Barking, declaring that foreign merchants residing in London 'brought wools to the undoing of Englishmen';[27] an attempt was made by the authorities to find the offender, principally by scrutinising the handwriting of every literate citizen. The complaints of city merchants against 'aliens' were perennial but then, in the following year, more decisive and dangerous action was taken.

A London broker (the word was in general use by this time), John Lincoln, approached the popular warden of the Franciscan community of Grey Friars by the City wall and asked if he would preach against the abuses of the foreign merchants; Henry Standish declined, but another priest obliged. During Easter week he delivered a sermon in the fields near St Mary Spital, in which he declared that 'this land was given to Englishmen'.[28] In the same period a mercer is reported to have threatened certain Lombard rivals that 'by the Mass, we will one day have a day at you'.[29] And that day came. There had been threats and insults directed against foreign merchants since the sermon in the Spital fields, and on 28 April some 'aliens' were attacked by apprentices in the London streets. All the reports suggested that there was to be a riot on May Day itself, and that the foreigners were to be murdered. There was also talk of freeing prisoners held in the compters of Poultry and Wood Street. At seven o'clock on the evening of 30 April, Thomas More attended a meeting of the City authorities in the Guildhall; as both under-sheriff of the City and a member of the king's council, he was arguably the most important figure to deal with the encroaching crisis. From the Guildhall he rode either to Westminster or the cardinal's dwelling, York Place, where he consulted with other members of the council. It was decided that an immediate curfew should be ordered, and at 8.30 More came back to the Guildhall with that demand. The aldermen returned to their wards with the news that no citizen 'should stirre out of his house, but to keep his doores shut, and his servants within' until the next morning.[30] But it may already have been too late. One city official tried to break up an apprentices' sword game of 'bucklers' in Cheapside, thereby creating a minor riot. By eleven o'clock that night a crowd of artisans, apprentices and children ran through Newgate Market and down St Nicholas Shambles, just to the north of St Paul's churchyard; More with other officials met them at the corner of St Martin's, and attempted to persuade them to disperse.

It is at this moment that drama, or popular legend, enters history. In a late sixteenth-century play, *Sir Thomas Moore*, one long passage has been ascribed to Shakespeare; it is concerned with this confrontation between More and the crowd at the corner of St Martin's. He steps forward and calls out to the apprentices: 'Good masters, hear me speak.' More then goes on to calm the people with a homily on the need for order and obedience together with a pointed reference to the fact that, if they were banished, they would become in turn 'straingers' in a foreign city. His entreaties succeed and the apprentices declare that 'Weele be ruld by you master moor.'[31] The evidence supports Shakespeare's authorship of the fragment but, in any event, this dramatic episode confirms the importance of the event in London's history and suggests the esteem in which More himself was held by its citizens; it is not often that a condemned traitor to his king is praised, some fifty years after his death, as a popular figure.

On this particular occasion, however, Shakespeare nodded. More's attempts to calm the crowd succeeded momentarily but then some stones and clubs were hurled at the official party; one serjeant-at-arms was hit and shouted furiously, 'Down with them!' Thereupon a full riot ensued. The houses of foreigners were attacked and ransacked, especially those of the French, who in this period were particularly disliked, while several 'straingers' were injured. The sporadic violence and destruction continued until the early hours of the morning, but at five o'clock the earls of Shrewsbury and Surrey (together with other noblemen) rode through the streets of the city and restored order; three hundred were arrested and, on the following Monday, eleven were sentenced. Four prisoners were to be hanged, drawn and quartered at various sites of London (two at the Standard in Cheapside, close to More's house) and the other seven hanged at other positions in the city.

There was an appropriately theatrical sequel to the riots of May Day. The three hundred condemned men and women, with halters around their necks, were led in to the king's presence at Westminster Hall; Henry sat upon a raised platform and listened as Cardinal Wolsey pleaded for their lives. He refused. Then all of them fell down upon their knees crying, 'Mercy, gracious lord, mercy!' The queen knelt, too, and begged her husband's forgiveness for the unhappy offenders. Wolsey himself 'besought his Majesty most earnestly to grant them grace'[32] and, eventually, Henry consented to their pardon. Wolsey announced it to them with tears in his eyes; all of them took off their halters and threw them up to the roof of the hall. 'They jumped for extreme joy,' according to one witness and altogether 'it was a very fine spectacle'.³³ More, dressed in black for the solemn occasion, looked on.

But he was involved in foreign, as well as domestic, adventures. The affairs of Europe were like Mahomet's tomb, suspended between heaven and earth; there was no open warfare but there was no general peace. There were intrigues, doubtful treaties and, as always, troubling rumours. It was in this atmosphere, in the summer of 1517, that More joined a diplomatic mission to Calais to negotiate about various commercial disputes that had arisen between the merchants of both countries, and to deal with questions of piracy on the seas where English and French seem to have been equally at fault. It was not an assignment that More welcomed. He was to reside in Calais for three months, dated from the beginning of September, and was to involve himself in the complicated processes of French law. There were also reports of plague in Calais. But his role as a member of the council incurred responsibility such as this and, before he left London, he asked the Mercers to report 'any injuries or wrongs done unto them by Frenchmen'.³⁴ He was soon complaining of the tedium involved in the negotiations, however, and letters to the council from More and the other commissioners – even in their incomplete state – are filled with detail. There are various references to 'provisions' and 'ordinaunces', 'complayntis' and 'certeficacions', 'communycacions' and 'quereles'.³⁵ The favourites of kings, as Erasmus said ironically of More's plight, can expect such advantages.

There were, however, genuine benefits. Soon after his arrival at Calais he received from Erasmus a diptych, which displayed painted images of Peter Gillis and of Erasmus himself on two wooden panels. It was a tribute to the friendship between the three men, which had in particular fostered the publication of *Utopia*, but it was also a celebration of humanist learning itself. Erasmus is the image of contemplative and scholarly life, while Gillis holds a letter from More and looks out into the world. This double portrait was painted by Quentin Matsys, then the most famous portraitist in Antwerp, whose extraordinarily delicate realism announced a profound and revolutionary change in portraiture; it was as though men and women were seeing themselves clearly for the first time. The fine nervous features of Erasmus seem momentarily at rest, as he writes with a reed pen his paraphrase of Romans;³⁶ upon the shelf behind him is his *New Testament* as well as a copy of St Jerome's Vulgate. Erasmus is indissolubly linked to that other great scholar, and the entire conception of Matsys's portrait owes something to the orthodox images of St Jerome in his famous study (although the lion is missing). Here, in iconographic form, is the history of true scholarship. Gillis holds the letter from More in one hand, while the other rests lightly upon a copy of *Antibarbari* by Erasmus; volumes of Seneca and Suetonius lie on the shelves behind him. The references are clear enough, but what we also see upon the painted panels is that combination of startling realism and resonant historicism which was also characteristic of the new learning. That is what More meant when, in a set of verses, he praised Matsys as '*Veteris nouator artis*' ('the reviver of old art').[37]

More was delighted by the gift, so timely a reminder of his 'humanist' world in a place and period where he was embroiled in legal and commercial matters, and at once wrote both to Erasmus and Gillis in praise of a work which would act as a perpetual token of their presence in his life; he was '*coniunctus amore*',[38] united in love with them. In the painting Erasmus wears a ring on the forefinger of his right hand; it had been presented to him by More. Indeed throughout his life More was notably generous, and his contemporaries seem delighted to have offered him gifts in return, even if they were not always so magnificent as the diptych. In this period, for example, Cuthbert Tunstall sent him a fly suspended in precious amber shaped as a heart. It was an age in which friendship between men could take elaborate forms.

While he attended the negotiations at Calais, a second edition of his *Utopia* emerged from the press of Gilles de Gourmont in Paris; the publication had been supervised by a young English scholar who had worked for Erasmus at Cambridge, Thomas Lupset, and seems designed to promote the work to a larger audience of clerics, administrators, scholars and lawyers. In the same period as the publication of *Utopia* Froben issued another edition of the Lucian translations which More and Erasmus had prepared; these include emendations and corrections, for the printer, in Erasmus's hand. Three months later Froben issued the third edition of *Utopia*, together with More's epigrams; this was also printed and published under the supervision of Erasmus. So, with the ready assistance of his friends, More's earliest works were introduced to the world; these also became the works upon which his European reputation depended. There were to be no more written in this ironic and spirited style, since for the rest of his life he was engaged only upon texts of polemic and devotion. The young scholar and wit, the scourger of ecclesiastical and regal abuses, was to be covered by the mantle of the royal councillor and heretic hunter. There were occasions, even now, when he seemed oddly embarrassed or anxious about what we might term his secular productions. He even went to the length of lying to the Archbishop of Canterbury, William Warham, by claiming that *Utopia* had been printed without his knowledge; since he had sent the manuscript to Erasmus, and worried anxiously over the plans for publication, it was a bold fabrication. More may have been nervous of the prelate's reception of this satirical text; but the episode suggests the distance that he was willing to keep from his literary pursuits. He never was a scholar or writer in the fashion of Erasmus or Vives; he was an occasional poet and satirist who was not in the least unwilling to turn his hand to 'official' publications of a more solemn nature. Here, in Calais, we may mark the transition. More is in his thirty-ninth year, and over the next few months he came to the decision which would affect the course of his life.

Yet even while he contemplated his future, an incident took place in Europe which would prove decisive for his career. In the autumn of 1517, on the eve of All Souls when relics were displayed to the faithful, Martin Luther is supposed to have nailed a placard containing ninety-five theses for debate to the castle church in Wittenberg. His questions on the doctrine of indulgences and on the remission of sins were placed upon the church door as part of what one biographer has called 'scholastic routine';[39] certainly it was academic practice to publicise debate in this manner, but Luther's complaints and questions were taken up by the whole of Germany and his words were quickly in the mouths of princes, merchants and populace. 'It is mere human talk to preach that the soul flies out [of purgatory] immediately the money clinks in the collection box ... All those who believe themselves certain of their own salvation because of letters of pardon, will be eternally damned, together with their teachers.'[40] The significance of the Articles was such that Erasmus sent a copy of them to More in the spring of the following year. In the meantime Luther had written to a friend, declaring that he longed 'to obtain the *Utopia*'.[41] The two men were already aware of each other's presence and capacities; soon they would be at each other's throats as they struggled over the future of their Church.

More left Calais in December, but before returning home he rode north to Bruges to meet Richard Pace. Pace had been in the vicinity for several months, his principal task being to create or finance a military alliance against France. What was the purpose, then, of More's journey to Bruges? It is likely that he brought secret news of the negotiations with France, which might compromise Pace's own activities. But it may be that they had other business to discuss – in the following year they would both be working closely and directly with the king.

It was Erasmus who first noted the change. More, he wrote in the spring of the following year, is now '*totus . . . aulicus*',[42] wholly a courtier, and attending continually upon Henry. In the next sentence he hints that Richard Pace may have been partly responsible for his change of status. More had moved from the position of councillor in the Star Chamber to that of councillor attendant – literally attendant upon 'His Majesty's Honourable Person', part of the travelling court which followed Henry from palace to palace, and *de facto* a member of the Privy Chamber.[43] He always contended that he accepted his new post reluctantly – '*invitissimus*'[44] – and mentioned that even the king joked with him about his initial unwillingness. Erasmus, in letters to friends, gives the impression that More was practically forced to take the position. That is an overstatement, but there are reasons why More would have had misgivings about his new appointment. He was forsaking the life of law and, unlike his father, he would never move forward to the posts of serjeant-at-law or judge. He was also giving up his position in City politics and City administration, while at the same time suffering from possible loss of earnings. But, perhaps more importantly, his position as councillor attendant meant that he had much less time for his family and that he would be apart from them when he followed his master to Windsor, or Ampthill, or further afield.

His constant proximity to the king meant that he became a figure of much authority and power, but there were more significant reasons for royal service. He truly believed the king to be divinely ordained, the proper source of the harmony and blessings of the 'commonwelth'. Henry represented spiritual, almost magical, power. In that sense it became More's duty to serve him. Perhaps the element of sacrifice in the choice, made it all the more pleasing to him; once more he could subdue his own inclinations, just as he subdued his flesh, in the service of a higher order. Yet he knew himself well enough to know that he might serve as a counsellor to his monarch and, a few years later, declared it necessary that every man of 'good mynde' should give 'good aduyce towarde his prynce and his countrey'.[45] It is fair to take this as a measure of More's own feelings on becoming a councillor attendant: he would be in the very best position to advise and persuade the king to follow his own highest instincts and better judgements. He could only have been heartened when, on his entering the king's service, Henry himself told him that he should serve God first and his master second.

His first role in Henry's court was as a hearer of 'poor men's suits'; this was a relatively old office by means of which the 'poor' (the term was somewhat elastic) could sue for justice without facing the costs of formal litigation. Thus More, normally with one other councillor, would receive petitions or 'requests' on such matters as enclosures, wardships, contracts, marriage settlements, and the whole paraphernalia of early sixteenth-century English life. More's reputation for fair and swift justice made him the obvious choice for such a post. As the court moved on in 1518 through Windsor, Newhall, Hampton Court, Richmond, Abingdon, Woodstock, Southampton, Greenwich and Eltham, More heard from suitors who had been cheated or oppressed, deprived of land or inheritance, prevented from enjoying customary rights or unlawfully expelled from ward or guild. Within a year, however, Wolsey had established a committee in Whitehall to hear these suits of 'poor men', so great was the press of business, and More was released to assume more complex and sensitive duties.

It had been in many respects a difficult year. He had arrived at court with Richard Pace, who had returned to take up his post as the king's secretary. Henry had welcomed them with 'very wise and substantial precepts',[46] but More was actually not paid until the following summer; only after he presented a petition to Henry was his salary of £100 a year honoured and backdated to the autumn. He formally resigned as under-sheriff of London only after he had received payment; his last official duty for his old city was to greet the papal legate, in Cheapside, with a brief Latin oration. His resignation as under-sheriff at this time suggests, perhaps, that even at this late stage More did not consider his post at court to be safe or permanent. Certainly his position does not seem to have been altogether assured, since Richard Pace was obliged to write to

Wolsey on his behalf requesting him to make sure that More received from the household staff 'daily such allowance of meat and drink as the king's Grace hath granted'.[47] More was being forced to buy meat in town for his servants, which was 'intolerable'.[48] There is a picturesque vignette of More and Pace sitting down to eat, surrounded by others carding or dicing, and, later, pitching arrows over the screens in the Hall.[49] It is reminiscent of a description by Erasmus of the foolish courtiers who 'go to Dice, Tables, Cards, or entertain themselves with Jesters, Fools, Gambolls, and Horse-tricks'.[50] It seems likely that Wolsey (with the help of Pace) had been responsible for More's transition to this sportive court; the young lawyer was reliable, industrious, clever and, perhaps most important, apparently without ambition on his own account. He could be trusted, in other words, to remain loyal to Wolsey while faithfully fulfilling his duties to the king. Soon enough, then, he was at the centre of affairs.

XVIII

He Sat upon a Throne of Gold

THE image of Henry VIII is preserved for ever in the portraits of Hans Holbein. The legs are set firmly apart, subduing the ground upon which he stands, as if he could straddle the world; the confident forward stance is amplified by the right arm beside his hip, while the left hand rests lightly by his dagger; the full and rubicund face gazes outward, challenging spectators to avert their eyes. It is a picture of majesty, eliciting both awe and fear; the slightly etherealised and religiose portraits of earlier English kings have been replaced by the robust presence of one whose physical body is itself an image of a prospering body politic. Henry wished to be viewed in the absolute fullness of health and majesty, the confidence of his whole posture matched only by his fabulously bejewelled robes. He sat upon a throne of gold, beneath a golden canopy.[1] He was dressed entirely in scarlet, purple, crimson and white – a doublet of white and crimson satin, hose of scarlet and a vast mantle of purple velvet with white satin lining. His cap of crimson was looped with gold, his mantle had a great golden cord with golden ornaments upon it; around his neck was a gold collar, with a diamond the size of a walnut; another gold necklace, encrusted with smaller diamonds, was draped over his shoulders. And his fingers were covered with rings. No Roman or Egyptian ruler could rival such magnificence. Here was another Apollo, covered in gold.

Henry also prided himself upon his legs and, in a typical scene from his court, once demanded of the Venetian ambassador if the king of France had such good limbs. Then he opened the front of his doublet and, placing his hand upon his thigh, exclaimed, 'Look here! and I also have a good calf to my leg.'[2] That most of his portraits show those legs is not simply a matter of personal vanity. The vitality and beauty of the king are necessary aspects of his magnificence and of his divine status; just as in the *Timaeus* Plato extols the combination of physical and mental beauty as an image of the divine harmony of the universe, so the splendour of God's anointed is revealed by his bearing in the world. That is why Henry placed so much emphasis upon fencing, dancing and jousting as the games of court. There may also be a further connotation; the emphasis upon the size of the legs may reflect upon that of an adjacent member, and thus be a token of the king's virility. The evidence of Henry's armour, however, demonstrates that the painter felt obliged to lengthen them.

But there are other aspects to Holbein's art. In the painting known as 'the 'Thyssen portrait', Henry is given a sardonic and almost guileful expression. His eyes are slightly averted, his somewhat thin lips compressed, but at the same time he evinces a confidence and *hauteur* that seem to give an added lustre to the pearls and jewels with which his robes are encrusted. There is a wilfulness and ruthlessness in the pose of the head – an effect that only a master such as Holbein could achieve. Those qualities are depicted with less refinement in an engraving by Cornelius Matsys, the son of the man who painted Erasmus and Peter Gillis; in this engraving, published only after Henry's death, the king has been deliberately portrayed as porcine, devious and malevolent. It is the king of whom Thomas More spoke one evening, as he walked in his garden with his son-in-law after a visit from Henry – 'If my head could win him a castle in France . . . it should not fail to go.'[3] More was displaying his usual shrewdness, since all of the portraits depicting Henry's wilful magnificence were completed after More's execution.

There is one painting of Henry which can be dated to approximately two years after More entered royal service; the artist is unknown and the image is quite different from anything executed by Holbein. It shows a pensive and refined young man, magnificently dressed but somehow suggesting a depth of interior temperament. It is too close to the stereotypes of previous royal portraits to be taken at face value, but it is at least a reminder that the king who persuaded More to enter court was in certain respects distinct from the king who killed him. Henry was twenty-seven when More became councillor attendant; he was a proficient linguist, an excellent musician and a student of theology who had developed a fine Latin style. He had also shown much skill as a mathematician, in earlier years, and was fascinated by the new speculations of astronomers. Soon after entering court, More described his master as a courteous and benevolent monarch who increased daily in both erudition and 'virtus'.[4] The Venetian ambassador offered a similar impression. 'He is affable,' he wrote to the Signory, 'gracious; harms no one; does not covet his neighbour's goods, and is satisfied with his own dominions.'[5] Contemporary reports advert to his beauty, his well-proportioned frame and his athletic prowess as both hunter and jouster; these were of course also the conventional attributes of a chivalric king and suggest the extent to which the young Henry could be seen as the epitome of royal virtue. His great love of music and dancing – he was a performer on both the organ and lute, as well as a composer of such songs as 'Pastyme with Good Companye' – also contributed to the impression of a well-tempered prince who bestowed harmony upon his realm. His apparent generosity of spirit was celebrated in various anecdotes; he was almost killed by the Duke of Suffolk in a jousting accident, for example, 'but the king said that none was to blame but himself'.[6] He was also exceptionally pious and attended several Masses each day.

Yet who knew better than More the deception of mere show and semblance? The chronicler of Richard III's feigning and the author of a commonwealth where all outward magnificence is rejected might have concurred with Machiavelli's incisive description of the young king as 'ricco [rich], feroce et cupido di gloria'.[7] There were already portents of that thirst for glory. More had heard Henry declare, at a great conference in Blackfriars, that 'the Kings of England in time past have never had any superior but God alone'.[8] To attend Mass so frequently was an act of loyalty and almost filial respect. Two years previously, Henry had ordered the imperial crown to be stamped upon the coins used by the occupying forces in Tournai, and the same device was also blazoned upon a royal pavilion just two years after his accession to the throne. It cannot be assumed, then, that More suffered from any illusions on becoming a councillor attendant. Some years later he advised Thomas Cromwell that, in serving the king, 'ever tell him what he ought to do but never what he is able to do ... For if a lion knew his own strength, hard were it for any man to rule him.'[9] This is similar to the recommendation given by Thomas Wolsey to another royal servant: 'I warn you to be well advised and assured what matter ye put in his head; for ye shall never pull it out again.'[10] Wolsey, too, dwells upon the cupidity of the king

– 'rather than he will either miss or want any part of his will or appetite, he will put the loss of one half of his realm in danger'.[11] Both men spoke of a man whom they knew intimately, but perhaps even they could not then have guessed the carnage and destruction which would follow their own deaths. In this earlier time, however, at the beginning of More's service, the indomitable self-will of the king could perhaps be mistaken for authority and his extraordinary self-belief recognised only as courage.

The court itself formed the penumbra of the king's presence. It was in many respects highly structured and hierarchical, yet it was also based upon informal associations and connections; it was the arena for spectacle and display, but also the centre for secret negotiations and clandestine meetings; it was the high point of power and of game; it was the site of betrayal and arrest, but also of music and dancing. For the next eleven years Thomas More remained one of its most significant and powerful figures. He was a member of the Chamber, but his continual attendance upon the king meant that he was *ex officio* a member of the Privy Chamber. These might be described as the king's private offices and are to be distinguished from the Household, which dealt with more general matters of food, accommodation and entertaining. More's affairs at court would have been conducted within a set of rooms literally 'behind the scenes' of the great theatrical and ritual displays which comprised so much of royal life. Here were the present or presence chamber, the withdrawing chamber, the privy chamber itself and a set of lavishly tapestried and gilded 'privy lodgings' which included the king's bed chamber and raying chamber. The privy chamber was staffed by approximately six 'grooms of the chamber' and administered by the 'groom of the stool';[12] but it was also the abode of Henry's seven or eight 'minions' of noble or gentle birth. Among them all, among the attendant guards and ushers and pages, walked 'Master More'. It was a world within a world, an intimate and lavishly appointed centre of royal government.

The collective name for those around More was, in the fifteenth century, 'a threat of courtiers'.[13] One contemporary described the court as 'quesy' and 'unstable'. 'It is hard trusting this wylle worlde,' he continued, in which 'every man is here ffor himsylff'.[14] Erasmus had attacked court follies in *Moriae encomium*, where are to be found 'nothing more indebted, more servile, more witless, more contemptible' than the courtiers themselves.[15] It was a world of faction and patronage, 'affinity' and 'worship', where competing groups intrigued in order to gain access to the king and where offices could be bought and sold. 'Affinity' is a word that has now lost its force, but it helps to define that intricate network of association and relationship which characterises sixteenth-century English society. 'Advancement in all worlds,' as one observer remarked, '[is] obtained by mediation and remembrance of noble friends.'[16] A man's 'worship' was in a literal sense his honour or repute, but it included the visible tokens of renown; the retinue of a nobleman, the servants of a lord, the sumptuousness of dress, even the gold and silver plate displayed in a household, all contributed to this 'worship'. It is related to that sense of life as drama which is so much part of late medieval Catholic sensibility, and is also intimately associated with the rituals and devices of the court itself.

Chambers could be treated like theatres, with tapestries and hangings introduced for certain scenes; halls could become arenas for elaborate allegorical performances. Lords and ladies of the court would enter upon pageant cars; one vehicle is covered with trees, flowers and fruit to represent a wooded mount, while another is pitted with rare minerals, coral and gold to signify a desert place. Thomas More looks on. There were mummeries, and revels, and jousts, and disguisings. The king, embellished in gold and diamonds, sets up a challenge. A winged horse speaks words of peace. Trees grow from painted rocks. To the sound of trumpets a 'spell wagon' enters, together with four gentlemen dressed in robes of blue and gold. These lords and ladies are extravagantly arrayed, in crimson satin and damask gold, cloth of silver and yellow sarcanet, playing the parts of Ardent Desire or Lady Pity or Lady Strangeness. The ingenious dance goes on, as 'one moves tranquilly, without agitation, in the most gracious fashion'[17] to the sound of tabors and viols, flutes and recorders, virginals and trumpets. The harp was particularly fashionable in this period, the harmony of its strings reproducing the order of the equally fashionable 'basse Daunce'. Above the sprightly dancing partners hangs suspended a model of the universe, the eleven circles of the eleven heavens turning together. At one great triumphal banquet in July 1520 the noble guests were supposed to look up and gaze upon a *mappa mundi* of the elements in glorious display. (A great wind brought it down as a token, perhaps, of a fickle and unstable natural world.) They are all members of a society where form and formal elaboration are instruments of authority. There is power in the appearances, whether that of an amber mountain or a portrait of the glittering king.

There was another aspect of the court, which found its centre in the queen. Catherine of Aragon was no less pious than intelligent; a product of that Spanish 'renaissance' which had emphasised the importance of female education, she patronised those scholars and humanists who, like More himself, were another adornment of royal power. Her piety also had a Spanish flavour. Under her robes of state she wore the habit of the third order of St Francis; she attended Mass each day and spent several hours in her private chapel, kneeling in prayer upon its stone floor. When a girl was cured of convulsions by a vision of Our Lady, Catherine and Thomas Wolsey travelled on pilgrimage to the site of the visitation, which had already been turned into a shrine. Thomas More, in every sense the faithful courtier, advanced the cure as an example of miraculous intervention.

There was one influential book which was soon to establish certain ideal rules of such courtly conduct. Baldassare Castiglione's *The Book of the Courtier* was read by two of More's most famous contemporaries, Thomas Wyatt and Thomas Cromwell, and Catherine's nephew, the Emperor Charles V, kept it by his bed together with Machiavelli and the erotic prints of Bellini. It was not printed in volume form until 1528, but, since it had already been widely disseminated in manuscript, it is likely that More knew of its existence even if he was not fully acquainted with its precepts. Yet he hardly needed to read the entire treatise; in part, he embodied it. *The Book of the Courtier* is not so much a study of court etiquette as a manual for virtuous living. 'Just as,' Castiglione wrote, '. . . there exists the idea of the perfect Republic, of the perfect King and the perfect Orator, so there exists that of the perfect Courtier.'[18] Service to a king or prince becomes, therefore, the model for all good conduct in the world; to be a courtier, like More, was to occupy an illustrious and at times almost solemn position. So it is that, in the course of four evening conversations at the court of Urbino, Castiglione defines the ideal courtier as a man of learning and of virtue, a pleasing orator and dutiful servant, a charming companion and prudent counsellor who combines fortitude with temperance and modesty. The Mantuan writer concludes with a moving evocation of the Platonic desire for spiritual beauty, at which point More might have substituted the idea of sacrifice and obedience to God. Yet there can be no doubt that he fulfilled many of Castiglione's more exacting requirements. Erasmus described him in precisely the same terms – in a letter written the year after More became a councillor attendant, his friend reports him to be a wise counsellor and agreeable companion to the king. He added that Henry could hardly bear to be separated from him; this may be an overstatement but it is at least partially confirmed by More's son-in-law, who entered the household of Bucklersbury during this period. Roper relates how the king would detain More in talk of geometry or divinity and how, sometimes, they would go upon the roof of the palace to discourse upon the 'motions, and operations' of the stars.[19] It is an apt image of the time, when the concern for astronomy and mathematics, cartography and horology, determined the new face of the universe. Roper also observes how More would often 'sit and confer' with Henry upon 'worldly affairs', and how after dinner he would 'be merry' with both king and queen.[20] Of course More knew all the formulas of courtesy to superiors – 'yt may lyke you' and 'yt may please you' among them[21] – and recognised, too, that 'men must make courtesy to them, & salute them with reuerence, & stand barehed before them, or vnto some of them knele peradventure to'.[22] He could have learned from Cicero's *De Officiis* the moral value of decorum, but his own innate sense of irony conformed to Castiglione's belief that 'joke, with an element of irony, is very suitable' in court conversation where it can be 'both grave and pungent'.[23] Erasmus had also described how More's judgement and good sense helped to reconcile private quarrels and to promote good fellowship; this description is supported by an entry in the State Papers, where he is recorded acting as a mediator between Sir Arthur Poole and the Earl of Arundel.[24] More might here again have been taking Castiglione's advice on the need for 'harmony'[25] in the affairs of life and state.

For a time he remained 'Master More'. An instructive contrast might be made with a younger contemporary at court, Thomas Wyatt, a poet as well as courtier. More must have known him well, but he never mentions him. Where More tended to deal with matters of trade or treaty, Wyatt was despatched on missions to the Pope or the emperor. Wyatt was also Marshal of Calais for a time. He took part in tournaments and he also translated Plutarch for the queen. He was a grander and more expansive figure than More, a better poet but not necessarily a better man. We must think of More as dealing with him directly, and perhaps intimately, in the course of his duties. Wyatt's own evocations of court life are filled with lamentations upon its craft and corruption, its 'colours of device' and the devotion of courtiers to 'Venus and Bacchus all their life long'.[26] It is curious to consider More writing a treatise on 'last things' while serving in a world where Wyatt, at a slightly later date, was composing his own lines of plangent dismay at 'the press of courts'. In his poetry Wyatt was trying to define English verse, and indeed himself, in terms of an inheritance which included Seneca and Plato; his work is in that sense complementary to that of Castiglione. It is testimony, if nothing else, to the richness of experience at the centre of Tudor life.

Castiglione was always aware of court society as a game in which each courtier must fulfil a role to the best of his ability. It is a world in which words become a form of artifice, where men and women even speak of themselves as if they were literary figures. In certain senses it is a strikingly optimistic vision, equivalent to that of Pico della Mirandola; each person can create himself (or, sometimes, herself) through the power of words or appearances. The court was the one arena of the nation where human contradictions could be amended, where Christian belief and classical wisdom, allegory and argument, male and female, modesty and pride, might all be reconciled. Yet the harmony is necessarily fragile and may be brief indeed, as Wyatt evokes:

> Always thirsty yet naught I taste
> For dread to fall I stand not fast.[27]

More's distinguished career suggests that he flourished in such a setting. His dramatic skills and his dialogues, in which he consistently played roles for the benefit of an argument, reinforced his success as both orator and diplomat, but his preoccupation with the study of rhetoric was of no less significance. That discipline presumes a public world, and audience, while at the same time establishing the rules of performance within it. Rhetoric also encourages the display and promotion of fictional narratives, as a means of graceful persuasion. To be effective in the world, even while playing a part, is the mark of an unusually clever man such as Thomas More. No doubt he delighted in the game. It is likely that he was galvanised and excited by the affairs of the world even, or especially, when he realised their emptiness.

More's private feelings about 'worldly pomp & vanyte' are not in doubt. Only four years after entering the king's court he composed a private treatise for his household in which he compares worldly authority to that of 'the tapster ... in the marshalsye' prison.[28] Certainly it is possible to see Henry, or Wolsey, in such a part. More never seems to have disclosed his feelings about those of noble birth who crowded the court and among whom he moved, except for a brief remark in the same treatise. Having a coat of arms, he wrote, is 'as if a gentleman thefe when he should goe to Tyburne, wold leve for a memoriall the armes of his auncesters painted on a post in Newgate'.[29] Why should we 'envy a poore soule, for playing the lord one night in an interlude'?[30] That More himself was entitled 'armiger', and was therefore able to bear heraldic arms, seems only to complicate and deepen our understanding of his part in the radiant court of Henry VIII.

XIX

My Poor Mind

IN *A Dialogue of Comfort Against Tribulation*, written in the prison cell which was his last home on earth, More condemned the 'round bisy mase of this divill that is callid besynes'.[1] Yet he had walked through that maze of business, that 'folysh myserye' as he termed it, for much of his life. It was not long after he joined the court, for example, that he found himself at the centre of England's administration. He became the king's second secretary and, since the principal secretary, Richard Pace, was for a long time out of the country on secret diplomatic business, More was soon the regular mediator of the correspondence between Henry and Wolsey. Some of More's own letters to Wolsey have survived, the first of which dates from the summer of 1519, and they are of great significance in ascertaining the nature of his role and relationships at court. His simplest function was as an amanuensis; he would be called into the king's presence and would write letters to his dictation. He would then make a fair copy (as well as a second copy) and present it for the royal signature. He also read aloud to the king communications from Wolsey, and on one occasion the cardinal even urged him 'to take your tyme that ye may dystynctly rede' matters of 'gret importance'.[2] Sometimes the communications were of such consequence that More was still working 'late in the nyght' or writing back to the cardinal 'aboute mydnyght'.[3] He invariably addressed Wolsey as 'your good Grace', with Henry invoked as 'his Grace' or 'the Kingis Grace', characteristically concluding as 'Your most humble seruant and mooste bounden beedman'.

The letters are concerned with urgent matters of war and peace, with details of army movements as well as secret negotiations, and there can be no doubt that More was entirely trusted by both men. He was one of only two or three courtiers who had attained that position of confidence. But one of Henry's letters can suddenly turn from high matters of state to a detail of ecclesiastical patronage; in the same way More can remain perfectly clear and measured about official business, while on occasion introducing a private note which suggests that he was altogether at ease with his masters. On the cardinal's good health he passes on the king's message that 'he saith that ye may thank his counsel thereof, by which ye leue the often takyng of medicines'.[4] Henry claimed to have foreseen a foreign cardinal's duplicity, and asks More to remind Wolsey 'wherby he thinketh your Grace will the bettre truste his coniecture hereafter'.[5]

Only once does More venture his own opinion in the correspondence between the two men; when Henry seems to be moving towards war and More interjects 'I pray God send his Grace an honorable and profitable peace'.[6] There is no evidence of More's advice being sought or offered, but there are stray signs of his participation in the great debates of the period. 'And whan,' he wrote to Wolsey in one long letter, 'I was abowte to haue shewed his Highnes sumwhat of my pore mynde in the matter . . .';[7] he was interrupted on this occasion, but the reference does suggest that his 'pore mynde' was sometimes employed. He may not have been a forceful or opinionated counsellor, however, since, as Wolsey informed the king, More was 'not the most ready to speake and solicite his own cause'.[8] In turn both of his masters are ready to compliment him and commend 'my pore service'.[9] But the cardinal once wrote to him, on a certain diplomatic matter, that 'I am in noo smal perplexite howe the same may be continued';[10] it may be an oblique message to the king, but it may also be an implicit request for More's advice. It is impossible to be sure of such things, of course, but it may be supposed that More on occasions played more than a secretarial part.

Yet Wolsey was the principal agent in such matters. More is continually passing on compliments to him from the king, in which More himself sometimes joined; 'hit is for the quantite one of the best made lettres,' he said of one diplomatic communication concocted by Wolsey, '. . . that ever I redde in my life'.[11] There are various references to the cardinal's 'labor, travaile, study, payne and diligens',[12] and it becomes clear that Henry was often ready to defer to his advice. Letters from the king were sometimes 'devised by the prudent caste of your Grace',[13] and Wolsey was often asked to devise 'the moost effectuall meanys'[14] to expedite policy. It was not that Henry lacked self-confidence; the overwhelming impression of the king's letters is that of a man swift and certain of his judgement in most personal matters, but more wary and circumspect in the great affairs of state. Impressions are sometimes so strong that we might be listening in the next room: 'Nay by my soul that will not be, ffor this is my removing day sone at New Hall. I will rede the remenaunt at night.' So Henry replied to a request from More. Of Wolsey, he once exclaimed: 'He has hit the nayle on the hed.'[15] Here are some phrases taken from a conversation between More and the king:

'Nay veryly, Sir, my Lord hath yit no word . . .'

'No had? I mych mervaile . . .'

'Sir, if hit lyke your Grace this mornyng my Lord Grace had no thing herd . . .'

'Mary, I am well a paied thereof . . .'

The king laughs. 'And his Grace answered me that he wold take a breth therin.'[16] And so it goes on, this invaluable record of the relationship between three highly dissimilar men – each of them, in their own way, intelligent and watchful – in which friendship and formality, irony and authority, secrecy and service, are strangely mingled.

More's work as royal secretary was not confined to the correspondence between Wolsey and the king. If a member of the Council had important news for Henry, they would generally write to More. He also received the foreign post and was one of the principal agents in dealing with foreign courts and ambassadors; such was his legal expertise that it is likely he read over the first draft of treaties or diplomatic instructions. He held the ciphers for secret correspondence and maintained the diplomatic registers. He controlled access to the king, at least in epistolary matters, in a period when such access was of paramount importance; to be physically close to the king was in a sense to imbibe power and More, even though he often denied it, became a very powerful man indeed. He was responsible for checking various grants and appointments; he signed warrants and witnessed royal documents.

His influence is also attested by the fact that he assumed control of the king's 'signet seal', which was the visible token of royal authority permitting many forms of expenditure. He was involved in other financial transactions for the king, such as the securing of manors and estates, and on many occasions acted as the court's official Latin orator. In addition, he was asked to advise on private matters; at one point, for example, he was involved in deciding the best form of education for the king's illegitimate son.

If he helped to administer the channels of patronage, he also benefited from them: on several occasions he successfully requested posts, for members of his household and for others close to him, in the administration of both City and court. Certainly he was soon considered influential enough to be the recipient of what might now be termed 'begging letters' from some of the most important people in the kingdom. Much of his private correspondence was destroyed at the time of his imprisonment, but there does survive one reply from More to a request by John Fisher; the bishop of Rochester wished to arrange an ecclesiastical appointment for one of his priests and More confirmed that he had obtained the king's agreement. He went on to say that his influence with Henry was extremely small,[17] but this may be taken as a pardonable and almost ritual under-statement. It suits his generally reticent and 'diplomatic' manner, however; when the Venetian ambassador attempted to extract information from him, 'he did not open, and pretended not to know in what the difficulties consisted'.[18]

More's formal administrative powers are easier to define. He had been appointed as a member of Wolsey's commission on enclosures even before he entered the court, and the author of the strictures against that practice in *Utopia* might well have played some part in Wolsey's ultimate decision to prosecute those who had enforced enclosure 'contrary to the statutes and law of the realm'.[19] More also remained a member of the king's council and continued to perform various legislative and judicial duties. He was still attending the Court of Requests, both at Westminster and in the king's court; there is a record of one judicial matter resolved by him at 'Grenewich'.[20] He had ceased to practise law on his own behalf, but there were occasions when he still agreed to act for the Company of Mercers. He was appointed to various commissions of inquiry, and, since he attended the Council of the Star Chamber, he became a regular traveller to Westminster. He could have taken the boat from Greenwich or Three Cranes Stairs, the landing closest to his house in Bucklersbury; in Hollar's panorama of early seventeenth-century London it is clearly visible, with skiffs and boats bobbing at the edge of the water by the stone parapet. Then he passed Bridewell and Whitefriars before coming up to the King's Stairs at Westminster itself. More has left his own vivid recollection of the journey to

Westminster, completed on horseback, where he came upon a group of 'poore folke' begging for alms by the abbey; the press of them was so great (and no doubt the odour) that he was 'fayn to ryde another waye'. But he lingered, and praised the monks for their bounty. 'No thanke to them,' one of the poor muttered, for the monks received their money from 'landes that good prynces haue gyuen them'.[21] More replied that this was better far than that the princes should take it from them again. And so on to the Star Chamber.

It is not possible fully to document More's itinerary for these early months and years of service, but certain episodes survive in contemporary accounts. He was with the king at Abingdon and Woodstock in late March and April of 1518, for example, at a time when the monarch and his court were moving from place to place in order to escape the contagion of the plague and sweating sickness. The plague itself had visited Oxford, only a few miles from both royal residences, and More was asked to enforce the precautions which had been taken in London the year before; all infected houses had to display a small bundle of hay for forty days and any inhabitant of those houses had to carry a white rod some four feet in height when he or she walked abroad. It was not a popular measure, but three children from Oxford had already died of the disease; its virulence did not abate throughout the summer and More's friends became concerned for his health. The Countess of Salisbury even sent him some medicines. He in turn must have been fearful for the safety of his own household, ensconced in the middle of the city, yet it was his obligation to stay beside the king. Such were the blessings (as Erasmus might have repeated) of royal service.

There were disturbances of another kind in Oxford at that time. Public lectures in Greek had been established at the university in the previous year, and already there were signs of opposition to the new learning. A group of those more inclined to orthodox scholastic teaching called themselves 'Trojans', as opposed to 'Greeks', and one of their number delivered a sermon of great wrath against the newly introduced studies. More was by now one of the most prominent exponents of those studies in England, and his role at court gave him a position of particular power; so he felt obliged to compose a magisterial remonstrance to the proctors and masters of the university. His letter exudes authority and self-confidence, which could only have been acquired from his status as the king's servant. Erasmus claimed later that Henry specifically encouraged the study of Greek by those who were inclined to that learning.[22] It is in this context that More's letter to the university, dated 'Abingdon. 29 March', can best be understood. It begins with an attack upon the 'Trojan' preacher – he is not named, but is likely to have been a Franciscan monk – and continues with an encomium on the merits of 'seculares literas'[23] as a way of advancing true knowledge and virtue. But he ends with what can only be described as a veiled threat that if the university does not suppress these emerging factions[24] then others with more power will do it for them. This famous epistle is not only a perfect example of formal rhetoric, and therefore a suitable production from the pen of a courtly Latin orator. It also marked More's most enthusiastic celebration of the possibilities of good letters, which suggests that his support of a central humanist programme of studies had the additional encouragement of the very people whom he mentions in his letter – Warham, Wolsey and Henry himself. There is a sequel to this episode, narrated by Erasmus, when a 'theologus' preached before the king; he, too, attacked the study of Greek. The king apparently smiled at Richard Pace, another supporter of the new learning, and then asked More to engage in a disputation with the theologian. After More had delivered what must have been a formidable oration his opponent knelt before Henry and begged to be excused a response. He had attacked Greek studies while filled with the spirit of folly,[25] replied the king, rather than that of Christ. It all ended in humiliating defeat for the hapless preacher who, according to Erasmus, was banished for ever from the court.

It sounds too neat to be altogether true, but it emphasises an important aspect of More's career in this period. It has sometimes been surmised that his humanism did not survive his transition to the realpolitik of court life, but this was clearly not the case; indeed it seems to have been strengthened and amplified by his close association with king and cardinal. Certainly, in these first years of royal service, More became a spirited advocate of humanism as well as a firm defender of Erasmus. He wrote two further, and much longer, letters in response to critics of that scholar. One was addressed to Edward Lee, a theologian and Londoner with whom More had been acquainted for many years, while the other was directed against an unnamed monk whom recent research has revealed to be John Batmanson; Batmanson was previously of the Charterhouse, where More had known him. He had admired both men and, since they were both younger than More himself, his assault upon their arguments is touched by a certain frustration that the precepts of the new learning had failed to convince them. The principal point of contention was Erasmus's recension of the New Testament. In his *Novum Testamentum* he had published parallel Greek and Latin texts, freed of solecisms or false readings, while at the same time adding his own notes at the back of the volume. For many theologians the revision of the Vulgate was an act of impiety, and there were occasions when Erasmus did implicitly challenge the accepted orthodoxy of certain beliefs. But for the Dutch scholar it was an attempt to free Christian doctrine of unsound interpretation and unhelpful scholastic accretion; it was an attempt faithfully to reveal the true piety and practical spirituality of the Gospels.

These letters are also interesting for their passages of cutting irony and sarcasm, typical of More, which on occasions turn into open abuse. At one point he describes Batmanson as an ignorant and unknown little monk who has a foul tongue.[26] He also delivers a fierce attack upon the follies of monasticism. It would perhaps be more correct to say that he assaults false monasticism, except that his is almost a general diatribe against those who prefer to stay in one place '*spongiae*' – like a sponge – and look for an escape from the troubles of the world by avoiding '*negocia*' and '*laboribus*'.[27] In fact '*negocium*' was the word he used for 'besyness', which he would later condemn as the work of the devil. But here it is extolled as an alternative to the monk's sequestered stagnation. He was of course at this period immersed in 'besyness' himself, and it is very likely that his assault upon monasticism was a way of affirming or excusing his own commitment to court life.

Yet, even as he attacked others, he himself was being criticised. The French poet and courtier Germanius de Brie or 'Brixius' had been the subject of some unflattering verses by More seven years earlier in which the Englishman had chastised the Frenchman for false heroics in a poem concerning a sea-battle between the two nations. The later publication of these verses in the first edition of More's *Epigrammata* (together with the third edition of *Utopia*) seems to have aroused the fury of Brixius who in the early months of 1520 issued *Antimorus*. It is a long poem, followed by a prose commentary, in which More's reputation as grammarian and rhetorician is attacked in the most spirited and venomous terms. Brixius called him a 'moron', in the usual pun on his name, as well as bitch and barbarian; in his prose postscript he described in vivid

detail the solecisms and faulty metres in More's Latin verses, with the
injunction that he should really try to learn the language properly. It
was a strong attack by one courtly humanist upon another, but the
most wounding and dangerous assault was upon More's position
rather than his pride. Brixius commented upon More's celebratory
poem on the accession of Henry VIII, and professed astonishment
that he should have chosen to denounce the previous king; a son
would prefer to hear his father praised, and '*metuo tibi*' ('I am afraid
for you').[28] If Henry realises what you have written, you are likely to
be expelled from England. This could be construed as an attack upon
More's loyalty to the Crown, and More knew it – in what great
danger you might have placed me,[29] he replied, if Henry had believed
you. This was the reason why More wrote at once with a long and
bellicose letter to Brixius, in the course of which he exonerates the
dead king and pretends that various unnamed councillors took
advantage of his sickness. There was no real evidence for this, of
course, but it was the best defence he could mount; at the same time
he in turn accused Brixius of plagiarism, vainglory, and such obvious
fabrication of the truth that he was likely to bring the new learning
into disrepute. Brixius was indeed an exponent of that learning and
was greatly admired by, among others, Erasmus. So, in an almost
technical sense, More lectured Brixius upon his fundamental breach
of decorum in using the wrong type of rhetoric for the wrong
purpose. If it is a case of one royal servant attacking another, it is
also an example of the representatives of two kings in a form of
shadow jousting.

   That is why the letter evinces a sense of purpose, and responsibility, which affords a fresh insight into More's role. In his letter to
Brixius he asserts that, in his advice to the king, he follows the
precepts of reason rather than the allurements of flattery; he is intent
upon praising true virtue, even if in the process he forfeits the good
opinion of '*vulgi*',[30] which can be translated as the people, the masses
or the vulgar crowd. It is interesting, then, that More should also
regret the publication of some of his earlier verses on the grounds
that they were not quite '*severa*'.[31] In a letter to another scholar he
asks that his correspondence not be published until he has had time
to revise it; otherwise his unguarded remarks might be used against
him by his critics. Seriousness or gravity was clearly now an
important aspect of his public personality, and indeed some poems

were excised by him from the edition of *Epigrammata* that was published by Froben at the end of 1520.

He also furnished an addition to that volume, by including a verse epistle which he had written to his children. It was a genuine expression of his love for them, and confirms the impression of the letters which he wrote to Margaret while he was absent from home on official duties. He particularly asks about the progress of her studies, and it is again clear that he took great pride in her attainments as well as those of other members of his household. In this period, for example, he employed Nicholas Kratzer to give his children further schooling in astronomy and geometry. But the most agreeable touches are perhaps the most private; when Margaret requested a small loan, for example, he replied that, the more often she asked, the more pleased he became. Even at the height of his 'besyness', the family living in Bucklersbury remained close to the centre of his life.

That household was certainly flourishing and, in this period, being extended in the familiar Tudor way of marriage and alliance. His future biographer, William Roper, the son of an old family friend, lodged at Bucklersbury upon entering Lincoln's Inn, and within three years was betrothed to Margaret. At the same time Sir John More was, apparently effortlessly, ascending the judicial hierarchy; he was knighted in 1518, the year in which his son became a councillor attendant, and two years later was promoted to the King's Bench. Legal historians have suggested that his advancement owed as much to his son's powerful position as to his own legal abilities; but the case cannot be proven. There were, in addition, wider connections between Bucklersbury and the public world. More's brother-in-law, John Rastell, had come down from Coventry and had established himself as a printer and bookseller; he had moved his shop from Paul's Chains and was now conveniently placed at Paul's Gate, by the archway into the churchyard. Rastell was equally involved in public affairs: he had arranged pageants on behalf of the City and had also played an important part in building English fortifications in France. But if he was a man of eminence, he was sometimes an unlucky one. He had planned and fitted an expedition to the New World, sailing with two ships from Gravesend in the summer of 1517; certain members of the crew, however, had no intention of voyaging to what Thomas More once called that 'ferme lande and contynent, dyscouered and founden out wythin this fourty yeres laste passed'.[32] They were happier with shorter, and generally piratical, voyages; so Rastell was left in Ireland, where he spent two years before returning to London as a litigant against them. The More family was directly involved in these incidents, since Sir John More had stood surety to the Crown for the voyage and now owed 250 marks.

Another member of the extended household was soon also enjoying public eminence, largely as a result of More's own efforts. John Heywood had married John Rastell's daughter, who was thus also More's niece; in doing so, he had become part of the complicated structure which included Rastells and Ropers and Mores, and which would soon exert a formidable influence in law and religion. Soon after More had become a courtier attendant, Heywood was appointed as a groom of the royal household, denoted first as 'synger' and later as 'pleyar of the virginals'.[33] He 'became noted to all witty men', according to Anthony à Wood, and was 'very familiar' with Thomas More;[34] no doubt their friendship sprang from the fact that Heywood was particularly esteemed 'for the myrth and quicknesse of his conceits'.[35] He also remained faithful to the Catholic religion until his death in 1580, and it is not surprising that More became his particular patron.

John Heywood and John Rastell shared another characteristic which throws an interesting light upon the More household. They were two of the first known English dramatists, writing plays and interludes which survive still. It has been suggested that Heywood was the first 'proper' English playwright, but there is a better case for suggesting that Rastell built the first 'proper' English stage. It was set up in Finsbury Fields and was close to those other London theatres which predate the Globe, the Theatre and the Curtain. The plays of Heywood are more substantial and inventive than the interludes of Rastell, but they share an interest in disputation and debate of a kind derived from the educational methods of the period. Drama was still, in a sense, part of the rhetorical tradition of the universities and the legal Inns, and it is significant that the earliest English tragedy, *Gorboduc*, had its first performance at the Inner Temple. So it is likely that the scenes of court were succeeded by more domestic episodes when, in the hall of Bucklersbury, short dramas like Heywood's later *Johan Johan* or *The Playe called the foure PP* were performed. *Johan* is concerned with the lubricious activities of a bad priest, while *The Playe* comments upon the trade in such false relics as the wedding cup of Adam and Eve and 'the great toe of the Trinite'.[36] These were the comic matters which moved More and his household to laughter, together with that continual ribald facetiousness which was a mark of London humour:

> I shall bete her and thwak her I trow,
> That she shall beshyte the house for very wo.[37]

It is an apt quotation to put beside the image of More as the discreet and cautious counsellor.

XX

Eques auratus

IN the autumn of 1518, after the sporadic and inconclusive warfare of the previous years, Thomas Wolsey contrived a pact of universal peace which was generally known as the Treaty of London. His essential motive was to gain further honour for his prince and to establish England's central importance in European affairs; but there can be little doubt that the craving for peace, so brilliantly conveyed by Erasmus, was also a main context for his actions. Yet the making of policy was inseparable from spectacle, and there were some wonderful moments of theatre. When the general treaty was celebrated in St Paul's, Henry and Wolsey together with the legates from France ascended to the high altar where they simply whispered the articles of agreement; this was taken to mean by the Venetian ambassador that a proposed expedition against the Turks had been cancelled. Thomas More, now within the circle of power, would have known exactly what was happening. Once the ceremony was over, a dinner was held in the banqueting hall of York Palace, where the guests were surrounded by rich tapestries and great vases of gold and silver. Then, after dinner, they gambled with cards and dice.

The great game of nations continued with the betrothal of Henry's daughter, aged two, to the infant dauphin of France. There were now two kings and an emperor in uneasy alliance – Henry VIII of England and Francis I of France, together with Charles V who was Holy Roman Emperor as well as the ruler of Burgundy and Spain – and soon negotiations and elaborate preparations were made for them separately to meet in sumptuous array. Thomas More's role among the pomp and circumstance was as one of a small group charged to prepare treaties and to resolve outstanding disputes. With Pace and Tunstall, for example, he was commanded in the spring of 1520 to negotiate with the representatives of Charles in separate diplomatic and commercial matters; he and his colleagues were designated as '*consiliarii, oratores, procuratores, legati et commissarii*',[1] with each man appending his seal and signature to the final document in the chapel of Greenwich Palace. Even before the agreement had been concluded, More was ordered by the king to help in the preparations for Charles's arrival at Canterbury. He then became one of Henry's retinue which sailed to Calais in the early summer of that year for those negotiations with Francis I which have become known, iconically, as 'The Field of Cloth of Gold'.

There is a painting of the scene, by an unknown artist, which gives some indication of the magnitude and magnificence of the occasion. Here are palaces and towers and gateways, adorned with great statues and painted devices, all of them fabricated for the occasion; here are fountains, pouring forth beer or wine, as well as artificial lakes and bridges. Here are great lines of foot-soldiers, as well as nobles and retainers, while in the distance can be seen vast tents and pavilions of richly painted cloth. The principal French pavilion was covered in gold brocade and azure velvet,[2] while its interior was decorated in a zodiacal display with all the 'Orbes of the heauens'.[3] The English palace contained galleries, apartments and rooms on the grandest scale; its defending walls were of painted cloth, and some five thousand feet of glass were used in its construction. The kings of England and of France met in a valley which had been partially redesigned with artificial mounds; they approached each other with a retinue of more than two thousand men. Henry was covered in 'fyne Golde in Bullion',[4] and it was said that the French king was so dazzlingly arrayed that it was impossible to gaze upon him. There were also games and masques, dances and banquets, jousts where the contestants of the two nations sported various devices – the English bearing a 'heart on fire'[5] which was being quenched by a watering can. There was a High Mass conducted by Wolsey, during which a fiery dragon (or, according to some reports, a eucharist) was launched into the sky. It was a great spectacle denoting peace, and More was at the centre of it. The foreign legates described him as '*secretarius regius*'[6] and his signature is to be seen on a treaty between Henry and Charles, who had met soon after the French negotiations in order to make further secret agreements of their own. There was also, and typically, another family connection; More's brother-in-law, John Rastell, had been responsible for devising many of the ornaments and astronomical devices of the English palaces and pavilions.

It could not have been altogether an unwelcome occasion for More, in any case, since he met other courtly humanists during the great displays. Erasmus had arrived as part of the retinue of Charles V – the ruler for whom he had once written *The Education of a Christian Prince* – and the great scholar and antiquarian Budé was similarly accompanying Francis I. More had already corresponded with the French humanist; Budé had been one of those who furnished *Utopia* with dedicatory epistles, and as a measure of his gratitude More sent him a pair of English dogs, probably mastiffs, or 'Masterthiefs', which had become something of a national symbol. He professed to be even more grateful for Budé's treatise on ancient coinage, *De Asse*, which represented one of the first serious attempts to understand the true nature of classical civilisation. More himself collected ancient coins and seals as a visible token of the past, and in a letter to Budé he congratulated him for restoring the dead to life. But there were also the living to consider: Erasmus had brought with him to France a collection of polemical letters addressed to his opponent Edward Lee, which he probably gave to More on being formally reconciled with Lee in Calais itself.[7] So the accord of princes was matched by the union of humanists with, alas, equally fruitless results.

Soon after the negotiations at Calais had been concluded, More moved on with other councillors to Bruges, where various commercial disputes with the Hanse merchants were in need of resolution. More seems to have been unimpressed with the citizens of Bruges, considering them avaricious, and during a period of seven or eight weeks the negotiations with the merchants were prolonged, frustrating and ultimately unproductive. The Hanse merchants themselves were not charmed by More, however; they reported that he used more words than truth and employed sophistry, cunning and trickery in his conversations with them while retaining a calm demeanour and '*blando sermone*' ('temperate speech').[8] Yet More did manage to make one friend in the city; he was introduced by Erasmus to Francis Cranevelt, an assistant to the magistrates of Bruges who became well known for his achievement in learning Hebrew without any assistance. Some of the letters between More and Cranevelt have survived, and they are touched by passages of sexual humour which are not found elsewhere in More's correspondence.

In the early autumn of 1520 More finally was able to return to England after an absence of almost three months, and, as he wrote in one of his Latin poems, 'To Candidus', you will rejoice when you forsake the company of men and rest in the bosom of your knowledgeable wife.[9] He was now always surrounded by company and his eminence at court was such that, in the spring of the following year, he was granted the lucrative post of under-treasurer. In this role he was charged with supervising the work of the Exchequer, where the officials recorded the proper disbursement or collection of allowances and fees, grants and annuities, customs and receipts; he was obliged to draw up the annual accounts of the treasury and to look after the expenses of the king's council. By Henry's own commandment he was also responsible 'for costes and expences whiche shal behoue vs to haue and susteyne aboutes our howsholde and our greate wardrobe' as well as the payment of courtiers and servants; there is even a reference to the purchase of 'parchemente paper ynke wax bagges Canuas' for use at court.[10] It was hardly a sinecure, therefore, and on one occasion Wolsey was obliged to apologise to the king for More's absence from court for five days on the grounds that he was delayed at the Exchequer 'in consequence of great matters at the knitting up of this term'.[11] The under-treasurer was also given a knighthood, according to custom, and so in this period Master More was transformed into Sir Thomas More. He had become, in the words of the king, 'our trusty and wel bilouyd counsellor Thomas Moore now knighte'.[12] He was *eques auratus*, and was obliged to put on the chain of knighthood as well as to wear golden spurs while riding. He was a knight of cheerful countenance, but behind that assumption of rank there was still a living tradition of honour and chivalry which More would have imbibed from Chaucer, Malory and Lydgate; the 'parfit gentil' knight was one who loved 'Trouthe and honour, fredom and curteisie'.[13]

His annual salary as under-treasurer was £173 6s 8d; it was the second highest in the exchequer, but it was by no means his only source of profit. As a favoured servant of the king he became the recipient of various sinecures and grants which more than doubled his income. In 1520 he had received one half of the revenue to the royal exchanger, or keeper of the foreign exchange, who controlled the exodus of bullion from the country. At a later date he was granted a licence to export a thousand woollen cloths; he would have sold it on to a merchant in that commodity although for those who persist in believing that the author of *Utopia* spoke in his own voice it might seem an inappropriate gift to the denouncer of excessive sheep-rearing. More also purchased the guardianship of two wealthy landowners who were deemed to have lost their wits, Edmund Shaa and John Moreton; this testifies to his financial acumen, perhaps, but it also suggests that he had a genuine interest in observing or managing the insane who were believed to suffer from an excess of black bile. (He once referred to an inmate of Bethlem, just beyond Bishop's Gate, who laughed aloud at 'knocking of his own hed against a post';[14] there is every reason to believe that More visited this hospital of the deranged.) There were yet further sources of income. He received an annual 'retainer' from the Earl of Northumberland of £21, as well as other payments from a bishop and a lord; he was given a pension from the French king, the presentation of a canonry from Henry, and various sums for expediting the business of the Mercers; in the year after he was appointed under-treasurer, for example, he received twenty marks for helping to arrange protection for a fleet of merchant ships departing from the Low Countries. There were doubtless other transactions of this kind, but they have not been recorded. And then there were the lands. The king awarded him the manors of Doglyngton and Fryngeford, as well as some other property in Oxfordshire, and in the spring of 1522 he was granted the manor of South in Kent which had belonged to the Duke of Buckingham and which provided £67 each year in revenue. More was even accused of illegal enclosure, but successfully defended himself against the charge.

In this gift of Buckingham's manor lies a story of pride, treachery and death which is so resonant with Tudor fate and polity that More himself used it as an example. What if, he wrote in an unpublished treatise, 'thou knewest a great Duke', and envied him his estates and his worship, only to be informed that 'for secret treason lately detected to the king' his goods and estates were suddenly 'broken vp' and 'ceased', with the duke himself put to death?[15] This is precisely what happened to Edward, Duke of Buckingham, who in the spring of 1521 was charged with treason, convicted by his peers, and beheaded on Tower Hill a month after his arrest. There has been much controversy over his case, with certain historians assuming that it had been concocted by Henry and Wolsey to remove an innocent nobleman who was considered 'over-mighty' and who happened to be a claimant to the throne of England. In that sense it could be viewed as a harbinger of the king's suspiciousness and ruthlessness. It is not at all clear that this was the opinion of Buckingham's contemporaries, however, and we are left with the fact that More willingly took land from the estates of the attainted man. His own account of the 'great Duke' who suffers an equally great fall is employed by him as an example of human folly in a world of which only the end is certain and where 'deth shal take away all that we enuy any manne for'.[16] Yet he was not averse to profiting from some, if not all, of these enviable possessions. Here we come close to one of the complexities of More's life and career. He lived in the spiritual world as well as the secular world. In the former he practised individual prayer and penitence, while in the latter he derived his identity from the social hierarchy in which he found himself. One was a question of private, the other of customary, ritual. To be a good Christian, in both worlds, required obedience and the fulfilment of obligations – which included providing an inheritance for his descendants. One may be labelled piety, the other decorum; but they are both aspects of the same religious civilisation.

More was involved with the execution of the Duke of Buckingham in one other sense; his status as a Londoner was such that he was asked to address the Court of Aldermen in order to rebuke them for various disloyal reports and complaints on the manner of the duke's attainture. He returned to the same court, four days later, and remonstrated with the aldermen again. It is reminiscent of the scene in his own history of Richard III when, ironically, the previous Duke of Buckingham had spoken in favour of the king before the citizens at Guildhall; on that occasion 'the people began to whisper among themselfe secretely'.[17] These were not the only occasions when More was obliged to censure or rebuke the City authorities, but he nevertheless remained the 'specyall lover and ffrende in the Busynesses and Causes of this Citie'.[18]

He was a friend in the cause of Wolsey's foreign policy, too, and less than a year after his last visit he returned to Bruges. He stayed at the court of the Counts of Flanders, the Princenhof, although in earlier correspondence with Francis Cranevelt he had been enquiring about the rental of a private house with eight or ten beds – which suggests that he travelled with a relatively large retinue. Once again he was involved in wearisome dealings with the Hanseatic merchants, but he was also required to attend important business elsewhere. Before the negotiations had been completed, he rode to

Calais and joined the entourage of Cardinal Wolsey. His presence had been urgently requested by the king, who, in a letter to Wolsey on the subject of his 'grette affayris', 'desyrith Your Grace to make Sir Wyllyam Sandys, and Syr Thomas More, priveye to all such matiers as your Grace schall treate at Calice'.[19] They were serious matters indeed. Wolsey had travelled to Calais ostensibly to resolve the burgeoning conflict between Francis I and Charles V; king and emperor were already vying for territory, and whoever was deemed the aggressor would thereby have violated the Treaty of London and instigate English military action against him. But Wolsey had come with an ulterior motive; it had already been decided that, under the cover of negotiations, he would arrange a secret treaty with Charles V against France which would eventually result in a joint invasion of that country. These were the 'grette affayris', involving dissimulation and double-dealing, in which More was to participate.

More returned to Bruges with Wolsey in the middle of August 1521, and here the covert discussions with Charles began. In *Utopia* the character of More argues that the royal servant's duty is to lend good advice in order to guide affairs, tactfully and carefully, towards the honourable course. Raphael Hythlodaeus dismisses this as wishful thinking and suggests that a wise counsellor will simply be used as a disguise or cover for the wickedness and folly of others. It is impossible to be sure whether this was the situation in which More found himself at Bruges, but the evidence suggests that he was a willing or at least not unwilling accomplice in Wolsey's designs. It was his obligation to obey the commands of his king, after all, and no one possessed a stronger sense of duty. Yet there is no reason to suppose that he believed his masters to be acting foolishly or wickedly. There was always a strong possibility that Wolsey would be able to arrange a truce between the two warring parties. His Treaty of London had, in any event, maintained peace for almost three years; it was the French themselves who, in the spring of 1521, had begun offensive action. More was not always favourably inclined towards that nation, as some of his Latin verses demonstrate, and he may not have been so naturally or instinctively predisposed to peace as, for example, Erasmus. Erasmus belonged to no country; More was always a Londoner and Englishman. To enter a secret alliance with the emperor, which would be put in action if the negotiations failed, could well have seemed the most effective way of curtailing French power and thereby securing a prolonged peace.

More remained in Bruges after Wolsey's departure in order to continue the negotiations with 'the bodye of the Haunz';[20] there were the usual delays and prevarications and it seems that he left the city before any composition of the various disputes had been arranged. He rejoined Wolsey in Calais at the end of September and in the middle of the following month was despatched to England with 'urgent causes of consideration' to be delivered 'by word of mouth' to the king. It was a period of French military success and Wolsey was confronted by demands from Francis I to which he could not accede. He found time in his message to Henry, however, to commend More's 'laudable acquittal and diligent attendance'.[21] More may have been too assiduous, since on his return he immediately lapsed into a tertian fever and suffered three or four 'fittes'.[22] He experienced the strangest symptoms, too, feeling himself to be 'hott & cold' all over his body at the same time, and his doctors could prescribe no certain remedy. But then his adopted daughter, Margaret Giggs, remembered reading of his condition in Galen's *De Differentiis Febrium*, and eventually a remedy was found; with the help of his highly educated 'school', he had recovered by the middle of November.

There had been lighter moments in his long mission away from home. He had taken with him his household fool, Henry Patenson, 'a man of knowen wysdome in London and almost euery where ellys',[23] as More put it with a tincture of irony. More tells one story of him that provides an authentic vignette of late medieval city life. In Bruges it soon became apparent that Patenson was a 'man of specyall wytte by hym selfe and vnlyke the comon sorte', and some of the citizens (no doubt mainly children and apprentices) began to throw stones at him. Patenson gathered up the stones and then stood upon a bench, angrily proclaiming that everyone should leave the scene except those that had hurled the stones at him – then, he said, he could fire back at his known enemies. Unfortunately he had spoken in English and no one had understood what he meant. So the good people of Bruges merely laughed at him and began to stone him again. Whereupon he threw some back in retaliation, and broke the head of an apparently innocent bystander. Patenson went up to the man and asked him to bear his injuries bravely, because he had been given fair warning.

There was also the episode of 'Dauy a douche man',[24] whom More had retained and who 'wayted vpon me at Bruges'. He had told More that his English wife had died at Worcester two years before and recalled 'his bytter prayours at her graue'. More relayed this touching information to his wife and, on the day Davy was to marry for the second time, a letter arrived from Alice in London. She informed More that the supposedly dead and buried Mrs Davy was alive and had come to Bucklersbury searching for her errant husband. More summoned Davy, about to commit bigamy, and read out the letter to him. The rest can be put in More's words.

'Mary, mayster, that letter sayth me thinke that my wyfe is a lyue.'

'Ye beste, that she is.'

'Mary, then I am well a payed, for she is a good woman.'

'Ye, but why art thou such a noughty wreched man, that thou woldeste here wedde a nother? Dyddest not thou say she was dede?'

'Yes mary, men of worcester told me so.'

'Why, thou false beste, dydest not thou tell me and all my house that thou were at her graue thy selfe?'

'Yes mary, so I was. But I could not loke in, ye wote well.'[25]

The conclusion of this episode is not known, but More would have loved this kind of sharp retort. There is one last story from his residence at Bruges, which has often been cited as an example of More's own quickness of wit. A member of the emperor's court put up a notice, stating that he would dispute with any member of the English delegation on matters of law. More promptly published his question for debate – '*An averia capta in withernamia sunt irreplegiabilia?*',[26] which can be translated, equally unfathomably, as 'Can cattle captured in withernam be irrepleviable?' It is a highly technical question about the distraint of livestock in legal proceedings, and of course the putative disputant was quite unable to respond to the challenge. As a result he became an object of ridicule. Or so the story goes. But there is no reason to believe that a Dutch doctor or jurist would not have understood the concept of 'withernam'; it may be that More posed the question because it had some bearing on his negotiations with the Hanseatic merchants, and was thus embarrassingly unanswerable. In either case it demonstrates that superior sarcasm which he could readily deploy. It may have been in these somewhat combative circumstances that More defended his native language. Ambassadors from various countries had been praising their own tongues and condemned English as the worst.

More challenged them to utter a sentence in their own language, which he then perfectly imitated. 'Now I will speak but three words, and I durst ieopard a wager that none here shall pronounce it after me.' The phrase was 'Thwaits thwackt him with a thwitle'.[27] Who else but More could say it?

By the time he had recovered from his fever he was involved in early preparations for the war with France. In the spring of 1522 Wolsey ordered a great survey of the financial as well as military resources of England, while at the same time More was concerned with the internment of French enemy aliens. Charles V arrived in order to consolidate the treaties between himself and Henry, and at the beginning of June both men were met in London by 'diverse pagents', with the crafts standing in the array of their liveries and 'the freers, priestes, and clerkes, standinge in copes, with crosses, sensures and candlesticks'[28] all the way from London Bridge to Cheapside. More was chosen by the City authorities to deliver 'an eloquent Oration'[29] in praise of the two monarchs and in celebration of the 'comfort it was to their subjects to see them in such amity',[30] for which service he was granted £10 for the purchase of a velvet gown. Warfare was about to begin, but there was another and perhaps more dangerous enemy with whom More was soon to be engaged.

XXI

I Am Like Ripe Shit

WHEN Martin Luther proclaimed his theses at Wittenberg he was announcing, too, the triumph of his own self-awareness. The era of Protestantism, as it has been called, was inaugurated by the drama of one man's spiritual torment. It began when a bolt of lightning hurled him to the ground and, as he lay prostrate in the thunderstorm, instilled in him a great fear. 'Help me, St Anne!' he called out. 'I want to become a monk!'[1] Stefan Zweig described Luther as 'the only genuinely dramatic nature in German history', and the episodes of his religious reawakening have all the lurid emotionalism of that moment when, while participating in the Mass, he fell to the floor of the choir and raved as if in the grip of demonic possession. '*Non sum!*' he cried out. '*Non sum!*' It is not clear whether, in his frenzy, he spoke in German or in Latin; in English we may take it to mean 'I am not' or 'I am not present'. His was a character doomed always to live in lightning. In that respect he is strangely similar to another great German visionary, Jakob Boehme, the cobbler from Upper Lusatia who saw a vision of the universe in the sunlight reflected upon a pewter dish. Boehme was reviled and rejected by the burghers of the German cities, but his essential message remained intact 'to show how man may create a kingdom of light within himself'.[2] The spirit of Luther's writing, too, with its reliance upon paradox and dramatic conflict as well as its attentiveness to the whole struggling process of human becoming, anticipates the style of such German philosophers as Hegel and Heidegger.

Yet how different Luther was from Thomas More; they might even be cited as the two great figures representing the 'medieval' and the 'modern' worlds. Luther disobeyed his father completely and irrevocably, while More remained the model of filial piety. Luther abandoned the law in order to enter a monastery, where More had forsaken the Charterhouse for Lincoln's Inn. More moved easily within any institution or hierarchy to which he became attached; Luther was seized by violent fits of remorse and panic fear in any fixed or formal environment. It is hard to imagine More screaming out '*Non sum!*' during the Mass. More obeyed and maintained all the precepts of the law; Luther wished to expel law altogether from the spiritual life. More believed in the communion of the faithful, living and dead, while Luther affirmed the unique significance of the individual calling towards God. More believed in the traditional role of miracles; Luther saw visions. More's irony and detachment were very different from the intense seriousness and self-absorption of Luther. Yet one characteristic was held by them in common, even if it served only to embitter and inflame their dispute; as Luther confessed, 'he heard God's voice in his father's words'.[3] If one were to write the psychopathology of the Reformation, one might begin by examining the different reactions to that paternal voice as exemplified in the careers of Luther and More.

Luther's final revelation came to him in the Tower Room of Wittenberg, where a verse of St Paul led him ineluctably to the doctrine of justification by faith alone. It was at this point, of course, that he involved the world. The history of the events which led directly to the publication of Luther's ninety-five theses is well known; but his central assault upon the role and privileges of the Church was only just beginning and, three years after the events at Wittenberg, he published three pamphlets which entirely changed the religious discourse of the period. In the summer of 1520 appeared *An Appeal to the Christian Nobility of the German Nation*, in which he urged the temporal powers to lead and guide their communities outside the Roman jurisdiction. Three months later he published a short treatise, *Concerning the Babylonish Captivity of the Church*, in which he attacked the sacramental system of the Catholic faith and insisted that the gospels lent their authority only to baptism, confession and communion. His last and shortest work in this year of invective was entitled *On the Liberty of a Christian Man* and provided a succinct if startling account of his speculations on faith, free will and good works – with the doctrine that true freedom can be obtained by faith alone. Man receives grace through divine mercy, vouchsafed by faith, and good works do not earn merit or salvation. With the publication of these three pamphlets Luther lost the sympathy of those, such as Erasmus, who had seen him as a possible ally. He had gone too far in his attack upon the Church's authority, and its sacramental system, to be considered a humanist reformer. Pope Leo X issued a bull threatening excommunication, *Exsurge Domine*, which Luther publicly burned in Wittenberg together with some books of canon law. This has been taken by many historians to mark the first moment of the Reformation. Then, in January 1521, Luther was solemnly excommunicated and *ipso facto* damned.

The ecclesiastical authorities in England were already aware of the Lutheran heresies; there were reports, indeed, that Lutheran doctrine was being disseminated among the students of Oxford and Cambridge. Cuthbert Tunstall had written to Thomas Wolsey from Worms, where Luther publicly defied both pope and emperor, imploring him to forbid the importation of the heretic's books into England 'lest thereby might ensue great trouble to the realm and Church of England'.[4] The king himself took a central role in combating the new heresy; in 1518, the year after Luther had promulgated his ninety-five theses, Henry had started work on a book condemning the message of Wittenberg but he had never completed it. In the opening months of 1521, in the full glare of Luther's defiance, Henry set to work again upon a treatise in defence of the Seven Sacraments entitled *Assertio septem Sacramentorum adversus Martin. Lutherum*. It was a reply to the second of Luther's pamphlets, published in the previous year, and set a royal seal upon the attempts of the English clergy to extirpate the teachings of the erstwhile monk. It is not at all certain that Henry himself composed every word, but it is not beyond the bounds of possibility that he wrote most of it; he was a good Latinist and a not uninformed theologian. It is more likely, however, that arguments and materials were suggested to him by divines such as John Fisher and Edward Lee; at some point the papers were given to Thomas More for perusal, and he described his role as that of 'a sorter-out and placer of the principal matters contained therein'.[5] He put the book in order, therefore, but he also offered comments of his own; he advised the king, for example, to subdue his enthusiasm for papal primacy 'and his authority more slenderly touched'.[6] The king refused to do so in an exchange which, a few years later, would take on a darkly ironic aspect. On 12 May 1521 Thomas Wolsey walked in stately procession to the churchyard of St Paul's, where, in front of a crowd numbering some thirty thousand according to one contemporary account, the books of Luther were ritually despatched into the flames of a great bonfire. John Fisher delivered a sermon on the pestilence of the new opinions, and Wolsey held in his hand the unfinished manuscript of the king's own polemic against Luther. Catholic England had responded with horror and outrage to the reformer.

When Henry's book was completed it was presented to Pope Leo X, with a solemn oration professing that there was 'no nation which more impugns this monster, and the heresies broached by him';[7] the pontiff deemed it good and rewarded Henry, 'this great Prince', with the title of *'Fidei defensor'*. Martin Luther was not slow in presenting his opponent with a less welcome gift; he wrote a diatribe against Henry and, in defence of his own beliefs, did not scruple to describe the king as a pig, dolt and liar who deserved, among other things, to be covered in excrement.[8] Thomas More, as councillor attendant and royal servant, now entered the imbroglio. John Fisher was already composing a grand theological tract against Luther, but More was given a simpler task. He was ordered to reply on behalf of his master in the same vitriolic terms, trading text for text and insult for insult. It was a role not necessarily to his taste and he went to elaborate lengths to concoct pseudonyms for this *Responsio ad Lutherum*. He created a sub-plot in which the author of the book was a Spanish scholar, horrified by Luther's insolence and impiety; but some months later he altered his plan and the writer of the *Responsio* was named as 'Gvilielmvs Rosseus' or William Ross. There were various prefatory letters to add substance and detail to this subterfuge, which seems to have been designed only to shield Thomas More. Could the celebrated exponent of the new learning admit to composing what one eighteenth-century divine called 'the greatest heap of nasty language that perhaps was ever put together'?[9] Could a prominent royal servant and diplomat be revealed as 'having the best knack of any man in Europe at calling bad names in good Latin'?[10] It was not to be thought of.

More began *Responsio ad Lutherum* in February 1523, six months after Luther's assault upon the king had been published. He wrote a first version quickly – perhaps within six weeks – but then revised, and added to, a final draft which was published at the end of the year. The delay in publication may have been for political as well as stylistic reasons; there was talk of Luther recanting, of Erasmus launching an attack upon him and of the emperor controlling his unruly subject. More profited from the delay by consulting with a

German monk recently arrived in London, Thomas Murner, who was thoroughly acquainted with Luther's opinions. It has even been suggested that Murner wrote some of the *Responsio*, but this is highly unlikely. That he inspired particular passages, however, is certain. More also took the opportunity of clarifying his own opinions on the nature of the Church and of the papacy, and of re-evaluating the traditions of his faith in order properly to defend them. One long addition to the first version of *Responsio* marks an advance in More's ecclesiology that would have immense consequences for his later career. He had been discussing the matter of papal primacy with his Italian friend Antonio Bonvisi, and had at first argued that the papacy was 'inventyd of men and for a polytical ordre, and for the more quyetnes of the ecclesiasticall bodye, than by the very ordynance of Chryste'. After some days of study and thought, however, he changed his mind. He returned to Bonvisi and admitted that he had been wrong and that the papacy was indeed of divine origin; it 'holdyth up all'.[11] This was the rock upon which More would eventually be wrecked.

So his attack upon Luther was now consistent and complete. It is in one sense a long oration in which More assumes the role of a forensic lawyer pleading his case to jurors – '*Quaeso te lector . . . Ecce lector . . . Redeo lector . . . Audisti lector*'.[12] Much of the text consists of passages from the *Assertio* of Henry and the replies of Luther, interspersed with More's severe and caustic commentary. On the opening page, for example, he excoriates Luther's first and perhaps gravest offence in attacking the king himself '*nullius ordinis habita ratione*', without any respect for rank.[13] Yet there are other connotations; '*ordo*' signifies class or rank, but it can be taken to mean order, methodical arrangement, regularity and propriety. In the course of the *Responsio*, More suggests that these were also the objects of Luther's scorn and hatred. There is a wonderful letter by Luther, in which he celebrates a sudden vision of 'the sky and the vault of the heavens, with no pillars to support it, and yet the sky did not fall and the vault remained fast. But there are some who want to see the pillars and would like to clasp and feel them.'[14] Thomas More was one who needed pillars and the security of an ordered world; he spoke and argued as a lawyer, but in the *Responsio* he also introduces the concept of law as the defence against disorder and chaos. '*Vna est ecclesia Christi*',[15] he wrote, and that one church is guided by the workings of the Holy Spirit; it is the manifest, visible and historical faith of 'the common knowen catholic church' whose sacraments and beliefs are derived not only from scripture but also from the unwritten traditions transmitted by generation to generation.

What is it that Luther wrote? '*Hic sto. Hic maneo. Hic glorior. Hic triumpho.*'[16] Here I stand. Here I remain. Here I glory. Here I triumph. It does not matter to me if a thousand Augustines or Cyprians stand against me. It is one of the great moments of Protestant affirmation and became a primary text for the 'individualism' and 'subjectivism' of post-Reformation culture, but to More it was '*furor*' or simple madness. Only a lunatic, or drunkard, could express himself in such a fashion. More invoked, instead, the authority of the apostles and the church fathers, the historical identity and unity of the Catholic Church, as well as the powerful tradition of its teachings guided by the authority of Christ. Where Luther would characteristically write 'I think thus', or 'I believe thus', More would reply with 'God has revealed thus' or 'The Holy Spirit has taught thus'. His was a church of order and ritual in which the precepts of historical authority were enshrined. All this Luther despised and rejected. He possessed the authentic voice of the free and separate conscience and somehow found the power to stand against the world he had inherited. He was attacking the king and the Pope, but more importantly he was dismissing the inherited customs and traditional beliefs of the Church itself, which he condemned as '*scandala*'.[17] He was assaulting the whole medieval order of which More was a part.

There is one other instructive comparison. It is often said that those whom we hate most are those whom we most resemble, and there is a sense in which Luther and More are true counterparts. In particular Luther's early obsession with ascetic practices and his frantic reactions to the monastic life provide an exaggerated caricature of More's own early conduct. It might even be claimed that the force of Luther's piety and the almost elemental power of his nature took late medieval Catholicism to its limits – and thereby destroyed the delicate balances which had sustained it. More believed that a monster had been born, slouching away from Rome, but the 'mooncalf Luther' was a creature of the Church's own making.

Under the influence of Luther, More's perspective begins to alter. The formal ironies and cultural games of his early work are abandoned and there is no more satire at the expense of foolish friars or bogus relics. There will be no more epigrams, only polemics. There will never be another *Utopia*. In fact it might be said that More forces his celebrated treatise into the real world. In *Responsio* Luther becomes a highly inflamed version of the garrulous and improbable traveller, Raphael Hythlodaeus; the German reformer is also filled with absurd fantasies, and even imagines a society of Christians who are no more than '*Platonis ideis*'.[18] But More is no longer taking part in an elaborate literary exercise; he is fighting for the life of his world, which, he believes, will otherwise be extinguished by uncertainty and doubt. The battle between the two men is like an internalised conflict between the warring selves of sixteenth-century civilisation.

And how More did rage! *Furfuris! Pestillentissimum scurram! Pediculosus fraterculus! Asinus! Potista! Simium! Improbe mendax!* Martin Luther is an ape, an arse, a drunkard, a lousy little friar, a piece of scurf, a pestilential buffoon, a dishonest liar. '*HA. HA. he, facete, laute, lepide Luthere, nihil supra . . . Hui.*'[19] The unmediated demotic speech here will be of interest to anyone who wishes to know how the educated inhabitants of early sixteenth-century London actually sounded when they spoke in Latin, but More's grasp of colloquialism went much further. Someone should shit ('*incacere*') into Luther's mouth, he farts anathema, it will be right to piss ('*meiere*') into his mouth, he is a shit-devil ('*cacodemon*'), he is filled with shit ('*merda*'), dung ('*stercus*'), filth ('*lutum*') and excrement ('*coenum*'); look, my own fingers are covered with shit ('*digitos concacatos*') when I try to clean his filthy mouth. This is not, perhaps, the normal language of a saint; but More's scatological obsessions are shared by Luther himself. 'I am like ripe shit,' he once said, 'and the world is a gigantic arse-hole. We probably will let go of each other soon.'[20] 'A Christian should and could be gay,' he said on another occasion, 'but then the devil shits on him.'[21] More suggested in the *Responsio* that Luther celebrated Mass '*super foricam*' ('upon the toilet'),[22] and indeed Luther did state that he had once been visited by the Holy Spirit on the '*CI*'[23] or cloaca.

This particular kind of imagery is to be found in the bawdier verses and fabliaux of the period. It is related to the interest in 'babooneries', too, which mark the irruption of the grotesque into the sacred. It is this tradition to which More reverts when in one passage of the *Responsio* he invokes apes, and fools, and dogs, and in another where Luther is described as an ape dressed in purple. It is the reverse world of the medieval imagination, filled with frantic symbols of fear and disorder. There are passages in More's treatise which are close to Rabelais – another monk who, like Luther, renounced his profession for literature. When More has an image of the holy eucharist stuffed with sausage meat,[24] he is close to the sensuality and spirituality of the contemporaneous French novelist who deployed the grossest types of sexual and scatological imagery.

More was a model of tact within his own family, however, and his inherent patience and forbearance became evident when his son-in-law, William Roper, began to espouse Lutheran doctrines in Bucklersbury. He allowed his daughter Margaret to marry Roper, even though the young man was at that time filled with 'Luthers newe broached religion'. When his son-in-law went so far as to indulge in 'open talke and companying with diuers of his owne sect',[25] he was summoned before Wolsey himself. The prelate released him with a 'friendly warning', no doubt because of the family connection, but Roper remained in heresy. More tried to persuade him by argument and debate, but at no point asked him to leave the household. Finally he took his daughter into the garden. 'Megge,' he told her, 'I have bourne a longe time with thy husband . . . and still geuen to him my poure fatherly counsaile; but I perceaue none of all this able to call him home; and therefore, Megge, I will no longer argue nor dispute with him.'[26] Instead he took to praying for 'son Roper', who, perhaps as a result, recanted his heresy and returned even more fervent to the Catholic communion.

It was in the context of his household, too, that More then composed one of his most powerful treatises. It is a meditation on the four last things – 'deth, dome, pain, and joy',[27] which can be translated as death, judgement, hell (or purgatory) and heaven – and remained unpublished in his lifetime, simply because it was a devotional manual for the use of his family. It is emphatically a late medieval production, displaying the true sources of More's piety in the religious practices and principles of his childhood. It is in the spirit of the skeletal effigies adorning ornate tombs, and in the manner of medieval homilies such as the *Poema Morale* and medieval sermons on death which emphasised the physical facts of human decay when a man's 'bake begynnythe for to croke downwarde to the erthe that he came of'.[28]

All of these elements are present in More's treatise, where the reader is exhorted to 'fantasys thyne own death . . . thy hed shooting, thy backe akyng, thy vaynes beating'.[29] But there are also touches which are peculiar to the adult More. In this little work, addressed to those closest to him, there was no need for pseudonym or elaborate preface; he even abandoned his customary form of dialogue and spoke forth freely. When 'the very face sheweth the mind walking a pilgrimage', as he wrote, we ask 'a peny for your thought'.[30] More's thoughts when his mind went on this pilgrimage to the gates of death were of the world itself as a vast prison, with 'some bound to a poste, some wandring abrode, some in the dungeon, some in the upper ward, some bylding them bowers and making palaces in the prison, some weping, some laughing, some laboring, some playing, some singing, some chiding, some fighting'.[31] It is an effective passage and, written at this time when he was both courtier and diplomat, it reveals his true feelings about those like Henry and Wolsey 'making palaces' in this gaol of a world. There is another connotation, too, which reflects the ecclesiology of More's reply to Luther. In the *Responsio* he celebrates the historical continuity and traditional rituals of the faith; but might that sense of an overpowering institution lead to a vision of the world itself as a prison? If you must earn merit, a proposition that Luther emphatically denied, then you must also labour. Yet, for More, this is not necessarily a dark vision. 'If we be not in spirit mery',[32] we will fail in our duty to ourselves and our neighbours; and here, once again, he recommends the proper playing of a role in this 'stage playe' of existence. Why, for example, should we 'envy a poore soule, for playing the lord one night in an interlude'?[33] So a meditation on the four last things and on this fallen world leads to joyfulness rather than sorrow; it acts as a further incentive, also, to the coherent and cheerful playing of a part on the earthly stage.

More's treatise was medieval in style as well as in theme; in returning to the piety of his London childhood, he reverts also to the techniques of alliteration which were at the centre of old Germanic prosody and which found their finest expression in England during the fourteenth century. It was the metre that More would have heard in nursery rhymes, ballads and oral poetry of all kinds. In the *Responsio ad Lutherum*, More uses a phrase which now seems as strange as alliteration itself – 'a dog, when goaded, will usually laugh'.[34] The image of a laughing dog is thoroughly medieval. It evokes those pictorial images which furnish the rich detail of ordinary medieval life; there are illustrations in which a farmer carries two wooden buckets upon a staff, a boy scares away crows, a woman spreads out a linen cover to dry in the sun. It is an art that never loses its interest, however mundane the activities which it depicts, because the ordinary world is known to be shaped by spiritual forces. There are certain phrases of More's which possess the same resonance, some of them as simple as that describing a man who 'getteth hym to the fyre & shaketh hys hatte after a shoure of rayne'.[35] He also mentions a slogan which was often chalked on London walls – 'D.C. hath no P.'[36] – and which 'toucheth the readiness that women hath to fleshly filth, if she fall in drunkeness'. Graffiti are as old as the city itself. Here are More's contemporaries '*digito purgamus nasum*',[37] picking their noses, and scratching their head, and cleaning their fingernails with a pocket-knife. And then, in the tavern, they dance. When they sing they do not say plainly 'gyf me a spade' but 'gyf me a spa he ha he ha he-hade'.[38]

There is an anecdote about More which has that same medieval note. He was sitting with his dog on the roof of his gatehouse, meditating, when a madman came up behind him and tried to hurl him to the ground; they struggled, and More suddenly cried out, 'Stay. Let us throw the dog down and see what sport that will be.' The man stopped, and threw over the dog. 'This is fine sport,' More said. 'Let us fetch him up, and try it again.' Whereupon the lunatic hurried down the stairs to pick up the animal; More fastened the door, and cried for help.[39] It is a strange story, related by John Aubrey in the seventeenth century, and is perhaps apocryphal; but it is so strange that it is hard to imagine it being invented.

The laughing dog in *Responsio ad Lutherum* might conceivably have been laughing at More since More's great opponent, Luther, has been described as 'the first Protestant at the end of the age of absolute faith'.[40] The denial of tradition in the partial destruction of the Catholic Church, together with the loss of faith in purgatory and in the living presence of the dead, strongly suggest that history itself was being forsaken; it is as if the memory of the past had to be erased before the next leap forward could be taken. The cult of the dead, so prominent in late medieval worship, was discontinued. The concept of immutable and complex law, manifest in elaborate structures and hierarchies, evinced in unwritten codes of honour, duty and mutual obligation, was gradually eroded. From the wreckage of this universal consensus emerged the sovereign state and, as Luther had so firmly asserted, individual faith or conscience.

This departure from the customs of a thousand years was part of a general dislocation of values. It can be traced in the attention to privacy in domestic life, the substitution of simple for complex spaces in religious architecture, the abandonment of canon law in the universities, the theory of national empire promulgated by Henry, the word 'state' displacing '*res publica*' or 'commonwealth'. What emerged in England was an energetic and male-dominated society of commerce and of progress, together with its own state church; it was a religion of the book and of private prayer, eschewing all the ritual, public symbolism and spectacle which had marked late medieval Catholicism. The age of More was coming to its close.

XXII

Long Persuading and
Privy Labouring

A MID the reports and preparations for war against France,
More was chosen by Henry and Wolsey to be the Speaker of
the 1523 parliament. He was formally 'elected' by the
Commons on Saturday, 18 April, though there was never any
question that he was other than a royal servant placed to charm or
cajole the members to do the king's will. It was customary for the
Speaker to be formally attached to the monarch, either as a member
of his Household or Council, and More was perhaps the obvious
choice. But here again there appears that odd motif in his public
career which is so important to any understanding of his character.
He did not seek; he acquiesced. He took on, apparently willingly and
cheerfully, the most demanding posts without any private schemes or
ambitions of his own. He was indeed the king's true servant, and was
duly appointed an MP for Middlesex before his election as Speaker.

There is an engraving (taken from a miniature) of the opening of
this 1523 parliament in Blackfriars, the house and church of the
Dominican friars stretching north from the Thames up to Ludgate;
the engraving shows the king on his dais, covered by a canopy, with
the Archbishops of York and Canterbury below the steps at his right
hand. Before him, sitting in rows, are arrayed the bishops and the
abbots, the barons and the earls. In the middle of the floor between
them the judges sit upon their woolsacks. There is a figure standing
by the bar at the very bottom of the illustration; this is Thomas
More, and beside him stand other members of the 'Common House'.
There was of course a formal ritual of petition and rejection in the
appointment of a Speaker, but in his opening address More
volunteered his own plea for freedom of speech among his fellow

members, where many who are 'boisterous and rude in language see deep indeed, and give right substantial counsel'.[1] So he urged Henry 'to take all in good part, interpreting every man's words, how uncunningly soever they be couched, to proceed yet of good zeal'.[2]

The parliament had been called to raise money for Henry's projected invasion of France, and for the cost of continual skirmishing on the Scottish border. Wolsey spoke, at its commencement, of Henry's desire to guard 'his honour and the reputation of this his realm' by keeping 'his oath and promise' to Charles V and therefore prosecuting war against his 'ancient enemy, the French King'.[3] The cardinal had exacted money in the previous year, but now demanded that a very large sum be raised in further taxes and forced loans. As the king's close counsellor and under-treasurer in charge of royal finances, More would have collaborated with Wolsey to ensure that parliament voted the king's way. Certainly, throughout the summer and autumn of the previous year, More had been deeply involved with his two employers in reporting all the preparations for war as well as transmitting news or instructions to the various parties. The first example of the combined efforts of More and Wolsey came two weeks after parliament had opened: angered by the Commons' delay and by reports of their hostility to the king's demands being 'blown abroad in every Alehouse'[4] Wolsey entered the Commons with a large retinue. Some members had demanded that he appear with only a few retainers, but More had persuaded his colleagues to allow him unimpeded access. He is said to have argued that the 'Alehouse' reports might then be believed to come from Wolsey's own servants, if they were present at the deliberations, though it is likely that he and Wolsey arranged this show of power to overawe the Commons. Wolsey berated the members for their reluctance to comply with the king's financial requests and demanded that a subsidy or tax of £800,000 be raised. More strongly supported Wolsey's demand, but his colleagues proved less accommodating; they suggested the establishment of a committee to find ways of reducing the sum, whereupon the cardinal replied that he would 'rather have his tongue plucked out of his head with a pair of pincers' than make any such suggestion to the king.[5] He then descended upon the Commons for a second time, and once more demanded the full amount. There was a 'marvellous obstinate silence' at this,[6] and Wolsey demanded replies from individuals whom he knew. 'How say you?' Still he received no answer, and finally he turned to the Speaker. More fell upon his knees and begged that his colleagues be excused, since to debate with Wolsey 'was neither expedient nor agreeable with the ancient liberty of the house'.[7] More then claimed that he could not answer for them, since he was not sure of their general conclusions upon the matter. So the deliberations were once more adjourned.

Clearly this was now the occasion for More to deploy his skills as a mediator and negotiator; by the middle of the following month the 'Common House' did finally vote a large sum of 'supplies' to the king, but not without a great deal of polemic and division. One letter from a member of that parliament throws a vivid, if indirect, light upon the conduct of More. There had been 'the grettiste and soreste' argument, 'debated and beatten xv or xvi dayes to giddir'[8] with the possibility of the parliament being completely split. Eventually, the more powerful force prevailed: those members of the Council, 'the Kings servaunts, and gentilmen, of the oon partie' were 'in soo long tyme . . . spoken with and made to sey ye'.[9] The Speaker of the Commons would have helped to 'make' them 'sey ye', perhaps, according to the letter, against their 'hert, will, and conscience'. They made up the majority of the MPs, or at least they were 'the more parte . . . assembled', and the grant was agreed. 'I have herd no man yn my lif that can remember that ever ther was geven to any oon of the Kings auncestors half so moche at oon graunte.'[10] Yet it was still not enough for the cardinal and so one of the king's servants, Sir John Hussey, Master of the King's Wards and Chief Butler, harried his colleagues into enlarging the grant – 'for the whiche,' according to Edward Hall, 'Sir Ihon Huse had muche evill will'.[11]

This had already been a long parliament, but after a recess of three weeks it met again at Blackfriars for further wrangling on grants and taxation. The burgesses of the towns accused the knights of the shires of being 'enemies to the realme', but More negotiated between them and 'after long perswadyng and privie laboryng'[12] an agreement was reached. Another member, Thomas Cromwell, complained that he had endured a parliament that had continued for seventeen weeks, in which 'we haue done as our predecessors haue been wont to doo, that ys to say, as well as we myght, and lefte where we begann'.[13] But he was not wholly right. Cromwell had been opposed to the invasion of France and had composed a long speech outlining the reasons against it, but the king had obtained the funds necessary for war. Wolsey and More, together with other of the king's servants, had been successful.

There is a story, first told by William Roper, of Wolsey berating More in York Place for failure. 'Would to God you had been at Rome, Master More, when I made you Speaker!' To which More is supposed pleasantly to have replied, 'Your grace not offended, so would I too, my lord.' He then added, equally pleasantly, 'I like this gallery of yours, my lord, much better than your gallery at Hampton Court.'[14] Wolsey is then supposed to have tried to despatch More as ambassador to the Imperial court in Spain, as a sign of his displeasure at his conduct as Speaker, but the king disapproved. It is in accord with certain other implausible Roper stories that are designed to detach More from Wolsey and all secular preoccupations. And it is reminiscent of another anecdote, which at least has the merit of humour. Wolsey is said to have rounded on More, exclaiming, 'By the mass, thou art the veriest fool of all the council.' To which More replied, 'God be thanked the king our master hath but one fool in his council.'[15] Actually, Wolsey was so pleased with More's conduct of the Speakership that he asked the king to reward him with an extra grant of £100, in addition to the conventional fee of the same amount and the various emoluments to be picked up by the Speaker in assisting individual bills, such as the one forbidding the hunting of hares when snow was upon the ground. He also became one of the collectors of the parliamentary subsidy in Middlesex. As More put it, I 'shalbe dayly more and more bounden to pray for your Grace'.[16] If there is any possible truth in the story of the conversation between Wolsey and More in York Place, it may be that it was staged for the benefit of certain people who 'overheard' it; itself unlikely, the theatrical manoeuvre would at least be in keeping with the characters of both men.

The additional payment of £100 was timely, since More was engaged in two property speculations. In the summer of 1523, while parliament was still in session, he purchased Crosby Place in Bishopsgate Street for £150. It is described in the indenture as a 'grete Tenement . . . with sellers sollers gardeyn'[17] – a 'soller' being a kind of parlour – and at the same time More bought 'ix other measuages therunto adioyning'. John Stow described Crosby Place itself as 'very large and beautiful, and the highest at that time in London'.[18] It was a truly grand house, with a great hall, a parlour known as the 'Council Chamber' and another great room known as the 'Throne Room' because of its association with that Duke of Gloucester who murdered his nephews. More had had occasion to mention it in his history of Richard III, as 'Crosbies place in Bishops gates strete wher the protectour kept his household'.[19] More purchased it from John Rest, who happened to be lord mayor of London when More was one of the under-sheriffs, and then sold it on eight months later to his great friend Antonio Bonvisi, at the considerably higher price of £200; Bonvisi, in turn, eventually leased it to William Roper and William Rastell. The reason for these elaborate transactions is not easy to guess, but it may be that More had originally bought the property on behalf of his family as well as Bonvisi. The Italian merchant may also have been paying him, indirectly, for other services rendered. In the following year More purchased twenty-seven acres of land in Chelsea for £30, and seven and a half acres of land in Kensington for £20. It was in Chelsea that his great house was being constructed; it may have been greater than even his means allowed, since in this period he borrowed more than £700 from the king himself.

Wolsey, as a token of gratitude, continued to grant him preferments. In the summer of 1524 he was appointed High Steward of Oxford University and in the following year he was given the same post at Cambridge. These were judicial and financial, rather than academic, appointments. He was involved in trying serious offenders within the jurisdiction of either university, but he was also concerned with what he described as business affairs.[20] From his enthusiastic letter of acceptance to the congregation and masters of Oxford, it is clear that he had successfully performed such services for his university in the past. On one occasion he was informed that the merchants of Oxford were charging unfair prices to the poorer scholars, and he insisted that the burgesses of that city return the money to him; he then distributed it among the same scholars. Another story concerns his relationship with the students of the time. Because he was a famous and powerful man, known for his skill in disputations of any kind, he was visited by young men from both universities. He would engage in friendly debate with them, but if they proved unequal to the task 'then, lest he should discomfort them, would he by some witty device courteously break off into some other matter and give over'.[21]

His assistance was also on a more private level when, with the approval or assistance of Wolsey, he was able to procure a readership at Oxford for Juan Luis Vives. Vives was a Spanish humanist who had been introduced to him by Francis Cranevelt during the negotiations at Bruges in 1520; he was fourteen years younger than More, but was even then working on an edition of Augustine's *City of God*. This connection would be strengthened over the next few years as Vives composed a number of treatises on themes, such as good government and the education of women, which were central to More's own concerns. Vives first came to England in 1523, and it became for a while the principal home of this young wandering scholar whose memorial stone is now to be found hidden beside a Bruges canal. More admired him and spoke ruefully of the younger man's resourcefulness and productivity. He told Erasmus that he felt very ashamed in comparison;[22] he considered himself less successful in the cause of good letters, and probably he blamed this upon his general business in the affairs of the world. Yet he could serve that cause indirectly and he asked one of his children's tutors, Richard Hyrde, to translate the treatise of Vives upon the education of Christian women. More himself then corrected it before publication. He must have been instrumental, too, in persuading Wolsey to grant Vives a readership at the newly established Cardinal College at Oxford. There is a further connection of interest. Through More's agency Vives joined the circle of pious scholars around Catherine of Aragon, who eventually entrusted her compatriot with the education of her daughter. There is an anecdote of Vives and the Queen of England, sailing by barge upon the Thames from Richmond Palace to the Bridgettine house of Syon; it was a short journey down river, but there was time for reflection. After a life of some drama and hardship, Catherine said that she wished only for a tranquil life; but if she had to decide whether to endure great fortune or great calamity, she would choose the latter as the more spiritual course. As the barge drifted towards the landing-stage at Syon, perhaps she already had some inkling of her unhappy fate.

We might then follow the ever-flowing river to Westminster, where More was at work. He regularly attended meetings of the king's council there, though much of his time was spent on various small committees established by Wolsey to promote the administration of justice. He was, for example, deputed to a special Star Chamber court which dealt with cases from Middlesex; he was a member of an inquiry into the conduct of a judge who eventually 'was deposid hys office',[23] and was appointed to various commissions attempting to control the vagrants and prostitutes of the city. It was a world he had known well during his eight years as under-sheriff of London. He also investigated the cloth trade, identified grain supplies and became the commissioner of sewers along the bank of the Thames from Greenwich to Gravesend. He still found time to assist the affairs of the City, of course, and remained highly influential there; he arranged for one of his servants, for example, to be granted the post of sword-bearer to the Lord Mayor.

But his real power and influence remained in his proximity to the king. While other courtiers waited in galleries and passages, hoping to catch the attention of the monarch as he passed, More was always beside him. A mark of his authority is to be found in his presence at the ceremony ennobling Henry's illegitimate son, Henry Fitz Roy, where More 'read out the letters patent granting the earldom'.[24] He was also the royal orator on formal diplomatic occasions, and at this time the Venetian ambassador reported him to be 'a man of singular and rare learning, and in great favour with the king and cardinal'.[25] Wolsey's proposed changes to the Royal Household in 1526, known as the Eltham Ordinances, illustrate the nature of that 'favour'. More was named as one of the four counsellors obliged to attend 'what place so ever his highness shall resort' with 'two of them at the least' to be in the king's dining chamber 'every day in the forenoon by ten . . . and at afternoon by two'.[26] More was also given the task of examining any petitions made to the king in the course of his travels. That these ordinances were never employed does not affect the obvious esteem in which More was held. Further evidence of his intimacy with the royal family is contained in an exchange of letters between Vives and Erasmus, in which Vives mentions that Henry and Catherine had admired the Dutch scholar's *De Libero Arbitrio* – '*non dubito*,' he wrote, they will discuss your book '*cum Moro*'.[27]

There were other discussions with Henry of a more importunate nature. After his duties as Speaker had been completed he returned to the side of the king, as his secretary, and became once more involved in the highest and most secret matters of state. For it was, now, a time of war. Much of that warfare, and the motives behind it, can be gauged from More's letters to Wolsey; he wrote at the dictation or instigation of the king, whose voice can almost be heard examining the details of the 'Great Enterprise' against France. He spoke to More of his determination to set aside Francis I, as his father had vanquished Richard III at Bosworth; he talked of 'th' Emperor' and 'the Duke of Burbone',[28] who, in the autumn of 1523, joined with him in an invasion of France. There was a great flurry of letters in

September when Wolsey and Henry agreed that 'my Lord of Suffolke' should end his siege of Boulogne and march 'in to the bowellis of Fraunce'.[29] The king had been opposed to the notion, for good practical and strategic reasons, but he allowed himself to be persuaded otherwise by Wolsey and his commanders. He insisted, however, that the country be open for 'burnyng and spoile'[30] – without 'the profite of the spoile' the English soldiers would become discouraged 'and theyre capitayns shall haue mych a doo to kepe theym from crying, Home! Home!'[31]

More's hopes for peace had now foundered. Although he speaks of it only twice in his own correspondence of this period – once to Wolsey and once to Cranevelt – it is certain that his instincts lay in that direction. Yet, when some had argued in Council that England should not intervene in the wars between the French king and the emperor, Wolsey had said that wise men took to caves when it began to shower, while the fools stayed in the open and were 'wasshed with the raine'; but when the wise men came out from their shelter, ready to 'vtter their wisdome', the fools 'agreed together against them, and ther all to bete them'.[32] France and the emperor would, in other words, one day fall upon England if Henry did not at this stage assert his strength and influence. 'I trust we neuer made warre as reason wolde,' More said later, 'but yet this fable for his parte, did in his daies helpe the Kynge and the realme to spende many a faire peny.'[33]

The siege of Boulogne was lifted and the Duke of Suffolk marched with the English soldiers towards Paris; he came within seventy miles of the city but the familiar lack of money and supplies, as well as problems of bad weather, determined that he would go no further. There were sporadic mutinous outbreaks among his men, and in the winter of that year the orders were given for a retreat to Calais. The adventure had by no means matched the triumph of Henry's predecessor at Agincourt, but it had proved that he could gain 'fre entre'[34] into the heart of France; it may have even been enough to assuage his appetite for glory. The cost of prolonged warfare was proving very high, in any case, and Wolsey's attempts to raise money were meeting severe resistance. It was at this time, then, that the diplomatic and reticent More became involved in secret negotiations with an envoy from France. In the spring of the following year a Genoese friar, John Joachim, travelled to London and stayed with Antonio Bonvisi at Crosby Place. Joachim became well known to More over the eighteen months of his stay, especially since under cover of business he had come to arrange a secret treaty between Henry and the French king. This was of course in direct contradiction to the terms of the alliance with the emperor, and so there were all sorts of covert explanations and double-dealings involved during Joachim's presence in England. In these, too, it can be assumed that More played a part. Certainly he collaborated with Wolsey in another, somewhat devious, plan. A courier, carrying letters from the Imperial ambassador to the emperor, was detained just outside London and was taken to More's house; More promptly opened the letters, read what should have been privileged diplomatic despatches, and then sent them on to Wolsey. Another courier from the ambassador was also intercepted, and the ambassador himself called before the Council to explain the nature of his missives to Charles V. These were highly irregular incidents, but relations between allies and combatants were now becoming so complicated and ambiguous that duplicity was part of the game. That was why, in this period, More wrote that all *'priuatas sollicitudines'* ('private cares')[35] were completely overwhelmed by collective disasters and concern for the public welfare.

In the early months of 1525 the battle of Pavia had set the seal upon Imperial ascendancy: the French king was captured and some eight thousand of his troops killed. But Charles V was not magnanimous in victory; there had been great official rejoicing in London on news of the defeat of Francis, yet the emperor refused to assist Henry in any further invasion of French soil. So it was time finally to change sides, and More was deputed to be one of the principal negotiators in arranging a proper truce with France. It was More, also, who signed as one of the witnesses of a final treaty in the summer of 1525. For his part in successfully concluding the new alliance, the French king (or, rather, his proxies) granted him an annual pension of 150 crowns. So ended England's active participation in warfare; Henry would not intervene militarily in European affairs for another two decades.

Throughout these years of turbulence and division More continued to work in close collaboration with Henry and Wolsey, just as he had done when he was Speaker of the Commons. He was one of the three or four people in the kingdom who realised the true direction of affairs; in particular, he knew the extent to which Henry and Wolsey were playing devious games in order to protect England's position in European matters. Perhaps this is reason enough to explain his involvement in various dubious strategies: he was genuinely concerned that the safety and honour of his country be protected. Of course he preferred peace to war, and he may have believed that Wolsey's policy was designed to create peace. And, if modern historians are to be trusted, he may well have been correct in that belief. Whether More was an active maker of policy or a particularly brilliant counsellor who obeyed the orders of his superiors as a 'bounden duty' cannot now be established, although the available evidence suggests the latter.

Some of that evidence emerges in the period when More was engaged in negotiations with the French ambassadors. An envoy who had been sent on a parallel mission to Spain, Sir Richard Wingfield, died in Toledo in the summer of 1525 from a fever. Wolsey learned in August that 'it hath pleased Almighty God to call Mr Wingfield out of this present life'.[36] One of the posts which Wingfield had held was that of chancellor of the Duchy of Lancaster and, later in the year, it was offered to More; he in turn resigned the office of under-treasurer, which was granted to Sir William Compton. A smaller duchy appointment, also previously held by Wingfield, was given to Sir William Kingston; but it is a measure of More's influence that William Roper, one of the More household, became Kingston's deputy.

The post of chancellor of the Duchy of Lancaster was not an ancient one, having been established in the early fifteenth century to protect and preserve the income from royal lands, but it was important; in the reign of Elizabeth it was described as 'one of the most famous princeliest and stateliest pieces of the Queen's inheritance'.[37] The estates of the duchy lay in Lancashire, Yorkshire and Staffordshire, as well as in Kent and parts of London itself; there were also some thirty or forty livings within the gift of the chancellor of the duchy and his salary has been reckoned at £160 (with various additional unknown sums).[38] In no sense, then, was this a demotion of More at the behest of a jealous Wolsey, as previous biographers have suggested. Since More possessed greater independence and judicial authority in this new role, it might even be considered a promotion as a result of his successful negotiations with the French earlier in the year.

His first responsibility was to preside in the Court of the Duchy Chamber, in an upstairs room of Westminster Hall, and for the next four years he heard cases of trespass, theft, arson, tolls, elections and murder, as well as the various suits over the ownership of land. 'In ffull humble wyse Complanynge', the clerk of the court at Wigan testified that one defendant in an action for debt had seized the records of the court and 'Threst them' into the eyes of the clerk. Then, 'contenuynge in hys ungracyus fury Tok a gret Staf in hys hande . . . and said that yf eny of them ull come nere hym that he should Brayn them'.[39] More ordered him to appear before him at Westminster. A farmer of the king's coal mines in Burnley complained that about eighty tenants, pleading ancient rights, 'brake and hewed in pieces' the coal beds there.[40] One defendant argued that they had used no violence and carried no weapons except those that 'had staves with them as they used when going to Church, for it was a procession day in "gange" week'.[41] It was the day to walk the bounds of the parish, but such a pious excuse did not conciliate More; commissioners were sent to investigate the matter and, over a year later, he gave the judgment. 'Memorandum, it ys ordered that every of the persones above namyd shall pay to the kynges farmor ii s iii d for every fother [or cart-load of coal] above expressid.'[42] It is signed in More's own handwriting 'Thomas More, knight'. He also wrote memoranda to himself on matters of law, he questioned individual petitioners, brought patent books into the Duchy Chamber 'by his own hand',[43] and on one occasion 'callythe hastily for the sute of the obligaceion therffor'.[44] Eminently practical in his conduct of the court, energetic and conscientious as ever, More was becoming the greatest administrator of his generation.

It was in his more general capacity as royal counsellor that he led a raid upon the Steelyard in the early weeks of 1526. This was the home of the Hanseatic merchants, where they lodged and kept their stocks of grain, or wax, or linen; it was situated by the river, with a stone gate of three arches facing Cousin Lane and a wooden crane by its landing-stage. It was a Friday evening, and the merchants were about to sit down for dinner in their hall when Thomas More, together with councillors or noblemen and their armed retainers, burst upon them; the keys of the door were taken and the hall closely watched. More then rose to address them, and from contemporary accounts it is possible to furnish the details of his speech. 'There is no need to be alarmed at our coming here. We have been sent by the Council and by his grace the lord cardinal. You know that one of your number has lately been imprisoned for clipping the king's coins. We of the Council would not be highly concerned about this matter, but we have received reliable news that many of your number possess books by Martin Luther. We are also informed that you import these books and so cause great error in the Christian faith among his majesty the king's subjects.' After he had finished speaking he ordered that three named merchants be immediately arrested, and demanded that a list of all others be brought to him early on the following morning. On that next day he returned to the Steelyard and asked for any Lutheran books on the premises to be given to him; the chambers of the merchants were then thoroughly searched. Eight of their number were taken to Westminster and brought before Wolsey, who lectured them severely and forbade any member of the Steelyard to leave England within the next twenty days.

More had invaded the Steelyard in order to uphold a 'monition' issued by the Bishop of London fifteen months before; Cuthbert Tunstall had forbidden the publication or importation of any book containing Lutheran doctrines. But they were not to be extirpated easily and at the end of 1525 a doctor of divinity, Robert Barnes, preached against the worldly wealth and power of the Church. He was promptly accused of heresy and brought to London for trial. By the second month of 1526, Barnes and four of the German merchants were brought to St Paul's on 11 February and forced to kneel in the aisle with faggots tied to their backs; Wolsey presided over the Mass and John Fisher preached a mighty sermon against the new heresies. He was not easily heard, however, 'for ye great noyse of ye people within ye church'.[45] The guilty men were then conducted to Paul's Cross in the precinct of the church, where, despite heavy rain, they threw their faggots into the flames of a large fire; these bundles of wood were a potent symbol of the death they might have endured in Smithfield. At the same time volumes of Lutheran doctrine were also despatched into the flames.

It is clear that More was closely involved in the detection of heresy; as High Steward of Oxford and Cambridge universities, also, he must have been particularly vigilant about its dissemination among the scholars; there were official 'visitations' of both Oxford and Cambridge, when certain men were interrogated and certain rooms searched, but they proved inconclusive. He is also likely to have been involved more directly in the battle against Luther. In the summer of 1526 Henry wrote a scathing answer to a somewhat apologetic letter from the famous heretic, but the king's response is couched in terms so close to the vocabulary and arguments of More that it might well be More's own work. When Luther is accused of encouraging 'a bold lyberte of leude lyueng',[46] for example, the alliteration and sentiment are identical with those of *Responsio ad Lutherum*. More suffered a minor embarrassment, however, when his own daughter's translation of Erasmus's *Treatise of the Paternoster* was brought before the Vicar-General; its publisher had neglected to show or 'exhibit' it to the ecclesiastical authorities, and so was technically at fault. It was wholly a production of the More household; Margaret Roper had translated the work and the tutor Richard Hyrde had contributed a preface. Within a few weeks of its withdrawal from sale, a second edition was issued; this contained the arms of Cardinal Wolsey, as well as the legend *'cum privilegio a rege indulto'*. More had acted swiftly.

Despite the precautions, Lutheran tracts continued to find their way into England – often by being smuggled in the goods of Antwerp merchants. In the autumn of 1526 Cuthbert Tunstall felt obliged to issue a second and more solemn 'monition' against heretical literature; in particular he inveighed against Tyndale's translation of the New Testament, which had been published in Worms at the beginning of that year. The book had reached London soon after and was being distributed privately. Robert Barnes, who had recanted publicly at Paul's Cross and who was still kept under house arrest in an Augustinian friary, sold a copy of it to some Lollards for 3s 2d. This was what Tunstall denounced as the 'pestiferous and pernicious poison, dispersed in our diocese of London'.[47] In the following year he gave More permission to read, and keep, heretical volumes so that More might be able to respond to them with books of his own.

In fact More was already at work, fighting a polemical campaign against heresy which would last for the rest of his life. A short Lutheran tract by John Bugenhagen, entitled *Letter to the English*, had found its way to its addressees at the end of 1525; almost at once More produced a sharp reply. This was not some private decision, however; it is clear that he and Tunstall worked closely together in the attempt to expunge Lutheran doctrine, with the king and cardinal also playing a prominent role. That is why More's *Letter to Bugenhagen* was never published; it was superseded by the king's own letter to Luther. But More's unpublished piece of polemic has peculiarities of its own. It was apparently written under the guise of anonymity, but there is nothing generalised about the attack. More truly believed Lutherans to be *'daemonum satellites'* ('agents of the demons') who must, if necessary, be destroyed by burning.[48] Already, in these early days of English heresy, he was thinking of the fire. It is a measure of his alarm at the erosion of the traditional order that he should, in this letter, compose a defence of scholastic theology – the same scholasticism which in his younger days he had treated with derision. This was no longer a time for questioning, or innovation, or uncertainty, of any kind. He blamed Luther for the Peasants' Revolt in Germany, and maintained that all its havoc and destruction were the direct result of Luther's challenge to the authority of the Church; under the pretext of '*libertas*' Luther preached '*licentia*',[49] which had in turn led to rape, sacrilege, bloodshed, fire and ruin. He also denounces Luther for marrying a nun. This was truly the whoredom of Babylon, and there is almost a lubricious note in his description of his opponent's behaviour. Luther '*volutatur incestu*' and '*clunem agitat*';[50] he writhes in incest and wriggles his bum even as he preaches on virtue. In More's writing hatred and anger are never far from sexual or scatological imagery.

How close such imagery was to the surface of his life is evident in two other works of this period. Both emanate from the More household and both are touched by a licentious humour that is not normally associated with the calm piety of that family. *A Hundred Merry Tales* was published in 1526 by John Rastell, More's brother-in-law, and it is believed to be largely the work of More himself; he had already written 'Meri Gestes' in his youth, and this production bears the marks of his humour. *The Twelve Mery Jests of Wyddow Edyth*, published in the previous year, springs directly from the household. It is partly set within the More family, and is purportedly written by one of More's servants; it is possible that this somewhat lascivious poem is also the work of More, who as royal counsellor could hardly append his own name to it. It is the story of a bawdy old party, Edith, who manages to extort money from men by pretending to be a widow of means. She purported to be of 'great inheritaunce' and 'mouable substance not a lyte',[51] thus touching upon a central preoccupation of the period. The narrative of her twelve adventures is humorous enough, with moments of vernacular which still light up the page:

> Then fare wel, honycombe, til I se you againe
> God be with you, and shield you from the raine.[52]

During her tenth adventure she arrives at the More household where she 'deceiued three yong men . . . that were seruants to Syr Thomas More'.[53] There were candles in the chamber where she stayed, and an attendant 'tymbred her fyres'; another servant stood behind her at dinner, dispensing malmsey and ale. In these affluent surroundings she once more starts work. She tries to beguile one young servant with tales of her wealth, and then resorts to direct action.

> Therwith she imbraced him: be mery, sweet hart;
> She turned her arse in his lap, & let a great fart.[54]

This sets the scene for the rest of the story; her duplicity is discovered and, as a revenge, the servants secretly feed her 'Pouder Sinipari' which gave her strenuous and abnormal diarrhoea. At which point, still in the household, she is placed in chains for three weeks where her distress was no doubt unabated. These mishaps not only presage More's later treatment of heretics, but they also provide that strange combination of scatological imagery and repressive control which seems to be related to More's own sardonic humour. One other detail has not yet been mentioned, but it is important. Edith had travelled to Battersea before beginning her tenth adventure and was rowed in a wherry across the river:

> At Chelsay was her arrival
> Where she had best cheare of all
> In the house of Syr Thomas More.[55]

XXIII

Thy Foolish Face

A drawing of the More family at Chelsea, by Holbein, survives still. It is a preliminary sketch for, or copy of, a larger tempera painting which was destroyed in the mid-eighteenth century. Another painted version was completed by an English artist at the end of the sixteenth century, but of course it is not as suggestive as the Holbein original. The principal members of the household are preparing for their devotions in a room on the first floor of the house – Elizabeth Dauncey, Margaret Giggs, Sir John More, Anne Cresacre, Thomas More, John More, Henry Patenson the fool, Cicely Heron, Margaret Roper and Alice More. They have been placed by Holbein in subtly fluent arrangement, as if to emphasise the harmony of their spiritual and scholarly discourse. They are sitting in a spacious, well-timbered and modern room, with a few touches of Holbein's pencil to suggest that there were rushes upon the floor. It is clearly meant to be an exact representation of the interior. On the left side of the drawing, against the wall, is a sideboard which has a canopy above it; a salver, a vase of flowers, a bottle and some cups have been placed there, but Holbein has also sketched a viol beside it with the inscription 'clavichord and other instruments are on the shelf'. On the wall, above the seated figure of Thomas, there hangs a weight-driven clock and pendulum. It would have possessed only an hour hand. To the right there is an interior canopied porch which leads to another room, while within the right wall is a diamond-latticed window and sill. Upon the sill are two or three books, piled against each other, as well as a salver, a candlestick and a jug.

The expressions of the sitters have a certain gravity and seriousness. Margaret Giggs leans forward to point out a passage in the devotional work she is holding but Sir John More, seeming to ignore her, gazes forward with some interior preoccupation. Thomas More sits beside him in furred robe and cap, wearing the Tudor livery chain; in the painted copy of 1590 a dog, which seems to be a spaniel, lies at his feet. Elizabeth Dauncey is pregnant; the young John More is noted by Holbein to have a 'brown' complexion of a standard London type; Dame Alice More kneels at a prie-dieu. Holbein has added a note beside her – 'This one shall sit' – so perhaps she had complained of discomfort. All the women in the drawing are dressed in the height of fashion and the room itself is evidence of wealth and learning; it is curious, perhaps, that although the sitters hold works of devotion there are no religious images upon the walls.

It is likely that the painting was commissioned to mark Thomas More's fiftieth birthday, and Holbein has taken that opportunity to create a family group worthy of Erasmus's description of it as an English, perhaps spiritualised, version of those Neoplatonic academies which had flourished at Florence and elsewhere. Holbein would have had occasion to learn of the More household in some detail from Erasmus himself, since he had painted two portraits of that scholar only two years before. More pertinently, perhaps, Holbein had already executed woodcuts for *Utopia*. The artist had arrived in England from Antwerp at the end of 1526, presumably carrying a letter of introduction from Erasmus, and it has often been suggested that he stayed at Chelsea. There is no evidence for this, except for the drawing itself, but there is confirmation of More's enthusiasm for Holbein's work; in a letter to Erasmus, he extolled him as '*mirus . . . artifex*'.[1] That wonderful artist in turn created, at the request of More, what has been described as the first great work of secular portraiture in Northern Europe. It is conceived as a record of familial history, a pictorial archive or 'tree' which reflects More's own profound sense of tradition; but it is also a study of intimate relations, touched by spiritual awareness and enlightened by knowledge.

They had come to Chelsea at some point in 1525 or early 1526; the date is uncertain because More also owned land and property in Butclose (just west of the present Royal Albert Hall), where the family might have stayed while the great house was being completed. Chelsea, or Chels-hithe, had a reputation for healthy air; Jonathan Swift stayed there two centuries later and wrote to Stella of the sweet odour of its countryside. The village was approximately two miles from the city and was approached by crossing the Westbourne river on horseback while avoiding the marshy fields and creeks which were known to be the haunts of footpads. It was also possible, of course, to travel there by means of barge and wherry; that may indeed have been one of the reasons why More chose the spot, since it was almost equidistant from the royal palaces of Greenwich and Richmond. The Thames at this point, however, was known to be particularly rough; the villagers spoke of the water 'dancing' to the sound of drowned fiddles.[2] The river itself was filled with salmon, perch, carp and so many other varieties of fish that the people along its banks characteristically earned their living as fishermen. The view from More's house on the Chelsea side, across the Thames, was of the woods and pastures of Surrey filled with wild duck and water-fowl, while beyond rose the hills of Clapham and of Sydenham. Yet London was always clearly visible, with the steeple of St Paul's rising above the roof-tops; indeed More created or preserved an 'eminence' in his garden from which the prospect was at its best. He never wished to lose sight of his own earthly city.

He purchased land in the area now bordered on two sides by the King's Road and the river, and on the other by Milman's Street and Old Church Street; there had been a farmhouse or small manor house on the site, which was pulled down to make way for More's larger dwelling of Tudor red-brick. It was grand indeed with a frontage of some 164 feet, with a porch and two bays, and two sets of casement windows on either side. Holbein described it as dignified without being overtly magnificent.[3] We may approach it in imagination, as we leave the river-side and walk through the gardens towards it; there were two gates and two gatehouses in front of us, approximately 300 yards apart, while the gardens were filled with a variety of trees and herbs and flowering shrubs. In particular there was a mulberry tree, because its name is *morus*, as well as rosemary and lilies, gillyflowers and sweet cabbage roses. There was an orchard with its apple trees and pear trees, plums and apricots and spreading vines. The house was approached by a path, with a few steps leading up to a front porch decorated with jasmine and honeysuckle. This entrance led directly to the interior, where, on the right-hand side, were wooden screens; these protected the great hall, at the eastern end of which was a raised dais where the More household ate. It was a large room, more than seventy feet in length, and rose up to the beamed and timbered roof. On the first floor, looking down into the hall, was a covered gallery with oriel windows. A door by the raised dais led to the staircase and chapel; the chapel, like the hall, could be viewed from above while the rooms on the first floor comprised the bedchambers and '*cubicula*'. The servants' quarters as well as kitchen, buttery and pantry were on the left-hand side of the house, opposite the great hall.

In the grounds of the house More also built a library and private chapel which became known as the 'new building'; there was also a gallery here, and no doubt in his library he kept a desk and candlestick so that he might work late into the night. He required a private chapel in order literally to fulfil the injunction of Thomas à Kempis that 'If thou desirest true contrition of heart, enter thy secret chamber and shut out the tumults of the world'.[4] As More himself later wrote, it is necessary for a man to 'chose hymselfe some secret solitary place in his own house as far fro noyse & companye as he conveniently can, and thyther lett hym some tyme secretely resort alone ymagynyng hym selfe as one goyng out of the world'.[5] He must fall prostrate before God, keeping in front of him 'some pitifull image of christes bitter passion', and there confess all his faults. In particular he must declare the temptations of 'his worldly frendes' and say in his heart '*Inimici hominis domestici eius*',[6] which has generally been translated as 'And a man's foes shall be they of his own household.'[7] It would have been in this private chapel, away from the eyes of his own family, that More scourged himself with a leather thong.

There was also a small village church close to his estate, which had been built in the twelfth century and dedicated to All Saints; soon after his arrival in Chelsea, More restored its largest chapel as a 'family chapel'. A gate and arch separated it from the chancel, with carved capitals on either side in an 'Italo-English' style that is reputed to be the work of Holbein. On the eastern capital have been carved More's coat-of-arms and crest, together with the date '1528', while the other bears the emblems of a holy water pail, prayer book, tapers and crossed candlesticks, which were the instruments used by More during his participation in the ceremonies. More would have prayed in the chancel while Alice More, according to the ruling of the council of Nantes, remained at her devotions within the chapel itself. The vault of the chapel was also restored, and it was designed by More to be his family's last resting place. He had the remains of his first wife transported from St Stephen Walbrook, and he composed a fine epitaph in which he expressed the wish that he and Dame Alice might one day lie beside her.

He was a frequent and active member of the little congregation, taking part in the processions and performing as an altar-server at the Mass. It seems that he even donned a surplice and sang in the choir; when the Duke of Norfolk berated him for performing such a humble role, he is reported to have replied, 'My master the King cannot be displeased at the service I pay to his master God.'[8] It may be apocryphal, but it neatly summarises the hierarchical order which he served. It is even reported that he sometimes kept the king waiting until the Mass was completed; such piety was formidable indeed. There is a story of his walking the bounds of the parish on foot, together with the rest of the congregation; he was offered a horse because of his rank as knight, but he is supposed to have answered, 'My Lord went on foot. I will not follow him on horseback.'[9] There were also occasions when, in processions, 'he would carry the cross'.[10] He walked, too, on pilgrimages to the shrines outside London; that of Our Lady of Willesden was held by him in particular veneration.

His daily routine at Chelsea did not differ significantly from that of Bucklersbury. He retired to bed at nine o'clock, and rose at two in the morning; he worked and prayed until seven o'clock in the morning, when he heard Mass before embarking upon the duties of the day. This energetic regime was sometimes mitigated by after-dinner slumber – dinner being customarily eaten at midday – but, as he wrote in the dramatic guise of one of his dialogues, 'you wote well I am not wont at after none to slepe long, but evyn a litle to forget the worlde'.[11] His diet was not so heavy, either, but consisted of the plainest fare with water; he was accustomed to eat the first dish placed before him, and nothing else. He favoured 'powdered biefe or some such like salte meate'[12] and did not, in the manner of his contemporaries, gorge upon a variety of meats and puddings, though Erasmus suggests that he did on occasions enjoy a dish of eggs or fruit. On Fridays and holy days, according to his early biographers, he spent the entire day abstaining within his private chapel. A great deal of his time was spent with the king and council, however, and the rigours of his life at Chelsea must be seen as a retreat from the cares of the world that otherwise surrounded him. His entire household joined him when he returned home to his devotions; he led them in morning and evening prayers, which included the penitential psalms and the litanies of the saints. During their meals one of the family would read a passage from the Scriptures, which would then become the subject of general conversation. If it sounds altogether pious, it should not be forgotten that the earthly mishaps of the widow Edith also occurred within the Chelsea household.

So More lived on a grand scale appropriate to his rank and position, withdrawing himself regularly in order to engage in private prayer and mortification. He described his own position accurately, when he wrote of a man 'that hath unto riches no love, but having them fall abundantly upon him, taketh to his own part no great pleasure thereof, but, as though he had it not, keepeth himself in like abstinence and penance privily';[13] such a man will employ his wealth in maintaining a true Christian household and in 'setting other folk a work'.[14] If he does this with a clear conscience and good heart, he is to be praised as much as the man who forsakes his wealth. Certainly More performed charitable works. He is reported to have visited the poorer inhabitants of the village, and given liberally of his money; when his official duties prevented him from dispensing alms, he instructed other members of the family to take his place. If he heard of a neighbouring woman beginning her labour, he would kneel down in prayer until the moment of delivery. He often invited those in need to join his family at dinner, and he brought the sick or the dispossessed into the shelter of his house. He maintained a poor widow, Paula, for example, who had lost everything in the law courts of London. It is likely that news of his charitable endeavours spread further than Chelsea: one of his earliest biographers, Thomas Stapleton, described how More eventually established a separate house for the poor, the infirm and the elderly, which in his absence was supervised by his daughter Margaret.

It was his solemn duty to act in this manner – all aspects of his life were matters of obligation. But a more private note emerges in a letter which he wrote to his wife, from the king's court, on hearing news that his barns and part of the house itself had been accidentally destroyed by fire. He resigned himself to God's will and was 'bounden not only to be content but also to be glade of his visitacion';[15] this was cold comfort, perhaps, for Alice More, who had to deal with the situation. He instructed her to take the entire household to church, 'and ther thanke God'.[16] But he also offered more worldly advice. 'I pray you to make some good enserche what my poore neyghebors have loste' and promise to reimburse them, since 'I shuld not leve my selff a spone[;] there shall no poore neghebore of myne berre no losse by eny chaunce hapned in my howse'.[17] His farm had suffered severe damage from the fire, but he ordered Dame Alice not to discharge any workers there until they had found new masters – 'I wolde not that eny man were sodenly sent away he wote nere whyther.'[18]

More sits with his family, in the Holbein drawing, his somewhat ugly hands hidden by the sleeves of his furred robe. But it is not just the portrait of a single family; it also affords a glimpse of a great network of money, patronage and power. In 1516 Alice More's daughter (and therefore More's only stepdaughter) had married a wealthy landowner, Thomas Elrington, who happened to be a cousin of More's first wife; he owned properties in Kent and Middlesex, Yorkshire and Hertfordshire, and his grandfather had been a central member of the court of Edward IV. But he was not so wealthy that he did not desire a royal appointment, and Thomas More arranged for him to be granted a position in the Treasury at the time he himself was under-treasurer. Elrington died at the end of 1523, transforming his wife into a very rich widow; in the following year she married another landowner, Sir Giles Alington, for whom Sir John More had been a trustee until he came of age. So the family associations and mutual bonds were maintained.

It was in Alington's private chapel, also, that the next set of alliances was formed. At a service in Willesden, More's two younger daughters were married in a double ceremony, for which a special dispensation had been granted; Elizabeth was joined to William Dauncey, whose father had been 'general surveyor'[19] and then a member of the king's treasury, while Cicely married Giles Heron, whose father had been the king's 'treasurer of the chamber'.[20] Heron, also, had been a ward of More. Some of the principal members of the royal household were, in other words, allying themselves in a formal manner. After his marriage to Elizabeth, William Dauncey even advanced in royal favour; he was granted two leases within the Duchy of Cornwall, under More's direct control, and in 1528 he became 'one of the tellers of the Exchequer . . . with the usual fees'.[21] In the following year both Dauncey and Heron were returned as members of parliament for Thetford; interestingly this was the only occasion in the king's reign when Thetford was represented in the Commons and, equally significantly, Thetford was part of the Duchy of Cornwall. Thomas More had simply arranged their election with the assistance of the Duke of Norfolk.

His other son-in-law, William Roper, also managed to be elected to that parliament, as a member for Bramber in Sussex. Roper was not overtly connected to the royal household, but instead he represents that other network of posts and preferments which the More household controlled; he was a lawyer, and the editor of Spelman's legal reports has described the process by which the More household and its dependants transformed the King's Bench into 'virtually a family business'.[22] John Roper and Sir John More had worked closely together in the past and, on his father's death, William Roper succeeded him as 'Protonotary' or clerk of the pleas of the King's Bench. This was an eminent and well-rewarded position, which in turn William Roper bequeathed to his own son. Primogeniture is the key to a hierarchical society. William Roper was also the grandson of Sir John Fineux, who had been until November 1525 Chief Justice of the King's Bench, and Roper's sister eventually married another Chief Justice. Other of More's relations, including the Rastells and the Heywoods, were also involved in the administration of the King's Bench. There is nothing sinister about these arrangements, however, since the King's Bench remained an authoritative and highly regarded source of law. The Ropers and the Heywoods and the Rastells, who can properly be described as 'the second More circle', were excellent lawyers and administrators who had – in the circumstances of the period – quite naturally come together and aligned themselves one with another. So at the king's court, in parliament and in the law courts Thomas More had taken up a central and highly influential role. It was said, by Erasmus, that no one became a member of the household without attaining good fortune. More also looked after his extended family in direct ways; he leased Bucklersbury to his adopted daughter Margaret Giggs, after her marriage to John Clement, and gave Butclose to the Ropers.

What, then, might they have said to one another as they posed for the Holbein drawing? Only Margaret Giggs appears to be talking in the work itself, although Sir John More is ignoring her. Anne Cresacre seems to be looking on with a faint expression of disapproval. More himself is the most calm and benign figure among them, yet his reported conversations with the members of his family were not necessarily benevolent. He was not averse to mocking the size of his wife's nose, for example, although his own was not inconsiderable. There was also the occasion when Anne Cresacre asked for a pearl necklace, and subsequently More presented a box to her. 'I haue not forgotten,' he said.[23] Inside there were no pearls, however, only a string of garden peas; it was clearly designed to instruct his daughter-in-law on the themes of pride and vanity. She 'allmost wept for very greefe'[24] but it was 'so good a lesson' that she never forgot it. The story may not be reliable, since Anne Cresacre is wearing a necklace of real pearls in the Holbein sketch, but it is certainly very like More's manner in the world. He instructed his children 'to take vertue for their meate, and play for their sawce'.[25] One of his favourite phrases in the Chelsea house, at a time of misfortune or sickness, was 'we must not looke to goe to heauen at our pleasure and on fotherbeds',[26] to which, perhaps, he appended his customary phrase, 'I assure you'. But such composure could not always be maintained; when his eldest daughter was visited by the sweating sickness he wept and prayed and vowed that, if she had died, he would 'never have meddled with worldly matters after'.[27] His love for Margaret was the most profound and significant passion of his life. He watched her grow into the most erudite woman of her age; he educated her and he trained her in virtue. He truly nurtured and cherished her female nature; there are occasions, as at the time of her sickness, when they seem even to share the same identity. Behind the calm and ironic demeanour of the man, there was a capacity for powerful and morbid feeling.

There are some other figures in the Holbein drawing who have yet to be mentioned. The briefest outline of a man can be seen in an adjoining room; he is sketched as if seated, with a window behind him, and can be taken to represent More's secretary. John Harris played the role of a confidential clerk; he took down letters to More's dictation, vetted his manuscripts and generally assisted him in the affairs of the world. According to Cresacre More, More would 'for the most parte in his greatest affaires and studies ask his man Harris his aduise and counsell; and if he thought the contrarie better, he would willingly submit to his opinion'.[28] John Harris read aloud passages of scripture during meals on holy days, and on occasions acted as his master's agent. More had an additional servant, John à Wood, who took care of personal dress and private needs. Once when Harris berated More for the state of his shoes, he replied, 'Ask my tutor to buy me a new pair.' The 'tutor' was John à Wood, and it seems that More also valued his advice highly in matters besides his appearance. He in turn looked after Wood and Harris with affection and consideration – 'we be bounden to loke to them & prouide for their nede', he wrote of his household servants, and look after them 'yf they fall sik in our seruice'.[29] There is also the story of a former servant who overheard some merchants 'slander and raile against his old maister', and immediately travelled to Chelsea in order to inform him of their false reports. More only smiled, however, and said that their arrows were of no consequence – 'so none hit me, what am I the worse for that?'[30]

Henry Patenson, the fool, is dressed fashionably in cap and robe; he has an open benign face and is gazing thoughtfully into the middle distance. His is almost a medieval presence in this modern household, since the post of resident fool dates from the twelfth century. Henry VIII had his own fool, Will Somers, whose jests and adventures are recorded in various dialogues; he called his master 'Harry' and, having made the king laugh, happily laid 'doune among the spaniels to sleep'.[31] Nothing can be further from the modern imagination than the idea of retaining a 'simple' or 'folysh' man for the amusement and edification of a family. Yet it was a role of much subtlety, since the fool was considered to be divinely blessed; in the words of St Paul, 'the wisdom of this world is foolishness with God'.[32] Erasmus, in his *Praise of Folly*, had already made it plain that the foolish are indeed wise compared to the ordinary wisdom of the world, and More seems to have been delighted when he was chided for his 'folly' by the Duke of Norfolk and ridiculed as a 'fool'[33] in Coventry. He was a fool as Socrates, and Lucian, were fools; they were the true scholars of humanity, who in their folly refused to countenance the follies of the age. When Richard Pace was criticised for wearing a fool's coat at a masquerade More is supposed to have replied, 'No, no. Excuse him. It is less hurtful to the commonwealth when wise men go in fools' coats in jest, than when fools go in wise men's in earnest.'[34]

The Fool is malleable and can play many parts, as More himself did; he can also speak the truth by means of humour. Henry Patenson was a fool by nature, whereas More was a fool by art. Someone lost a purse and set up a sign in St Pauls, 'Whosoeuer hath found a purse . . . ' More saw the notice, and put his own name beneath it. So the man hurried to his chamber and More solemnly took down the details of his name and age. 'My friend,' he said then,

'I am sorry for your loss, but I do not have your purse and I do not know where it is.'

'Why then, if it may please you, did you write your name?'

'So I may know you again another time: for if you cannot keep your own purse, you shall not keep mine.' He then gave the man forty shillings and dismissed him. The Franciscans wished to be considered as fools; to know oneself to be foolish is to avoid the sin of pride. That is why it is best to deprecate oneself and secretly rejoice that one is 'laughed down as a fole'. It is a means of avoiding the wrath of God, but it is also a way of displaying the true nature of human beings upon the earth which no furred robe of state or golden chain can conceal. That is why More maintained Henry Patenson as a permanent member of his family in Chelsea – poor Henry, who was reputed to be crazed after a fall from a church steeple. When his fool knelt in the chapel with hazel nuts on a string as a rosary, More was no doubt inclined to repeat the words of the epitaph upon one of the king's own fools named Lobe:

> And Lobe, God have mercye on thy folyshe face;
> And Lobe, God have mercye on thy innocent sowle.[35]

There is one last figure in the Holbein drawing which is worthy of notice. The artist has drawn a small monkey, tied to a chain, who seems to be clambering up the dress of Alice More. She is reading her devotional manual, and is so accustomed to the animal's presence that she pays it no attention. More is known to have kept an entire menagerie, and among his 'pettis' were a fox, a weasel, a ferret, and a monkey as well as several rabbits and birds. Erasmus noted how he loved to observe their character and behaviour, and it may be from this habit of close attention that More is able to describe the process of artificial incubation in *Utopia*; perhaps direct experience prompted his remark that newly hatched chickens follow the nearest human being. He also observed birds, of which he had many breeds, and may have been the source of Erasmus's phrase in *Colloquies* that 'they have their kindnesses and feuds, as well as we'.[36] He is without doubt the origin of that scholar's disquisition on the monkey and the weasel. When the monkey became ill he was taken off his chain, and spent some of his time watching the efforts of the weasel to seize the rabbits in their wooden cage. Finally the weasel managed to prise loose the hutch so that it was open at the back; all at once the monkey ran over to it and, climbing upon a plank, managed to restore it to its former safe position. The story appears in the *Colloquies*, also, and its lesson of primatial compassion is explicitly set in the household of Thomas More.

More sometimes employed his animals as metaphors. In particular he chose the image of the monkey to denote the heretic as 'an olde ryueled ape',[37] the devil's pet kept on a chain 'to make hym sporte, with mokkynge and mowynge'.[38] Of course More kept his own monkey upon a chain, and at the same time he imprisoned heretics within the gatehouse of Chelsea; the purpose, in both instances, is to keep a tight control of instinct and irrationality as well as evil and folly. The monkey and the fool can also be related, since in both instances More is able to contain unreason within a secure and formal setting. But what if Henry Patenson were to turn truly mad, and the ape to break its chain? This is More's vision of the world after Luther, a world about to emerge all around him.

XXIV

You Are but One Man

THERE was a moment, during certain revels at Cardinal Wolsey's palace of Hampton Court, when a band of maskers plucked off their visors and revealed their true identity. It was the third day of the new year, 1527, and one of their number was the king. The art of concealment and feigning was a memorable aspect of court entertainments in this period, whether it was expressed in allegory or in real intrigue. Disguising was a device, but it was also a necessity in a world established upon spectacle and appearance. But there was to be a true surprise later in this year, when the dancers of state paused for an instant and took off their masks. One of their company was Anne Boleyn.

She had been accustomed to such a life since her childhood, having been despatched to the French court at the age of twelve. She had returned to England at the beginning of the war against France and had been, as it were, within the king's sight for five years. He had been involved in a sexual intrigue with her sister, however, before he turned to her in the early months of 1526. During the summer of that year Catherine of Aragon was becoming apprehensive; by the winter, Henry had decided. Apparently on grounds of religious scruple, in that he had married his dead brother's wife against the injunctions of Leviticus, he had determined that his marriage should be annulled. Early in the following year Cardinal Wolsey was instructed to begin secret proceedings which would expedite the matter of annulment, but this private legatine court adjourned after two weeks at the end of May without any sentence passed. In the following month Henry approached Catherine herself with the news that they had been unlawfully married for the last eighteen years. It is said that she collapsed in tears, but there are also reports that she knew precisely what had been happening.[1] The Imperial ambassador had already been informed and the news passed to her nephew, the Emperor Charles V. It soon emerged, also, that Catherine had been instructed on issues of canon law which could materially serve her cause.

This is the moment that Thomas More entered the famous arena of the king's 'divorce'. Although he was not officially acquainted with Henry's scruples until the autumn of that year, he was in the confidence of both Wolsey and the king, when very few others were; he himself said, in a letter written at a later date, that he was aware of the king's reading of Leviticus. He may not have been formally asked to give his attention to the subject, but he knew. Yet someone was also secretly informing and advising Catherine. It may have been John Fisher, who as Bishop of Rochester became her most impressive and outspoken supporter, but it might have been More himself. He was close to her and to her entourage; he admired her piety and applauded her learning. Catherine returned his loyalty and is reported to have often told her husband that 'of all his councillors More alone was worthy of the position and the name'.[2] More knew his 'bounden duty' was to the king, however, and he is most unlikely to have acted in a manner which might anger or compromise his master. If his loyalties were divided, no courtier could have guessed the mind's construction from the face.

Holbein's memorable portrait of Thomas More was painted during, or immediately before, these spring and summer months of 1527. He is dressed as a great counsellor and wears the heavy gold chain of Tudor livery over a black velvet cloak which has a brown fur collar; beneath it he wears a doublet of red velvet, while his short dark-brown hair is firmly held within a black cap. The catalogue of the Frick Collection in New York, where the painting now resides, notes that a few strands of grey hair are also visible. On the forefinger of his left hand can be seen a gold ring inset with a bloodstone, while his right hand holds a dispatch or sheet of paper. His right arm lightly rests against a ledge of stone and there is a bright green curtain draped in folds behind him. It is being held partly open by red cords, and there is a glimpse of clear sky – or of an empty space – beyond.

In certain respects More's appearance, in this half-length portrait, resembles Erasmus's famous description of him. His complexion is fair but not pale. Erasmus describes the eyes as '*subcaesii*' or 'bluish grey',[3] although in the Holbein portrait they seem closer to a brownish grey; Erasmus also notes that the eyes were flecked or tinted in some way, yet the painting shows him to be clear-eyed. He has a broad forehead and what appears to be a somewhat short or squat neck; an eighteenth-century writer declared that his 'scull was a small one',[4] perhaps having seen the severed head in its last resting place. He was a man of middle height only – which, by contemporary standards, would make him rather short. There are wrinkles over the bridge of his nose, as well as at the corners of his eyes; surprisingly, perhaps, he has the stubble of a beard of three or four days' growth. This may be an indication of what Erasmus meant when he said that his friend had been from childhood '*negligentissimus*' in matters of dress and appearance.[5] Erasmus alluded to Ovid's *De Arte Amandi*, and in particular to a line which suggests that More's dress was not always of the cleanest: 'But let the gowne be well fittynge, and clyne wythout ony spot.'[6] Ovid also suggested that the mouth and teeth be clean and the nails without dirt, and it is to be expected that More obeyed at least those injunctions. But he wears his clothes of state with the indifference of an actor. That is why the most striking aspect of the portrait lies within the lucid clearness of the eyes.

Holbein was aware of the physiognomical aspect of portraiture, and probably was here emphasising More's acuity and sharpness of judgement. The chin and jawbone signify the active powers of the will, and in the portrait they are somewhat pronounced. The nose is large, while the lips are thin and compressed, which suggests a powerful instinctive passion that is kept in check. A sixteenth-century treatise upon Aristotle's physiognomical beliefs is also suggestive. A long nose with a tip declining slightly towards the mouth, like that of More's in the portrait, denotes a 'secretive, modest and trustworthy' character; a dimpled chin is also the token of a 'secretive' nature.[7] Of course Holbein was too great an artist to delineate in so mechanical a fashion the attributes of his sitter; these characteristics are simply the background features which remain thoroughly dependent upon his own interpretation of More. Erasmus once wrote that it would take the skill of another Apelles to do justice to his friend, but it cannot be said that Holbein has failed to do so.

There are two preliminary sketches for the completed work. In one of them More's visage is as composed and reserved as that of the portrait, but the second drawing is altogether freer and looser: he has a gentler and more benign countenance, with a slightly mournful but open gaze. There is nothing so wistful or fugitive in the painting itself. More sits in front of the half-drawn curtain, attired as a man of power, but his expression is almost unfathomable. Some have found within it traces of anxiety and sensitivity, as if he might already see his own fate unfolding before him, but others have recognised the essential cheerfulness and conviviality of the man. Some find evidence of imperiousness in the portrait, while others have discovered irony and ingenuity. He might be sad, or simply grave; or, as others have suggested, he might be about to laugh. There may be a hint of that stubbornness and severity which his religious opponents ascribed to him, but this may instead be an indication of that clever sharpness which emerged in his ironic asides. There may also be caution, and frugality, and self-distrust.

Holbein has fashioned a great portrait precisely because of these unanswered and unanswerable questions. His is a study in ambiguity and detachment, with the inscrutability of More's expression as a direct representation of his reticence and impenetrability. Holbein did not know that under the gold chain and velvet doublet More wore a hair shirt which chafed and broke his skin. But once it has been imagined there, the true value of the painting emerges. This is the portrait of a private self dressed as a public image, with the contrast between a secret inner life and rhetorical public role creating this enigmatic and inscrutable figure.

If More played no ostensible part in the matter of the king's disputed marriage during this period, he was a necessary and visible agent of Wolsey's diplomacy. The pre-eminence of Charles V had once again forced England into an uneasy embrace with France, and in the early months of 1527 More was one of the central figures in the negotiations for a new treaty. These proved successful, and he was also one of those who signed the document at the end of April. The French envoys were then invited to a tournament, followed by a great banquet and disguising at Greenwich Palace. On that same day of pomp and ceremony, 6 May, imperialist troops entered Rome and wreaked such havoc within the city that the details were not forgotten for a hundred years. Old men were disembowelled and young men castrated, women raped and tortured, children tossed onto the points of swords before being butchered. The corpse of Pope Julius II was dragged from its ornate tomb and paraded through the streets. The living pope fled to the castle of St Angelo, where he remained a prisoner. It would be tempting to dwell upon the extraordinary disparity between the magnificence of Greenwich and the massacre of Rome, but these occasions are related in much more complicated and ambiguous ways. The English king wanted the Pope to grant him an annulment of his marriage; the Pope was imprisoned by the emperor, Charles V; Francis I and Henry VIII had formed an alliance against the emperor. All the fragments of polity were in the air at the same time and Wolsey was supposed to conjure them into a shape pleasing to his master.

That is why he also needed More's assistance and counsel. It had been decided that the cardinal, with a great retinue that included More, should travel to France where he would solemnly ratify the treaty with the French king himself. Wolsey rode on a mule out of London, crossing London Bridge at the head of a large concourse before making a stately progress to Canterbury. It was an extraordinarily wet summer, and we may see them proceeding slowly through the rain. He stayed in the town for three days, celebrating Mass for various occasions – the vigil of St Thomas on 6 July and the feast day of the Translation on the seventh – always kneeling on a bench 'covered with carpets and cushions'.[8] In the second week of July they crossed over to Calais. There then ensued the whole panoply of the diplomatic process, which in its essentials was derived from an earlier chivalric age. There were the solemn entries into each town where they were welcomed by persons of 'rank and distinction'.[9] There were the set speeches and the formal presentation of credentials, public processions and ceremonial audiences, all of which were accompanied by Masses as well as more secular festivities. It was not until the beginning of August, therefore, that Wolsey arrived in Amiens, where he was greeted by the French king. Francis also greeted More and, later, Wolsey and More made a ceremonial visit to the queen mother. Two weeks after their arrival the treaty of peace was finally solemnised in the cathedral. (In that church More saw the supposed head of John the Baptist in a crystal case; he did not seem to doubt the authenticity of the relic and noted only the absence of its 'nether iowe'[10] or lower jaw.) The English envoys remained in Amiens until the end of the month, and then began their slow journey home. More himself did not return to England until late September.

Then Henry approached him. More had repaired to Hampton Court, where the king was staying, at which time 'sodaynly his Highnes walkying in the galery, brake with me of his great mater';[11] he declared that his marriage to Catherine had been contrary to the laws of the Church, of God and of nature itself. The king 'layed the Bible open byfore me, and ther red me the wordis that moved his Highnes and diverse other erudite persons so to thinke, and asked me ferther what my selfe thowght theron'.[12] The 'wordis', in translation, are these: 'Thou shalt not uncover the nakedness of thy brother's wife: it is thy brother's nakedness'[13] and 'If a man shall take his brother's wife, it is an unclean thing . . . they shall be childless'.[14] This was the first occasion upon which the matter was directly broached to More. Although he distrusted his 'pore mynd', 'I shewed never the lesse as my dewtie was at his commaundment what thing I thowght vppon the wordis which I there red'.[15] His answer could not have been wholly satisfactory, since the king ordered him to 'commune ferther' with certain royal advisors and to read a 'booke' on the need for an annulment, which was even then being compiled.

So at the king's instigation More had become publicly, if indirectly, concerned with the 'great matter' which was to dominate policy for the next five years. It involved issues of substance and of interpretation, of theological argument and diplomatic manoeuvre; it concerned precedents and statutes and bulls. Had Catherine's brief marriage to Arthur, the older brother of Henry, been consummated? Was there an 'impediment' of 'public honesty' which could set aside her union with the king? Was their child, Mary, therefore illegitimate? Was it a question of divine law that could not be altered, or of 'positive law' that might be modified? These were grave questions indeed, and More could not have been unaware that there was also the risk of king contending against pope. He said later that 'I neuer medled' in the affair, since 'the mater was in hand by an ordynary processe of the spirituall law, whereof I could litle skyll'.[16] But even if he never directly intervened in the legal process, he may have offered informal suggestions and advice. In this context it is also significant that in the autumn of 1527, and again in the following year, More's friend Juan Luis Vives returned to England in order to support and counsel the queen.

The scene is worthy of Molière or perhaps of Marlowe. Henry seems genuinely to have convinced himself that he had incurred divine displeasure by marrying his dead brother's wife and that as a result he had merited the biblical punishment of conceiving no male issue from the forbidden union. Yet at the same time he was pursuing Anne Boleyn with gifts and letters. It would not take a cynic to suggest that his desire for an annulment was prompted by sexual as well as religious reasons. But this was the point that could never be made in public. Those around Henry, including More, were compelled to enter an unacknowledged pact of silence about his motives. Catherine's whole life was being betrayed, too, but nothing could be said of that matter. The atmosphere of court had become difficult as well as delicate and those, like More, who supported Catherine of Aragon had to tread cautiously. One of the games being played was that of waiting, since they hoped that the king's attraction to Anne was nothing more than infatuation. There was, however, one further problem. There is some evidence to suggest that Anne, who had grown up in the society and culture of French humanists, already espoused what could be called a 'reformist' attitude towards church matters based upon an intense reverence for the New Testament. She was by no means a Lutheran, and was indeed much closer to Erasmus; but, in the climate of the time, her position was significant.

It is likely to have been in this period that Henry made his famous visit to More's house in Chelsea, where he walked in the gardens with his arm around his counsellor's neck. The king's affection may or may not have been genuine on that occasion, but More probably shuddered at the touch; scrupulous and reticent as he was, he would have wished to keep his distance in order to preserve his integrity. He also had doubts of a more general kind, doubts which he expressed while walking along the riverside at Chelsea with William Roper.

'Now would to our Lord, son Roper, upon condition that three things were well established in Christendom, I were put in a sack and here presently cast into the Thames.'

'What great things be those, sir, that should move you so to wish?'

'In faith, son, they be these. The first is, that where the most part of Christian princes be at mortal wars, they were all at an universal peace. The second, that where the Church of Christ is at this present sore afflicted with many errors and heresies, it were well settled in a perfect uniformity of religion. The third, that where the King's matter of his marriage is now come in question, it were to the glory of God and quietness of all parts brought to a good conclusion.'[17]

Warfare, heresy and the annulment, then, were the three concerns which moved together in More's mind. Although it would be too much to claim that he foresaw the Reformation and its consequences he had at least noticed a dangerous tendency in English policy which it was his duty to avert. At a slightly later date Wolsey himself was to speak of 'infinite and imminent perils',[18] but More had already glimpsed them. That is why his conduct over the next two years, before he was appointed Lord Chancellor, must be seen steadily and as a whole. The king had asked More to engage in further study of his 'great matter'. The central question concerned the extent of papal power and, in particular, of the ability of the Pope to waive the injunction of Leviticus. One of Henry's arguments consisted of the claim that divine law had made his marriage abhorrent to God and that no pope had the authority to abrogate that law. The Pope had, in any case, granted annulments in the past; Henry's request was not unwarrantable and there was no reason to believe that it would be denied. Papal authority was not yet at the centre of the controversy, although in the end it did become the principal issue. In a letter to Thomas Cromwell, some years later, More claimed that 'by this continuaunce of these x yere synnys'[19] he had been considering the question of 'the prymatie of the Pope'.

He had addressed the problem in *Responsio ad Lutherum*, but only in a partial fashion; he was already well acquainted with the behaviour of bad or weak popes and may at one stage have inclined towards a 'constitutional' or 'pluralist' view of church authority, with the Pope himself as *primus inter pares*. But eventually papal supremacy became for More a question of faith. It was not for him, therefore, a minor or peripheral matter. He read the New Testament, as well as the writings of such holy doctors of the Church as Jerome, Cyprian and Gregory; he also examined the records of the general councils. The conclusions he then reached after his study were those which he soon applied to all other matters of religious conscience. Papal primacy had been instituted or established 'by the corps of Christendom';[20] it was manifest through 'the general counsell of the whole body of Christendome' or the 'whole catholike church lawfully gathered together in a generall counsell',[21] which was itself governed by 'the spirit of God'. Here is the creed of a man who was guided all his life by the powers of institutions and hierarchies. He was also, as a late medieval lawyer, an exponent of customary as well as statutory law; that is why he believed in the power of the inherited traditions and beliefs of the Church. On the matter of papal primacy, in particular, it had been 'corroborate by continuall succession more than the space of a thowsand yere at the leist'.[22] In that sense it did not matter 'whither the prymacie were instituted immediately by God or ordeyned by the Church';[23] it had become a matter of consensus and authoritative tradition.

But More knew well enough the limitations of any theory. In the great debate between king and pope, for example, two forms of authority were placed in confrontation without any certain result. The Pope prevaricated, owing to the unfortunate international situation which had left him a virtual prisoner of Catherine's nephew, and there were weary months of messages and meetings. In the summer of 1528 Cardinal Campeggio had been dispatched from Rome, in order to establish a legatine court in London which would decide the matter of the king's annulment. But he did not arrive in England until the autumn, so slow was his progress, and there followed a further eight months of negotiations. The career of Wolsey seemed linked to the result of the case, however, and a 'memorandum' was drawn up for the king's attention by a noble courtier, Thomas Darcy, which declared 'that never legate nor cardinal be in England' and 'that it be tried whether the putting down of all the abbeys be lawful and good or no'.[24] Although not directly involved in these events, Thomas More remained alert to every movement and decision – the attempt to drive Catherine into a nunnery, the appointment of various scholars and lawyers to defend her in the legatine court, the sudden disappearance and appearance of significant documents, the warnings of Wolsey to the Pope that the Church in England would be destroyed, the pious if self-serving public declarations of Henry, the veiled threats to accuse Catherine of sedition, the rumours of the Pope's death which then proved to be unfounded. The fury and impatience of the king were everywhere apparent, dominating all aspects of English policy.

This was the setting for a great drama at Blackfriars, which materially affected the destruction of the Church in England and helped to decide More's own fate. The legatine court, established to assess the validity of the royal marriage, was formally opened on the last day of May 1529 in the parliament chamber of Blackfriars, while the king and queen were residing close by in Bridewell Palace; a wooden bridge over the Fleet River connected the two great establishments. The parties involved, Henry and Catherine, were summoned to appear before the court on Friday 18 June. There then followed, through that hot summer, a series of scenes and tableaux which were worthy of the attention that Shakespeare later devoted to them in *All Is True*. Two days before she was asked to appear at the

court, Catherine summoned eight bishops and the Archbishop of
Canterbury in order to declare before them that she wished to revoke
the whole matter to Rome. More did not attend this solemn meeting,
but there is good reason to suppose that he was present in the
Blackfriars court two days later when the queen delivered a formal
protest against the process she was being forced to endure. There was
further business of 'protestation' and 'appeal', so the cardinals asked
her to return three days later when they would deliver their
judgments on the matters laid before them.

A large audience of courtiers and interested parties witnessed the
events of the following Monday when Henry, Catherine and Wolsey
all appeared in the court at Blackfriars. Henry was beneath a 'cloth
of estate' and Catherine sat some distance away; before them were
the Archbishop of Canterbury and the other bishops, while on
opposite sides had been arranged their various counsels. A witness
recorded the beginning of the drama.

'King Harry of England, come into the court!'

'Here, my lords.'

'Catherine Queen of England come into the court.' She rose
without replying, according to this contemporary witness, and
walked over to the king. Then she knelt down at his feet and, 'in
broken English',[25] begged him for 'pity and compassion'. 'Wherein
have I offended you?' she asked. She went on to say that 'I loved all
those whome ye loved only for your sake' and declared that she had
been a virgin when she was betrothed to him.

The king lifted her up, but she fell upon her knees again; he is
supposed to have declared that only his love for her had prevented
him before from mentioning his doubts about the marriage and he
added that, if the legatine court determined that it was valid, he
would gladly and willingly be reunited with her. He lifted her up
again and she left the court. On such a vivid occasion it is pardonable
that contemporary observers should season their reports with a little
hyperbole, but although surviving accounts differ on the number and
order of speeches certain episodes are clear enough. Wolsey rose and
begged the king to confirm that he, the cardinal, had never been 'the
chief mover or first inventor of this matter unto Your Majesty, for I
am greatly suspected of all men herein'.[26] The king graciously
confirmed this fact, and himself delivered a speech upon the nature of
his scruples about his marriage. But there was one less benign
moment which repays attention if only because of its connection with

More. John Fisher, the Bishop of Rochester, was Catherine's counsel and supporter; he had already written to her, offering advice and encouragement, and played an altogether open part in the affair. This was precisely the role which More himself could not perform, but he supported Fisher's stance. Both men were confined to the Tower and put to death for the same cause, six years after these events, and for that reason the small incident in Blackfriars is significant. At one point in the proceedings Fisher rose and indignantly denied that he had signed a document encouraging the king to put his case to the Pope. Henry was momentarily surprised but was then heard to say, 'Well, well, it shall make no matter; we will not stand with you in argument herein, for you are but one man.'[27] And how could one man withstand the might and majesty of the king?

The court at Blackfriars was to remain in session for another month, but some three weeks before its adjournment More was obliged once again to travel as an ambassador. All of Wolsey's great schemes of power and influence were beginning to fall apart; Francis I and Charles V were moving towards a separate peace, and the exclusion of England would have been a considerable embarrassment for the cardinal who believed himself to be the power-broker of Europe. On the last day of June, More and Cuthbert Tunstall, with two other envoys, were dispatched to Cambrai with instructions to derive what advantage they might from a difficult situation. Cardinal Campeggio believed that they had also been ordered 'to promote the interests of the Pope and the Holy See';[28] this may be seen as part of the great game being played out at Blackfriars. Wolsey was obliged to remain in London, tending the king's 'great matter', but More and Tunstall were practised negotiators. They were both also famous and powerful men; More's 'diet' each day, for example, was a munificent 26s 8d.

They had two principal duties on this embassy. They were to ensure that imperial debts to Henry continued to be paid and that the trade between England and the Low Countries was not threatened. Their letters from Cambrai survive only in fragments, but the tenor of negotiations becomes clear in a careful reading. 'And as for lending of any more monay . . . hit shuld be no wisdome . . . And aftre moche reasonyng on both sides of these two maters, noo thing agreing in any point . . . Whereunto we aunswered that we had great maruaile [marvel] that they shuld make stikking or make any question therin . . . we gaue them a shorte and plaine aunswere . . . a resolute answere . . . shuld thinke it straunge . . . And in this case standeth the affairs . . .'[29]

In one of his dialogues More employs the terms of a game of chess – 'half a checke in this point . . . matyd me . . . it is but a blynde mate'[30] – to chart the course of a debate. The same metaphor can be used to describe the negotiations at Cambrai, which proceeded by delicate manoeuvre and deliberate delay. All the parties realised that trade between England and the Low Countries should not be interrupted, but Henry's honour was also at stake. It was important that moneys owing to him from previous treaties were still paid and that England's high place in the game of nations was maintained. There were frustrations and difficulties, as the letters of the envoys demonstrate, and certain negotiations between the representatives of Francis and Charles were not divulged to More and his partners. Separate agreements were made between Henry and the major participants, however, and a 'general peace' between all the nations was proclaimed at the beginning of August. It could not be said that England's role in previous years had been altogether glorious, but More and his colleagues had successfully salvaged some honour from the wreckage of Wolsey's grand schemes.

This diplomatic mission was of some significance to More, since it was the only public event which he chose to commemorate upon the tombstone in the Chelsea church where he hoped one day to rest. His epitaph recorded this occasion 'when the leagues between the chief Princes of Christendom were renewed again and peace so long looked for restored to Christendom'.[31] The league lasted for almost fifteen years and represented the best chance for the general peace which More and Erasmus, with the other humanist scholars, had earnestly anticipated since the beginning of the century. He mentioned one other honourable public duty in the course of his epitaph: he had always been '*molestus*' or troublesome to heretics.

XXV

Foolish Frantic Books

MORE had already been given permission to read heretical books but, by the spring of 1528, the dissemination of these forbidden texts could not be halted. Tyndale's English version of the New Testament, in particular, was a cause for concern; when it was ritually consigned to the flames in the autumn of 1526, the fire provoked controversy even among the faithful. Tyndale's tendentious translation of such key terms as *'presbyter'* and *'ecclesia'* was too abstract a matter for most to understand, compared to the spectacle of the Scriptures being put to the torch. Yet hundreds of copies were still being smuggled into England from Antwerp, Worms and Cologne; they could be purchased in Coleman Street, or Honey Lane, or Hosier Lane, or the house of Simon Fish by the White Friars. The same Fish impersonated Wolsey at a disguising in Gray's Inn, and was afterwards 'highly rebuked and thretened'[1] by the cardinal, who knew nothing of the young man's proselytising. The episode suggests, if nothing else, how religious and political dissent might together ferment in those young men who, above all, desired change.

At the end of 1526 Tyndale caused to be printed his interpretation of Paul's epistle to the Romans, in which he used that central text of the reformers to affirm Lutheran doctrines of grace and redemption. In the same period More wrote a letter to Erasmus, from the king's palace at Greenwich, in which he pleaded with him to complete a work against Luther, of which only the first volume had been published; there is a sense of urgency about More's entreaty that suggests he might also have been conveying the impatience of the king. But it is important to recognise, also, that for More and his colleagues this was still in large part an intellectual debate. Although there was no popular appetite for Lutheran doctrine – suspected 'heretics' were ostracised and derided in London – the ecclesiastical authorities feared that the sources of learning might be corrupted. A circle of Cambridge scholars met at the White Tavern (at least this was the name by which they were eventually known) in order to discuss and disseminate reformist ideas. Some of them – Coverdale, Ridley and Latimer – were to play so formative a role in later events that the importance which the authorities attached to the universities can readily be understood. There were also younger men among them who were fired by the prospects of change and reform; as More put it, 'yonge scolers be somtyme prone to newe fantasyes'[2] and become 'newfangly mynded'.[3]

In the following year Wolsey and Tunstall took more deliberate action when a Cambridge scholar, Thomas Bilney, was brought for trial on the grounds of preaching heresy in London and elsewhere; he abjured and bore the faggot, but remained in prison for eleven months. More had interrogated a confederate of Thomas Bilney's and had also attended the trial. He gives such circumstantial detail of the case that it is clear he was already engaged in what would now be called surveillance and entrapment among the leather-sellers, tailors, fishmongers and drapers of London. He envisaged small groups of people, perhaps three or four at each clandestine meeting, gathering at midnight in locked rooms, a 'nyght scole'[4] of evil and sedition. One of their number would read aloud from the Scriptures, or from texts smuggled into the city. Sometimes whole families worshipped together, but more often city merchants and apprentices would meet together in a 'conventicle' organised by a disaffected priest or scholar. We read, for example, of Thomas Geffrey, tailor; of John Medwall, a scrivener's servant; of Matthew Ward, a merchant adventurer; and of Robert Ward, a shoemaker by Fleet Street; all of whom were arrested and forced to recant their heretical beliefs. John Foxe, in his *Actes and Monuments*, mentions approximately thirty Londoners who abjured and suffered public penance, but there were others. These small assemblies may be compared to the banned radical groups in late eighteenth-century London, as well as to the puritan millenarians of the 1640s, and capture the inherent spirit of civic revolt.

Within three months of Bilney's trial, a concerted assault upon presumed heretics was conducted by More and his ecclesiastical colleagues. More wrote to the Oxford authorities, for example, and demanded that one 'Henry the mancypull of Whyte Hall' be put under close arrest and brought to him in London; he insisted at the same time that they 'handle the matter so closelye that ther be of hys apprehension and sendyng vpp as lytyll knowleg abrode as may bee'.[5] Such secrecy was necessary so that More could question the man without alerting any other Oxford 'heretics', who might fly or conceal their books. On the order of the council, More also personally searched the house of one of Tyndale's patrons, Humphrey Monmouth, who later confessed that 'al the lettres and treatyes that he sent me . . . I did burne them in my howse'.[6] In the same period an Oxford scholar, Thomas Garrett, was arrested and questioned; as a result of these interrogations, the rooms of certain other scholars were searched and a hundred banned books were discovered. Six students were then summarily imprisoned for some months in the fish cellar of Cardinal College, where it is reported that three of them died. In London and Colchester, too, there was renewed activity among the hunters of heresy; Lollards, as well as members of a clandestine group of reformers known as the Christian Brethren, who disseminated Tyndale's New Testament, were arrested and forced to abjure.

But it would be wrong to suggest that there was some generally violent wave of reprisal or repression; those proved heretical were compelled to bear the faggot, or were placed in the stocks, but there were no burnings. The authorities were intent upon removing possible sources of heresy and were not engaged in stifling a popular movement. No such movement existed. The conditions of the time, in any case, were not propitious. In 1528, one of the 'dere yeres' when the corn was scarce and the bread dear, More was part of a commission appointed to search for grain supplies in barns or outhouses; he himself disclosed that he was feeding one hundred people each day at his house and farm in Chelsea.[7] During that summer there were also virulent outbreaks of the plague and the sweating sickness; the courts at Westminster were suspended and the king fled. The whole time seemed out of joint, and it is significant that More should believe the 'lakke of corne and catayle' to be a 'sore punishement' from God 'for the receypte of these pestylent bokes' of heresy.[8]

Yet still those books were smuggled into England. Jerome Barlowe's *The Burying of the Mass* was a verse attack upon 'the papysticall secte', but it was followed by two more substantial and significant works. Tyndale's *Parable of the Wicked Mammon* was succeeded by *The Obedience of a Christian Man*. In these treatises Tyndale expounded Lutheran doctrines, in particular the belief in justification through faith alone and the opinion that a temporal prince should also exercise ecclesiastical power. It is not surprising, therefore, that in this year More was asked to launch a fierce reply to what he called these 'folysh frantyke bokes'. Cuthbert Tunstall's licence, for the reading of heresy, was the merest formality; the two men were close friends and it is likely that More suggested a counter-offensive in the vernacular in order to warn and advise '*simplicibus et ideotis hominibus*'[9] (which can roughly be translated as 'the man in the street') on the perils of alien creeds. If Lutheranism could be denounced as a foreign doctrine, then the patriotic citizens might immediately disown it. More was already busily employed at Westminster and at court, but the rebuttal of heresy was seen by him as a paramount duty; he mentioned once the need of a man to 'wryte by candellyght whyle he were halfe a slepe'.[10] The danger was too great for delay.

He called them by many names – these 'new men', 'new named bretherne', 'evangelycall fraternyte', 'new false sect' of 'our evangelycall Englysshe heretykes'. He linked them to the plague and to the abhorrent violence of the Peasants' Revolt in Germany, as well as to the sack of Rome. Heresy was a poison, an infection, a contagion attacking the body of Christendom. They scorned the sacraments of the Church and derided the notion of purgatory; they encouraged sexual licence and were intent upon bringing 'all out of order'.[11] They denied the eucharist and reviled the Mass. They believed that the Church of Christ was fundamentally corrupted and should be swept away. More knew that all the certainties of inherited belief and the prevailing social order would thereby be destroyed; it would be tantamount to the collapse of the entire structure of the world. This was the Antichrist, and very soon More was talking about 'the daye of Iudgement' and 'dredefull dome'.[12]

More's first defence of the Church, *A Dialogue Concerning Heresies*, was written in this year of dearth and sickness; it was a topical book in every sense, filled with local detail and circumstance. The narrative opens with the description of a scholar from one of the universities questioning More on matters of faith. He has read Tyndale and knows about the preaching of Bilney; he is a thoroughly modern young man who is 'nothynge tonge tayed'[13] and is veering towards the doctrines of Martin Luther. At a little before seven in the morning, More takes him into 'my study'[14] at Chelsea and begins a dialogue which ultimately convinces the young man to remain within 'the comen fayth and byleue of the hole chyrche'.[15] It is a conversation, almost a drama, but it does not share the irony or the ambiguity of *Utopia*. More adopts the role of a polemicist and propagandist, rather than that of a scholar concerned with good letters and the new learning; as a result the main interest for the contemporary reader lies in its language rather than in its argument. It was the first book which More had published in the vernacular, and it displays the living speech of the period leaping 'lyke a flounder out of a fryenge panne in to the fyre'.[16] Running through the stories of juggling and baking bread, songs 'of Robyn hode' and ballads of love, are phrases that bring the people closer to us: 'the lytle apple of myne eye . . . as bare as a byrdys ars . . . that can perceyue chalke fro chese well ynough . . . to proue the mone made of grene chese . . . one swalow maketh not somer'.[17]

But if some of the phrases and stories are immediately recognisable, others are mysterious. Who will now, for example, 'tourne a plum into a doggys torde in a boyes mouthe'?[18] And was it 'alway that the cat wynked whan her eye was out'?[19] There is mention of a church where there were models in wax of male and female genitalia hanging upon the walls, while near the altar were 'two rounde rynges of syluer, the one moche larger than the other. Thrughe whiche euery man dyd put his preuy membres at the aulters ende. Not euery man thrughe bothe but some thrughe the one and some thrughe the other. For they were not bothe of a bygnes.'[20] The church was in Flanders, but it might as well have been in London. There were always wonders to be seen there, and More recounts how some handkerchiefs woven by the Virgin Mary had been found concealed in a tabernacle at Barking Abbey. The thieves of London prayed to the robber who had hung on the right side of Christ; they called upon 'Dysmas' to help them in their crimes. The *Dialogue* reveals a world of miracles and pilgrimages, of painted images and wonderful relics, of a true Church commanding all. More celebrates, in a double sense, what was essentially and primarily an oral culture. He employs it in the dialogue itself, but he also uses it to defend the traditions of the Church; they have been transmitted by word of mouth, 'by onely wordes and prechynge . . . by mouth amonge the people'.[21] That is why More considered it dangerous to rely upon the written Scriptures, but it is also why he employed the form of dialogue.

There is a public truth which can be debated, rather than some private and individual truth to be found in secret musing.

It is perhaps too late now to sift through the dust of forgotten controversies, but it will be instructive to describe More's conclusions. The Catholic Church was a visible church, with its own hierarchy and known places of worship, rather than a fleeting sect of believers; it was a Church with a proven tradition of faith reaching back for fifteen hundred years, which was transmitted in both oral and scriptural form. It possessed the authority of the apostles and the church fathers and had been guided by the Holy Spirit since the resurrection of Christ. It was a historical faith, established upon a consensus of the faithful. Its teachings were manifested in papal or conciliar decrees, whereby general opinion and traditional belief were given dogmatic force 'and so comen downe to our dayes by contynuall successyon'.[22] Its divine origin was proved by miracles and reinforced by pilgrimages. It was the mystical body of Christ, comprising the living and the dead. For More it was the vehicle of God's purpose and the paradigm for all earthly law and authority. But if it was the model of unity and continuity, it now found itself in a world which seemed to be breaking down. There had been heresies and heretics before who 'lefte the common fayth of ye catholyke chyrche preferrynge theyr owne gay gloses',[23] but the situation of Christendom had never been more perilous. The Turks had moved as far west as Hungary and might one day threaten Rome itself, while the heretics of Germany and Switzerland were intent upon a more insidious destruction of the established order. It is no wonder that present events seemed to More to be an anticipation of 'domesday'.

The whole theme and purpose of his *Dialogue Concerning Heresies* had been to celebrate that common culture which was under threat; by employing the stories and proverbs that were in the air around him and by drawing upon the resources of the medieval tradition of caricature and speech he was implicitly appealing to his audience to consider what would be lost if Christendom fell into schism. A religion and a way of life might disappear. More's prose is highly significant in that respect. As a Latinist he has a tendency to break up the periods of Cicero with the expletives of Terence, thus creating a colloquial and on occasions harsh style; as a writer of English he presses that advantage home, and reflects what he once called the 'comen custume and usage of speche'.[24] On the bad reputation of priests, for example, he writes that 'If they be famylyer we call theym lyght. If they be solytary we call theym fantastyke. If they be sadde we call theym solempne. If they be mery we call theym madde . . . they say that yf a woman be fayre than is she yonge and yf a preste be good than he is olde.'[25] There are many examples of this quick demotic throughout More's writing, but his is not simply an ear which caught the inflections of the London streets. He is also part of a tradition of devotional and homiletic literature which has been traced back to the religious treatises of the eleventh century and even, indeed, to Aelfric and the supposed writings of Arthur. His use of balanced and alliterative sentences is a clear token of his medieval affinities – 'hys open lyuyng in lechery wyth his lewd lemman the nunne'[26] is one such example – but the vigour of his writing owes some debt to the long history of the London sermon. It should be recalled that More's vernacular works were, in large part, intended for an illiterate audience and were therefore to be read aloud.

But it would be wrong to suggest that his was a simple colloquial or dramatic style. He resorts both to brevity and to amplification; he mixes ornate diction with plain speech. He seems to wander through examples, but in the midst of simile or metaphor he always sustains the momentum of his argument. He puts on voices – imitating the speech of a Kentish man, a Yorkshire man, or a German – and then reverts to his own. He was devoted to the traditional order but, in linguistic terms, he is a great innovator. Some of the words and phrases he introduced into written English include 'fact', 'taunt', 'shuffle', 'anticipate', 'paradox', 'pretext', 'obstruction', 'monosyllable', 'meeting', 'not to see the wood for the trees', and 'to make the best of something'.

He wrote very quickly and neatly, marking the page with careful underlinings and revisions. The absence of large-scale emendations suggests that he knew what he wished to say and revised only in order to add clarity or emphasis to his points; he changed sentences, but rarely altered arguments or long sections of prose. Indeed, he wrote in large structural units, which could be moved to different parts of the narrative. The common method of erasing words was to 'scrape theym out' with a small knife,[27] but More deleted them with a delicate cross-hatching of lines. In similar fashion he creates his own persona in the dialogue; he had to remain calm, confident, and meticulous, in the rebuttal of false doctrine. That is also why he carefully proofread the first edition of *Dialogue Concerning Heresies*; it was printed by his brother-in-law John Rastell, 'at the sygne of

Thomas More, as Lord Chancellor of England, calm and
inscrutable even at the height of his power; beneath the rich
gown he is wearing a hair shirt.

Below: Desiderius Erasmus, the great Dutch humanist whom More called 'my derlynge'. He in turn addressed More as 'sweetest Thomas'.

Opposite: Peter Gillis, the public servant of Antwerp in whose house and company More conceived *Utopia*. This double portrait was sent to More by Erasmus as a tribute to the friendship between the three men.

John Fisher, the devout Bishop of Rochester who was denounced as a traitor by Henry VIII. He was created a cardinal but 'the head was off before the hat was on'.

Below: Thomas Cromwell, the king's abetter in the destruction of the monasteries. He is recorded as saying, 'I will either make or mar'.

Martin Luther, the greatest exponent of the Protestant conscience, who compared himself to 'ripe shit'.

Below: Thomas Cranmer, Archbishop of Canterbury, the able, amiable and ambitious proponent of the king's 'great matter'.

John Colet, Dean of St Paul's and the founder of St Paul's School; he had a reputation for contentiousness and, like many of More's London friends, was somewhat theatrical in manner.

Thomas Wolsey, the brilliant and resourceful cardinal who became More's greatest patron. 'Neuer,' More wrote after Wolsey's death, 'was he saciate of heryng his own prayse.'

The sanctified image of King Henry VII; his legacy of authoritarian and overwhelming power helped to bring More to the scaffold.

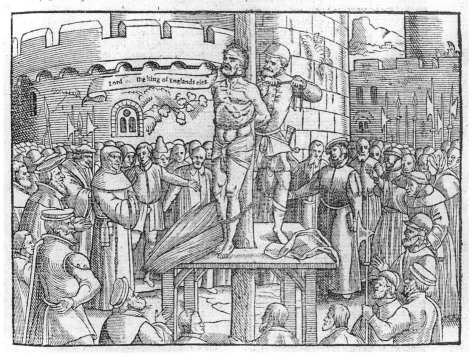

The burning of William Tyndale, the pious and learned translator of the Bible whom More described as 'a beste' with a 'brutyshe bestely mouth'. This was the fate to which More consigned several heretics.

King Henry VIII, painted the year after More's execution.
'If my head could win him a castle,' More had said, 'it should not fail to go.'

the meremayd at Powlys gate next to chepesyde'.[28] Because he had already asked for the 'examynacyon and iudgment' of men such as Tunstall and Fisher and had as a consequence already 'put out or chaunged'[29] certain things, his additions at this later stage were not large. A second edition was printed two years later by his nephew William Rastell, who had established his business by St Bride's churchyard, and for this More added passages emphasising the danger of heretical books; the titlepage states that it had been 'newly ouersene' by him. One sentiment remains unaltered, however. There can be no 'couenant' with the heretics, and at the last they must be 'punyshed by deth in ye fyre'.[30]

In the early months of 1529 a small tract was 'sown' in court circles, to use the word of Cardinal Campeggio, which even came to the attention of the king himself. It was entitled *Supplication for the Beggars* and had been written by the same Simon Fish who had once impersonated Cardinal Wolsey at a Gray's Inn disguising. Fish had wisely moved to Antwerp after this event, from which place he issued his violently anticlerical pamphlet. He accused the English clergy of rapacity, of grabbing as much land and as many tithes as they could while in the process reducing the kingdom to beggary. He declared that they owned one third of the property of the kingdom and had debauched 100,000 women. He also accused them of attempting to filch the authority of the king and 'translate all rule power lordishippe auctorite obedience and dignite from your grace vnto theim'.[31] Fish's humble suggestion to Henry was that he should assert his 'hyghe power' against this evil generation of priests, with the further implication that he could appropriate church property. It was an interesting suggestion, given the frustration and uncertainty of Henry's relationship with Rome.

More may have known about certain private matters concerning this subject. Anne Boleyn had obtained a copy of the book, according to John Foxe, and presented it to the king. Then Henry 'kept the booke in his bosome 3. or 4. dayes'[32] and was told that Fish, this strident supporter of his 'auctorite', had already fled the country 'for feare of the Cardinall'.[33] But there is an ambiguity here, since Foxe also suggests that the book was read to the king by two merchants; the monarch is then supposed to have replied that when you remove a lower stone from a wall, an upper stone might follow. It has also been recorded that the book Boleyn gave to the king was Tyndale's treatise, *The Obedience of a Christian Man*, which similarly argued that the king's authority should be extended over ecclesiastical affairs. According to this version, Henry is reported to have read it and then declared: 'This is the book for me and all kings to read.'[34] In either case, the tendency of events was clear enough. Heretical and anticlerical books were being countenanced at court, even while public measures against their distribution were being strengthened.

More acted rapidly and within weeks, perhaps even days, of reading *Supplication for the Beggars* he composed a reply approximately ten times the length of the original tract. He called it *The Supplication of Souls* and addressed it 'To all good Crysten people',[35] although there is no doubt that it was also addressed to the king himself. There are passages when it shows signs of being hastily written but in certain respects it is an extraordinary performance, in which More dramatises the voices of those souls still being licked by purgatorial fire. Simon Fish had suggested that Masses for the dead were only another means of wresting money from the living, but More's souls 'in most pytouse wyse continually calleth' for prayer and remembrance. There are some wonderful descriptions of their agony in More's best late medieval manner – 'the gay gere [clothes] burneth vppon our bakkys: and those prowd perled pastys [ornaments dangling from the hair] hang hote about our chekis'.[36] This is not some 'feynyd fyre payntyd on a wall', but a true token of life after death. Purgatory was visualised by More's contemporaries in direct and dramatic terms; it is a large open area, with neither ascending nor declining ground, marked by invisible boundaries. Here devils and human beings cohabit. In one celebrated Cistercian treatise, the landscape is depicted with shadowy meadows, wheels of fire and freezing rivers.[37] The dead call out for the living to save them from torment and, as More asks in his account, would you not reach out to snatch your mother from the fire? When the souls of purgatory 'vomyte, yet shall they vomyte styll and neuer fynde ease therof'.[38] 'Remember our thurst,' they call, 'whyne ye syt & Drynke.' Although More is concerned to emphasise the close and sometimes terrifying communion between the living and the dead, he is equally intent upon reaffirming the importance of tradition and of inherited belief. At this point in his career he resembles St Augustine, himself a man of law who had turned his rhetorical skills into polemic against his religious enemies. Augustine had, for example, composed vitriolic and unfair attacks upon the Donatists and the Pelagians in a spirit close to that of More. Augustine has been described as perhaps 'the first theorist of the Inquisition',[39] and More would perhaps have been happy to be placed in the same company.

But he also had a more immediate purpose. If Henry had indeed read Tyndale's *Obedience of a Christian Man*, he would have been told that he was appointed by God to protect and guide the Church of his country – and whoever resisted him 'resisteth God'.[40] That is why More responded so fiercely to Simon Fish's pamphlet. He repeatedly emphasised the power and authority of the king, far beyond that of convocation or the 'spiritual arm' of parliament, and then strenuously denied that the clergy were filching any of the wealth of the kingdom. This was plainly an effort to reassure Henry, and More berated Fish for daring 'to take vppon hym to gyue counsayle to a kynge'.[41] But it was not simply a matter of presumption. More believed that the attack upon the priests was a partially concealed attempt to introduce Lutheran heresies within the kingdom, so that the wreckage of the clergy would be followed by the destruction of the Mass and the sacraments. And what then would follow but the riot and warfare which had already afflicted Germany? The seizure of church lands would be succeeded by the theft of other property, and the assault upon the Church would encourage an attack upon all forms of authority. The forces of innovation and sedition would spread, 'and at laste bryng all the realme to ruyne and thys not wythout bochery and fowle blody handys'.[42] More was warning Henry against these siren voices of the anticlerics, which would inevitably lead to the destruction of his realm. That is why his metaphors during this period are those of expulsion and rejection. He wrote in his *Supplication* of stopping up a gap 'all redy with such a bush of thornys as will pryk theyr handys thorow a payre of hedgyng glouys'.[43] Yet still volumes of heresy were passing through those gaps into England – a book by William Roye on Lutheran doctrine, a book by John Frith on the Antichrist who sits in Rome, a book by Simon Fish on false sacraments, a revised English primer designed to promote the Protestant cause. The time was at hand, however, when More would act more directly and more violently.

XXVI

We Poor Worldly Men of Middle Earth

ON his return from Cambrai, in the third week of August, More found that all was changed. The legatine court had already been adjourned and it seemed likely that Henry's case would be revoked to Rome. Wolsey had failed in his master's 'great matter'. More visited him on 23 August with news of his successful mission, but within a few weeks the cardinal had gone. On 9 October he was indicted on a charge of praemunire and arrested for treason. More would have known about the king's growing disaffection with his Lord Chancellor, since there had been rumours to that effect circulating since the late spring of the year. Various forces had played their part, among them the influence of Anne Boleyn and her family, as well as the failures of Wolsey's foreign policy. But the plainest fact seems to be that after the débâcle of the annulment proceedings Henry wished to teach the Church, both in Rome and England, a lesson in power. That is why he appointed a layman as Wolsey's successor. That, paradoxically, is why he chose Sir Thomas More.

On 17 or 18 October 1529, Wolsey surrendered the Great Seal, 'contented to obey the King's high commendment';[1] the cardinal loudly lamented his fate, weeping amid his retainers and invoking the example of the early martyrs. 'But if I had served God as diligently as I have done the King,' he is reported to have said, 'He would not have given me over in my grey hairs.'[2] An inventory was made of his possessions, and all his golden bowls and plates, his satins and his cloths of silver, were laid out upon long tables. The seal itself, the authentic impress upon acts of state, was taken in a bag of crimson velvet to the monarch. There then began a week of discussion and negotiation over Wolsey's successor, with the king's council meeting the day after the surrender of the seal and reconvening with the king at Greenwich four days later.

Some report that William Warham, the Archbishop of Canterbury, was suggested; others say that the Duke of Norfolk refused to countenance the appointment of Suffolk, and that Cuthbert Tunstall might have been chosen as a 'compromise' between the various factions. More was certainly present during these sittings of the council – his name is appended to one of its declarations – but we cannot say with what surprise, or misgiving, he received the news on Monday 25 October that he was to be appointed as the next Lord Chancellor of England. On that same day the king gave him the Great Seal, and on the following morning More was led in procession 'thorowe Westminster hall up into the Chauncerie'[3] accompanied by the great lords of the realm, both spiritual and temporal. He was escorted to the marble seat of judgment, and then the Duke of Norfolk delivered a speech in praise of his wisdom and virtue; in particular he mentioned More's conduct of the negotiations at Cambrai, where he 'so woorthily handled himselfe' that 'all Inglande was bounde to him'.[4] More replied in words that are no longer extant, although one of his earliest biographers dilates upon a speech in which he is supposed to have discussed the 'heavier burdens' that he had to assume and to have reflected ruefully upon the 'unhappy fall' of his predecessor.[5] This may be a dramatic invention, however, in the manner of Sallust or Tacitus. The words of More's oath of office do survive, and the new chancellor swore not to 'suffer the hurte nor disherytyng of the kyng or that the rightes of the Croun be decreysed by any mean'.[6] He left Westminster Hall amidst the panoply of office; a gold sceptre with imperial crown was borne by an official on his right side and, on his left, another attendant carried a book.

Why had Henry chosen a man who had found it impossible to endorse the king's 'great matter'? Of course More's reputation was considerable, both as diplomat and statesman; his skill as a lawyer and his success as Chancellor of the Duchy of Lancaster were also of paramount importance. He was well known for his caution and discretion, while his fame among the humanist scholars and administrators of Christendom lent him additional authority. One of his great opponents paid tribute to the 'wisedome and lerning that is in him, but also the great auctoritie and experience',[7] and there was even a grammar prepared for children that included a litany of More's praises as an exercise in translation. 'Moore is a man of an aungels wyt & syngler lernying' is one phrase to be parsed, together with 'a man of merveylous myrth and pastymes & somtyme of as sad gravyte as who say a man for all seasons'.[8] As Speaker of the Commons he had proved that he could deal with the vicissitudes of parliament, and the clergy had already chosen him as their polemicist in the fight against heresy. Perhaps most importantly, he had worked closely with the king for more than ten years; Henry believed that he could rely upon his loyalty and good judgement as the proceedings against his marriage continued their serpentine course. But by appointing a layman as chancellor for the first time in almost a hundred years, Henry was also reasserting his own power over that of the Church. Wolsey's fall and More's appointment, therefore, were directly associated with the king's desire to separate himself from Catherine of Aragon.

According to More, the king broached the subject with him soon after the ceremony in Westminster Hall – 'sone after which tyme his Grace moved me agayne . . . to loke and consydre his great mater'.[9] It is significant that More should be approached at the time of his appointment; the king needed to learn no lessons from Machiavelli, as his subsequent words to his new chancellor might also imply. He asked More to ponder the question of the annulment and, if persuaded, 'wold gladly vse me among other of his counsailors'.[10] But he declared that More should follow his conscience and repeated the injunction that 'I shold fyrst loke vnto God and after God vnto hym'. He was clearly anxious to enrol More into his cause, however, since he assigned the Archbishops of Canterbury and York as well as other dignitaries to persuade him of the merits of his case. But More proved obstinate, or merely impassive, and listened with great care to the various arguments without once changing his mind. He believed the original papal dispensation to have been valid and the marriage sound. Henry was disappointed but in More's words, was 'neuer the lesse graciouse lord'.

So why had he accepted the post of Lord Chancellor, when he was fully aware of the pressures which would be applied to him? He may have had little choice in the matter but, in any event, no choice was necessary. He was fulfilling his life's work, or, rather, his work in the world; the chancellorship was the culmination of the process which had begun at the time of his birth. All the stages of his youthful study and adult career converged at this point, and we may imagine the spiritual presence of Archbishop Morton somewhere about him when he accepted the Great Seal. To be elevated to the most powerful official position in the country would also greatly please his wife and, most importantly, his already ailing father. By becoming Lord Chancellor of England 'young More' had amply fulfilled his filial responsibilities.

The Spanish ambassador, Eustace Chapuys, reported to his masters that everyone was 'delighted' at the promotion of More because 'he is an upright and learned man, and a good servant of the Queen'.[11] The knowledge that More supported Catherine of Aragon was not confined to the ambassador, and indeed may have played some part in Henry's decision to appoint him as chancellor. The king was aware of Catherine's popularity, particularly among the people of London, and to have More by his side was a way of protecting himself against accusations of malice or falsehood. Such an 'upright and learned man', known to favour the queen, was a visible warrant of the king's holy intentions. More would have been sensible of this device, but he had equally powerful motives of his own. As Lord Chancellor he would be in a position to assist the queen, albeit in a discreet manner, but he might also be able to protect the Church against the possible wrath of the king. It could even be argued that More accepted the post precisely in order to defend and maintain his Church in an age of anxiety. It was his 'bounden duty' to do so. It was the greatest obligation in a life filled with obligations.

He wrote a short letter to Erasmus after his elevation, but it is not altogether of a cheerful or optimistic nature. He told his old friend that he had been promoted without any warning and required sympathy rather than congratulation. The reason he gives for his acceptance of his new role is that it was vitally concerned with 'rei Christiane' or the affairs of Christendom.[12] He does not advert to his private feelings on this momentous change, but they can be gathered from a remark elsewhere in his writings. In times of apparent success or prosperity it is important that a person 'by lesse lykyng the false flateryng world set a crosse vppon the shypp of his hart, & bere a low saile theron, that the boysteouse blast of pride blow hym not vnder the water'.[13]

Thus he set sail upon the ocean of affairs. He was working now as part of a triumvirate around the king; Thomas Howard, Duke of Norfolk was lord treasurer, and Charles Brandon, Duke of Suffolk was soon to be appointed lord president of the council. The royal secretary, Stephen Gardiner, was also influential and in the foreground there was Sir Thomas Boleyn, newly ennobled as the Earl of Wiltshire. The most powerful figure was Norfolk, however, whose position was further secured when his daughter married the Duke of Richmond, the king's illegitimate son; he was also the uncle of Anne Boleyn, and therefore has some claim to being the courtier closest to the king. He was a short, spare man, perpetually suspicious, conscientious but ever anxious. From the beginning he and More cooperated in the affairs of state and they were, in particular, united in their desire to defend the 'old faith'.

The first test came in November with the summoning of parliament in order to consult the powers and interests of the nation at a moment of transition. The fall of Wolsey, who had administered the affairs of state for almost fifteen years, had naturally provoked a bout of anticlericalism – at least among those groups, such as the lawyers and London merchants, who were not disposed to think well of the clergy. The king wanted to use the session as the quickest way to waive his debts, while the new Lord Chancellor wished to affirm the principles by which his policy would be guided. There were, in addition, matters of domestic legislation to be resolved. On 3 November a great procession made its way to the church of Blackfriars; Archbishop Warham of Canterbury walked beside Sir Thomas More, who wore the vivid scarlet robe of his new office. Who could have believed, on that winter's day by the river, that this particular parliament would not be dissolved for seven years; and that, in the course of its eight sessions, the 'comen knowen catholick church' would be wholly changed? Before the end of its deliberations, too, the new Lord Chancellor would be beheaded on Tower Hill.

In the parliament chamber of Blackfriars, and in the presence of the king, More opened the proceedings with a speech in which he declared that 'divers new enormities were sprong amongst the people' which required the passing of new laws 'to reforme the same'. He then denounced his predecessor, Wolsey, for 'fraudulent juggeling and attemptes' and described him as 'the great wether which is of late fallen'.[14] It has sometimes been suggested that More was here guilty of ingratitude to his once great master, but his was essentially a rhetorical performance on behalf of the king. He could hardly have dismissed as inconsequential the matter of Wolsey's fall, and there might have been an additional urgency in his condemnation, since at the time there were rumours that the cardinal might somehow, one day, be reinstalled into the king's favour. This was not an outcome which either More or Norfolk desired. For there was urgency, too, in More's demand that new laws be passed to deal with various of the problems that had emerged in recent years.

When parliament reconvened at Westminster three days later, it soon became clear that the forced departure of Wolsey had indeed aroused resentment against the worldliness and power of other priests. Various articles of complaint, for example, came from those members of the 'Comen House' associated with the London mercers; the clergy were accused by them of taking too much money for 'mortuaries' and 'probat of testaments'. There were also priests who acted as stewards for bishops and deprived honest men of employment; there were priests who lived in the palaces of the rich and noble without attending to the needs of their parishioners; there were priests growing fat upon the vices of pluralism and non-residence. A special committee of MPs then announced a number of measures designed to remove these abuses. More heard John Fisher, in the Lords, denounce the proposals as an attempt to bring the clergy into the 'contempt and hatred of the layetie'; he also condemned the members of parliament for lack of faith, which charge they indignantly denied. But Thomas More might not have been as vociferously opposed to reform as the bishop. At a later date he described his severe 'correccyon' of bad or wayward priests, for example, and boasted that 'there was no man . . . into whose handes they were more lothe to come'.[15] He knew the temper of the times and he understood the paramount need of keeping the Church free from scandal. The members of the Commons were not attacking the Church but, rather, abuses within the Church; this was at least a possible interpretation, even if subsequent events might suggest that it was the beginning of a much more fundamental process of change. In the event, the proposals were never fully implemented; they were filtered through committee, most likely under the guiding hands of More and Norfolk, and were finally passed by the Lords with various provisos and modifications that remedied certain abuses without greatly affecting the privileged position of the clergy.

The first session of this parliament was actually more notable, and more notorious, for its secular legislation. Its most urgent business was concerned with the cancellation of the king's debts, raised in past years by various levies and exactions, but the measure was passed only after much argument and complaint in the Commons. There were also proposals which bear the direct impress of More's legal acumen; a very complex piece of legislation on the inheritance of land known as 'the statute of uses', for example, was discussed but eventually deferred. Instead More reached an agreement with the peers which simplified the law while at the same time protecting the king's financial interests. Yet he also looked further ahead and, in the opening speech to parliament, generally remembered only for its ritual attack upon Wolsey, he denounced various 'erroribus et abusibus' existing within current secular and spiritual legislation.[16] Of course he was particularly dismayed by the spread of heretical literature, but he was also likely to have entertained the possibility, at least, of legislation designed to reform certain aspects of the Church itself. There is a petition to the king, drawn up by Thomas Darcy, in which complaints about the power of the clergy are said to be upheld by 'your Chancellor'.[17] In subsequent articles promulgated against Wolsey, of which More was the chief signatory, it is claimed that the cardinal suffered the 'great pox' but had nevertheless blown upon the king 'his perilous and ineffective breath'. After the forced departure of Wolsey, More was intent upon reform which would improve both the spiritual health and economic fortunes of the nation. The younger man who wrote *Utopia*, with its preliminary discussion of good and bad government, survived still. More's ambitions were large, as his speech to the parliament suggests, and the years of his chancellorship might indeed have been marked by the emergence of a reformed Catholic nation. But if that was his aim, the time was against him; his distance from the king on the 'great matter', in particular, would lead to a diminution of his power.

The beginning, however, was auspicious. More was instrumental in passing an Act which restored the judicial capacities of the Star Chamber in the interests of equity. He sat in that court even while parliament was in session, and there is a record of his committing a man to prison 'for his obstinacy'.[18] Throughout this period, indeed, he was busily engaged in all the affairs of state. In the first week of December, for example, while parliament was still sitting, he was involved in hard negotiations with the Spanish ambassador on matters of trade; More, as usual, prevailed. In that same week he had also signed the bill against Wolsey, entreating the king to act so firmly that the cardinal could never 'vex and impoverish' the nation again.[19] The regal decision upon Wolsey's future had yet to be made but the fact that the petition was also signed by Lord Mountjoy, another 'humanist' from the early days of the century, suggests that there was a genuine belief in the possibility of reform under the new Lord Chancellor's guidance. At a great dinner to commemorate the feast of St Simon and St Jude, in the court of the Lord Mayor of London, More was listed first in the order of precedence. He sat beneath a rich cloth of arras; he was alone at the head of the table, with the great dukes and lords of the land sitting below him. Here, in striking form, is the measure of his new authority.

For thirty-one months Thomas More embodied the law of England. He was the presiding figure in Chancery and in the Star Chamber; he was known as 'the keeper of the king's conscience' and, in that capacity, he was permitted to apply equity and moral judgement to the strict application of the law. William Roper depicted him as so practical and energetic a judge that the entire 'backlog' of cases from Wolsey's administration was cleared; apparently he was so assiduous that there were days when there were no cases remaining for him to investigate. The reality was more complicated and more interesting.

The distinction between the Courts of Chancery and of Star Chamber was a nice one; both dealt with civil actions, largely involving disputes over property and contracts, but the Star Chamber was primarily concerned with cases where criminality was also being alleged. Hearings in Chancery, however, reveal the very fabric of Tudor life. Robert Farmer, a London seller of leather, tricked a young man into the poor purchase of worsted cloth; Robert Eland was forcibly removed from the manor of Carlinghow by a rival claimant to the property; Richard Fisher complained that he had been illegally 'bound' to a London draper; Richard Boys, a skinner of London, was about to be falsely imprisoned for debts; John Parnell, a draper of the city, refused to deliver cloths and woad for which payment had already been made. More listens intently. He sits in his scarlet robe trimmed with lambskin, a brown cap upon his head, flanked by the Master of Rolls and the Masters in Chancery. Below them are the registrars and the other officers of the court; some of them sit around a table covered in green cloth, upon which are various rolled papers, folded writs, documents, waxes and seals. Behind the bar stand the serjeants, barristers and apprentices; the senior of them wear striped or 'party-coloured' gowns, while the others wear robes of single colour. A clerk scribbles down the words of Sir Thomas More, as he makes a point or delivers a judgment. A sealed paper is handed to him and, if we look carefully, we can see him writing upon it '*per se vel per atturnatum*'. The phrase represents one of his innovations as Lord Chancellor; he was willing to allow various interested parties to be represented in the court by their 'attornies' rather than being compelled to appear in person.

Unlike Wolsey, More brought to the practice of justice a huge resource of knowledge and experience. The cardinal had known much less about legal precedent and authority, which meant that his judgments were often erratic or overtly personal. This was indeed one of the complaints against him, and More had alluded to the problem in his *Responsio ad Lutherum*, where he had defined the relationship between magistrate and statute; no judge could decide matters at his own pleasure,[20] but must rely upon the framework of good and settled laws. There were differences of emphasis, too, which help to define More's new role more closely. Part of his duty as Lord Chancellor was to introduce the principles of equity into the system of justice and, by ordering his conscience 'after the rewles and groundes of the law',[21] to remedy manifest injustice or assist those who seemed to be thwarted by the strict procedures in the ordinary courts. The chancellor was, in a sense, '*procurator fatuorum*'; '*Morus*', the fool, had become the protector of the foolish. The courts of common law were 'grounded upon the maxims and customes and the rules of the law, and according to the process', but More was in a position to make his judgments 'grounded upon the lawe of reason and the lawe of God'.[22]

There was no necessary disjunction between the two, of course, but one incident in his tenure of the office suggests how practical differences might arise. He had been informed of some judges' complaints against his injunctions, and so he invited them to dinner in the council chamber at Westminster. He discussed with them all the cases that had provoked controversy, carefully going through the details of each one, until the judges themselves agreed that they would have acted in the same manner as More. He then proposed an informal arrangement; if the judges would 'upon reasonable considerations, by their own discretion' mitigate and change 'the rigour of the law', as in conscience they were already bound to do, then he would agree to grant no further injunctions. But after debating the matter the judges refused his offer. 'I perceive, son,' More explained to William Roper, 'why they like not so to do, for they see that they may by the verdict of the jury cast off all quarrels from themselves upon them.'[23] The judges refused to make individual or sensitive decisions, in other words, but instead relied upon the verdict of the jury as well as the strict application of legal precedent and procedure. This could not be the path taken by More. Nothing could better illustrate the quasi-religious nature of the law than the fact that part of his duty as Lord Chancellor was carefully to consider, and then to purge, the conscience of the malefactor. In the process More had to examine his own conscience, to ensure that his private judgement did not in any way flout or compromise the 'commen order and longe contynued law';[24] a suggestive analogy might be drawn here with More's similar phrase concerning 'the comen knowen catholique chyrche'.[25] It goes to the heart of the medieval dispensation which he was struggling to uphold.

More's growing isolation from the king's counsels meant that he had far more time to devote to his duties than ever his predecessor did; Wolsey had received 540 chancery petitions each year, whereas the average for More was 900.[26] It seems likely, then, that plaintiffs preferred the verdict of Thomas More rather than that of a jury. There were other contrasts which might be drawn with the practice of Wolsey. More was a cautious exponent of the law and it was his habit to examine bills very carefully before issuing writs of subpoena or *corpus cum causa*. He involved himself in cases more directly and he was also much sterner with those who disobeyed his injunctions. A measure of that strictness emerges even in his treatment of his own household. In the case of *Giles Heron* v. *Nicholas Millisante*, in bundle 643 of early chancery proceedings, More 'made a flatt decree against' his son-in-law.[27] As More had once said to William Roper, 'were it my father stood on the one side and the devil on the other, his cause being good, the devil should have right'.[28] Sometimes he sat in the hall of Lincoln's Inn, sometimes he sat at his own home in Chelsea, where plaintiffs came to plead their case with him. Here was a lawyer who had reached the pinnacle of his profession, dispensing justice with equity in a manner which the prelates of the Church, his predecessors, had never been able to achieve.

One judicial anecdote from Chelsea, of a trivial kind, illustrates that mixture of good humour and common sense which marked his public life. A beggar-woman had lost her dog, which had subsequently been adopted by Alice More; the beggar eventually discovered where the animal had been taken and complained to the master of the household. But was it truly her dog? So the Lord Chancellor set up a test; he asked his wife and the beggar to stand at opposite ends of the great hall and to call for the dog, which had been placed between them. The animal ran to the beggar and was returned to her. But Alice More bargained with her and bought the dog for a piece of gold – 'so all parties were agreed; everie one smiling to see his manner of enquiring out the truth'.[29] His practicality in this matter resembles another occasion when a judge complained of the ease with which pockets could be picked in London; More then arranged for the judge's own purse to be taken. The story offers an instructive moral that More himself understood well; the greatest judge is not above the weakness and folly of the world, but is a simple Christian in need of salvation. One other anecdote will suffice. A learned and perhaps portentous attorney, Mr Tubbe, had asked More to sign a subpoena; it was only after he had left the court that he realised the Lord Chancellor had simply written across it 'A tale of a Tubbe'.[30] Not all such stories are proven – they might not, for example, stand up in a court of law – but their survival suggests the general impression that More made upon his contemporaries.

More once even joked about a heretic. He had imprisoned him in the porter's lodge of his house at Chelsea, where, for punishment, he had kept him in the stocks; it is not clear whether the man's head, hands or feet were confined within the small holes. When the prisoner escaped More instructed his porter to mend this wooden frame of torture, in case the man should try to get back in again. He was informed that the heretics were jubilant over the escape and wrote in reply: 'neuer wyll I for my part be so vnreasonable, as to be angry wyth any man that ryseth if he can, whan he fyndeth hym selfe that he sytteth not at hys ease.'[31]

This is just one of many reports of his behaviour as the hunter of heretics. From John Foxe's *Book of Martyrs* and other post-Reformation sources we learn that he tied heretics to a tree in his Chelsea garden and whipped them; we read that he watched as 'newe men' were put upon the rack in the Tower and tortured until they confessed; we learn that he was personally responsible for the burning of several of the 'brethren' in Smithfield. Stories of a similar nature were current even in More's lifetime and he denied them forcefully. He admitted that he did imprison heretics in his house – 'theyr sure kepynge'[32] he called it – but he utterly rejected claims of torture and whipping. There were only two occasions when he had ordered beating. A child of his household had once been instructed by a heretic and had begun to spread a blasphemy about the holy eucharist to another young servant; More, on hearing of this, caused him to be whipped 'lyke a chyld before myne houshold'.[33] It was customary to beat a child before the entire family, but this seems to be a different More from the one who chastised his own children with peacock feathers. The other case involved a madman, lately out of Bethlem, who practised 'many madde toyes and tryfles' in church; during the silent moments when the priest was about to hold up the eucharist, he would creep behind kneeling women and, in a medieval parody of the elevation, lift their gowns over their heads. More, 'beyng aduertysed of these pageaunts', ordered him to be arrested, tied to a tree in the village of Chelsea, 'and there they stryped hym with roddys therfore tyl he waxed wery'.[34] It is likely that this incident prompted the later rumour that he had tied heretics to the tree in his garden, a report that More specifically rejected, 'as helpe me god'.[35] He was not a man falsely to invoke the deity and it can be believed that the heretics whom he detained and interrogated suffered 'neuer . . . so mych as a fylyppe on the forhed'.[36]

More began his campaign against the 'brethren' almost as soon as the parliamentary session had ended. In the first month of the new year, through the agency of the council, he issued a proclamation against heretics and heretical texts; he commanded every office-holder in the country to search them out, and issued a list of prohibited books of which the ownership would bring immediate imprisonment. The whole power of the realm, from the greatest sheriff to the humblest Dogberry constable, was now directed against the 'newe men'. In a letter to Erasmus he confirmed that he found them to be odious, and announced his determination to be as active against them as lay within his power; he told his old friend that the future of the world itself was in peril. It is not clear whether Erasmus shared these passionate sentiments – he may have agreed with St Bernard that in matters of faith it was better to persuade than to impose – but he understood the nature of More's hatred for '*seditiosa dogmata*'.[37] 'Seditious' is precisely the point since, for More, heresy was a form of disorder on every level. His duty to his religion and to his country came together, lending him a double strength and authority.

The first burning of his chancellorship was in no way connected with him, but his comments upon it are suggestive. Thomas Hitton was a Catholic priest who, after embracing the doctrines of Luther and of Zwingli, became an evangelical 'runner' between England and the Low Countries; he carried communications between the brethren of London and Antwerp, while at the same time distributing forbidden books. He was found, curiously enough, loitering in Gravesend; he was suspected of stealing some linen cloth which had been hanging on a hedge close by, but during a search letters 'vnto the euangelycall heretykes beyonde the see'[38] were discovered in the concealed pockets of his coat. It was only a month after More's proclamation against heresy and, in this new climate of suspicion and persecution, Hitton was brought before the Archbishop of Canterbury. Under interrogation he firmly proclaimed the tenets of his new-found faith. 'The masse he sayed sholde neuer be sayed . . . Purgatory he denyed . . . no man hath any fre wyll after that he hath onys synned . . . all the images of Cryste and hys sayntes, sholde be throwen out of the chyrche . . .'[39] Here was an abominable heretic indeed, and the archbishop dispatched him to the secular powers for punishment. He was burned at Maidstone, the first of the 'newe men' in England to be consigned to the flames. Thomas More derived a certain satisfaction from his fate or, rather, from the purging of that 'spiryte of errour and lyenge' which had taken Hitton's soul 'strayte from the shorte fyre to ye fyre euerlastyng'.[40]

In the month after Hitton's burning, More found a new ally in the war against heresy. John Stokesley succeeded Tunstall as Bishop of London and immediately became known as the hammer of heretics or, in the words of one of those whom he pursued, a 'blody bisshop crysten catte'.[41] The two men collaborated closely – on occasions Stokesley interrogated suspects in More's house at Chelsea – and there is a great deal of evidence to suggest that they successfully set up a network of spies and informants within the capital. In his own writings More takes great pleasure in explaining how he intercepted letters or interrogated witnesses; he describes in detail certain people and certain houses which were being closely watched. One heretic had secret friends 'at the sygne of the botell at Botolfes wharfe',[42] for example, an inn only a few yards from London Bridge. More knew that the mistress of this inn, 'the good wyfe of the botell of Botolphs', had a pronounced limp; he knew that she had previously allowed two renegade nuns to sleep 'in an hygh garet' of the house and had then smuggled in two men to lie with them; he also informed his readers that the good ale-wife 'is nat tong tayed'.[43] He added, perhaps rather chillingly, 'I haue herd her talke my selfe.'[44] His surveillance was exact in every particular, and he went so far as to warn the heretic residing at Botolph's Wharf that he had been seen disguised 'in a mertchauntes gowne wyth a redde Myllayne bonet'.[45]

More's position as a layman defending the Church was unique; his closest colleagues were now not the king and his courtiers, but the clergy. In the spring of 1530 he and his wife received a 'letter of confraternity' from the Benedictine foundation of Christ Church, Canterbury, and in the same period he was the only secular member of an ecclesiastical commission which met at Westminster to discuss heretical literature. More was particularly commended for his 'dylygent and longe consyderacyon',[46] a diligence that was reinforced when a further proclamation against heretical books was issued in June. More had once agreed upon the need for a translation of the Bible into the vernacular, but this proclamation gave as a reason to ban all such translations 'the malignity of this present time, with the inclination of people to erroneous opinions'.[47] More was becoming harsher and stricter.

The first fruit of this new repression arrived that autumn, when a number of people were arrested for owning banned books. More interrogated them in Star Chamber and then consigned them to the Tower, the Fleet or the Counter. The condemned heretics were forced to ride, facing the horses' tails, with various of their texts pinned to their clothing. They became, as it were, living books of heresy; during the journey from the Tower to Cheapside Cross, the citizens obliged by pelting them with rotten fruit and dung. One prisoner's servant was so alarmed by his employer's condition that he drew up a petition to the parliament, where it was believed there were men more favourable to the cause of reform; More summoned the servant and consigned him to the Fleet prison. Subsequently he launched a sudden raid upon the house of John Petyt, a wealthy merchant who resided in Lyon's Quay, just a few yards from the notorious inn at Botolph's Wharf. More led a search for heretical volumes, but it is reported that he could find no incriminating material; instead he relied upon the testimony of a priest who declared that Petyt had helped to finance the publication of Tyndale's books. Petyt eventually died as a prisoner in the Tower.

An interesting aspect of this unhappy case is that Petyt was a close friend of, and collaborator with, Thomas Cromwell, who was even then framing anticlerical legislation for parliament. There were reports that the king himself favoured a vernacular Bible and had studied various heretical texts, and that Cromwell had already made contact with certain of the 'newe men' in Antwerp and elsewhere. That is why the severity and urgency of More's conduct were a direct response to political, as well as spiritual, affairs.

More has left a record of his own conduct in such raids as that on the merchant's house by the river. There was a man named Richard Webb who had been denounced by various informants and whose name had emerged in More's interrogations of certain heretics. So More ordered 'a doser' or dossier to be prepared and summoned Webb to appear before him. The intricacies of the case, in which Webb was betrayed by one of his fellows, are less interesting than the words and demeanour of More on such occasions.

Richard Webb: I have heard that those who are true and plain in examination with you have always found you good and favourable.

Thomas More: If I find you true, then you will find me favourable. But I fear that your answers are not all true.

Richard Webb: Sir if you find any of my answers false, never be a good lord to me and never trust me while I live.

Thomas More: Is Bristol in Holborn, and is six weeks half a year?

With this remark the prisoner realised that part of his testimony had been undermined. 'Then downe he fell vppon hys marybonys, & pytuously prayed me to forgyue hym that one lye.'

Richard Webb: In good faith, sir, there is not in all mine answers any one thing untrue but that.

Thomas More: Well, Webb, in faith if that be true, then will I wink at this one and let it go for none.

Richard Webb: I would not be so mad to say as I do, and forsake your favour so foolishly.

Thomas More: Well, when saw you Robert Necton?

Richard Webb: Now by my soul, sir, as I have showed your lordship upon my oath, I saw him not this half year to my remembrance.

Thomas More: Was yesterday half a year ago? And were you not with him at saint Catherine's? Are you not now shamefully forsworn?[48]

And so it goes on, with More probing and sometimes taunting his prisoners with information gathered from his spies. He epitomised, in modern terms, the apparatus of the state using its power to crush those attempting to subvert it. His opponents were genuinely following their consciences, while More considered them the harbinger of the devil's reign on earth. How could there be moderation in any confrontation between them? He was, in large part, successful; he managed to check the more open expression of heretical opinion and thereby prevented it from being accepted piece by piece or gradually condoned. He also disrupted the community of 'newe men' in Antwerp and helped to diminish the flow of banned books into England.

The following year, 1531, was the time of burning. It was inaugurated by a macabre episode, with which More was not personally involved. A last will and testament had been judged heretical; the corpse of the perpetrator, William Tracy, was dug up and then ceremonially burnt. More was concerned with living heretics, however, and a few months later he became involved in the case of Thomas Bilney. He was known as 'Little Bilney' because he was 'of little stature and very slender of body';[49] he was also a fervent and devoted man, who preached the gospel in leperhouses and in prisons. He had recanted in the time of Wolsey, and was one of those who bore the faggot at the great ceremony by Paul's Cross in 1527, but he had since relapsed into heretical opinions. After examination the suspect was given into the custody of the ecclesiastical authorities, who pronounced him guilty of heresy and sent him back to secular officials for punishment. He was burned in the Lollard's Pit, outside Norwich, and was supposed to have recanted once more before the flames reached him. It is said that he had inured himself against the pain of fire by putting his hand over a lighted candle in his prison cell. But his apparent recantation became a highly contentious matter, involved with the sensitive question of the king's ecclesiastical authority, and More launched a swift if not very subtle Star Chamber investigation to stifle any possible controversy. Although this scheme was effective More felt obliged to defend the official account of events in the polemical work he was then writing. He declared that God 'of hys endles mercy brought hys body to deth',[50] but in the process saved Bilney's soul.

He approved of burning, therefore, and in that respect was no different from most of his contemporaries. He remarked that heresy in England – 'a good catholyke realme', as he could still put it[51] – had for centuries been 'punyshed by deth in ye fyre'.[52] He was correct, of course, and as early as 1210 we read of an Albigensian being consigned to the flames. There were less severe punishments available; some heretics had been burned on the left cheek, or obliged to wear clothes embroidered with a red cross for the rest of their lives. But burning was the natural remedy for those who refused to recant or who later relapsed. Lollards were burned in the fifteenth century, and it has been calculated that in the hundred years before More's chancellorship there were in the region of thirty fires.[53] So his actions were not exceptional, and it might be argued that his severe stance was a reaction to the menaces of the period. There is no doubt about his tenacity of purpose, for example, when he declares 'And after the fyre of Smythfelde, hell dothe receyue them where the wretches burne for euer';[54] they are 'well and worthely burned'.[55] These men anticipated the Antichrist who, as far as More was concerned, might soon be born among the wreckage of the world. Their words might tempt poor souls into eternal damnation. They had to be prevented by all and any means.

The condemned heretics were led to a wooden platform, some three feet from the ground, and were bound to the stake by a heavy chain; the bundles of sticks were then piled around them so high that their limbs were partly concealed from the circle of spectators. The mayor called out 'Fire the faggots!' and '*Fiat justitia!*' ('Let justice be done!'); then the executioner, after testing which way the wind blew, lit the wooden pile with a torch. There are many woodcuts of the proceedings, in some of which the church of St Batholomew can be seen behind the Smithfield fire. A large crowd is always gathered around the stake; on occasions the devout people have to be restrained by officials on horses and men brandishing halberds. A bench is erected for the benefit of 'nobles' who wish to view the interesting proceedings. Other people watch from open windows as the body of the condemned man, charred and melted by the flames, topples forward from its chain onto the fire. The timing of that moment was never certain, however; one heretic took forty-five minutes to die, and John Foxe records of him that 'when the left arm was on fyre and burned, he touched it with his right hand, and it fell from his bodye, and he continued to pray to the end wythout mouyng'.[56]

There were other burnings after that of Bilney, but not before More inflicted damage at the centre of the network of brethren. More received information that George Constantine, a 'carrier' of forbidden books, had secretly travelled to London. After investigations and searches, Constantine was discovered and taken to Chelsea, where he was placed in the stocks in order to await questioning by the Lord Chancellor. His interrogation lasted for several days, and, as More declared, there may have been no physical punishment except for that of the stocks. But there is a letter concerning Constantine, written to Thomas Cromwell from one of those suspected of heresy, which throws an interesting light on the nature of More's investigations. The correspondent, Stephen Vaughan, had been informed that More displayed a 'clear desire in his countenance and haviour to hear something of me';[57] Vaughan then noted Constantine's 'imminent peril and danger' before adverting to 'tortures and punishments'. Vaughan did not suggest that More himself inflicted these – he referred to unnamed 'ministers' – but he went on to mention 'threatenings of tortures and punishments'.[58] Here, in the realm of subtle threat and innuendo, we must imagine More.

Constantine talked. In More's words he 'vttered and dysclosed dyuers of hys companyons'[59] and he revealed the method of smuggling 'those deuelysshe bokes whyche hym selfe and other of hys felowes hadde brought and shypped';[60] he told More the name of the shipman and the secret marks placed on bundles of heretical material. This was a great *coup* for More, who at once went to work. Many books were seized and burned, but volumes alone were not sufficient. Constantine had named Richard Bayfield, a defaulting Benedictine and trader in banned books; he was arrested and, again in More's words, 'the monk and apostata' was 'well and worthely burned in Smythfelde'. More had joked with Constantine about Archbishop Warham's former policy of buying up the stock of heretical books in Antwerp; this tactic had served only to enrich the brethren, and the Lord Chancellor's stringent measures were intended to provide a more powerful lesson. And then Constantine escaped – or, as seems more likely, he was allowed to escape after providing such good service to the old faith. Less than three weeks after the burning of Bayfield, More dispatched another heretic to Smithfield. The house of a London leather-seller, John Tewkesbery, was found to harbour banned books; he had recanted two years before but now, after at least two public examinations led by the Lord Chancellor, he was sentenced to death. More declared that he had reverted to heresy as a dog returns to its own vomit, and so he was 'burned as there was neuer wretche I wene better worthy'.[61] Now he lay in hell, 'an hote fyrebronde burnynge at hys bakke, that all the water in the worlde wyll neuer be able to quenche'.[62] He was soon joined in that inferno by Thomas Dusgate, burnt for heresy in Exeter.

Yet there were still certain constraints upon More. A leading Lutheran and English exile in Antwerp, Robert Barnes, was given 'safe conduct' by the king to travel to England and remain for six weeks; it is not hard to discern the reason for this apparent welcome of a heretic, since, only a few months before, Barnes had written *A Supplication unto King Henry the Eighth*, which combined a generally anticlerical diatribe with an assault upon the authority of the Pope – 'can not the pope erre? lett hym rede his awne lawe.'[63] There were also familiar theological arguments drawn from Luther, but the king was now interested in theology only in as far as it concerned himself; this was a period when Henry seemed about to sever the ancient bonds of England with Rome and he was willing to listen to those who could provide cogent scriptural or doctrinal reasons in defence of his action. That is why Barnes was allowed to remain in London during the last weeks of the year.

Although More did not approve, he could do nothing but keep a close watch upon Barnes. He could perhaps frighten him a little by intercepting letters and questioning those whom the exile met; but, fundamentally, he was helpless in the face of this heretic. Barnes safely left the country and, as More wrote in a subsequent polemic against *Supplication*, 'lette hym go thys ones, for god shall fynde hys tyme full well'.[64] He was more cordial towards a German scholar of Zwinglian sympathies, Simon Grynaeus, who had travelled to England in order to pursue his study of Plato's texts. More made no effort to impede his movements but as a precaution he asked John Harris, his own servant, to accompany Grynaeus everywhere.

One of More's last triumphs came in the destruction of James Bainham, whose marriage to the widow of Simon Fish, author of *Supplication for the Beggars*, had cast grave doubts upon his orthodoxy. He was also a member of the Middle Temple, at a time when lawyers were becoming the most vociferous opponents of clerical power. More pounced upon him. He was taken to Chelsea and interrogated; More called him 'Baynam the iangler'[65] or empty talker, which suggests that the questioning was not altogether successful. Foxe reports that he was whipped and then put to the rack in the Tower, but this is most unlikely. It is true that Stokesley joined the interrogations at More's house, however, and eventually Bainham confessed to the ownership of heretical books. He was then offered the choice of recantation or the fire, but he prevaricated and joined the thirty or forty other Lutherans who were said to have been consigned by More to various prisons within the city.

Two months later Bainham formally abjured and was released, but his faith or conscience proved too strong; he relapsed into heresy, was taken up by the authorities, and 'The last day of Aprill, 1532, one Baynam, gentleman, was burnt in Smythfeild for heresie'.[66] According to the *Book of Martyrs*, Bainham, when tied to the stake, declared that 'I come hither, good people, accused and condemned for a heretic, Sir Thomas More being my accuser and my judge'. He then read aloud the articles of his faith and the citizens cried out: 'Set fire to him and burn him!' To which the condemned man replied, 'God forgive thee, and show thee more mercy than thou showest to me; the Lord forgive Sir Thomas More; and pray for me, all good people.' Then he himself prayed 'till the fire took his bowels and his head'.[67]

Bainham the 'jangler' appears in the book that More was writing at the time of the Smithfield fires. It is entitled *The Confutation of Tyndale's Answer* and has the distinction of being the longest religious polemic in the English language. In the spring of 1531 William Tyndale had issued *An Answer unto Sir Thomas More's Dialogue*, in which he used a rebuttal of *Dialogue Concerning Heresies* to mount a larger assault upon the rites and sacraments of the Church. Almost immediately More began to compose his *Confutation of Tyndale's Answer*, which, in the space of half a million words, attempts to answer Tyndale point by point. These books represent the most important dialogue within English religious discourse, perhaps of any age. The confrontation between Tyndale and More embodies the struggle between the opposing tendencies of the period – inner prayer and belief against communal worship and ritual, faith against works, the direct inspiration of scripture against inherited orthodoxy, redemption through Christ rather than the sacramental system. Of course it would be entirely wrong to see these tendencies as of equal force, or weight, at this moment of transition.

The brethren remained a very small sect indeed, and the people of England were as notably pious as before; but More sensed the danger. If the king were to defy the Pope, and to use the Lutherans for purposes of his own, then the fate of Germany might be visited upon them all. There was also a more general change which he could not have observed or anticipated except in the shape of the Antichrist; others have preferred to describe it as the emergence of the modern world.

More had reached such a pitch of nervous intensity that he could not rest from the fight; his whole life and duty lay now in his battle to protect the Church. Late at night, after his extensive duties as chancellor were completed, he sat up by candlelight in his library at Chelsea; he wrote quickly, almost furiously, composing thousands of words each week through the summer and winter of that year. That is why the *Confutation* is conceived in the form of a dialogue, in More's characteristic manner, as if the atmosphere of public disputation had to be maintained.

William Tyndale: Marke whyther yt be not true in the hyest degree . . .

Thomas More: Tyndale is a great marker. There is nothynge with hym now but marke, marke, marke. It is pytye that the man were not made a marker of chases in some tenys playe.[68]

It is dramatic and colloquial speech, as the protagonists confront each other upon the stage of Christendom itself. More has the advantage of humour in the exchanges, with the intentional use of ribaldry and insult as a way of belittling those opponents gradually growing in strength. He adopts the language of the 'comon peple' as a way of confronting Tyndale's own vivid use of demotic.

William Tyndale: Iudge whyther yt be possible that any good sholde come oute of theyr domme ceremonyes and sacramentes.

Thomas More: Iudge good crysten reader whyther yt be possyble that he be any better than a beste oute of whose brutyshe bestely mouth, commeth such a fylthye fome.[69]

His use of current phrases, as well as proverbs and anecdotes and stories, conveys his belief that the old faith is part of the customs and traditions of the people, whereas the heretics embrace only 'new-fanglynes'.

William Tyndale: But that the apostles gaue us any blynde ceremonies, whereof we coulde not knowe the reason, that I denye and also defye.

Thomas More: Forsoth saue for the ryme I wolde not geue a ryshe, neyther for his denyeng nor for hys defyenge.[70]

The *Confutation* was intended to be read aloud; the manner of the narrative is designed to ensure that short sections can be extracted and read to a group of people. That is why More's imagery is close to the popular sermons of the period and why he mentions both specific locations and individual citizens. He needed to capture the attention of his auditors in order to emphasise the pressing danger of these heresies.

William Tyndale: More muste nedes graunte that chyrche is as comen as ecclesia.

Thomas More: Fyrst I say that mayster More must not nedys graunte thys to Tyndale neuer a whytte.[71]

The argument here is over a crucial point of translation, and at such points in the narrative More tries to anticipate every line of attack, to leave nothing undecided or undefended, to quibble and question and define and distinguish until his opponent sinks exhausted under the weight of his cross-examination.

William Tyndale was himself a grave and learned scholar; he was a courteous and unworldly man but, if he was diffident on his own account, he was fervent for the truth. He was also a wonderful exponent of a plain English style, as any reader of his biblical translations will know, and there was some justice in his attack upon More as a mere poet, a juggler of words who 'biteth, sucketh, gnaweth, towseth and mowseth Tyndale'.[72] More was a sophister who dealt in 'taunts and mocks',[73] a charge which was also levelled at him by others who denounced his resort to farce and 'feyning'. This was always the principal criticism directed against him and it suggests, perhaps, the image he gave to the world. But if they found fault with him for not treating Tyndale 'with no fayrer wordes nor in no more courteyse maner',[74] the other complaint was, in More's own words, that 'my writyng is ouer longe, and therfore to tedyouse to rede'.[75] His explanation for this repetitiveness lay in his need continually to concentrate upon certain key themes and doctrines so that the good Christian 'Shal not nede to rede ouer any chapyter but one'.[76] Where men like Barnes typically wrote brief tracts, with their points succinctly made, More felt obliged to reply with discourses which try to stop up every gap, close any loophole, destroy every argument, with an urgency that is palpable upon the page; it is as if he were intent upon out-shouting or deafening his opponents. There is perhaps a more private reason, too, for the length and elaboration of his polemic. He writes all the more volubly and excitedly here because he could not properly speak out in council or at the court; his polemic was a form of compensation for his incapacity as a maker of policy.

The central theme of the *Confutation* is that there is only one true Church, the visible and orthodox communion of Catholics. Throughout its history its members have been frail or weak, but that in no way affects its authority as Christ's mystical body upon the earth. It is the permanent and living sign of Christ's presence, sustained by inherited custom and maintained by traditional knowledge. It is a visible, extensive and palpable community rather than a few 'brethren' gathered in secret rooms. Just as parliament was considering plans for the reformation of abuses among the clergy, More was insisting that the sinfulness or folly of individuals – even the wickedness of a bad pope – in no way affected the divinely instituted *sanctitas* of the Catholic Church. There were covert messages here to the king as well as to the members of parliament, but no one chose to listen to them.

A more general interpretation can also be offered. When More writes of 'one fayth in the howse of god',[77] he is at the same time invoking the medieval society of the household. Among the articles of his creed, in other words, are the precepts of the world in which he grew up – a world where communality and tradition were no less important than external ritual and inherited faith. Indeed they cannot be separated one from another without a general dissolution of 'the comen knowen catholique chyrch'.[78] Yet William Tyndale was possessed by an alternative vision of private belief and individual grace; he made the distinction between 'an hystorycall fayth' and 'a felynge fayth',[79] with all his trust residing within that 'sure felynge' which is vouchsafed to those when 'god shall wryte yt in theyr hertes wyth his holy spyryte'.[80] His was a powerful statement of individual redemption, but one that More rejected utterly as the shortest way to pride and anarchy. More was fully acquainted with the frailty of 'we pore worldely men of mydle erth',[81] therefore, and from this awareness springs much of his irony and humour. From it, too, comes his overwhelming desire for discipline and external authority.

What if that authority should, then, disappear in some new age of the world? The presiding image of *The Confutation of Tyndale's Answer* is that of 'Tyndales great Mayster Antecryste'.[82] This was not for More some bugbear to scare children, but a real and pressing threat. Martin Luther had married a Cistercian nun, Katharina Bora, or, in More's words, 'toke out of relygyon a spouse of Cryste'[83] and it was generally believed 'that Antecryste sholde be borne betwene a frere and a nunne'.[84] So the beast might be about to come forth, and on two occasions More adverts to the approaching horror, when 'the great archeheretyke Antycryste come hym selfe whyche as helpe me god I fere be very nere hys tyme'[85] and 'now very nere at hande'.[86] This was the terror which he was preparing himself to face; he truly believed that Luther and Tyndale were the false prophets or disciples of the great beast. It is now possible, perhaps, to understand the feverish haste and urgency of his work, a clamancy which is not untouched by a sense of weariness and feeling of doom. There are times when More begs his 'good cristen readers' not to study any heretical books; he even implores them, in one remarkable passage, not to read his own in case the very mention of false beliefs might contaminate or confound them. This was the pass to which he had come; he abhors the mention of heresy even as he launches a huge barrage of words against it.

There was another reason for his weariness and sorrow. In the winter of 1530 his father, Sir John More, died; he had not quite reached his eightieth year, according to Erasmus, but until the end had seemed wonderfully alert. Family history reports that he died from eating 'a Surfeit of Grapes',[87] which does not suggest fading health; on his own epitaph More preferred to believe that his father died 'having witnessed his son made Lord Chancellor of England'. His son-in-law recalled that, in the moments of his father's death, More 'with tears taking him about the neck, most lovingly kissed and embraced him, commending him into the merciful hands of almighty God'.[88] This is the first report of More's tears, which would be plentiful in the years that followed. And then he grew sick. After the death of his father he began to suffer from some disease of the chest;[89] he also confessed that he began to feel himself growing very old.[90] His was a severe and in a literal sense morbid reaction, yet not perhaps unexpected in a man who used the image or metaphor of 'the father' as the token of social order and authority. By strange chance Cardinal Wolsey, under arrest at the king's command, died within two or three days of John More; in their joint passing we might see the demise of the old order itself.

More's father was buried in the church of St Lawrence Jewry, a few yards from the family home in Milk Street, and had asked that his funeral be 'not to pompiously perfourmed'.[91] The coffin was sprinkled with holy water before being lowered into the stone tomb; the mourners, arrayed in special gowns of black, white or russet, held lighted torches at the moment of interment. It was generally believed that thirteen was the optimum number for those present, in commemoration of the last supper, but for so grand a man as Sir John More there may have been many others. There was then a funeral feast, in honour of the living and the dead, as John More entered the great communion of souls. He became a spiritual member of what More, in the fourth book of his *Confutation*, had called 'thys great knowen congregacyon'.[92] But a great change had come upon More himself when he wrote those words; he had resigned as Lord Chancellor and, in horror at the collapse of the established authority of his Church, he had retreated to Chelsea.

XXVII

Infinite Clamour

AT three o'clock of a spring afternoon in 1532, Thursday 16 May, Sir Thomas More was admitted to York Place 'beside the village of Westminster', as the official report of the ceremony puts it. It had been Wolsey's home but it now belonged to the king. He was taken to the garden, where the king awaited him. In the presence of the Duke of Norfolk, More then ceremoniously handed to Henry VIII the pouch which contained the Great Seal of England. The king graciously received this symbol of office, and granted More leave to bestow the rest of his life in preparing his soul 'in the service of God'.[1] 'And for the service which you before have done me,' Henry went on to say, 'you will find me a good and gracious lord unto you in any suit which should concern your honour or pertain unto your profit'.[2] Yet he bestowed none of the customary honours on the resignation of his chief counsellor. More's own feelings are not fully known, although at a later date he suggested that if a man 'seeth the thinges that he shuld set his hand to sustayne, decay thorow his defaut & fall to ruyne vnder hym' then 'I in any wise aduise hym to leve of that thing . . . give it ouer quyte & draw hym selfe aside, & serve god'.[3] This is precisely the task which More set himself, as his own world fell 'to ruyne'.

The public events leading up to More's resignation will be familiar to those interested in the progress of the Reformation and the development of England as a commercial nation-state, but in the context of Thomas More's life they may be seen in a less familiar perspective. On More's appointment as Lord Chancellor in the autumn of 1529, the king had broached with him his 'great matter' of the annulment and had asked him to consult a group of scholars and theologians who were already advancing his cause. Although More was not persuaded by their arguments, his sense of loyalty and perhaps also of prudence was such that he never read any books opposing the king but 'gladly' studied many which supported his master's case. Among the band of committed scholars were Stokesley, Foxe, Lee and Cranmer; they were in no way deterred by More's refusal to join them, and had indeed already been instructed to gather supporting documents as well as learned opinions favourable to the monarch. The English universities were the first to express their support, in the spring of 1530, but not without much questioning and controversy; Thomas Cranmer, who was in these years rapidly emerging as the king's most active scholar, had composed a treatise on the subject of the doubtful marriage which was then put to the congregations of both universities. Finally they agreed that it was 'more probable'[4] that the king's scruples were justified; he should not have been allowed to marry his dead brother's wife, if it was indeed true that she had been carnally 'known'. More believed, of course, along with many others, that Catherine's claims to virginity at the time of her second marriage were true. But he had been chancellor of both universities and knew that bribery and patronage were not unwelcome visitors to academic life.

The king was not intent on seeking scholarly approval alone and, in the middle of June, he summoned a great meeting of lords and prelates to place their signatures and seals upon a letter to the Pope; this epistle urged Clement to accede to the request for an annulment, but it was couched in so hostile a tone that many of those assembled could not agree to its terms. It is probable that Henry adverted to his belief that he might act without the Pope's consent. In any event the letter was redrafted and, in more humble words, urged the Pope to 'declare by your authority, what so many learned men proclaim'.[5] This ornate and gilded document was then sent to Rome where it produced little, if any, effect. The most notable name absent from the list of signatories is that of the Lord Chancellor, Sir Thomas More. Although he may have refused to sign, it is more likely that his opinions were so well known that he was not asked to put his name to the letter; but already it is possible to sense the isolation and exclusion into which he would eventually be drawn. And, where pleading failed, threat might take its place. In the following month fourteen prelates, most of whom had taken Catherine's part in the great argument, were accused of breaches of praemunire legislation. The charges were ostensibly related to Wolsey's period of office, but they were clearly directed against the opponents of the king's 'divorce'. It was rumoured at the time that More was most unhappy with this legal chicanery and had thought of resigning his post, but for the moment nothing happened. He must have calculated that any abrupt or irreversible decision would hurt the cause of Catherine; so he remained in a position where he might affect, if not make, policy.

The course of events grew clearer month by month, as the king became informed of his possible legislative and spiritual independence. In the late summer of this year a collection of documents, together with supportive 'determinations' from certain foreign universities, was presented to the king. It was known as the *Collectanea satis copiosa*, and marshalled evidence from the Donation of Constantine to Geoffrey of Monmouth's *History of the Kings of Britain*, from Anglo-Saxon scrolls to conciliar records, in order to suggest that as the ruler of a traditional empire Henry had inherited the power of ecclesiastical jurisdiction within his domain. It was an ancient argument, concerning the concept of 'Albion' and 'the matter of Britain', but for Henry it was simply a means of asserting his authority over the Pope. He annotated the various manuscripts delivered to him and over a period of some months seems genuinely to have convinced himself that he was head of the faith in England. More was aware of the course of events, but still he held his ground; Henry was all the while pursuing his case at Rome, and seemed uncertain about the precise direction of his policy. It was More's duty to wait, and to watch.

Henry ordered a second round of visits to the universities of France and Italy while at the same time, in mid-September, he issued a proclamation against the entry of any papal bulls detrimental to the king's concerns. This was a direct assault upon the authority of the Pope, and More openly expressed his disagreement. He was almost dismissed at that point and, according to diplomatic dispatches, the king now began to complain that More had not signed the general petition to the Pope on the subject of the marriage; the Spanish ambassador reported that 'the Chancellor, I hear, has spoke so much in the queens favour' that he might be forced to resign.[6] There was a further complication, of which More was not unaware. Henry had discovered that the discussions of the Privy Council had 'got wind' and were being disclosed to Catherine and her supporters.[7] More was nominally the senior member of that council, but is it possible that suspicion fell upon him?

At a great council in Hampton Court, convened that autumn to discuss the king's marriage and to prepare for the next parliamentary session, Henry's proposals on the country's ecclesiastical sovereignty were not welcomed; a contemporary report discloses that, as a result, 'the king was very angry, and adopted the expedient of proroguing parliament till the month of February'.[8] One of the reasons that More remained in office is because there were still many nobles, lawyers and prelates who shared his beliefs. So parliament was prorogued – in the event only until January – but, before the new session opened, the king took Thomas Cromwell into his service. From this time forward, the conduct of policy became more coherent and skilful, as events drifted away from More. The portrait of Cromwell by Holbein depicts the resolution and pugnacity of the man; he does not possess that mysteriousness which the half-opened curtain behind the image of More seems to imply. The artist has caught the reflection of thought upon the face of his sitter, but there is a determination stamped upon Cromwell's features which suggests that thought will soon turn into action and practical decision.

He was born in Putney and his father, according to conflicting and sometimes malicious reports, had been a blacksmith or fuller or even a brewer. Cromwell himself had become a soldier, a banker, a merchant; he was one of those men who seek their fortune in other countries and among alien customs. But the adventurer finally came home and, after marrying an heiress, took up the life of a London banker and merchant. He was a member of the parliament of 1523, when More himself was its Speaker, and at that time he came to the attention of Wolsey; the cardinal recognised in others gifts similar to those he himself possessed, and Cromwell became one of his most trusted and efficient servants. It is also important to recognise that his sympathies were with the 'newe men' and the reformers, even though they had to be partly concealed until circumstances were more propitious. There is an illuminating anecdote, told by Wolsey's servant, of Cromwell's behaviour after the cardinal's forced resignation. He found 'Master Cromwell leaning in the great window with a primer in his hand'.[9] He was weeping, with indignation or self-pity, at the prospect that he was likely to descend with his erstwhile master. 'I cannot tell,' he said, 'but all things, I see before mine eyes, is as it is taken.' By which he meant that the opinions and interpretations of others were paramount. So he had come to a decision. 'I do intend,' he added, 'God willing, this afternoon when

my lord hath dined to ride to London and so to the court, where I
will either make or mar . . . I will put myself in the press to see what
any man is able to lay to my charge of untruth or misdemeanour.'[10]
This statement testifies both to his shrewdness and his courage; there
is also a perhaps apocryphal story that he recommended that a
staunch defender of the 'old faith' read Machiavelli rather than old
books.

The fall of the 'great wether', as More had called Wolsey, did not
in fact affect Cromwell's career; he had unique powers of organisation and administration which would have been invaluable to any
sovereign or great minister. So, by the end of 1530, he had become
an important member of the king's council. Certainly he was actively
preparing parliamentary business on an ambitious scale. He is likely
to have been the source of Henry's threat to charge all the English
clergy with breach of praemunire, for example, on the ground that
their ecclesiastical courts deferred to Rome rather than to England.
But Cromwell prepared much more detailed and elaborate proposals
which encompassed public, as well as religious, reform. There is a
document, dating from this period, that contains draft bills and items
of proposed legislation. Many of those measures are clearly designed
to curb the power and the abuses of the clergy: a 'great standyng
counsayll'[11] is suggested to establish limits on the jurisdiction of
church courts, and any attempt to criticise the anticlerical legislation
of the last parliamentary session is to be deemed illegal. There are
other items of a similar nature, but the author or authors of the
document also turn their attention to secular affairs. A scheme of
public works is proposed to curb unemployment, for example, and
urgent attention is to be paid to the problems of inflation and rural
decay. It is not likely that More approved of all these plans, but he
might well have supported the programme of public renovation. Yet
he was no longer in a position to help or to hinder; the initiative had
passed to Cromwell, who was indeed the man for a new age.

There is one recognisable author of this parliamentary proposal,
since much of its writing is in the hand of a lawyer named
Christopher St German. He had been a member of the Middle
Temple, and was now in his seventies; he had also been acquainted
with Sir John More and had been published by John Rastell, so he
would have been well known to the Lord Chancellor. He was the
most eminent legal theorist of his period but, unhappily for More, his
principal purpose was to systematise the common law of England

and in effect to diminish the jurisdictional powers of the Church. In *Doctor and Student*, the last part of which was published in the same year as Cromwell entered the king's council, St German asserted the claims of common law over canon law; property was not a divine gift, for instance, and any disputes over estates or inheritance should be removed from the church courts. His essential argument consisted in the declaration that the law of the realm, rather than ecclesiastical law, should be pre-eminent. This was one of those rare books which appeared at precisely the right moment, and the septuagenarian scholar found himself quickly translated into the councils of state. He may have been present at the meeting in Hampton Court and he was certainly given the task, by Cromwell or by the king himself, to draw up proposals for legislation. In the same year that he drafted these measures to confine the powers of the Church, as well as to check its abuses, he published *New Additions* to his earlier work which affirmed the sovereignty of the king-in-parliament as 'the high sovereign over the people, which hath not only charge on the bodies, but also on the souls of his subjects'.[12] The fact that St German's legislative proposals were not enacted in the parliament of 1531 does not detract from their significance. Henry now had legal and constitutional, as well as historical, support in his struggle to assert his throne over the papacy.

Parliament's next session opened in the middle of January 1531, in an atmosphere of rumour, threat and suspicion. Catherine and her supporters were apprehensive, while Anne Boleyn was triumphant in her disdain for 'the queen or any of her family'.[13] It is also possible to detect signs of new belligerence on the king's part. The convocation of the clergy was summoned from Canterbury to Westminster, where Henry challenged them in two respects. He demanded £100,000 in order to recoup the cost of his fruitless negotiations with Rome, and at the same time threatened to indict the spiritual leaders of the English Church for breach of praemunire in respect of their association with Wolsey. The members of the convocation first prevaricated and then surrendered. They agreed to give Henry the money and sued pardon. In exchange they asked for a restatement of traditional clerical privileges, which Henry refused. At this point the guiding hands of Cromwell and St German can be glimpsed behind the assertion of the king's will; far from acceding to the demands of the clergy, Henry acted in a manner which shows that he had been a close reader of the legal scholar. He widened the terms of praemunire

to threaten the very existence of ecclesiastical courts in England, and
also demanded that he be termed 'sole protector and supreme head
of the English Church and clergy'.

The direction of the king's policy was now becoming clear and the
Bishop of Rochester, John Fisher, made a significant announcement
to the House of Lords on the matter. 'We cannot grant this unto the
King,' he declared, without abandoning 'our unity with the see of
Rome . . . we renounce the unity of the Christian world; and so leap
out of Peter's ship, to be drowned in the waves of all heresies, sects,
schisms and divisions.' The acceptance of regal supremacy would
represent 'a tearing of the seamless coat of Christ in sunder'.[14] This
was a defining statement, but at this early stage the king did not seem
inclined to press the matter too far. After prolonged negotiations a
modifying clause was added to the king's new title – '*quantum per
legem Dei licet*'; that is, as far as the law of God allows. This was
then put to convocation, which responded only with a sullen silence.
Archbishop Warham then announced: '*Qui tacet consentire videtur*'
('Whoever remains silent can be assumed to agree'). The king's new
title, or authority, was tacitly accepted; but it had been imposed
upon an unwilling Church, which remained apprehensive and
uncertain.

The extant records of More's official business in this period show
him to have busily engaged in his judicial duties; but, as leader of the
Lords and senior member of the Council, he was perfectly aware of
the development of policy. He was even, nominally, a participant in
it. Within days of Henry winning the title of 'supreme head' from
convocation, the Spanish ambassador reported that 'The chancellor
is so mortified at it that he is anxious above all things to resign his
office'.[15] He chose not to do so, or was persuaded by his friends and
allies that it would not serve the cause. His own reasons for
remaining in office are clearly depicted in another Spanish dispatch.
The Emperor Charles V had written him a letter of support and
encouragement for his efforts on Catherine's behalf; but More
declined, in the most polite terms, to receive it. At first he managed
altogether to avoid the Spanish ambassador, Eustace Chapuys; when
he eventually received news of the imperial missive, he implored
Chapuys not to deliver it to him. 'He begged me for the honour of
God to forbear, for although he had given already sufficient proof of
his loyalty that he ought to incur no suspicion, whoever came to visit
him, yet, considering the time, he ought to abstain from everything

which might provoke suspicion; and if there were no other reason, such a visitation might deprive him of the liberty which he had always used in speaking boldly in those matters which concerned your Majesty and the Queen.' More went on to pledge his most 'affectionate service' to the emperor.[16]

Certain conclusions can be drawn from this appeal. Clearly there had been no occasion when he had shown any disloyalty towards the king, whatever his own opinions may have been; this in turn suggests that Henry considered him to be an effective and trustworthy Lord Chancellor. Indeed his fidelity afforded him the privilege of offering advice which might not necessarily please the king. There were occasions when he came close to the limit of his master's tolerance, and he had already once been threatened with dismissal. Nevertheless, he was still so good a servant that he could speak out where others remained silent – although it is likely that he did so in the guise of impersonal or theoretical counsel, in which his own feelings were not involved. That ability to offer disinterested advice would be jeopardised by any communication with the emperor. More's assurance to Charles V of his 'affectionate service', however, suggests that all was not as it seemed; he had his own objectives, which could only be pursued gradually and secretly. This is not to suggest that he was in any sense engaged in treachery or betrayal; he believed that part of his role as Lord Chancellor was to purge the conscience of the king in exactly the same manner as those of the malefactors who appeared before him in Chancery. In his conversation with Chapuys, More had indeed invoked 'the welfare, honour and conscience' of his master; he was able to speak out on the queen's behalf, for example, precisely because Henry trusted More's good faith, if not his opinions, in these matters. It was a difficult as well as an ambiguous role and More was the only man in the kingdom who could have played it. He also knew well enough the dangers of his strategy; when John Fisher spoke against the king's assumption of supremacy, according to Chapuys, 'he and his followers have been threatened with death, by being cast into the Thames'.

A few days after his conversation with Chapuys, at the end of March, More read out a statement to the House of Lords on the subject of the king's marriage. He declared that Henry had not pursued an annulment 'out of love for some lady' but, rather, for reasons of conscience and religion.[17] It is likely that the king had already persuaded himself that this was the truth, and More was doing no more than play the role of a lawyer putting his client in the best possible light. The favourable opinions of the universities were then read out to those assembled, and a formidable case was made. One great scholar of More has confessed that 'the academic stature and the professional integrity of Henry VIII's adherents were almost unimpeachable'.[18] So More was in no sense compromising himself by these statements in the House of Lords. But then he was asked for his own opinion and, according to an account of the proceedings, he replied that 'he had many times already declared it to the king; and he said no more'.[19] It is interesting to note that he had declared his opposition, or neutrality, 'many times' to Henry; yet the king still obliged him to act as his representative on the matter.

After the address to the Lords, More, with a company of peers and prelates, proceeded to the 'comen House', where he spoke again. 'You of this worshipful House, I am sure, be not so ignorant but you know well that the king our sovereign lord hath married his brother's wife, for she was both wedded and bedded with his brother Prince Arthur.'[20] More clearly spoke against his own belief here, since he was himself convinced of Catherine's virginity. He went on to say that 'Wherefore the king, like a virtuous prince, willing to be satisfied in his conscience, and also for the surety of his realm hath with great deliberation consulted with great clerks, and . . . the chief Universities of all Christendom to know their opinion and judgment in that behalf.' At this point the clerk of the Commons read out these opinions and judgments. More concluded his performance by declaring that 'the king hath not attempted this matter of will or pleasure, as some strangers report, but only for the discharge of his conscience and surety of the succession of his realm'.[21] His son-in-law reports that after this episode More wished to resign on the grounds of poor health; he asked the Duke of Norfolk for his help in persuading the king to release him from his increasingly compromising and unpalatable duties. Henry was using him in a deliberate or cunning fashion, and he knew it. Yet More stayed, subduing his private inclination for the sake of the great struggles ahead. The parliament deliberated on such matters as the wool trade, the treatment of vagrants and the punishment for poisoners; the Church had not been attacked and the session came to an end without any further resolution of the king's 'great matter'.

It was a spring and summer of faction. From the dispatches of Eustace Chapuys it is possible to follow More's increasingly troubled path through court and council. He reported that the Lord Chancellor was already well known in England as 'the father and protector of the Emperor's subjects',[22] by which he probably meant the merchants and bankers of Spain or the Low Countries; but it may be also a covert reference to those who wished to defend the old faith. More is also recorded to have expressed his dismay 'in a very piteous tone, of the blindness of those princes who refused to assist Your Majesty against so cruel and implacable an enemy' as the Turks;[23] this was a clear reference to Henry, whose obsession with the 'great matter' was such that he refused to notice the great and pressing danger of the Turkish invasion of Christendom. This was certainly another of More's preoccupations. It was a further token of the advance of Antichrist and it was believed by many people that the Lutherans were not necessarily opposed to the Muslim onslaught; it was one way of destroying the old Church. There was also a rumour, faithfully reported by Chapuys, that Henry was prepared to declare war against Charles. Yet More had taken the trouble of reassuring the ambassador's secretary that in England 'there were no preparations or power to do so'.[24] More's reputation for reticence was such that these oblique comments about the king might even be construed as hostility.

The growing triumphalism of Anne Boleyn and her adherents was everywhere apparent to him. The royal mistress had evinced 'such demonstrations of joy as if she had actually gained Paradise'[25] at the time the king acquired the title of 'supreme head' of the Church in England; she had already ordered to be embroidered upon the coats of her liveried servants the phrase '*Ainsi sera, groigne qui groigne*' ('It will happen, whoever grudges it'). At the end of May a party of royal councillors visited Catherine at Greenwich in order to persuade her to abandon her cause; they were not successful. Then, on 11 July, Henry left her for ever. This is the private atmosphere in which the king prosecuted his public campaign by issuing the 'determinations' of the universities (with an accompanying treatise) and in which Thomas Cromwell laid plans for the next session of parliament. But if Anne Boleyn and her allies were triumphant, they were not yet omnipotent. There were powerful forces ranged against them, forces who might yet persuade the king to check his personal inclinations for the sake of the realm and the old faith.

More was not alone at this stage, therefore, although he was the most visible and perhaps most effective member of what has lately been termed as the 'faction' supporting Catherine of Aragon. There were women of noble birth who took her side – the Duchess of Norfolk, Margaret Pole Countess of Salisbury, Gertrude Marchioness of Exeter and the Countess of Derby among them. There were courtiers and members of the household such as Sir Henry Guildford and Nicholas Carewe. There were great nobles of the realm such as the Earl of Shrewsbury and Lord Darcy, as well as the Seymours and Arundells, who were determined, in the phrase of the period, to 'uphold the queen's rights'. Two of the burgesses of London, William Bowyer and Paul Withypool, publicly represented what was a general City sympathy for Catherine; many London clergy followed the example of Dr Coke, priest of All Hallows in Honey Lane, by preaching against the king's course. There were the bishops of Ely, Bath, Norwich and St Asaph, who supported the efforts of Cuthbert Tunstall, William Warham and John Fisher. There were many members of the lower house of convocation deeply opposed to any annulment, and there were parliamentarians who met at the Queen's Head Tavern, in a passage off Fleet Street, in order to plan their strategy against the king and Anne Boleyn. In parliament, too, were a number of members who might be termed More's 'allies' or affinity. Yet some of the most effective opposition came from the religious orders closest to the royal family itself, the Bridgettines of Syon Abbey and the Franciscan Observants at Greenwich. The Austin Friars and Carthusians of London were also opposed to the king's 'great matter'. These were significant forces indeed, arrayed against a small group of people who owed everything to Henry's patronage – Thomas Cranmer, Thomas Audley, Thomas Cromwell as well as Anne Boleyn and her family. In retrospect it might seem that the spirit of the age, or the force of history, or some other deterministic concept, was also with them; but at the time the power and resourcefulness of the Aragonese 'coalition' helped to persuade More of the merits of remaining in his post. Catherine, and the old faith, might still be rescued.

On the first day of the new year, 1532, Henry VIII and Sir Thomas More exchanged festive gifts; More presented the king with a walking stick inlaid in gold leaf and in turn he was given a great golden bowl. Two weeks later the parliament met, in a session which would decide the course of the Reformation and determine More's own fate. The struggle began in earnest in February when a bill was presented to the parliament through the agency of Cromwell; it was designed to put pressure on the Pope by denying him much English revenue paid as 'annates' by new bishops. At the same time indictments were laid against the privileges of several leading clergy. The direction of policy seems clear, but in practice the situation was thoroughly confused. Henry was still courting the Pope even as he threatened the English Church. The lower house of parliament, in the words of Norfolk, was filled with the 'infenyte clamor of the temporalyte . . . agaynst the mysusyng of the spiritual jurysdiccion',[26] yet at the same time the bill depriving the Pope of annates was strongly resisted; the king himself visited Westminster on three occasions in order to secure the passage of the legislation, and in the end it was passed only when he demanded that the members of the Commons physically stood up to be counted. Those opposing and those supporting his measure were instructed to go to opposite ends of the chamber, thus creating the first recorded parliamentary 'division'. It was not an auspicious beginning, however, for Cromwell's schemes against the power of the clergy. Thomas More presided over the Lords for all this period, where he had also witnessed strong resistance to the king's demands. There must have seemed an opportunity for conciliation or compromise, and More was no doubt ready to put all his skills into the most urgent business of his life.

But then Thomas Cromwell struck again, on this occasion by introducing a petition which complained of the injustice involved in trials for heresy; here, of course, he was attacking the methods and procedures close to More's own conduct. The 'Supplication of the Commons Against the Ordinaries' ranged over the whole field of ecclesiastical jurisdiction and in large part reflected Christopher St German's theoretical objections to the clerical courts. The chronicler of this parliament, Edward Hall, reports the agreement of the Commons that 'all the griefes which the temporall men were greved with should be putte in writyng and delyvered to the kyng, which by great advyse was done'.[27] In the middle of March the members of the Commons accordingly submitted a petition to Henry which explained 'how the temporal men of this realme were sore agrieved with the cruel demeanoure of the prelates and ordinaryes [the secular clergy], which touched both their bodyes and goodes';[28] they then implored the king to establish 'your jurisdiction and prerogative royal' thereby bringing his subjects, both clerical and lay, into 'perpetual unity'.[29] The specific complaints and charges were, on any close scrutiny, unjustified; but that was not the point. Cromwell and his agents were obliged to maintain their campaign against the clergy, if only because it had seemed to be losing any of the momentum which it had once possessed. The Commons, however, delivered their supplication to the king only to request that the parliamentary session be forthwith prorogued. The king rebuked them for their nonchalance and then passed the supplication to Archbishop Warham and convocation. He was assuming the role of supreme mediator between all his subjects.

More realised well enough the pressing danger: his entire career as Lord Chancellor and prosecutor of heresy was being undermined, and it might be that by parliamentary statute heretics would soon be able to 'swarm' in the streets without any check. The Commons did adjourn, over the holy period of Easter, but the days of late March and early April were filled with strident controversy. The Church was being seriously threatened and some of its more outspoken members were already fighting back. William Peto was head of the Franciscan Observants at Greenwich and in the Chapel Royal he preached to the king in the manner of Savonarola. 'Your Highness's preachers are too much like those of Ahab's days, in whose mouths was found a false and lying spirit. Theirs is a gospel of untruth . . . not afraid to tell of license and liberty for monarchs which no king should dare even to contemplate.'[30] Once again the king's desire to annul his marriage was being implicitly aligned with his wish to curb the powers of the Church. Peto then delivered his most solemn rebuke. 'I beseech your Grace to take good heed, lest if you will need follow Ahab in his doings, you will surely incur his unhappy end also, and that the dogs lick your blood as they licked Ahab's – which God avert and forbid!'[31] On the next Sunday a more amenable preacher, Hugh Curwen, accused Peto of being another Micah speaking evil to kings – 'Thou art a dumb dog, or else art fled.' No sooner had he uttered these solemn words from the pulpit of the Chapel Royal when Henry Elstow, the guardian of the Greenwich Observants, spoke out to rebuke him. He reminded the preacher that Peto had fled only so far as a provincial council in Canterbury, and then accused Curwen of being 'one of the four hundred lying prophets, into whom the spirit of lying is entered: thou seekest by proposing adultery to establish a succession. In this, thou art betraying the King to everlasting perdition!'

This was a significant moment, when the king's opponents found their voices. The Earl of Essex, sitting with the king, shouted out. 'You shameless friar! you shall be sewn up in a sack and thrown into the Thames, if you do not speedily hold your tongue!' Elstow replied finely: 'Make those threats to your fellow courtiers. As for us friars, we make little account of them indeed, knowing well that the way lieth as open to heaven by water as by land.'[32] Peto and Elstow were popular preachers, with a holy mission to mingle with all of the people, and in that sense they represented a real threat to Henry's stratagems. A sermon in London could become a great public event, and the volatility of the populace was well known. That is why official papers of the time display evident unease at the prospect of controversy stirred by the words of priests and friars. There were also the presses. A treatise by Catherine's chaplain, entitled *Invicta Veritas*, had been imported, while various ultra-orthodox sermons and treatises were reissued with warnings against the 'false and subtyll deceites'[33] of the heretics.

This was the atmosphere in which parliament reassembled on 10 April, with the supplication of the Commons not yet answered by the prelates. More sent for one of the members who supported the queen's cause, Sir George Throckmorton, and received him 'in a little chamber within the Parliament chamber where, as I do remember, stood an altar or a thing like unto an altar whereupon he did lean'.[34] More was at that moment holding a conversation with a conservative bishop, but he broke it off. Throckmorton was one of those who met at the Queen's Head tavern to plan their strategy and now, before the most fateful events of the session, More wished to encourage him. 'I am very glad,' he said, 'to hear the good report that goeth of you and that ye be so good a catholic man as ye be; and if ye do continue in the same way that ye began and be not afraid to say your conscience, ye shal deserve great reward of God and thanks of the king's grace at length and much worship to yourself.'[35] It is unlikely that Throckmorton was the only member to be summoned by More in order to be told to stand firm, and the evidence suggests that there was now an organised attempt to thwart the king's will. Throckmorton, for example, had already been instructed in the same manner by Father Peto, whose stern sermon to the king had led to his confinement within Lambeth Palace; it was here that Peto urged Throckmorton to serve the queen's cause 'as I would have my soul saved'.[36] Throckmorton also conferred with three others supporting the cause of the queen and the old faith, Nicholas Wilson, Richard

Reynolds and John Fisher. It is perhaps significant that More had told him that the king would thank him 'at a later date'; clearly he believed that this struggle would be of some duration and that any favourable outcome would take time. But there was no time.

Ten days after the opening of parliament the convocation of the clergy gave their answer to the 'supplication', which was no answer at all; it simply reaffirmed the rights and duties of Christ's Church on earth. A more substantial document was presented a week later, but this second answer proved no more favourable to a king who was all the time testing the extent of his new-found power; he handed the letter to the Commons with the remark that 'We think this answer will smally please you, for it seemeth to us very slender'.[37] His anger was also directed at those members of the Commons, such as Throckmorton, who openly expressed their support for Catherine.

The king's distrust of the bishops and his displeasure at what seemed like organised opposition to him in parliament, meant that More and the Aragonese loyalists were losing ground. There were rumours of bills or statutes designed to strip the Church of its powers, and on 8 May a deputation of prelates implored the king to defend their ancient liberties. Two days later he delivered an unexpected and unwelcome reply; in return for royal favour and protection, he demanded that all legislative power be given into his own hands. On the following day he maintained the pressure upon an increasingly hapless clergy by summoning members of parliament into his presence. He displayed to them the oath which prelates made to the Pope at the time of their consecration and addressed them with stern words. 'Well beloved subjects, we thought that the clergie of our realme had been our subjects wholy, but now wee have well perceived that they bee but halfe our subjects, yea, and scarce our subjects.'[38] He then instructed the Commons to take action. Two days later the clergy began to debate a possible compromise, yet still Henry made more demands. A bill was being prepared by Thomas Cromwell, which would have transferred the powers of the Church to parliament. Eustace Chapuys noted, on 13 May, that 'The king also wishes bishops not to have the power to arrest persons accused of heresy'.[39] This was at the heart of More's concerns, and at this juncture he expressed his thorough opposition. 'The Chancellor and the bishops oppose the bill as much as they can,' Chapuys continued, 'at which the king is exceedingly angry, especially against the said Chancellor.'[40] More had come out into the open at last.

His decision was a token of the urgency, or danger, of the situation; but already it was too late. The king had found his power, under the guidance of Thomas Cromwell, and now pressed the clergy into final surrender. He again prorogued parliament and on the following day, 15 May, convocation accepted his demands in a document known as the 'submission of the clergy'. Effectively he destroyed any independence which the Church still enjoyed, by insisting that all ecclesiastical law required royal assent and that canons or constitutions could be changed only with his approval. He, not the Pope, was truly the head of the Church in England. On the day after the clergy submitted, Thomas More resigned as Lord Chancellor.

He had failed in almost all of his objectives, and in a polemic he was then completing he wrote that 'Our sauyour sayth that ye chyldren of darkenes be more polytyke in theyr kynde then are the chyldren of lyght in theyr kinde. And surely so semeth it now'.[41] He also condemned 'traytors' at court and berated convocations 'of theyr dewty so neglygent';[42] clearly he believed that the débâcle was the result both of secular conspiracy and clerical incompetence. It is true that the clergy had voluntarily surrendered to the king, rather than being obliged to do so by parliamentary statute, and in that sense the 'submission' was without the absolute force of law. But this was small comfort. The 'faction' or 'coalition' which More had helped to organise had been unable to check the course of events. The Church had lost its independence and papal authority had been fatally compromised; the authority of More, also, had been undermined. It is possible, indeed probable, that Henry was waiting for his resignation. The two men met for the last time in the garden of York Place; More handed back the great seal, bowed, and withdrew.

XXVIII

All the Beasts of the Woods

THOMAS More, having resigned as Lord Chancellor, approached Dame Alice More in her pew at church; he stood before her, with his cap in his hand, and asked, 'May it please your Ladieship to come forth now my Lord is gone.'[1] The purport of this family story is clear enough, in its mixture of self-conscious irony and grave humour. His behaviour in the months ahead, however, suggests that he relished his fall from power as a blessed release from the perils of pride or worldliness and thus as an act of saving grace. His fool, Henry Patenson, put it his own way when he said that 'Chancellor More is Chancellor no more'.[2] It was in this period, too, that he composed the epitaph for the stone tomb where, he trusted, he would one day be allowed to rest; it was a conventional preparation, of course, but it suggests also that More believed he might soon die. William Roper records that in the period after his resignation he had discussions with his family on the nature of martyrdom; 'upon his faith,' More said, 'if he might perceive his wife and children would encourage him to die in a good cause, it should so comfort him that for very joy thereof it would make him merrily run to death'.[3] The irony here, however, is that they in no sense encouraged him to embrace that fate and never understood why he chose to do so.

His epitaph opens simply with 'Thomas More, a Londoner borne, of no noble famely' and then proceeds to enumerate his official posts in the service of a king extolled as 'the defender of the faith, a glory afore not herd of'; he professes his own competence in such offices and ends with his decision to be relieved from 'the business of this life' in order to prepare his soul for immortality. More told Erasmus that he had composed these lines *'ambitiose'*, in order to 'show off';

but it is significant that he nowhere mentions his own writings. It was as if *Utopia* had never been composed.

In a little Latin poem he completed at the same time, he scorns any hope of remaining upon this earth for very long.[4] Now that the glory of the world had departed he wished for a secluded, even monastic, life and there are family anecdotes which suggest his desire for plainness. His son-in-law reports that he gathered 'all of us that were children to him',[5] and explained that his income was now so greatly reduced that he needed their advice how they might 'live and continue together as he wished we should'. There was silence, and so More answered his own question. 'Then I will show my poor mind to you,' was one of his customary and favourite phrases. He believed that they should all now contribute to the cost of the household, and that they should also modify their 'diet' by degrees. It is also reported that the family were so straitened that they were obliged to burn bracken or fern to warm themselves, but this is unlikely. He remained an affluent, if not wealthy, man with the income of a king's councillor (which he retained until 1534) and estates in Oxfordshire, Hertfordshire and Kent. Alice More also had a large private income, from her previous marriage, as well as land of her own. But although the legend of More's poverty is insupportable it is true that he could not live in the munificent style of previous years; his children went to their own properties and he was obliged to reduce the size of his general household. In a letter to Erasmus, written in the early summer of this year, he explained that his doctors had advised him to lead a restful and secluded life.

The three letters of this period, two of which are addressed to Erasmus and the third to another European humanist, are characteristic of More; they seem to reveal, yet manage to conceal, the truth of his life. He declares in each of them, for example, that he resigned his office as Lord Chancellor as a result of his poor health and that the king had accepted his resignation most reluctantly. This might be described, in the language of our age, as the 'official' explanation, which concealed all the hostility and distrust involved in his departure. More did not feel obliged to give a more truthful explanation, if only because his letters would be shown to others, but there is a touch of ambiguity which would not have escaped Erasmus's attention. More writes that his '*pectus*'[6] was afflicted; this would ordinarily and properly be taken to mean that he suffered in his chest, but the word can also be implied to mean 'courage' or 'conscience'.

There is one other insistent topic in this correspondence which, unsurprisingly, concerns his battle against the heretics. He describes his delight on hearing a report that two of their leaders had died – namely Zwingli and Oecolampadius – and goes on to amplify his hatred and horror of the heresies spreading everywhere. It remained the greatest battle of his life and, deprived of the chance to imprison or to burn, he returned to angry and elaborate polemic. The first part of his *Confutation of Tyndale's Answer* had been published in the spring, just before his resignation, and now he began working on a second part, which was longer and more closely controlled. In particular, during this period of grave threat to the English Church, he emphasised the unity and traditional authority of the Catholic faith; he wished to defend, therefore, precisely those aspects of it which Henry was challenging. It was in this period, too, that the bishops wanted to repay him for his work in parliament on behalf of the clergy, as well as for his polemical writings; in the words of William Roper, 'they agreed together and concluded upon a sum of four or five thousand pounds at the least, to my remembrance, for his pains to recompense him'. But More refused the gift, telling Tunstall and others that 'I wolde rather haue caste theyre money into the Temys thenne take yt'.[7] He wrote later that 'loke I for my thanke of god that is theyr better, and for whose sake I take the labour and not for theyrs'.[8] He was also aware that Tyndale had accused him of avarice, and clearly wanted to avoid any such unfounded charge. Instead, he simply 'carried the Crosse in procession in his parish Churche at Chelsey'.[9]

Yet the Church itself was changing. Archbishop Warham died in the summer of 1532 and it eventually became clear that Henry had chosen as his successor the relatively unknown and untried Thomas Cranmer. This was the man for the Boleyns, since he was the scholar who had always followed the king's orders and had even translated a treatise justifying Henry's desire to annul his marriage. The old faith was again under renewed assault; Thomas Cromwell was even then drawing up proposals for the next parliament which would further subdue the powers and privileges of the Church, and at the same time he was compiling notes and lists of all those who opposed the king. Through his agent in Antwerp, Stephen Vaughan, he was also in contact with Tyndale and other 'newe men'. One of them even returned to England after More's resignation, with the expectation that Lutheran reformers would no longer be persecuted with the same fervour. John Frith arrived in the summer and quickly proved himself to be a young scholar of skill and eloquence; it seems likely that Cromwell had some wish to turn him into a representative of the king's cause. But Frith had come too soon. Henry had named himself the supreme head of the English Church and for that reason alone he could never condone heresy; he believed himself to have acted according to ancient custom, and therefore had to be seen as a true defender of the faith. That is why he still needed the tacit support of Thomas More, even in retirement, and why he could not allow himself to be compromised by Cromwell's association with the 'bretherne'.

In the autumn of the year Frith was arrested and taken to the Tower, in which confinement he wrote two or three short treatises on the new faith. One of More's informants, probably a member of the network which had flourished during his chancellorship, obtained a copy of one of these works and brought it to Chelsea. It was, in More's words, 'a false folysshe treatyce agaynste the blessed sacrament of ye aulter'.[10] The eucharist was the symbol of divine presence within the material world, and a token of Christ's mystical body on earth; this of course was also the Church itself, and so the transubstantiated bread was a visible sign of the eventual redemption of the world. When More read Frith's denial of what was for him a sacred truth, he reacted immediately by writing a reply which was then distributed among his friends. It was reported by the brethren themselves that More was so incensed with Frith that he exclaimed that his treatise 'sholde coste hym the beste bloude in hys body'.[11] This was indeed a calumny, given More's relative powerlessness, and he went to great trouble at a later date to explain precisely what he had meant; he had declared only that 'I fere me sore that Cryst wyll kyndle a fyre of fagottes for hym, & make hym theirin swete the bloude out of hys body here, and strayte frome hense send hys soule for euer into the fyre of hell'.[12] The vision of flames was constantly with him at this time, and one of the most arresting images in his 'letter' to Frith evokes the fire of heresy that 'begynneth to reke oute at some corner . . . burneth vp whole townes, and wasteth whole countrees . . . lyeth lurkynge styll in some old roten tymber vnder cellers & celynges'.[13]

More was still a master of prose and it may well be that the force of his polemic helped send the young scholar to his death among the flames of Smithfield seven months later. More's letter to Frith had a private circulation partly because 'I wolde wysshe that the comon people sholde of suche heresyes neuer here so myche as the name'.[14] But there was another reason why he arranged that his reply should reach the eyes of only the most influential citizens. There is nothing in More's life, at this stage, that did not have public ramifications. He knew that Frith was being held in loose confinement and that he was being actively courted by Cromwell and his agents as a possible supporter of the king's 'divorce'; More's attack was a way of exposing him. Frith was a dangerous heretic who threatened the nation, 'where as the kynges gracyouse hyghnes lyke a moste faythfull catholyke prynce, for the auodynge of suche pestylente bokes' had already banned 'suche poysened heresyes'.[15] It was a means of warning Cromwell not to go too far, and perhaps also of reminding Henry himself of his spiritual duties. If he colluded with heretics, he might even lose his kingdom.

The same tactics determined the writing of his next polemic, which was directed at Thomas Cromwell's strategy. At the end of 1532 Christopher St German, the author of various legislative proposals yet to be enacted, published a treatise 'concerning the diuision betwene the spirytualtie and temporaltie'. Here he pursued his central aim of raising English common law above canon law, and of removing all forms of secular jurisdiction from church courts; in particular St German criticised the procedure in trials for heresy. Although the book's author had not been revealed, More knew precisely who had written it, and he started at once upon a reply to St German's arguments. Indeed, the anonymity of the treatise served More's purpose; instead of attacking by name someone close to the king's council, he was answering an unknown opponent. He could never be seen as striking at Henry's own policies, especially as he had pledged to retire from temporal business, but there was no harm in a good 'catholyque' man contradicting the mad proposals of an unnamed scribbler.

The apologye of syr Thomas More knyght provides more than a simple rebuttal of St German. In some of his most artless, or at least plainest, prose he defends his own conduct as a polemicist before delivering a sustained and impassioned warning about the true state of the realm. 'Good catholyque folke'[16] were too complacent or too accommodating, for example, allowing heretics 'boldely to talke vnchekked'.[17] More's frustration and impatience are everywhere apparent; he believed his 'good cristen reders' to be true members of the old faith, but few seemed to be aware of the threat to their practices and beliefs. That is why he still wrote in the vernacular, repeating the same arguments and addressing the same themes, in an exhausting and almost single-handed fight against the 'bretherne', as well as against those who supported them for political purposes. He conveys the fear or anger of a man who feels himself to be outnumbered by those, such as Cromwell and St German, who wished to change the nation's polity. The horror of their enterprise is conveyed by More in his image of a procession at Corpus Christi, bearing the blessed sacrament, being attacked by a gang of villains who 'cache them all by the heddys, and throw them in the myre, surplyces, copys, sensers, crosses, relyques, sacrament and all'.[18] It was in this context that More turned to the arguments of St German, calling him 'Syr Pacifyer' in ironic tribute to his efforts to widen the divisions between the people and the clergy. He accused his opponent of wiliness, hypocrisy and wilful imposture in an attempt to subvert the Catholic Church. In one of More's most unusual pieces of demotic, he writes that the nation 'maye fall so farre downe downe down downe'[19] that it might never rise again.

The year of More's resignation, and the submission of the clergy, was a year of omens and of portents. In the spring two giant fish were found in the Thames and were considered to be 'a prodigy foreboding future evil',[20] and there were in London fourteen suicides within as many days. John Stow reports that two priests of Allhallows in Bread Street fought that summer in the church itself, and wounded each other; whereupon the church was closed for a month and the priests consigned to prison. On three occasions the blessed sacrament was stolen from London churches. Thomas Cranmer, returning from Italy to be installed as archbishop, saw comets each night in the sky and reported how others had seen a horse's head on fire, a flaming sword, and 'a blue cross above the moon'.[21] Cranmer believed such phenomena to herald some 'great mutation'. It was at this time that the brothers of the London Charterhouse beheld a huge red globe suspended above their church and there were further sightings of comets casting a strange light upon the sixteenth-century world below.

There are periods in English history when omens and predictions take on a rare significance and the years of the Reformation, beginning even now, are filled with rumours of legends and ancient prophecies. The prognostications of Bede and the myths of Geoffrey of Monmouth obtained common currency; the legend of Mouldwarp was resurrected, and there was much speculation about the dun cow, the dragon, the wolf and the eagle. Henry would be driven from his kingdom; the priests would rule for three days and three nights; the white lion would kill the king; the Pope would arrive in England.[22] This was not some eccentric activity on the margin of events; the Bridgettines of Syon studied the prophecies of Merlin with great attention, while the Spanish ambassador reported that the English might rebel against the established order on the strength of such predictions.[23] It is not difficult to understand the connection between prophecy and the old faith; at the time of its greatest trial, the adherents of the Church turned to popular legend and superstition as a way of bolstering their cause. It was the faith of the country, after all, and in its own defence it could invoke the old myths and beliefs of Catholic England.

There is no better example of the power of this popular belief than the curious career of the young woman known variously as the 'Holy Maid of Kent' or the 'Mad Nun of Kent'. Elizabeth Barton is of significance here, if only because More was suspected of colluding with her against Henry; he was certainly informed about all her activities and he sought her out on at least two occasions for conversation. She might almost be called the unacknowledged partner of his endeavours in maintaining the Church, not least by her formidable defence of the populist and pietistic aspects of the old faith at the time when they were being mocked by the Lutherans as mere superstitions. Her public life began in trance and miracle. She was a seventeen-year-old servant in a Kent household when, succumbing to a serious illness, she began to speak in rhyming prophecies. She was vouchsafed a vision of a chapel, two miles from where she lay; she was taken there, and for seven days lay in a trance before a statue of the Virgin. She prophesied once more, on awakening, and was questioned by a special commission established by the Archbishop of Canterbury. It found no fault with her and her visitations were deemed to be genuine; a thousand people took her in procession to the little chapel, which then became the object of cult and pilgrimage. At her own request she was admitted to a convent in Canterbury, where her visions and clairvoyant trances increased both in number and fervour.

Elizabeth Barton then became a controversial figure in the history of the period. Her messages and prophecies were conveyed by a group of priests who ministered to her, and soon she 'was brought into a marvellous fame, credit and good opinion of a great multitude of the people of this realm'.[24] This was the description employed in an Act of Attainder eventually brought against her, but she obtained that unhappy fate only because of her opposition to the king. When it became clear that Henry wished to annul his marriage with Catherine of Aragon, and to marry Anne Boleyn, Elizabeth Barton's visions became more troubled. She prognosticated much evil to the realm, and such was her reputation that she was granted interviews both with Wolsey and the king himself. She warned the cardinal that if Henry abandoned his wife his kingdom would be in great danger. She informed the king, to his face, that he would remain on his throne only seven months after his marriage to Anne Boleyn and that Mary, the daughter he was about to bastardise, would one day reign. The 'holy maid' or 'mad nun' also had several interviews with Catherine's courtiers, as well as members of those powerful factions which supported the queen's cause. She has now almost disappeared from history, but contemporary reports reveal the extent of her significance. Certainly she was considered a great threat to the cause of reform. Cranmer stated that 'truly, I think, she did marvellously stop the going forward of the King's marriage by the reasons of her visions'.[25] The king was convinced of her influence, and told the French ambassador that she had 'seduced the Queen and Princess; hence . . . their disobedience'.[26] It was also said, in a later proclamation, that the Pope had been persuaded to oppose the king 'principally by the damnable and diabolical instrumentality of the said nun and her accomplices'.[27] John Fisher wept when he listened to her, because he believed he was hearing the voice of God.

She first emerges in an unambiguous light at Canterbury itself. In the early autumn of 1532 Henry was once more engaged in those spectacular and flamboyant games of dynastic politics which came so instinctively to him; he was about to travel to Calais and then, on French soil, conclude a set of agreements with Francis I. The English king's principal purpose was to apply further pressure upon the Pope in the matter of the annulment, and, perhaps to bolster the belief in his case, he travelled in state with Anne Boleyn. He had already taken the precaution of giving her the title of Marquess of Pembroke, in case she should feel inferior to those 'brave hearts' of England who also accompanied him. The retinue stopped at Canterbury before travelling to Dover and there, in the walled garden of the abbot of St Augustine's, the king and Anne Boleyn took their healthful recreation. Elizabeth Barton was revered by the priests and friars of Canterbury, so it was not difficult for her to enter the same garden.

She came through a back gate and, according to the official account, harangued Henry to the effect 'that in case he desisted not from his proceedings in the said divorce and separation but pursued the same and married again, that then within one month after such marriage he should no longer be king of this realm, and in the reputation of God should not be a king one day nor one hour, and that he should die a villain's death'.[28] It is sufficiently dramatic to be apocryphal, but extant documents testify to the essential truth of it; there was, in any event, a tradition of holy women whose sanctity afforded them access to princes or to kings. Yet it was not a tradition which Henry would necessarily wish to continue.

A few weeks after this brief encounter one of Elizabeth Barton's circle or entourage, Richard Risby of the Franciscan Observants at Canterbury, stayed at More's house in Chelsea. After supper, just before he retired to his chamber, Risby spoke to his host of 'the Nunne, gyvinge her high commendacion of holiness'.[29] More knew that she had held, in the past, private conversations with Wolsey and the king; he was also aware that, on one occasion, through the agency of the Archbishop of Canterbury, she had sent to the king a roll of paper containing rhymed prophecies and other such matter. Henry had shown it to More, who, in his customary precise and neutral manner, had declared that this record of her trances showed nothing 'I coulde eny thinge regarde or esteme' except as the work of a 'righte simple woman'. He knew the stories of 'a myracle . . . shewed vppon her' but 'I durst not nor woulde not be bolde, in iudginge the matter'.[30]

Now everything had changed, yet More was as circumspect as before.

Richard Risby: It is wonderful to see and understand the works that God has wrought in her.

Thomas More: I am very glad to hear it, and thank God therefor.

Richard Risby: She has been with Wolsey, in his life, and with the King's Grace too.

Then Risby went on to discuss a revelation vouchsafed to her concerning the now deceased cardinal; God placed three swords in his hand 'which if he ordered not well, God wolde laye it soore to his charge'.[31] The third of these swords, according to Risby, concerned the 'great matter' of the king's marriage. At this point More interrupted him.

Thomas More: I will not hear of any revelation of the king's matters. I doubt not but the goodness of God shall direct his highness with his grace and wisdom, that the thing should take such end, as God shall be pleased with, to the king's honour and the surety of the realm.

Richard Risby: God has especially commanded her to pray for the king. Wolsey's soul has been saved by her mediation.

There the conversation concluded and Risby retired to his chamber in More's house.

Now that he was away from Westminster, he heard news only from friends and relatives. It is unlikely, for example, that he was aware of the secret marriage of Henry and Anne Boleyn a week before the opening of parliament in February 1533; by then Anne was already pregnant, and there may have been an even shorter and more private ceremony at some point in mid-November of the preceding year. The deed was, at any rate, done; all of the king's efforts in parliament and convocation were now designed to confirm Anne's status as wife and queen. In March Thomas Cromwell presented an Act in Restraint of Appeals which ratified the sovereignty and independence of the national Church while declaring, in a preamble, that England was an ancient empire which owed no allegiance to 'foreign princes or potentates'.[32]

Although the English clergy was largely protected from the power of parliament, this Act marked the withdrawal of England from what More had always called 'the common knowen catholyque church'. He understood this well enough and, from the relative obscurity and powerlessness of his Chelsea retirement, he may have helped to organise the final act of opposition to the king's will. Certainly those who had already supported Catherine of Aragon's interests now rallied against this last and latest measure: there is an extant list, in the handwriting of Thomas Cromwell, which notes down the names of those members who opposed the Act. Among them are William Roper and William Dauntsey as well as Sir George Throckmorton and two other members 'of Chelcythe' or, in the words of one parliamentary historian, 'the Chelsea group'.[33] So Cromwell considered those associated with More to be an identifiable circle of malcontents. But the Act was passed and the defenders of the old faith were defeated. Cromwell summoned Throckmorton and, in the presence of the king, ordered him to 'stay at home and meddle little in politics'.[34] The More household itself remained active, however, but in another sense. John More, the only son, published two translations of continental works that reaffirmed the unity of the whole Catholic Church and restated the central importance of the holy eucharist in its sacramental life. His was an effort to rebut heresy and schism – with the perhaps oblique reminder, to the king, that they could not be separated. More himself continued his career of frantic polemic with his *Apology*, containing an attack upon Christopher St German, published at the time parliament was debating the Act of Appeals.

But his was a lonely voice and, two weeks after Cromwell had presented his Act, Thomas Cranmer was installed as Archbishop of Canterbury. Under his presidency, at the beginning of April, both houses of the convocation of clergy pronounced the marriage between Henry VIII and Catherine of Aragon to be invalid. Unauthorised preaching was now forbidden and Bishop John Fisher, after his furious attempts to oppose the king's will, was arrested. Almost immediately Cranmer began to prepare another court hearing, into the validity of the king's first marriage. But, even before the expected verdict was reached, on 'the 12 day of Aprill, Anno Domini 1533, being Easter eaven, Anne Bulleine, Marques of Pembroke, was proclaymed Queene at Greenewych, and offred that daie in the Kinges Chappell as Queene of Englande'.[35] More and his supporters had lost everything.

It was, for them, a time of crisis. John Fisher, after being eventually released from custody, sent a secret appeal to the Spanish emperor for an invading force to be dispatched to England. Eustace Chapuys, the ambassador, also urged some form of armed invasion; he told his master that, at this juncture, the people were so alienated from Henry that an attack would easily succeed. It is significant, too, that Fisher and Chapuys had agreed not to speak to or even recognise each other in public. Thomas Cromwell later claimed that there had been a conspiracy against the realm, involving both More and Fisher; in the case of the bishop, he was not far from the truth. In this same period the 'holy maid', Elizabeth Barton, secretly met the papal envoy in Canterbury and told him that if Pope Clement agreed to the annulment 'God would plague him for it'.[36] She had already conversed with the papal envoy to Scotland, who, according to later reports, had promised her that Clement would do all he could to drive Henry from his kingdom. In this atmosphere of increasing tension Father Rich, of the strongly Aragonese Friars Observant at Richmond, visited More in Chelsea. Their conversation was later reported by More to Cromwell himself.

Father Rich: Has Father Risby anything showed you of the holy nun of Kent?

Thomas More: Yes, and I was very glad to hear of her virtue.

Rich then made discreet efforts to enlist More in the nun's cause, but More was fully aware of the dangers of that course. He may not at this time have known of all her activities, but he must have guessed that she was coming close to treason.

Father Rich: Did he tell you of the revelations that she had concerning the king's grace?

Thomas More: No, for sooth, nor if he would have done I would not have given him the hearing. Nor verily no more I would in deed, for since she has been with the king's grace herself, and told him, methinks it a thing needless to tell the matter to me or any man else.[37]

Father Rich then left the house, without staying for dinner, his aims unaccomplished. But the matter did not end there, since More arranged to meet Rich on two other occasions when they discussed the visions and trances of the nun; he also had further discussions with Father Risby. Yet he remained prudent, believing that silence might save him. Of course he refused openly to support the king's cause and when, in May, Thomas Cranmer pronounced Henry's marriage to Anne Boleyn to be valid (and, therefore, that with Catherine of Aragon to be void) More volunteered a characteristic comment to his son-in-law. 'God give grace, son,' he said, 'that these matters within a while be not confirmed with oaths.'[38] He was uncannily and unhappily prophetic in this, but he was put to the test much sooner than he expected.

The day after the marriage had formally been declared lawful, Anne Boleyn was brought by water from the palace at Greenwich to the Tower of London; she sat in a boat of state, followed by the great barges of the City companies festooned with silk and cloth of gold; other boats carried grand effigies, from which issued flames and fireworks. On the king's own barge were placed the minstrels and the musicians making, in the words of a contemporary report, a 'marvellous sweet harmony'[39] upon the river. Then as the procession of more than three hundred ships turned towards the city, fusillades of shot and cannon sounded from both shores. It was the beginning of four days of splendour, leading to the coronation of the new queen in Westminster Abbey. But Thomas More, still a king's councillor, was not present at any of the proceedings. This was the point when Henry hardened his heart against him.

Three erstwhile conservative bishops, among them his old friend and colleague Cuthbert Tunstall, had already written to More and urged him to take his proper place at the coronation. They were so concerned for his attendance that they sent him twenty pounds with which to purchase a new gown for the occasion. They knew the peril in which he now stood and were desperately anxious for him to reach some kind of accommodation with the king. He kept the money, but still he refused to be present at the ceremonies. The true courage and spirit of the man now emerge. His own comments to the bishops also reveal the far-sightedness with which he observed the affairs of the nation. He told them, first, a story concerning the emperor Tiberius; he had enacted a law which exacted death for a certain penalty, unless the offender were a virgin. But when a virgin woman did eventually appear on that charge the emperor was unsure how to proceed. Then one of his council proposed the perfect solution. 'Why make you so much ado, my lords, about so small a matter? Let her first be deflowered and then after may she be devoured!'

Thomas More: And so, though your lordships have in the matter of the matrimony kept yourselves pure virgins, yet take good heed, my lords, that you keep your virginity still. For some there be that by procuring your lordships first at the coronation to be present, and next to preach for the setting forth of it, and finally to write books to all the world in defense thereof, are desirous to deflower you; and when they have deflowered you, then will they not fail soon after to devour you. Now, my lords, it lieth not in my power but that they may devour me. But God, being my good Lord, I will provide that they shall never deflower me![40]

This apt speech may have been partly rewritten by his son-in-law, in his biography, but the classical allusion and the resonance of deflower/devour are characteristic of More. He knew, by this stage, the power and the danger of the forces opposing him; 'they' are Cromwell and his agents, with the monarch in the recesses beyond, but More speaks of them here in the terms he usually reserved for heretics and 'demones'; is it possible he believed that the agents of the council were indeed devils sent to inaugurate the reign of Antichrist?

A month after the coronation, Thomas More decided to pay a visit to Elizabeth Barton, who was then residing at Syon Abbey. The Bridgettine fathers there had promised More that they would notify him of her next visit and there is a strong suggestion that this meeting with the 'holy maid' was of some urgency. They spoke alone, in a small private chapel. Did the nun reveal to him further prophecies about the downfall of the king and the reign of Queen Mary? Was he now inclined to believe her? More's own account, written later to exculpate himself, is circumspect. He stated that he introduced himself as one who did not wish to hear her revelations but, rather, ask for her prayers. He had heard of her virtue and in turn the nun replied 'that of me she had manye suche thinges harde, that allredy she prayed for me, and ever wolde'.[41] They discussed a woman from Tottenham who had been troubled by visions, which Elizabeth Barton had persuaded her to be false. Then the 'holy maid' or 'mad nun' told More of her own visitations from the devil, who had appeared 'in likenes of a bird . . . fleeinge and flickeringe about her in a chambre, and suffered hyme self to be taken'.[42] The devil was much on More's mind at this time and there is no reason to suppose that he disbelieved her.

As a young scholar and as a lawyer, he had displayed no real interest in the paraphernalia of popular piety; he seems to have had no extravagant devotion to the saints and no particular fondness for relics, but he had instead practised a Christological devotion. In the altered circumstances of the time, however, he had acquired a love and reverence for all the customs of the old faith. He and the nun were now in affinity, and did indeed need to pray for one another. Yet More remained cautious in his letter to Cromwell, insisting that 'we talked no worde of the Kinges Grace or anye great personage ells, nor in effecte, of anye man or woman but of her selfe, and my selfe'.[43] Herself and myself, both growing increasingly isolated in a world which had little place for them. At the end of their interview, More gave her a double ducat and asked her to pray for him.

Yet not all was as it seemed. After her interview with More, the holy nun had ridden to the mansion of the Exeters in Surrey. They urgently wished to hear her prophecies because they touched directly upon the fate of the Lord Marquess, Henry Courtenay. He believed himself to have good title to the throne, and it can be supposed that he wished to have the nun's support. It was declared, in later evidence to Thomas Cromwell, that she had fallen into a trance and in that condition given a term to the king's life; she was questioned by Lady Exeter and replied that 'in so many months that her husband should reign'.[44] This was very close to treasonable talk.

It is clear that More knew of the nun's departure and journey to Surrey, if only because he wrote a curious letter to her touching on the matters which she was discussing with the Exeters. He addressed her as 'Good Madam and My Righte Dearlie Beloved Syster in our Lorde God', and then humbly begged her to consider his advice in a particular matter; but before he delivered his 'poore mynde' he asked her to recall that 'I shewed you that I neither was, nor wolde be, curious of eny knowledge of other mennes matters, and lest of all of eny matter of princes or of the realme'.[45] More kept his own copy of the letter, and this inserted 'remembrance' seems to have been written for the eyes of any future investigator rather than the nun herself. But then he came to the point; some of her admirers 'happe to be curiouse and inquisitive of thinges that litle perteine vnto theire partes: and some mighte peraduenture happe to talke of suche thinges, as mighte peraduenture after turne to muche harme'. If his meaning was not already clear enough, he recalled the fate of the Duke of Buckingham, who, after being persuaded by a monk of his royal destiny, had been executed for treason. He then concluded by advising her once more of the dangers involved in talking 'with any persons' on 'suche maner thinges as perteyne to princes' affeirs'.[46] He had issued a specific warning, therefore, against her collusion or association with the Marquess of Exeter, who might, in turn, invite the fate of Buckingham.

It has sometimes been suggested that he was being less than candid in his assertion that he never discussed the 'matter of princes' with Elizabeth Barton. One member of the Syon Community, who later gave evidence against the nun, declared that More had spoken to her 'divers times' about her revelations concerning the king.[47] His evidence is tainted, however, to the extent that it is exactly the kind of thing Thomas Cromwell wished to hear. A biographer of Father Richard Reynolds, also of Syon, claims that More spoke to the nun on two separate occasions; this is not difficult to believe, but it does not necessarily suggest any collusion between them. A member of the More household gave evidence to the effect that Elizabeth Barton came twice to see him; she conversed with Margaret Roper and Giles

Heron on those occasions, since More himself 'would not speak with her at neither of both times'.[48] The most plausible interpretation of these reports is that More no longer wished to speak to her: he realised that she had gone too far in her talk of the king's deposition or death, and he kept away from her. He did not wish to be implicated in any religious or political conspiracy. Yet he had another reason for concern; the nun was a defender of the old faith and, if she were compromised, the cause itself would be placed in jeopardy.

In the summer of this year Cromwell wrote to the king about the 'holy maid'; Henry had asked for her activities to be investigated and Cromwell promised that with Cranmer he would test the 'dissymuled holyness and supersticious demeanoures of the Ipocryte Nunne'.[49] He also reported that two Friars Observant had been arrested, after secretly visiting Catherine of Aragon, and he suggested that they be put on the rack to discover their secrets. At this time More made another visit to Syon, where, discussing Elizabeth Barton with the fathers, he gave a highly ambiguous and complicated description of her revelatory claims: 'I assure you she were likelie to be verye bad, if she seamed good, erre I shoulde thinke her other, tyll she happed to be proved naughte'.[50] But his discretion did not free him from suspicion; even as Cromwell investigated Elizabeth Barton, so he also pursued Thomas More. His agent, Stephen Vaughan, had returned to Antwerp in order to learn more about the activities and supporters of two Franciscans who had fled London: Father Peto, who had once preached so vociferously in the king's presence, and Father Elstow were busily engaged in promoting works favouring the cause of Catherine of Aragon. They were compiling their own Latin treatise on the validity of her marriage and acted as distributors for books of a similar kind. Their work was in turn being financed and supported by sympathisers in London. 'They be so much helpen out of England with money,' Vaughan reported to Cromwell, 'but I cannot learn by whom.'[51] He did have suspects, however.

Fisher's tract against the annulment was to be found in Antwerp and 'if pryvey searche be made and shortly, peradventure in the howse of the same Busshop shalbe founde his first copie'. One of the friars helping to support Peto and Elstow was being financed by a certain merchant residing in London. Vaughan did not name him but it is at least possible that this merchant was Antonio Bonvisi, the close friend of More who most recently had been a sponsor at the baptism of John More's second child. The investigations were coming closer. 'Maister More hathe sent often tymes, and lately bookes unto Peto in Andwerp, as his book of the confutacion of Tyndale, and Frythe his opynyon of the sacrament, with dyvers other bookes. I can no further lern of More his practises, but if you consider this well, you may perchance espye his crafte.'[52]

Then came upon More various torments and fears of the night, 'forecasting all such peryls and paynfull deathes, as by any maner of possibilitie might after fall vnto me'.[53] As he lay in the dank sweat of his 'nightes feare' where fantasy 'dowbleth . . . feare'[54] he envisaged torture upon the rack and terrible pain inflicted by more ingenious instruments; he envisaged death by disembowelling, his heart torn out of his body and shown to him while he was still alive. He quotes from the words of the psalm, which he recited at the time. 'Thow hast good lord set the darknes, & made was the night, & in the night walken all the bestes of the woodes[,] the whelps of the lions roryng & calling vnto god for their meate.'[55]

XXIX

The Wrath of the King
Means Death

THERE was an occasion now when, as the More household sat down to their dinner, a sudden knock at the door roused them. It was a messenger from the king, demanding that More appear forthwith before the royal commissioners. Some of the household wept, knowing the reason for this summons, while others were braver or more restrained. More noted their responses to this unexpected intruder and reproved those who had lamented his likely fate.[1] It was not a royal summons at all; More had concocted the scene in order to test and prepare those around him for what might be a real ordeal. He had not been able to speak to them (not even to his wife) about his own night fears and daily anxiety; he was so inhibited about revealing the true state of his feelings that he had created a drama in order to convey his meaning.

Where matters of faith and order were concerned, however, he still felt compelled to speak out. Christopher St German had, again under the guise of anonymity, printed an attack upon More's *Apology* in which he accused the ex-Lord Chancellor of misrepresenting the processes of the law; he also accused More of bad faith and subterfuge. As soon as More read St German's *Salem and Bizance* he replied, composing his *Debellation of Salem and Bizance* within a few days. He could not keep silent; he had to go on, even if, and perhaps especially because, it was the last moment. St German had blamed the clergy for their treatment of heretics, with the insinuation that the behaviour of the priests had promoted the growth of heresy, and this More refused to admit. St German's own plans for reform of the church courts would encourage heretics and heresy while at the same time leading to 'the mynysshement and decaye of the catholyke

338

chrysten fayth'.[2] Here he writes of 'decaye' as if he knew what might be about to happen. His horror at the prospect is revealed in his story of the madman Cliff, who had attacked an image of the Virgin and Child placed upon London Bridge. In his folly he had snapped off the head of the Christ child. Some of those who dwelled in shops and houses upon the bridge surrounded him and asked why he had committed such a blasphemy. According to More, 'he began to loke well and erenestly vpon them and, lyke a man of sadnesse and grauyte, he asked theym, "Tell me thys amonge you there, Haue you not yet sett on hys hed agayne?"

"No. We cannot."

"No, by ye masse it is the more shame for you. Why speke you to me of it than?" '[3]

It is a story about the irrevocable nature of blasphemy and heresy, but it is also an indication of the extent to which Christopher St German (and, by implication, the heretics) blamed the clergy and others for their own actions. It had another pertinent message for More himself since he mentioned that in recent times a statue of St Thomas Becket, also upon London Bridge, was defaced and torn down. This was at the instigation of the reformers, who considered Becket to be no saint and martyr but a papal traitor within the realm. There is no doubt that More felt a strong attachment to his saintly namesake, now that his own life in opposition to the king so closely resembled that of the murdered archbishop. Yet his assault upon the legal recommendations of St German is not simply a theoretical and spiritual affair; his rebuttals still display his practical experience of the courts, and, once more, he uses the language of London as a way of refuting the more impersonal objections of his opponent. 'This is a very colde tale,' he writes, '& as dede as euer was dore nayle.'[4]

But More must have guessed that it was growing too late for the war of the books, especially since he knew that he was increasingly coming under the surveillance of Thomas Cromwell. St German's treatise, to which he had taken such violent exception, had been published by the king's printer. It was becoming dangerous, even in matters of legal argument and theory, to speak out. But he did so for one last time. As soon as he had finished the *Debellation*, he began work upon yet another polemic which celebrated the doctrine of transubstantiation. His new work was entitled *The Answer to a Poisoned Book*, the 'poisoned book' in question being an anonymous tract entitled *The Souper of the Lorde*. He published his

Answer only five weeks after he had begun its composition. Five months earlier Frith had been burned for heresy, with the direct authority of the king, and More may now have believed himself to be on safer ground in attacking heretics rather than Henry's legal advisers. Yet this last of his polemical works, this last gasp, is a disquieting and dispirited book. On its opening pages More has a vision of the 'corrupt cankar'[5] of heresy growing all around him, and he advises his good Christian readers thoroughly to exorcise the 'newe men' from their company – 'not so mych as byd theym good spede or good morow when we mete them'.[6] It is a treatise aimed not only against those who deny the sacrament but against 'al this hole wretched world',[7] which even then he might have been wishing to leave.

The *Answer* is written so swiftly and with such passion that the reader can glimpse the very movement of More's mind. 'But go to nowe . . . Let vs now to ye secund than . . . I saye no not all . . . to that say I agayne . . . I haue as you se so well auoyded his gynnys and his grinnes and all his trymtrams.'[8] And in that same hasty and forceful cadence it is also possible to glimpse the character of More unfolding upon the page; he is in turn clever and defensive, sharp and disdainful, with a tendency towards malice and towards pride. Within the text he continually invokes images of juggling and of subterfuge, of masked men and games of chance, as if he were truly revealing the treacherous and secretive nature of the time.

Even now, in solemn consistory, the Pope had condemned Henry's separation from Catherine and had threatened him with the terrible punishment of excommunication if he did not return to his first wife. The anger of the king can be gauged from his treatment of those within the kingdom who supported the papal cause. The households of Catherine and Mary were dissolved and, more significantly for More's own fate, Elizabeth Barton and her closest associates were arrested and taken to the Tower for interrogation. The nun was brought before the Star Chamber, where she was accused of high treason. Even the threat of excommunication was blamed upon her; the new Lord Chancellor, Thomas Audley, stated that the Pope had been seduced 'principally by the damnable and diabolical instrumentality of the said nun and her accomplices'.[9] The methods by which their statements and confessions were extracted from them can only be surmised, but on 23 November Elizabeth Barton and seven others were taken from the Tower to Paul's Cross, where she stood upon a scaffold and confessed that her revelations and visitations had been entirely fraudulent. More was among the crowd which heard her, and at once sent word to the prior of Charterhouse that Elizabeth Barton had at last been proved to be 'a false deceyvinge ypocrite'.[10] Did he also know, or guess, that Cromwell's interrogators had been trying to establish the nun's complicity with Catherine of Aragon and More himself?

He was now Cromwell's principal suspect in all matters pertaining to opposition to the king, and an incident of the period demonstrates the terrible insecurity of his position. One month after Elizabeth Barton's confession, the king's council distributed throughout the kingdom a book of *Articles* which defended the autonomy of the realm, denounced the excommunication of Henry and condemned the Pope himself as 'bastard, simoniac and heretic'.[11] Two or three weeks later, Cromwell received news that a reply had been published. At once he sent for More's printer, William Rastell, and questioned him closely about More's possible involvement in this disloyal response. He even used the publication of *The Answer to a Poisoned Book* as an indication of More's hostility to the *Articles*, until Rastell was able to prove that that polemic had been published before the *Articles* themselves had been promulgated. Yet Rastell was so alarmed that he asked More to write to Cromwell exonerating them both. More's letter is a masterpiece of disingenuousness; he signed himself 'Assuredly all your owne',[12] but he gave nothing away. He denied having written any hostile pamphlet, and, as for the *Articles*, 'of many thinges which in that boke be touched, in some I knowe not the lawe, and in some I knowe not the fact. And therefore would I neuer be so childish nor so plaie the proud arrogant fole . . . as to presume to make an aunswere to the boke.'[13] He also stated that 'I know my bounden duety, to bere more honour to my prince, and more reuerence to his honorable Counsaile' than to deem himself worthy to reply to any book issued by them. Of course he did not mention that he had replied to the works of Christopher St German, issued by the king's printer. And his response may not necessarily have convinced Cromwell. In the month in which he had interviewed Rastell he had drawn up a memorandum – 'To cause indictments to be drawn up for the offenders in treason & misprision concerning the nun of Canterbury', to which is added 'Eftsoons to remember Master More to the king'.[14]

Parliament was reconvened on Thursday, 15 January 1534, and at first concerned itself with specific or local legislation such as the paving of Holborn and the punishment for sodomy. But by the second week of February the king's more pressing concerns came before the two Houses. A dowry bill confirmed Catherine of Aragon's new and unhappy status, while the second Act of Annates emphasised the fact that the king and not the Pope elected the bishops of the realm. A few days later Elizabeth Barton, now the 'Ippocrite Nunne' rather than the holy maid, was indicted by an Act of Attainder which confirmed her treason; at the preliminary inquiry into her activities there had been cries of 'To the stake! To the stake!', which was the direction in which she now would surely go. But the drift of Cromwell's policies became clear when a bill was drawn up that included the names of More and Fisher among her accomplices. More's name had been included in the bill 'concerning the Attainder of Elizabeth Barton and others' at the last minute, apparently at the insistence of the king, and he was accused of 'misprision of treason' or concealment of treason on the grounds that he knew about Elizabeth Barton's dealings with the Marquess of Exeter. More was informed at once, by Fisher himself, and wrote to Cromwell asking for a copy of that bill, 'which sene, if I finde any vntrue surmise therein as of likelihode there is'[15] he begged leave to bring his suit to the king. But there is no doubt that the king and Cromwell were now using Elizabeth Barton to bring down their principal opponents; Cromwell informed William Roper, still a member of the Commons, that More had not only 'had communicacion' with the nun but had also 'gyven her aduice and cowncell'.[16]

This was tantamount to accusing him of treason, and More immediately dispatched to Cromwell a long letter in which he detailed all his knowledge of the woman he now called 'the lewde Nonne'.[17] He concluded by swearing that, as long as he should live, no man or woman would 'make me digresse frome my trothe and faithe'[18] towards God and the king. It is a measure of his anxiety as well as his pain, perhaps, that he referred to 'this disceace of myne'[19] which prevented him from writing in his own hand: it was the same disease in his 'breste' which had afflicted him since the death of his father.

After Cromwell received the letter he requested that More visit him for an informal conversation. More travelled, downriver, to Westminster. It was clear enough, from the letter and from other witnesses, that his dealings with the nun could not be construed as treasonable; so it seems that most of the interview was concerned with the issues of the king's marriage and the papal supremacy. The bill including his name had already been given a second reading, but at this stage it seems more likely that the king wished to coerce rather than to punish More. In particular he wanted him 'to relent and condescend to his request'[20] to compose a treatise in favour of the annulment of Henry's first marriage. When Cromwell questioned him about his attitude to the whole affair, More reiterated the policy of silence and non-involvement that he had always supposedly pursued; as he wrote in a subsequent letter to Cromwell, I 'neither murmure at it, nor dispute vppon it, nor neuer did nor will'.[21] This may have struck his interlocutor as peculiar from one who had helped to organise the 'Aragonese' opposition to the annulment and who had refused to attend the wedding of Henry and Anne Boleyn; but even if Cromwell suspected More of double-dealing, there was no evidence for any worse offence. On the second issue, of the papal supremacy, More was equally guarded. He explained to Cromwell that he had not been convinced of the matter until he had read the king's own treatise, *Assertio septem Sacramentorum*, in which the divine origin of the papacy was asserted. It was a shrewd hit but, before this interesting meeting ended, More begged Cromwell to impart to the king his utter faithfulness, truthfulness and loyalty.

A day or two after his return to Chelsea More composed two letters. One of them was to the king, in which he declared himself lying 'prostrate at your graciouse feet';[22] he begged Henry to consider if he could be capable of such 'monstrouse ingratitude' as to conspire against him and, if the king still trusted his fidelity, asked him to 'releive the turment of my present hevynesse, conceived of the drede and fere'[23] which the bill had instilled in him. He signed the letter 'Your most humble and moste hevy faithfull subgeitt and bede-man'.[24] The king did not believe his protestations of innocence, but there is nothing in More's conduct to suggest that they were untrue. He considered himself to be always pursuing the king's best interests; as he had said to his colleagues, Henry would 'in the end' thank them for their efforts on behalf of Catherine and of the old faith. His nicely trained sense of order and obedience made it impossible for him even to consider disloyalty, let alone treachery, and his polemics against St German as well as his early interest in the Nun of Kent were ways in which he hoped to keep Henry on the right and noble path of sovereignty. But his fidelity was construed as faithlessness, and his loyalty as treason.

The second letter was to Thomas Cromwell and seems designed to convey More's own written record of their conversation; it was one of his most characteristic devices, and shows the caution of his legal mind. In this letter he also adverts to the 'wofull hevynesse in which myn harte standeth'[25] as a result of being falsely accused of disloyalty. He had already learned from William Roper, however, that Cromwell was now urging the king to drop the bill against More – probably on the reasonable grounds that there was no solid evidence to connect him with the activities of the Nun of Kent. Although this afforded him some 'reliefe and cumfort',[26] it was by no means the end of the process. The king refused to remove More's name, but he did agree that the accused man should be allowed to defend himself in front of a committee of the Star Chamber. Even as the Lords began their third reading of the Bill of Attainder, which despite Cromwell's efforts still included the name of More, the suspect was summoned to Westminster once again.

He appeared before a small committee that included Cranmer and Audley, as well as Cromwell, and they began by treating him 'very friendly, willing him to sit down with them, which in no wise he would'.[27] This account comes from Roper, who must have heard it from his father-in-law soon after the meeting. Audley opened the formal interview by descanting on the honours and privileges which the king had granted to his former Lord Chancellor. More replied, equally graciously, that there was no man living 'that would with better will do the thing that should be acceptable to the king's highness'.[28] On the matter of the nun More simply rehearsed the extent of his involvement.

The second, and more important concern, was the marriage of the king to Anne Boleyn. More replied, as he had always done, that he had 'plainly and truly declared my mind unto his grace, which his highness to me ever seemed like a most gracious prince very well to accept'.[29] This was not enough to satisfy his auditors, however, who now abruptly shifted from affability to threat. They declared that 'never was there servant so villainous, nor subject to his prince so traitorous as he'.[30] They also threatened him with various forms of condign punishment but he responded, in the words of St Basil to the Arian emperor Valens who was trying to convert him with threats, 'My lords, these terrors be arguments for children and not for me.'[31]

The commissioners specifically accused him of persuading the king to write his *Assertio septem Sacramentorum* against Luther, the treatise that had unfortunately included an unambiguous defence of papal supremacy. More justifiably denied being the instigator of the project and repeated his remark to Cromwell that the king had in its writing actually persuaded More of the paramount importance of the papacy. There was little more to be said. The committee of the Star Chamber broke up without any result – 'thus displeasantly departed they', in the words of William Roper[32] – and More returned by boat to Chelsea.

On his homecoming, he walked with his son-in-law in the garden.

'I trust, sir,' Roper asked him, 'that all is well because you are so merry.'

'It is so indeed, son Roper, I thank God.'

'Are you then put out of the Parliament bill?'

'By my truth, son Roper, I never remembered it.'

'Never remembered, sir! A case that toucheth yourself so near, and us all for your sake. I am sorry to hear it. For I verily trusted, when I saw you so merry, that all had been well.'

'Wilt thou know, son Roper, why I was so merry?'

'That I would gladly, sir.'

'In good faith, I rejoiced, son, that I had given the devil a foul fall; and that with those lords I had gone so far as, without great shame, I could never go back again.'[33]

More's lapse of memory about the bill concerning his relations with the Nun of Kent need not be taken literally; in his letters to Cromwell and to the king, the matter of the 'wicked woman' clearly concerned him a great deal. But the Star Chamber committee had been less interested in Elizabeth Barton's activities than in More's attitude toward the king's new marriage and toward the theory of papal supremacy. And it was here that Henry personally wished to test his erstwhile servant. More had been able to convey his reservations – in that sense, as he had said, he could not 'go back' upon his words – but had done so without incriminating himself. He was relieved to have been able to disburden his conscience while remaining strictly faithful to the king. It was the first time he had been formally interrogated by his peers upon those affairs which troubled him so deeply, and he had calmly triumphed over his adversaries. He also had some reason to be sanguine, at least on one matter. The upper house of parliament, having heard that More had been interrogated privately in special committee, sent a memorial to the king 'whether it squared with the King's mind, that Sir Thomas More and the others named with him in the said Bill . . . should be called before the Lords in Parliament'[34] so that they might defend themselves. Clearly it did not seem just that so eminent a man should be imprisoned and stripped of all his possessions merely for being named in the bill.

The request did not please the king, who was anyway unhappy with the course of the Star Chamber interrogation which had revealed nothing to More's detriment; he insisted upon retaining More's name in the Bill of Attainder, and when Audley warned him that the entire bill might then be thrown out (thus freeing Elizabeth Barton as well as her 'accomplices') the king threatened to attend the proceedings in the upper chamber. He would, in other words, cow the Lords into submission. At this point, according to William Roper, his councillors fell upon their knees and begged him to reconsider; their argument to the king was that, 'if he should, in his own presence, receive an overthrow, it would not only encourage his subjects ever after to contemn him, but also throughout all Christendom redound to his dishonour forever'.[35] Eventually the king accepted the force of their arguments and More's name was removed from the bill; but not before Henry, in his anger, stopped his remaining income as a councillor.

Cromwell came up to William Roper in the chambers of parliament and gave him the welcome news; Roper was dining in London that day, so he sent a message to Margaret Roper who thereupon informed her father. He took the news gravely enough, with the reply 'In faith, Meg, *quod differtur non aufertur*' ('what is deferred is not avoided').[36] He expected Henry to find another way of reaching him, and in that he was a shrewd judge of his old master. He was, indeed, unwittingly echoing what Audley and his colleagues had already told the king; even though More's name had been taken out of the bill, 'they mistrusted not in time against him to find some meeter matter to serve his turn better'.[37] The Duke of Norfolk then met with More, in a last attempt to help him or suborn him.

'By the Mass, Master More, it is perilous striving with princes. And therefore I would wish you somewhat to incline to the king's pleasure. For, by God body, Master More, *Indignatio principis mors est.*' ('The wrath of the king means death.')

'Is that all, my lord? Then in good faith is there no more difference between your grace and me, but that I shall die today and you tomorrow.'[38]

And, soon enough, there was 'meeter matter' with which to serve up Thomas More to the king. Just two weeks after his appearance before the royal commissioners, an Act of Succession was put before the Lords; it pronounced the marriage between Henry and Catherine of Aragon to be 'void and annulled' and then, in a curious but consistent extension of policy, dealt with the matter of all such 'prohibited' marriages. It was claimed that no power on earth could sanction them, and in one sentence the Act thereby destroyed the jurisdiction and authority of the Pope. The succession was then established through the children of Queen Anne, followed by a list of offences of treason or misprision of treason to be incurred by those who 'slandered' or 'derogated' the royal family. Then came the stipulation that eventually took More to his death on the scaffold: all of the king's subjects 'shall make a corporal oath' to maintain 'the whole effects and contents of this present Act'.[39] More had anticipated the time when all would have to be 'confirmed with oaths', and he must immediately have understood the significance of this new development. The Act of Succession was also interpreted, even at the time of its promulgation, as the defining measure of what Cranmer later called 'this world of reformation';[40] so entered the language the term which would ever afterwards signify that great process of change which More understood and feared. On the day the Act of Succession was given its first reading, the brother of one MP wrote that 'after this day the Bishop of Rome shall have no manner of authority within the realm of England'.[41]

That Act was one of several which, in the course of this parliamentary session, would utterly destroy the dispensation of a thousand years. The proponents of change claimed that they were only restoring the ancient privileges of the English Church, but the evidence suggests that this was a theory devised merely to justify wholesale 'reformation'. The Acts of Annates, of Appeals, of Peter's Pence and of Dispensations brought the Church under the king's control in every particular, whether in the appointment of bishops, the preparation of clerical statutes or the visitation of monasteries. A new heresy law, in addition, abolished the old system of ecclesiastical justice that More had used and defended; it was also no longer deemed an offence to speak against the Pope. The first phase was complete.

In this period which witnessed the rejection of his beliefs, and the destruction of the very order to which he clung, More turned from polemic to meditation and prayer. He began to compose *A Treatise on the Passion*. It is in many ways a standard votive work, which combines the exegesis of biblical texts concerning the last days of Jesus with passages of devotion and exhortation. Yet he composed it in these weeks and days of change, and there are intimations within it of that evil and confusion by which he believed himself to be surrounded. When he writes of the Jewish elders who concealed 'worldly wynning' and 'pryuate malice' under 'the pretext of a great zeale vnto the common wealth',[42] it is hard not to trace a contemporaneous allusion. When he prayed that God grant him the grace never to 'giue mine assent to folow the sinful deuice of any wicked counsail',[43] he was also invoking the specific situation in which he then found himself. The treatise was, in this respect, a way of concentrating his mind and his faith in an age of anxiety; more deliberately, perhaps, it was also a means by which he prepared himself for his own death. The passion of Jesus 'of which he was so ferd, and for which he was so sorowful'[44] might then be seen as an object of release as well as devotion, since by meditating upon the torments of Christ More was better able to understand and endure those which he anticipated for himself.

Yet it would be wrong to consider *A Treatise on the Passion* as an entirely private and meditative work; everything which More wrote also had a public context and significance, and in this book there are obvious calls to 'christen readers' and 'good readers' to stand firm within their faith.[45] More believed, with much justification, that the destruction of the old religion was being undertaken at the behest of an arrogant and impetuous king, together with councillors who hoped to benefit from the disorder; the 'reformation' was being imposed, therefore, upon a nation which remained generally pious and devoted. The substitution of king for pope as head of the Church may not have seemed a particularly damaging or damning development, but More saw further and more clearly than most of his contemporaries; once the community of the faithful, the living and dead, was broken by schism then the faith itself would be placed in severe peril.

More prophesied that the time would come when the faith was so harassed and persecuted that 'it shall seeme that there shall bee than no chrysten countreyes left at all'.[46] This may be construed as the time of Antichrist, but his reign 'shal be but short'. Then Christ will come 'and finyshe thys presente worlde, and rewarde euerye good manne after hys good woorkes wrought in hys true catholike faythe'.[47] More may well have believed that he was witnessing the events which would lead to the end of the world itself. That is why he continually exhorted his compatriots to remain true to the old religion and why he came to the conclusion of his work with a great paean in honour of the blessed sacrament, that mystical body of Christ which in its earthly form the king seemed about to tear apart. But he never completed *A Treatise on the Passion*; his last words here are 'quicke liuely membres in the spirituall societie of sayntes'.[48] Before he could write the next sentence he was consigned to a cell in the Tower of London.

XXX

The Weeping Time

IN the first week of April 1534, More travelled on pilgrimage to Our Lady of Willesden; it was a church favoured by Londoners, and was well known to him. He stayed at the house of Sir Giles Alington, husband to his stepdaughter, and from there wrote to his secretary concerning changes to *A Treatise on the Passion*; 'thus much is perplex enough,' he concluded. He was concerned at this time to put his life in order and, a week before, he had arranged 'a conveyance for the disposition of all his lands' on his decease;[1] two days after the first conveyance, he bequeathed to the Ropers a portion of his estate. Evidently he was trying to protect the interests of his family, and no less clearly was he preparing for his own death. All the members of parliament had taken the oath of succession at the end of March, and More realised that soon he would be invited to follow their example. On 12 April, Low Sunday, he attended Mass in St Paul's; after it had been celebrated he left the church and walked to his old house in Bucklersbury where John and Margaret Clement now lived. But, on this occasion, he was being followed. He had been observed in St Paul's, and an official of the council tracked him down. Even while he remained in these familiar surroundings, he was handed a summons directing him to appear at Lambeth Palace on the following morning and there to take the oath of succession.

The moment, so long feared, had come. He returned at once to Chelsea and acquainted his family with the unwelcome but not unanticipated news. Then he spent most of the night in prayer. Early the next morning he attended Mass in the village church and was given holy communion; before he left his house for ever, he walked with his family in the garden. He told them that he was likely to be imprisoned and took his leave of them there; he would not allow them to accompany him to the landing stage where his boat was waiting, but closed the wicket gate and 'shut them all from him'.[2] Only William Roper was allowed to stay with him and, as his servants rowed them down the Thames to Lambeth, More remained deep in thought. Eventually he roused himself and whispered, 'Son Roper, I thank our Lord the field is won.'[3]

'Sir, I am thereof very glad.'

Roper later admitted that he did not know what his father-in-law had meant, and it is indeed a somewhat cryptic remark. It is susceptible of at least two interpretations. He had managed to conquer his natural feelings for his family, so that he would not be tempted to betray his conscience for their sake; the gesture of shutting the gate behind him is indicative of this. But he had also won the field on his own behalf; as the events of succeeding weeks will testify, he had managed largely to conquer his own anxieties and had determined how to conduct himself in all dealings with his adversaries. And so his boat came up to the landing stairs at Lambeth, next to the horse ferry; forty-four years before, More had come here with his father on entering the service of Archbishop Morton. The elaborate gateway to the palace had not then been finished, but now More passed through it in his last act of freedom. Other people had already assembled there to take the oath of succession before the king's commissioners, but Thomas More was the first to be called. He also noticed that he was the only lay person present, which must have suggested to him the importance that was being attached to his decision.

He was led before Cromwell, Cranmer, Audley and William Benson, the Abbot of Westminster. They asked him if he was now ready to swear the oath and he expressed a wish to see it; a small slip of parchment, beneath the impress of the Great Seal, was handed to him and he read it carefully. Then he requested a copy of the Act of Succession itself, which was given to him in the form of a 'printed roll'.[4] He read this, too, and in his precise way he compared the oath to the Act. The commissioners were waiting impatiently for his answer and, finally, after detailed consideration of both documents, he spoke out. 'My purpose is not to put any fault either in the Act or any man that made it, or in the oath or any man that swears it, nor to condemn the conscience of any other man. But as for myself in good faith my conscience so moves me in the matter, that though I will not deny to swear to the succession, yet unto the oath that here is offered to me I cannot swear, without the jeoparding of my soul to perpetual damnation.' It may be supposed that this statement, constructed in the manner of a lawyer to avoid prejudice, had been rehearsed during More's sleepless nights. All along he had known the opinion of his family. His wife had told him that 'God regardeth' the heart rather than the tongue and that the meaning of the oath thereby 'goeth vpon that they thinke, and not vpon that they say'.[5] But More was not capable of such dissimulation. Instead he made a careful point to the commissioners. 'If you doubt whether I do refuse the oath only for the grudge of my conscience, or any other fantasy, I am ready here to satisfy you by my oath. Which, if you do not trust it, why should you be the better to give me any oath? And if you trust that I will herein swear true, then I trust of your goodness you will not move me to swear the oath you had offered me, perceiving that for to swear it is against my conscience.'[6] So he was invoking the dictates of his conscience for his refusal, but at no stage did he explain what they were.

Lord Chancellor Audley then replied to him. 'We all are sorry to hear you say thus, and see you refuse the oath. On our faith you are the first that has ever refused it, and it will cause the King's highness to conceive great suspicion of you and great indignation toward you.' He then showed More a printed roll, with the signatures of the Lords and Commons inscribed upon it, but More simply reiterated his first statement. 'I myself cannot swear, but I do not blame any other man that has sworn.' He was then silent, and was asked to walk down into the garden for further reflection or meditation. But it was a hot day and he decided to rest in 'the olde burned chamber' on the first floor, which overlooked the garden and the river; this was a 'waiting' room, next to the guards' chamber, that had suffered a fire in the time of Archbishop Warham. As he lingered there he saw Hugh Latimer walking with some of the Lambeth clergy; Latimer was laughing and joking with the chaplains, putting his arm around the shoulders of one or two of them 'that if they had been women, I wolde haue went he had been waxen wanton'.[7] Latimer was of strongly Lutheran tendencies, and had been continually under threat of imprisonment because of his beliefs; but he was laughing now, in the knowledge that half of his cause was won. More looked on and perhaps raised his eyes to the ever-flowing river.

A fateful spectacle was then played out before him. Dr Nicholas Wilson, a scholar and divine, was escorted from the interview chamber; he was 'brought by me', according to More, 'and gentilmanly sent straight vnto the Towre'.[8] He, too, had refused to swear the oath; he had been 'brought by' More as living proof of what would happen to all recusants. There was, for them, only one ultimate destination. More later learned that John Fisher had also been taken before the commissioners and dispatched to the Tower for the same reason. The anxiety and threat were too great for some to endure and the vicar of Croydon, Rowland Phillips, well known for his orthodox opinions and his devotion to the old faith, swore to the oath and signed his name. More heard that he had then gone down to the 'buttry barre' and ordered drink 'either for gladnes or for drines [dryness], or else that it might be sene'.[9] He might also have called for drink, of course, as a way of slaking his conscience as well as his thirst. In a description of the scene to his daughter More used a phrase from the gospel of St John, with the clear implication that he himself was in the position of St Peter just before he denied Christ. Yet there would be no denial from him. More called all these events a 'pageant', and indeed it might have been devised as a theatrical scenario for the state of the realm – a reformer rejoicing, an orthodox cleric bowing to the king's will and a defiant scholar sent to the Tower.

It was at this point that he was once again led before the commissioners. They revealed to him the number of the London clergy who had sworn the oath that day, even as he had waited in the burned chamber, but he still would not be drawn. He simply repeated his position that he could not join them in their assent. They asked what particular aspect of the oath disturbed him. More replied that he had offended the king already, but 'if I should open and disclose the causes why, I shall therewith but further exasperate his Highnes, which I will in no wise do, but rather will I abide all the danger and harm that might come toward me than give his Highnes any occasion of further displeasure.'[10] His was a subtle strategy of silence and non-compliance, but it had its dangers. The commissioners immediately accused him of stubbornness and obstinacy, but More knew the law better than any of them. 'But yet it thinketh me,' he told them, 'that if I may not declare the causes without perill, than to leaue them vndeclared is no obstinacy.'[11] No man is obliged to condemn himself. Cranmer then intervened. More had agreed that the swearing of the oath was 'vncertain and doubtfull',[12] precisely because his own conscience did not match that of others; but since it was his certain duty to obey his prince, why not take the less doubtful course and swear? More saw the force of the argument and could reply only that 'in my conscience the trouth seems on the tother side'. The Abbot of Westminster then asked him to estimate the weight of his conscience, when opposed by so many of the clergy and the parliament, but More answered that he could claim in his support 'the generall counsail of Christendome'. This was his central argument; the derivation of 'conscience' suggests knowledge-with-others, which for More included the communion of the dead as well as the living. It was this understanding which afforded him the strength and confidence to continue what seemed, to almost everyone, a foolish and futile struggle.

Thomas Cromwell, recognising More's position to be unalterable, swore 'a gret oth' that he would rather have seen his own son beheaded than be a witness to More's refusal. The mention of a beheading here was surely significant. Cromwell went on to suggest that the king would now 'conceiue a great suspicion' against More, and that in particular the machinations of the Nun of Kent would be blamed upon him. Their conference ended soon after, with More apparently conceding that he might swear to the succession if the oath was differently framed. He did not elaborate upon the necessary alterations, but once more invoked the principle of human conscience and finally declared that 'me thinketh in good faith, that so were it good reason that euery man should leaue me to myne'.[13]

He was now, effectively, a prisoner. He had rejected the oath and was therefore to be charged with 'misprision of treason'. But he had refused to give his reasons for his fatal decision and, at this moment, he entered silence. Or, rather, silence entered him. In a sense it was no longer his own choice; he ceased to be aware of himself, and at this level of conscience or knowledge he became part of the larger world of faith and spirit. He had always followed the imperatives of duty and service, but now that duty had turned irrevocably from his society to his God. If the will of heaven is vouchsafed to a human being in a wholly private way, demanding an act of faith as it had once been demanded of Abraham, then he cannot speak to the world. The world will not understand.

But if he did not explain the specific legal reasons for refusing the oath of succession, it is perhaps possible to reconstruct them. He told his daughter later that he had refused the oath because it was 'not agreeable with the statute';[14] by which he meant that, in his careful consideration and rereading of the two documents, he had realised that the oath itself went far beyond the matter of the royal succession. It required obeisance not only to the Act of Succession itself, in other words, but also to 'all other Acts and Statutes made since the beginning of the present Parliament'.[15] This included all the antipapal legislation within the Acts of Annates, of Appeals, of Dispensations, and of Peter's Pence. If More had sworn the oath, as presented to him with this wording, he would have concurred in the forcible removal of the Pope's jurisdiction and the effective schism of the Church in England. This he could not do, even at the cost of his life. He might have been willing to swear to a differently phrased oath, as he had suggested, as long as it did not include any other matters.

After the formal interrogation was over More was delivered into the custody of the Abbot of Westminster, under whose supervision he remained for the next four days. The truth was that no one knew precisely what to do with him; his case was not like that of John Fisher, who had formally been 'attainted' through his association with the Nun of Kent, and there was some discussion among the king's commissioners about the proper course of action. Cranmer wrote to Cromwell suggesting that More (and also Fisher) should be asked to swear only to the Act of Succession itself, thereby avoiding all the problems of acceding to the other Acts; he also suggested that their compliance, if it came, 'should be suppressed' or concealed until the right moment for its publication. Their oath of loyalty to the new royal family would be advertised, in other words, for the maximum possible effect upon the king's opponents. The importance being attached to More, in particular, was clear. But when Cromwell put Cranmer's arguments to the king, Henry refused to countenance any such compromise; he argued, with some justification, that it might act as a precedent. What if any others refused to swear to the entire oath?

So More's last hope of freedom was gone. On 17 April he was sent by river from Westminster to the Tower of London. He was wearing his gold chain of livery, as a solemn token of his service to the king, and he was advised to deliver it into the safekeeping of his family; but he refused, with a characteristic piece of irony: 'For if I were taken in the field by my enemies, I would they should somewhat fare the better by me.'[16] The boat steered its course towards Traitor's Gate, where a great oaken wicket was opened to receive the prisoner.

The wooden gate may be taken as an image for a subsequent conversation.

More: Well met, my lord, I hope we shall soon meet in heaven.

Fisher: This should be the way, Sir Thomas, for it is a very strait gate we are in.[17]

At the landing stage beneath St Thomas's Tower More was met by the lieutenant of the Tower, Sir Edmund Walsingham, and by the porter of the wicket. It was an old custom for the porter to request the 'upper garment' of any new prisoner. More proffered him his hat and explained that 'I am very sorry it is no better for you'.

'No, sir,' came the reply, 'I must have your gown.'[18]

More would have known perfectly well the tradition of handing the man his gown, and his offering of the hat may be construed as an example of that humour which always emerged in the most grave situations. Sir Edmund Walsingham led him up the narrow spiral stairway, with its thick stone and worn steps, the darkness punctuated briefly by slits carved in the massive outer wall. It was fortunate, perhaps, that Walsingham was a 'good friend and old acquaintaince' of More's;[19] he took him to his cell, or chamber, and 'desired him that he would accept in such cheare as he was able to make hym'.[20] His famous prisoner replied that 'if any here like it not, turne hym out of dores for a churle'.[21] If I complain, in other words, then eject me from the Tower. It is not at all certain in which part of the building More was imprisoned, but it seems most likely to have been within the Bell Tower or the Beauchamp Tower. It is reasonable to suppose, however, that he was moved during the period of his imprisonment.

He was taken to one of those apartments which were reserved for the more influential or privileged 'guests' of the lieutenant. His was a pentagonal stone chamber, with a vaulted ceiling; it was some nineteen feet in height, with a floor space of approximately eighteen feet by twenty feet. The walls themselves were between nine and thirteen feet thick, the floor flagged with rough and uneven stone, the windows merely arrow-slits or 'loops'.[22] More's furnishings were of the simplest; they included a table and chair as well as a 'pallet' bed. There was a small brick stove, to heat this cold room, and More arranged for mats of straw to be placed upon the floor and against the walls. He described it as 'metely feyre' and 'at the lest wise it was strong ynough';[23] indeed he would not have necessarily been uncomfortable. His old servant, John à Wood, was allowed to attend him; board and lodging, for both of them, amounted to fifteen shillings a week, which was more than adequate for food and clothing.

Wood remained his faithful servant through the entire period of More's imprisonment and might himself, if anything else were known of him, provide an interesting study in loyalty and affection. But he is only ever mentioned as a silent attendant upon his unfortunate master. When Wood and More were first shown the prison chamber by Walsingham, for example, More insisted that his servant swear an oath to the effect that if he, More, ever said anything to the king's detriment then Wood must report his comments to the lieutenant of the Tower. His master was not held with any strict discipline, however; it was appropriate for a prisoner of his rank to be given permission to walk within the 'liberties' of the Tower and to stroll in its gardens. More's fascination for animals was such that he perhaps visited the royal menagerie, where he might refresh his memory of the lions which 'in the night walken'. Much more importantly, however, he was allowed to attend Mass each day to pray for his own salvation and for the spiritual comfort of those close to him.

He wrote to his daughter, Margaret, soon after his arrival in order to calm her fears. 'I am in good health of body, and in good quiet of minde,' he told her, and beseeched their creator to 'make you all mery in the hope of heauen'.[24] This letter was written 'with a cole', or piece of charcoal, because More then had no other pen. He wished to console them because he knew in what desperate need of comfort they stood; the house in Chelsea was searched on more than one occasion, and in a dialogue he composed in his cell a young man described how 'our pore famely be fallen into suche dumpes, that scantly can any such comfort as my pore wyt can give them, any thyng asswage their sorow'.[25] They spoke of More constantly, as Margaret told her father later, and repeated to each other the proverbs and *dicta* by which he had tried to fortify them.

Yet he also was obliged to console himself. It has been recorded that a new prisoner is so overwhelmed with feelings, on his first admittance to his cell, that he does not notice the hardness of his bed until the second night. We cannot hope to follow More's unwritten meditations, but on several occasions he accused himself of being 'faint-hearted'[26] and prey to many fears. There were the natural concerns for his family, who might now be reduced to penury; there was his constant anxiety for the safety and future of his Church. But he also suffered from the stronger and more deadly fear that he would not be courageous enough to sustain his lonely course and that he would, in the end, surrender. His great fear was of torture, of 'duresse and harde handelinge' and 'violente forceble waies'.[27] He confessed that he considered 'the very worst and the vttermost that can by possibilite fall',[28] and that he found 'my fleshe much more shrinkinge from payne and from death, than me thought it the part of a faithfull Christen man';[29] indeed he seems to have had some compulsion to dwell upon all the vagaries of anticipated torment.

The events of the outer world could only have confirmed these worst fears of isolation and death. His old friend Cuthbert Tunstall had been summoned to London and there complied with the king's wishes; newly consecrated bishops also swore an oath to maintain Henry as 'the chief and supreme head of the Church of England', while commissioners were being despatched all over the country to tend the oath of succession to the king's subjects. Three days after More was brought to the Tower, 'all the craftes in London were called to their halls, and sworne on a booke to be true to Queene Anne and to beleeve and take her for a lawfull wife of the Kinge'.[30] But, on that same Monday in April, there was a fateful event which touched More closely. On the same day that the City guilds pledged their allegiance to the king, Elizabeth Barton and the five priests who had supported her were taken from their cells in the Tower and lashed to wooden planks; their wrists were tied together, as if they were at prayer. More would have heard, if not seen, the proceedings – a large assembly of officers and councillors had gathered to watch the last journey of the traitors to Tyburn. The wooden hurdles, on which the 'holy nun' and her accomplices had been tied, were then hitched to horses which dragged them over the unflagged stones, cobbles, mud and mire of the city. It was the fate to which More knew he might be consigned. In this painful and ignominious position the condemned prisoners journeyed the five miles to Tyburn.

Elizabeth Barton died first, having confessed to being a 'poor wench without learning' who 'fell into a certain pride and foolish fantasy with myself';[31] she was hanged, but since there was no 'drop' in this period the public executioner pulled down upon the legs until she gave up her ghost. Her accomplices were not so fortunate, and an account written by a Franciscan some years later confirms that the priests suffered all the penalties of the law for treason. Each one was hanged until he lost consciousness, and then was revived so that he could watch as his penis was cut off and stuffed in his mouth; his stomach was then cut open and his intestines tossed in a cauldron of boiling water so that the dying man might smell his own mortality. Then the heart was plucked from his steaming body and held before his face. One of the victims is supposed to have cried, 'What you are holding is consecrated to God.'[32] Then all were beheaded, their heads parboiled to be placed upon poles on London Bridge. This was the fate, too, which More might expect. These were some of his night fears as he lay upon his pallet in the stone chamber.

Yet, even *in extremis*, there was a measure of consolation. He had taken with him to his prison chamber a copy of the New Testament as well as the Psalter and Book of Hours; from his references in his 'Tower writings' he is also likely to have had beside him such books of devotion as the *Catena Aurea* and the *Monotessaron* of Jean Gerson. In particular he meditated upon the testing of St Peter, the martyrdom of St Stephen and the passion of Christ. He wrote to his daughter that 'I neuer haue prayde God to bringe me hence nor deliuer me fro death, but referring all thing whole vnto his onely pleasure',[33] and, when she was eventually allowed to visit him, he told her that of all God's spiritual favours 'I recken vpon my faith my prisonment euen the very chief';[34] by which he meant that he had been granted the opportunity to withdraw entirely from the world and prepare his soul for eternity. The great fear of the faithful was of a sudden or unexpected death and thus of meeting the creator without 'schrift' or 'housel', the last confession and communion. More knew that he had at least escaped that fate.

In all outward aspects he remained patient and mild now, not caring even to speak against heretics; he knew that he was likely to die soon enough, but the prospect of death was not an unwelcome one. In the words of Thomas à Kempis, he had grown to love his cell – 'In this thy cell thou shalt find what abroad thou shalt too often lose ... thou must always suffer, willingly or unwillingly, and so shalt thou always find the cross ... endure patiently the contempt which is thy due ... I am not then worthy of anything but to be scourged and punished.'[35] More retained his hair shirt as he dwelled in his chamber, and is reported to have whipped himself for penitence; he fasted on the appointed days, sang hymns and prayed both day and night. Before he slept, according to one of his first biographers, 'he wrapt hym selfe in a linen sheet, like a bodie to be laid in a grave'. He no longer cut his hair and within a few months his beard emphasised the haunted and emaciated look which later (and no doubt posthumous) portraits reveal. When Pope Benedict XIII was imprisoned in Avignon, he vowed that he would not cut his beard until he had been released; this was an old oath, but it is clear enough that More never expected to regain his liberty. His hair began to show through his hood. This is a medieval expression which meant that he had fallen into misfortune, but it did not seem an unhappy fate to More himself. He had in a sense returned to the time of his early adulthood, when he had participated in the rituals and services of the London Charterhouse. He had become a monk at last.

In his Book of Hours he wrote one line above and below the woodcuts which depicted the progress of Christ towards his crucifixion; taken together these lines form a 'Godly Meditation' in which he absorbs the images of 'the passion that christ suffred for me' in order to render himself more worthy of divine grace. Each image, whether that of the 'crowning with thorns' or 'carrying the Cross', afforded endless material for More's contemplation as he considered his own last hours. He prayed 'gladly to bere my purgatory here' and to 'have ever afore myn yie my deth that ys ever at hand', finding in the sufferings of Jesus the inspiration to endure his own. So he divided each day into the cycles of prayer, the canonical hours which comforted and protected him. In his Psalter, also, More made his own annotations. The words of the thirty-ninth psalm proclaim the silence of the psalmist before the deceits and lies of his enemies; More wrote beside it a note that he must remain quiet, also, and bless those who conspire against him. He marked or 'flagged' certain verses, which could be brought together in a 'cento' prayer filled with images of tribulation and imprisonment; one passage from the sixty-ninth psalm is particularly emphasised with its verse 'I am become a stranger unto my brethren, and an alien unto my mother's children'. Against the verse of the eighty-seventh psalm, 'I am become as a man without help', More appended the phrase '*in tribulatione uehemente et in carcere*' ('in grievous suffering and in prison').

Yet the central allusion, occurring forty times, is to 'demones'; he places it repeatedly against those psalms which implore deliverance from the snares of evil men or ask for patience in the face of enemies. More wrote in the margin of the fifty-ninth psalm, which opens 'deliver me from mine enemies', '*uel demones uel malos homines*' ('either demons or wicked men'). For him, in the battle for his religion more than his life, there was little difference between the demonic agencies and those who tempted or tried to force him to forswear his faith. More knew from Augustine that demons might possess bodies composed of 'thick moist air' like that which rises from a heated bath; perhaps the exhalations of his prison chamber reminded him of their presence.

His annotations and marginalia were written in ink, the psalms being generally lightly marked with a stroke or word, so it is clear that More's use of charcoal at the beginning of his imprisonment was only a temporary expedient. He had been given writing materials and during these early months of confinement he composed a lengthy treatise entitled *A Dialogue of Comfort Against Tribulation*; in that respect, it springs directly from the threatened and attentive piety which is visible in More's annotations.

But this late and last dialogue has a private and self-communing, almost brooding, quality which distinguishes it from its predecessors. It is the strangest mixture of narrative and fable, filled with recollection and animated by a curious passion for the absurd or the bizarre. There are memories here of More's childhood and of children's games, of his schooldays and of the London Charterhouse, of early friends such as Linacre, of Wolsey and of Dame Alice, of sea voyages and jury rooms. There is a discussion on the nature of dream and reality which provides the most appropriate setting for some of the strangest stories More ever told. He narrates, for example, the short history of a woman who wished to 'angre her husband, so sore that she might give hym occasion to kyll her & than shuld he be hangid for her';[36] the man did indeed chop off her head and witnesses 'herd her tong bable in her hed & call horson horson twise after that the hed was fro the bodye'.[37] More mentions the act of beheading on several occasions, as if his own fears were striated throughout the narrative. He relates the story of a rich widow, for example, who wished to be beheaded by her neighbour and somehow taken for a martyr; she also wished 'the blody axe'[38] to be secretly conveyed to another neighbour's house, and so instigate a false charge of murder. More tells the tale of a man who wished his wife to crucify him, in remembrance of Christ, but was eventually satisfied by a scourging.

There are also stories of those with a manic desire to commit suicide, and a vignette of a sick woman who in the act of making love vomits over her companion. He evokes a fervent and fervid world of 'wakyng revelacion' and 'false dremyng delusion', a world in which all the horrors of frail humankind are displayed. It is the world of visions and illusions in which the 'mad nun' of Kent had dwelled, but it is also the world as seen from the vantage of a prison chamber. It is the world of artists such as Hieronymus Bosch and Pieter Breughel, with the same fascination for the deformed and the demonic, with the *facetiae* of natural life transformed into the giant marks of the flesh and the devil.

He was also writing to allay his own desperate fear of pain or torture, shut up in that straitened room, aware of all the temptations and delusions of the anxious mind. The *Dialogue* is set in 1528, two years after the first invasion of Hungary by Suleiman the Magnificent; he was poised to attack again and the conversation between an old and young inhabitant of that country, 'Antony' and 'Vincent', is ostensibly designed to bring comfort to those unfortunate Hungarians who seemed destined to suffer at Turkish hands. Yet his real subject lies much closer to home. When More writes of a time when our friends 'vnder colour of kyndred' become 'our most foes',[39] for example, he was describing the period in which he dwelled. In the guise of Antony More is also able to relive, or relieve, some of his own most powerful and unspoken reflections. He describes those who 'semed they neuer so good & vertuose before' were discovered to be 'holow light & counterfayte in dede';[40] despite his public wish not to meddle in any other man's conscience, it seems likely that he is here condemning those orthodox clergy who had signed the oath of succession. There are also a number of allusions to 'the lion'. This was already well known as an image of the king himself, but in More's writing the royal beast becomes curiously entangled with other figures. The Turkish 'persecucion for the fayth' is depicted as 'a rampyng lyon',[41] and at the close of this narrative, when More meditates upon the agonies of Christ, the devil suddenly appears 'runnyng & roryng like a rampyng lyon abowt vs'.[42] So we have the king, the Turk, and the devil encompassed in the same range of imagery; in More's peril and isolation, he has conflated all of the enemies of the faith into one demonic form.

Those who die for their faith are promised a martyr's crown and everlasting glory, but More was not so presumptuous as to believe himself worthy of them. Half of his struggle lay in preventing himself from rushing to such a death, and indeed many of his references in the *Dialogue* concern those who suffer from spiritual pride or are tempted into that dreadful vanity by the devil himself. There are further snares. In the course of the book he names the four great temptations of the faithful: the terror by night, the arrow that flies by day, the pestilence that wanders and the devils of noon. This last 'mydday devill' is the strongest and most to be feared, since for More it represents the open persecution of the faithful. So More invokes the protection of God, and in several passages he alludes to the 'pavis' or shield of His presence.

Antony compares himself 'to the snofe of a candell that burneth with in the candell styk nose . . . yet sodenly lyfteth a leme halfe an Inch aboue the nose, & giveth a praty short light agayne'[43] until it finally goes out. It is a pretty image, but it cannot disguise the weariness of a man who now looked towards death and reckoned 'euery day for my last'.[44] This late work is filled with sudden and perhaps inadvertent allusions to More's own constrained state, with images of 'a little narrow room', 'key cold', 'men [that] get owt of prison', and 'this wepyng world'. It is also a fevered world, of 'siknes' and 'phisike', of the memory of his own 'fittes' in earlier life, of vertigo upon 'an high bridge' and the 'toth ache', of 'drugges' and 'desease', of 'medycyns' and 'poticaryes'. What is this life but a vast chamber of the mortally sick, watched over 'by the great phisicion god'?[45] More's own condition, in extremity, is also the condition of the world. And what is the world, in any case, but a vast prison no different in nature from the cell in which More found himself? 'In this prison they bye & sell, in this prison they brall and chide, in this they run together & fight, in this they dyce, in this they carde, In this they pipe & revell, In this they sing & dawnce.'[46] Then God becomes 'the chiefe gaylour ouer this whole brode prison the world is'.[47] This dark and hard dialogue reflects a faith of equal severity and unambiguity, established upon principles of order and authority where God is both doctor and prison warden. More can then reflect, with a certain degree of irony, on his own likely fate: 'Now to this greate glory, can there no man come hedlesse. Our hed is Christ.'[48]

There was still humour to be found, even in his confinement; he was anxious but not sorrowful and he had occasion to write some short English verses or 'balletes'. The second of them is addressed to 'lady luck' and ends

> But in faith, I bless you again a thousand times
> For lending me now some leisure to make rhymes.

He had enough leisure, also, to write letters. He was well aware of John Fisher's presence in the Tower and through the agency of the lieutenant's servant, George Golde, various 'scrolls' were passed between them; they would not have been of a compromising nature, but Golde always took the precaution of burning them. 'There is no better keeper,' he used to say, 'than the fire.' According to both Fisher and More, on a later examination, they had simply exchanged the prayers and comforts which seemed appropriate in their similar circumstances. Only once did they discuss the 'king's matter' – in the summer of the year they both described to each other their attitude to the oath of succession. More explained that he had not sworn, but would say nothing further on the subject.

He was no more forthcoming with his daughter. At first he had been refused visitors, but Margaret had written a letter in which she urged him to follow her example and accept the oath. He had once said that 'all the pynch' was in the 'paine' of torture or death, but there was another kind of pain; he was deeply wounded and disturbed by her letter 'surely farre aboue all other thynges'.[49] Twice he mentioned that Margaret had 'labored' to persuade him and, although her letter is not extant, it is clear that she tried every kind of exhortation on the issues which touched his conscience. This was the hardest suffering of his imprisonment. It was not simply that More, so much a man of the household and the society established upon it, had been separated from his family; he also knew that they could not understand his avowal of the principles which had led to his arrest and imprisonment. He was truly alone.

At this point Cromwell decided that she might visit her father, perhaps in the hope that a little filial affection and persuasion might soften him. More, on seeing his daughter in the sad confines of his stone chamber, might come to understand the folly or futility of his own situation. So she journeyed from Chelsea to the Tower, and was taken to her father's cell. They wept and chanted together the Seven Psalms and Litany. 'The wepyng tyme,' he wrote, '. . . is the tyme of this wrechid world.'[50] When he asked about Dame Alice and the rest of the household Margaret reassured him, as she mentioned on a later occasion, that his wife was in 'good comforte' and all else in 'good order' with the family 'disposing them self euery day more and more to set litle by the worlde'.[51]

Then More and his daughter engaged in earnest conversation about his refusal of the oath. On this occasion he may have informed her that it was not appropriate to the statute, but on the more general question he made it clear that he could in no way be swayed from the dictates of his conscience. He told her that he had come to his fatal decision only after long consideration and after reflecting upon the 'very worst and the vttermost that can by possibilite fall'.[52] There was much more talk on what Margaret had called her father's 'scruple of his conscience',[53] most of it taken up in his rehearsal of the truths by which he was guided. Once more he affirmed the unity of Christendom as well as the inherited doctrines of those holy doctors and saints who, rejoicing in the presence of God, sustained the communion of the faithful upon earth. Margaret may have expressed her unease about More's health and at the manifestly unhealthy conditions of confinement, but he was inclined to bless his captors. Her husband reported his words as 'if it had not been for my wife and you that be my children, whom I accompt the chief part of my charge, I would not have failed ere this to have closed myself in as strait a room – and straiter, too.'[54] His last words, before Margaret left the cell, also deserve to be quoted here: 'God maketh me a wanton, and setteth me on His lap and dandleth me.'[55] He had become a child again, supported and protected by his true father.

Margaret made other visits and employed her maid, Dorothy Colley, to run various errands to the Tower. He had given his daughter a formal letter 'to all my louinge frendes', in which he told them that Margaret was to act as his proxy in the outside world. It is also likely that she smuggled out letters or pieces of his work and provided him with any books he required for his devotional writings. His daughter was, in the first two or three months, the only visitor allowed to enter his cell. But eventually his wife was also given permission to see him. Their son-in-law has an account of the meeting which is vivid but not necessarily inaccurate.

Alice More: What the good-year, Master More, I marvel that you have been always hitherto taken for so wise a man will now so play the fool to be here in this close, filthy prison and be content thus to be shut up among mice and rats.

She then went on to expatiate upon the delights of their Chelsea house.

Thomas More: I pray thee, good Mistress Alice, tell me one thing.
Alice More: What is that?
Thomas More: Is not this house as nigh heaven as my own?
Alice More: Tilly-valle! Tilly-valle!

Thomas More: How say you, Mistress Alice, is it not so?

Alice More: *Bone deus*, *bone deus*, man, will this gear never be left?[56]

'Tilly-valle', derived from the name of the demon Tityvillus, was the phrase for idle talk. It is in fact quite likely that his wife did converse in this manner to him. More himself described the occasion when Alice berated him for lack of ambition: 'will you sitt still by the fier & make goslynges in the asshis with a stikke as children do? Wold god I were a man, and loke what I wold do.'[57]

More also provided a scene from their dialogue in his prison chamber, when his wife lamented that the door was locked against him at night. 'For by my trouth,' she said, 'yf the dore shuld be shit vppon me, I wold wene yt wold stopp vpp my breeth.'[58] More 'laughed in his mynd' at that, since he knew that she always closed the doors and windows of her bedchamber before retiring. Roper adds another detail of their conversation, in which More again renounced all his worldly goods. 'What cause have I then to like such an house,' he said, 'as would so soon forget his master?'[59] The mixture of gravity and irony, with remarks which are in turn earnest or playful, is appropriate for one of their last conversations upon this earth. It was characteristic of an affectionate relationship in which both thought that they had the measure of each other; Alice More's practical sense was not incompatible with More's own deeply rooted piety, while his honesty and good judgement were a match for her apparent worldliness and worldly intuition. But, in the end, he became unfathomable to her. He became absurd. Or, perhaps, he became sublime. The routines and conventions of the world fell from him, like the linen cloth which the disciple of Christ threw off in order to escape his enemies, and the thin, bearded, spiritual man who looked at Alice More might as well have been a stranger to her.

But although he had renounced the world, the world had not forgotten him. There were still those, like his family, who believed that he might be relieved of his imprisonment and returned to Chelsea. The Mores were well connected, too, and in the late summer of the year Thomas Audley arrived at Horseheath, the estate of More's stepdaughter and her husband. Here the new Lord Chancellor 'took a course at a buck', to use the conventional expression, and then invited Alice Alington to visit him the following day at the house of his father-in-law nearby. The interview was carefully prepared by Audley, with the aim of discovering More's intentions or of obliquely applying familial pressure upon the prisoner. Like Polonius he might 'by indirections find directions out'.[60] Alice was of course happy to talk to him 'because I woulde speake to him for my father'.[61]

Alice Alington: I desire you humbly that you woulde, as I haue herd say that you hath ben, be still good lord unto my father.

Thomas Audley: It appeared very well [for him] whan the mater of the nonne was laide to his charge. And as for this other mater, I marvel that your father is so obstinate in his own conceite, as that every body wente forthe with all saue only the blynde bishop and he. And in goode faithe I am very glad that I haue no lerninge but in a fewe of Esoppes fables of the which I shall tell you one.[62]

He went on to tell two stories; the first concerned the folly of those who appear to be over-wise, and the second suggested the perils of an excessively scrupulous conscience. And then 'my Lorde did laugh very merily'.[63] It was not unusual for opinions and judgements to be conveyed by fables or parables rather than by any personal statement; but the conclusions of Audley were clear enough, and at least there was no suggestion that he believed More to be guilty of conspiracy. Alice Alington immediately wrote to her half-sister, Margaret, with the news of this disheartening conversation; and, on the next occasion Margaret was allowed to visit her father, she brought the letter for him. It was evidence that, as she put it, 'you are likely to lose all those frendes that are hable to do you any good'.[64] He smiled upon her. 'What, mistress Eve, as I called you when you came first, has my daughter Alington played the serpent with you, and with a letter set you to work to come tempt your father again?'

There then followed a long explication of his beliefs, all contained in what purports to be a letter from Margaret Roper to Alice Alington. In fact it looks like the work of More himself, who had frequently employed this fiction of authorship in order to speak his own deepest truths. The letter has been compared to Plato's *Crito* and *Phaedo*, dialogues on the last hours of Socrates, and there are indeed similarities between the two men in their respective prison cells. Socrates followed his conscience and spoke of a truth beyond the jurisdiction of the court which condemned him; he was urged to escape, but insisted upon his duty to uphold the process of the law. He also died with a joke upon his lips. But there the resemblance ends. More's letter is not meant to be a majestic and harmonious encomium on the principles of one man but, rather, a fundamental restatement of the objective truths to which he was attached. Socrates trusted in the immortality of the soul, but believed that no person of intelligence could know the exact nature of life after death; the dialogue concludes with a salute from Phaedo to this 'best, wisest, and most just of men'. More's letter, however, concluded in the manner with which he often ended his conversations: 'I full hartely praye for vs all, that we may meete together once in heauen, where we shall make merye for euer, and neuer haue trouble after.'[65]

He was now suffering from the effects of his confinement, and had spoken to his daughter 'of his diseases, both in his breste of olde, and his reynes now by reason of grauell and stone, and of the crampe also that diuers nightes grypeth hym in his legges'.[66] He reassured her that these symptoms of cramps and stones were no more severe than those before his incarceration, but in a letter to a fellow prisoner, Nicholas Wilson – whom he had last seen while resting in the 'burned chamber' of Lambeth Palace – he revealed that there had been two occasions when he believed he was about to die. In the colder weather the walls of his prison cell would become damp, and seem to 'sweat' in mimicry of human fever. John Fisher had already complained about the cold and the poor diet which had severely strained his own health; during the September of this year another eminent prisoner, the ninth Earl of Kildare, died in his cell. It was at this time that More's old friend Antonio Bonvisi gave him a camlet gown with which to warm himself as well as providing him with meat and drink. More, in return, sent him an elaborate and touching letter of gratitude in which he also alludes to the fact that he might never be able to write to him again. He was going to sign it 'Tuus T. Morus', your Thomas More, but declared that now 'I am not such a one that it forceth whose I am'.

He had been warned by Thomas Cromwell, through Margaret, 'that the Parlement lasteth yet',[67] by which Cromwell meant that further and heavier penalties might soon be visited upon him. More replied that 'if they would make a law to doe me any harme, that lawe coulde neuer be lawfull'.[68] But in this he was too sanguine, when the practice of the world was even then over-riding the theoretical concerns of justice. The Friars Observant of Greenwich and Richmond had already been 'putt out of their places',[69] and indeed the whole order was 'putt downe' because of its support for Catherine of Aragon.

In October Thomas Cromwell was named as Master of the Rolls, and a month later the seventh session of the 'Reformation' parliament opened; this session marked a further consolidation of the great social and cultural revolution which was taking place and, in addition, provided the fatal bills by which More and Fisher were eventually condemned to death. A second Act of Succession was promulgated with its own particular oath, thus remedying the defect which More had found in the first and too broadly inclusive oath. Of greater significance, an Act of Supremacy was introduced, proclaiming Henry to be 'the only supreme head in earth of the Church of England, called *Anglicana Ecclesia*'. In a further measure, the English Church was obliged to yield a tenth of its income to its new master. But there followed other proposals which touched upon More directly, as surely as if the king had run upon him in the tilting yard. A Treason Act went through the parliament, albeit with some difficulty, which for the first time made it a capital offence to 'maliciously wish, will, or desire, by words or writing' to deprive the royal family of their 'dignity, title, or name of their royal estates', or to declare the king 'heretic, schismatic, tyrant, infidel'. To call Henry a schismatic, therefore, would be to incur the penalty of a lingering death. There then followed two Acts of Attainder duly passed by the parliament; the first was directed against John Fisher and several others, but the second was aimed specifically and only at Thomas More. This Act denounced him for 'intending to sow sedition' by refusing the oath of succession and went on to accuse him of having 'unkindly and ingrately served our sovereign lord by divers and sundry ways'.

So the door of his prison was shut upon him. His manors and estates became forfeit to the crown – that of South, in Kent, went to George Boleyn – and his household apparently impoverished. Dame Alice More wrote to the king, as soon as the parliamentary session was over, beseeching him 'to remitte and pardon your moste grevous displeasure to the saide Sir Thomas', who now lay incarcerated 'in greate continuall sicknes of bodye and heuines of harte';[70] she repeated the family belief that his obduracy was 'a longe contynued and depe rooted scrupple, as passethe his power to avoyde and put away'.[71] It was, in other words, an obsession of the same pathological kind as those which he had described in *A Dialogue of Comfort*. It was a 'frantik fantasye' or 'develysh fantasie', to use More's own phrases in that book, which has the connotations of a diabolic temptation. He would not necessarily have thanked his wife for her diagnosis, therefore, especially since he had spent the last eight months in battling against those snares of the devil manifest in spiritual pride and the over-bearing desire for martyrdom.

Dame Alice also lamented that she was likely to be 'vtterlye vndone' if More's 'landes and tenementis' were confiscated; here we may suspect her of pardonable exaggeration, since she remained a wealthy woman from the inheritance of her first husband. She still possessed, for example, her estate in Hitchin. Her daughter and stepchildren had also profited from good marriages, although it is true that John More was now held to be responsible for his father's outstanding debts to the king. There are one or two subtle allusions in More's correspondence from prison which suggest that the more valuable 'moveable goodes' had already been quietly taken by the family from Chelsea; he cared nothing for himself now, but he was deeply anxious for the welfare of his household.

Just before the Act of Attainder was passed against him, More was thrust into much more rigorous confinement. He told his daughter, in a long letter, that he was being held in 'close keping' because of 'some newe causeles suspicion' and 'some secret sinister informacion';[72] he also warned her of the possibility that 'some new sodain searches may happe to be made in euery house of ours as narowly as is possible'. He had always suspected that his liberty had gone for ever, but the passing of the Act now determined his fate; he was for a time allowed no visitors, and was prevented from attending daily Mass in the chapels of the Tower. He had also become the subject of false rumours. A report reached him, from the outside, that he had indeed succumbed and sworn to the oath of succession; he denounced this story as a 'very vanitye'[73] and repeated once again that 'conscience is the cause' rather than 'obstinate wilfulness'.[74] He would also not have appreciated a remark volunteered by Erasmus a little time later – 'If only he had left theology to the theologians!' This is not perhaps as sympathetic as circumstances might have allowed, but it is a measure of the real distance between More and his old humanist friend. In this period of his more severe confinement, More wrote a memorandum to himself on the subject of perjury; he concluded, in the space of approximately four hundred words, that it would be wrong to betray a secret lawfully entrusted to him. But whose secret did he mean? Something conveyed to him by John Fisher? Or was it, perhaps, that Henry had privately informed him of something which had a material connection with More's refusal to take the oath? And of what, then, might such a secret consist? The rest is silence.

Now he began his last work. *De Tristitia Christi* is, as its title infers, a disciplined meditation upon the 'sadness' of Christ; it is a commentary upon certain verses of the New Testament concerned with the agony in the garden, the slumber of the disciples and the arrest of Jesus after his betrayal by Judas. Its last words – 'and they laid their hands upon Jesus' – might serve as an introduction to More's own imprisonment and likely death, but the treatise has a more general spiritual import. It was composed in Latin, so at the close of his life More was reverting to the larger community of the faithful; it is in turn ironic and passionate, filled with intensely dramatic moments upon which he elaborates in a style at once analytical and celebratory. His well-known fears of schism and heresy are included even in his exposition of Christ's suffering, and the slumber of the disciples is associated with the silence or inaction of the English bishops in the face of the destruction of their Church. In certain passages More compares the suffering of Christ's physical body with the destruction of His mystical body within the communion of the faithful. Yet the weariness and sorrow which More depicts here are also his own. He writes '*qui nihil sum*' ('I who am nothing')[75] and locates the tendency of the book in a phrase which means simply that life is a sad thing when compared to death.[76]

The pages of *De Tristitia* were smuggled out of his prison cell, probably in small batches, and they have become known as the Valencia Manuscript. From the evidence of this extant manuscript it is clear that he was not at all sure whether he would have the time or opportunity to complete it; sometimes he looked over a few pages at a later date but generally he revised as he went along, fashioning sentences and periods with the instinctive skill of a rhetorician. There are phases of Christ's suffering which touched him deeply, however, and in these passages there are manifold signs of hesitancy, revision and deletion. In his allusions to martyrdom, to the physical and mental pain attendant upon death, to the states of uneasy slumber and wakefulness which spring from anxious fear, More can be said to approach the very moments of his own death with terror and trembling. He seems weary and somewhat distracted when he deletes four lines at the beginning of the sixty-second sheet (there are 155 altogether, with approximately fifteen lines upon each) and revises a sentence that contains an entire litany of suffering, '*tristiciam timorem tedium et dirae mortis horrorem*'.[77] The last phrase can be translated as the horror of a terrible death. In his prison cell More shares the agony of Christ at Gethsemane. At one point in giving the example of Jesus as the paradigm of all martyrs,[78] More started to write that '*we*' will learn from him but then altered it to '*they*'. The association, however, was clear enough. Yet then he regains his fluency and, when describing the divine consolation which is offered to those approaching a violent death, his writing becomes firmer and bolder.

At the end of the Valencia Manuscript several sheets have been included which reveal that More was noting down short biblical extracts for his own comfort. The edges of these papers have been worn away, and it has been suggested that he kept this small compilation in his pocket when his books were eventually taken from him. And what are the central themes to be found here? He admonishes himself to forgive his enemies and to endure his suffering patiently, as Jesus did; he tells himself that he need not be afraid and that he must not save his own life unworthily. If he remains confident all temptations can be endured and, as he had often told his family, 'a man maye in suche case leese his heade and haue no harme'.[79] He also wrote a small treatise on the blessed body of Christ, so that by 'deuout meditacion' he might talk with him, as well as certain short prayers of supplication. He prostrated himself in his cell, meditating on the bloody sweat of Christ, hoping that 'I will heare what our lord will speake within me'.[80]

Perhaps the Lord spoke to him of a time, soon to come, when there would be no more lights and images, no more pilgrimages and processions, no guild plays and no ringing for the dead, no maypoles or Masses or holy water, no birch at midsummer and no roses at Corpus Christi. Yet More might already have anticipated that the 'reformation' of the last three years would lead ineluctably to the ransacking of the monasteries, the destruction of libraries, the pillage of those ornaments, vestments and jewelled relics which were part of the glory of medieval England. From the church of St Lawrence Jewry, where More had once worshipped and lectured, we read of the despoilation of 'an awter of wode with Carued images'; we learn of books and bells and silver plate, of vestments of 'old white silk embroidered with gold'[81] as well as capes of blue velvet and cloth of gold, of basins and stone altars and marble, all demolished or taken away. From the church of St Stephen Walbrook, where More had worshipped for many years, the communion cups, burial cloths and chalices were removed; the plate was sold to a goldsmith and the vestments purchased by sundry others.[82] In the other London churches which More had known all his life the stained-glass windows were destroyed and the painted walls defaced, all their gilded interiors whitewashed. At the same time, shrines were torn down and tombs removed. With the extinguishing of candles, came the end of such rituals as beating the bounds and the feast of the 'Boy Bishop'. This reformation did not occur quickly; it was a slow and difficult process, reversed and then advanced, working through three reigns against the natural piety and traditionalism of the people. Forty years after the death of More, it was complete.

XXXI

Peck of Troubles

THE defenders of the old faith were fast fading. John Fisher was ill and weary in his prison cell; he was so wasted and worn that there were times when he looked as if he were already dead. But the king sent doctors, to restore him to the health he needed for his trial and execution. In the spring of this year, 1535, three Carthusian priors were cast into prison and interrogated by Thomas Cromwell. One of those questioned was John Haughton, prior of the London Charterhouse where More had once worshipped and prayed. It had been his spiritual foundation in every sense, and the eventual fate of the monks was intimately related to his own. They were asked if they would accept their king as supreme head of the Church of England; they refused to swear such an oath and one of them, Richard Reynolds of Syon, added that 'he doth this as thousand thousand that be dead'.[1] Two weeks later they were committed to trial on the charge of high treason, which they strenuously denied. Richard Reynolds, on being questioned by Audley, declared that 'I am sure the larger part is secretly of our opinion, although outwardly, partly from fear and partly from hope, they profess to be of yours'.[2] The three priors were then condemned to be taken to Tyburn.

Two days after their trial in Westminster Hall, Edmund Walsingham came to More's cell and told him that Cromwell wished to speak with him. More put on his gown and walked out upon the stone gallery that connected the chambers of the Tower; he entered a room where Cromwell sat with four others. He was also invited to sit down, but he refused to do so. He was asked if he had read the new statutes, recently promulgated by the parliament; More replied that he had seen 'the boke' but had returned it shortly afterward. He had not studied it, or put it 'in remembraunce'.[3] He was then asked if he had at least read that particular statute confirming Henry as 'Supreme Hed' of the Church. 'Yes,' was all he said. Then he was told that the king now did 'demaund myne oppinion'[4] on that matter. He replied in his familiar fashion – he had in the past declared his mind to Henry himself but, having reserved his life for prayer alone, he now refused 'to medell' in such matters.

Cromwell then tried to kill More with kindness, professing the benevolent intentions of a king who would be willing to show mercy and allow his old servant to be 'abrode in the worlde agayne among other men as I haue bene before'.[5] But More no longer wished to exist in that world. 'My hole study,' he told the commissioners, 'shal be vppon the passyon of Chryst.' At this point he was sent out of the room and waited while they deliberated upon his perplexing and difficult case. For many prisoners the times of interrogation must have been marked by intense distress and anxiety, all the more discomfiting in these old chambers of stone, but it may be assumed that More tried to possess his soul in quiet.

He was called back and was immediately asked if he should not be as subject to parliamentary statutes as any other man. He replied, characteristically, 'I will not say the contrary.'[6] Then Cromwell touched one of the primary reasons for More's imprisonment, 'that my demeanour in that matter was of a thyng that of likelyhode made now other men so styffe therin as they be'. More knew what 'other men' he meant. The three Carthusian priors had been interrogated and had also refused to swear to the supremacy, giving reasons similar to those which More himself had employed. They were about to be killed for their obstinacy, and Cromwell was implying that More might be held partly responsible for their cruel and lingering deaths. This proved too much for him and he expressed his indignation in some of the most forceful terms he had ever used in the Tower.

Thomas More: I do nobody harme, I say none harme, I thynke none harme, but wysh euerye bodye good. And yf thys be not ynough to kepe a man alyue, in good fayth I long not to lyue. And I am dying alredy, and haue syns I came here, bene dyuers tymes in the case that I thought to dye within one houre, and I thank our Lorde I was neuer sory for yt, but rather sory whan I saw the pang past. And therfore my pore body ys at the Kyngis plesure, wolde God my deth myght do hym good.

Cromwell was gentler with him then and, after some further

subdued questioning on the statutes, he brought the interrogation to an end and said that 'reporte shulde be made vnto the Kyngis Hyghnes, and hys gracyous plesure knowen'. The lieutenant of the Tower was called and More was escorted back to his cell.

Within two or three days he wrote to his daughter with an account of this interview 'fearing leaste she, being (as he thoughte) with childe, shulde take some harme'. The news of his interrogation would have been passed to the More household and he wished to reassure them that it had no fatal or conclusive outcome. At the same time Dame Alice More wrote to Cromwell, asking that she might be granted an audience with the king in order to plead for her husband; it was clear enough that More himself was doing nothing to alleviate his apparently unhappy situation and it had become her responsibility to find some remedy or 'utterly in this world to be undone'.[7] It is unlikely that Cromwell replied to her but, instead, Margaret Roper was allowed once more to visit her father. It was no coincidence at all, however, that she was permitted to enter his cell on the day that the three Carthusian priors were dragged from the Tower to Tyburn. The spectacle of their journey towards a terrible death would no doubt bring even more pathos to her pleas. Not much could have been seen, from the slitted windows of his chamber, but from William Roper's later account it is clear that both father and daughter knew precisely what was happening outside the walls of the prison. 'Lo dost thou not see, Meg,' More said to her, 'that these blessed fathers be now as cheerfully going to their deaths as bridegrooms to the marriage?'[8] He then lamented that he was forced to remain 'in this vale of misery and iniquity' while others went before him to eternal grace. His daughter could not have been expected to derive much worldly comfort from his remarks but, of all the household, she best understood his spiritual longings.

He was closer to death than he may yet have suspected. At the end of May the king learned that the new pope, Paul III, had conferred a cardinal's hat upon John Fisher. To turn an apparent traitor into one of the princes of the Church was provocative, perhaps, and it is reported that Henry was enraged by the decision. As Holinshed puts it in his history, 'The hat came as far as Calais, but the head was off before the hat was on'.[9] At the beginning of June a commission was established to enquire into treasons, with Cromwell and Audley among its members. More was summoned before it on 3 June, and Cromwell informed him that the king believed him to be the 'occasion of muche grudge and harme in the realme'.[10] He was asked to give a plain answer to the oath of supremacy, a copy of which Audley had in the pocket of his gown, but More responded in his most cautious and precise manner. 'For if it so were that my conscience gaue me againste the statutes (wherein have my mynde giueth me I make no declaracion) that I nothinge doinge nor sayenge against the statute it were a very harde thinge to compell me to saye either precisely with it againste my conscience to the losse of my soule, or precisely againste it to the destruction of my bodye.'[11] He never wanted to be convicted of treason, because that would be to die for the wrong cause; he never wished to invite death too willingly, because that would be to die for the wrong reason. So More remained silent; his interrogators accused him of stubbornness, but for him it was the most carefully planned consistency. In the end Cromwell 'saide that he liked me this daye muche worse than he did the laste time',[12] and sent him out of the room.

When More had complained of the injustice of condemning either his body or soul he had, according to a later indictment, used the simile of a 'double-edged sword'; it so happened that, in front of the same committee, John Fisher employed precisely the same image. Collusion or, at the very least, communication between the two prisoners had always been suspected; the lieutenant of the Tower, Edmund Walsingham, was indeed criticised for placing them in too close proximity. So the use of a two-edged sword now seemed to cut against them both. Their servants were interrogated a few days later, together with Walsingham's own, in order to find evidence of any clandestine dealings. It had become a very serious matter. The servants themselves were imprisoned and Fisher's man, Richard Wilson, was threatened with hanging. Walsingham's own employee, George Golde, confessed that he had been the messenger for certain communications between the prisoners; he had been told by Fisher that the letters had nothing to do with the king's business, although they had nevertheless been burned. But these secret papers had, at least indirectly, everything to do with that business. Fisher had written to More on the import of the word 'maliciously' in the Treason Act; More had warned Fisher that they must give their own answers to the commissioners, so that they might not seem to collude. The rest was exhortation and prayer.

These were in no sense treasonable letters, however, and, given More's own extreme reluctance to say anything at all, the possibility

377

of treacherous complicity was always remote. From the testimony of those involved, it seems clear that More continued to decline to speak even to his fellow prisoner on the real matters of his conscience. The servants had agreed 'to deny any letters sent between them'[13] and, in the circumstance of their masters' plight, this must have seemed their only prudent course. But now that their subterfuge had come to light, they admitted that within the past few days Fisher had sent More half a custard. More himself had, a little before this, sent Fisher some apples and oranges as well as an image of St John. George Golde had also reported to Fisher that More 'was merry'.

Five days after Golde's testimony More was visited by a less welcome guest. Now that the evidence of his communications with Fisher had been disclosed, he was placed in even stricter confinement. The Solicitor-General, Richard Rich, came to his cell with orders to take away all of More's books and writing materials. As Sir Richard Southwell and two servants trussed up the books in one corner of the prison chamber, Rich engaged More in what might at first have appeared to be a bantering conversation. Both men were well known to each other, having lived in the same parish, and their families were closely associated. Southwell was also a family friend and may have been intending to deliver the confiscated books to Chelsea. But More and Rich were also prominent lawyers, and their legal relationship played a significant part in the conversation between them. The words used by them have been the subject of some debate. At his trial More strenuously denied speaking to Rich in the manner attributed to him, and his son-in-law's later version of their conversation is somewhat ambiguous. There is one extant document, however, which at least has the merit of immediacy: Richard Rich returned to Cromwell and reported what More had said. An official record was prepared, which still survives in damaged and mutilated form.[14] It begins 'Charitably moved the seyd Thomas More to be conformable'; at once the reader might be standing in the prison cell with the two men.

Richard Rich: Experience and lernyng & wysedome yt wer lyke as yf a man wold take . . . of water and cast yt in the Temmys.

Having opened with a compliment to More's superior abilities, the Solicitor-General then came down to the central matter.

Richard Rich: Ask . . . you this case if it were inactyd by Parlyament that I should be King . . . and who so ever sayd nay . . .

Thomas More: ... putt a nother hyer case whiche was this Sir I put case ... by Parlyment that God were not God ...

Richard Rich: ... that act was not possyble to be made to make God ungod but sir by cause your case is ... ye agre that ye were bound so to affirme & accept me to be Kyng ...

Thomas More: ... the cases were not lyke by cause that a kyng ... although the Kyng were acceptyd in Ingland yet moste Utter partes doo not affirme the same[.]

Richard Rich then broke off the conversation and remarked on More's 'concelement to the questyon' before wishing that 'Jesu send you better grace'. Then he left the cell taking with him all of More's books.

In the eventual indictment against More the salient words about the king being 'acceptyed' only in England were deemed to refer to the royal supremacy of the Church in England. More was, therefore, treasonably denying the king's title as Supreme Head. But in William Roper's later version More is reported as having said 'No more ... could the Parliament make the King supreme head of the Church'. This might be interpreted as meaning the Church universal and it would be self-evident that the parliament could not confer the papacy on Henry. No treachery, therefore, had been uttered. There are many problems with all three accounts of what would turn out to be, for More, a momentous conversation – not the least of them being that Rich clearly believed More to be still practising 'concelement to the questyon'. In Roper's account of the trial, however, More is reported as also making another point. 'And yet, if I had done so indeed, my Lords, as master Rich hath sworne, being it was spoken but in familiar secreate talk, nothing affirminge, and only in puttinge of cases without other displeasaunt circumstances, it cannot justly be taken to be spoken maliciouslye.' This is a highly significant remark, the accuracy of which is confirmed by the surviving official memorandum. Throughout their conversation both More and Rich used the phrases 'put case' or 'ask you this case'. This was the standard procedure of sixteenth-century lawyers. It was the method of their education; in Lincoln's Inn a junior barrister could be given any subject of debate and asked to 'put the case' for it. The private feelings or convictions of the individual lawyer were in no way involved; it was a highly theoretical and dramatic activity, in other words, calling for the wisdom and subtlety of the orator. That is perhaps why Richard Rich had opened his conversation with a

379

compliment on More's own experience and learning; they were both lawyers, about to engage in an abstract debate on the force and extent of parliamentary statute. It would be inconceivable to More that anything he said should be taken to express his individual convictions. He had abided by the rules of law all of his life and still could not imagine a world in which they might be distorted or abrogated. In this, perhaps, he was naive.

After his books and his writing materials had been taken away, he asked for the windows of his cell to be covered up. 'Is it not meet,' he is supposed to have said, 'to shut up my shop windows when all my ware is gone?'[15] He was, as George Golde told Fisher, in a 'peck of troubles'. Two days after the confiscation of his books he was interrogated again, but he was no longer faced by a commission of his peers; he was questioned in the most formal manner by two official investigators, complete with two witnesses and a notary. More would have known that this was the preliminary for his trial. He was asked whether he would obey the king as Supreme Head of the Church in England. 'I can make no answer.' He was asked whether he would accept the king's marriage to Anne Boleyn as lawful. 'I have never spoken against it, nor thereunto can make no answer.' He was finally asked whether he believed himself formally obliged to answer the question concerning the king as Supreme Head. 'I can make no answer.'

He did not have to wait long to discover the outline of his fate. Three days later, John Fisher was put on trial for treason and condemned to death. He was no longer the Bishop of Rochester, having been stripped of his see by the king, and it was as 'Master Fisher' that he listened as Sir Thomas Audley ordered him to be hanged, drawn and quartered at Tyburn.

Five days later, John Fisher was led from the Tower. The king had been told that the prisoner was now so frail and thin that he would not survive the journey on a hurdle to Tyburn, and accordingly his sentence had been changed to that of beheading on Tower Hill. He had been woken at five o'clock in the morning with this news, and, when he was told that he would be led to his execution at nine o'clock, he asked to be allowed to sleep a little longer. He awoke at seven and requested his servant to lay out a clean white shirt and a furred tippet. It was, he said, his wedding day. He was too weak to walk to the scaffold and instead was carried in a chair the short distance to the infamous hill. He carried his New Testament with him and opening it at random came upon a passage from the gospel of St John. 'Now this is everlasting life,' he read, 'that they may know thee, the only true God, and him whom thou hast sent, Jesus Christ.'[16] He climbed to the scaffold singing the *Te Deum*. When he took off his gown to prepare for death, the assembled crowd gasped at the sight of his gaunt and emaciated body. His head was off at the first blow and an extraordinary gush of blood issued from his neck: it seemed impossible that so much blood should come out of so skeletal a figure. His naked body was displayed at the site of execution, as the king had demanded; his head was then thrust upon a pike and placed in a small iron cage upon London Bridge. Here it grew 'ruddy and comely', and became such an object of wonder that Henry demanded that it be thrown into the river.

At the time of Fisher's execution Thomas Cromwell was drawing up certain notes 'to be remembered at my next going to the court'. One such 'remembrance' was 'To know his pleasure touching Master More'. There was another note also, 'What shall be done farther touching Master More'.[17] It seems likely, then, that the exact timing or nature of the prisoner's fate was still to be determined. Then, four days after Fisher's execution, a special commission was established to 'hear and determine' the case of Thomas More. This was the essential precondition for a bill of indictment to be drawn up against him; just such a *billa vera*, accusing him of treason, was laid before the commission two days later. It is a document of some two thousand words, outlining the various acts or occasions of More's treachery and accusing him of 'falsely, traitorously and maliciously' denying the right of the king to be Supreme Head. More had fallen prey to the new Treason Act and would be tried for his life.

XXXII

Call Forth Sir Thomas More

S IR Thomas More, you are charged with attempting to deprive the king of his lawful title as supreme head of the Church in England, which is treason. You did refuse to accept the royal supremacy in front of His Grace's commissioners on 7 May. You were in collusion with a convicted traitor, John Fisher, and it is known that letters passed between you. You again maintained your silence on the matter of the supremacy, when formally questioned in the Tower of London on 3 June. In a conversation with the Solicitor-General, Sir Richard Rich, you denied that the parliament had the authority to declare His Grace the head of the Church in England.

Duke of Norfolk: Sir Thomas More, ye see that ye haue heynously offended the Kinges Maiestie; howbeit we are in very good hope (such is his great bountie, benignitie and clemencie) that if you will forethinke and repent your selfe, if you will reuoke and reforme your wilfull, obstinate opinion that you haue so wrongfully mainteyned and so longe dwelt in, that ye shall taste of his gratious pardon.

Thomas More: My Lordes, I doo most humbly thanke your honours of your great good will towardes me. Howbeit, I make this my boone and petition vnto God as heartily as I may, that he will vouchsafe this my good, honest and vpright minde to norishe, mainteyne and vpholde in me euen to the last howre and extreme moment that euer I shall liue. Concerning nowe the matters you charge and challenge me withall, the articles are so prolixe and longe that I feare, what for my longe imprisonment, what for my longe lingring disease, what for my present weaknes and debilitie, that neyther my witt, nor my memorie, nor yet my voice, will serue to make so full, so effectuall and sufficient aunswere as the weight and importance of these matters doth craue.

A chair may be brought to him.

Thomas More: I plead not gilty, and reserve unto myself advantage to be taken of the body of the matter, after verdicte, to avoid this Indictment. Moreouer if thos only odious tearmes, 'Maliciously, traiterouslye, and diabolicallye' were put out of the Indictment, I see therein nothinge iustlye to charge me.

Touching the first article, wherein is purposed that I, to vtter and shewe my malice against the King and his late marriage, haue euer repined and resisted the same, I can say nothing but this: that of malice I neuer spake any thing against it, and that whatsoeuer I haue spoken in that matter, I haue none otherwise spoken but according to my very minde, opinion and conscience. And for this mine errour (if I may call it an errour, or if I haue been deceaued therein) I haue not gone scot free and vntouched, my goodes and chattels being confiscate, and my selfe to perpetuall prison adiudged, where I haue nowe beene shut vp about a fifteene monethes. Touching, I say, this challenge and accusation, I aunswere that, for this my taciturnitie and silence, neyther your lawe nor any lawe in the world is able iustly and rightly to punishe me, vnlesse you may besydes laye to my charge eyther some worde or some facte in deede.

The King's attorney: Marie, this very silence is a sure token and demonstration of a corrupt and peruerse nature, maligning and repyning against the Statute; yea, there is no true and faithfull subiect that being required of his minde and opinion touching the saide Statute, that is not deepelye and vtterly bounde, without any dissimulation, to confess that Statute to be good, iust and lawfull.

Thomas More: Truely, if the rule and Maxime of the ciuill lawe be good, allowable and sufficient then *Qui tacet, consentire videtur* ['he that holdeth his peace seemeth to consent'], this my silence implyeth and importeth rather a ratification and confirmation than any condemnation of your Statute. For I assure you that I haue not hitherto to this howre disclosed and opened my conscience and minde to any person liuing in all the worlde.

As for the second count against me. Would God that these letters were nowe produced and openly read; but forasmuche as the said Bishopp, as ye saye, hath burned them, I will not sticke truly to vtter my selfe, as shortly as I may, the very tenours of the same. In one of them there was nothing in the world conteyned but certaine familier talke and recommendacions, such as was seemly and agreeable to our longe and olde acquaintance. In the other was conteyned my aunswere that I made to the saide Bishopp, demaunding of me what thing I aunswered at my first examination in the towre vpon the saide Statute. Wherevnto I aunswered nothing els but that I had informed and settled my conscience, and that he should informe and settle his. And other aunswere, vpon the charge of my soule, made I none. These are the tenours of my letters, vpon which ye can take no holde or handfast by your lawe to condemne me to death.

The King's attorney: Yet the verye same aunswere concerning the double-edged sworde the Bisshopp of Rochester made, wherby [it] doth euidently appere that it was a purposed and sett matter betweene you, by mutuall conference and agrement.

Thomas More: I did not precisely, but conditionally, aunswere, that in case the Statute were like to be a double-edged sworde, I could not tell in the world howe a man should demeane and order himselfe but that he should fall into one of the daungers. Neyther doo I knowe what kinde of aunswere the Bishopp made; whose aunswere, if it were agreable and corresspondent to mine, that hath happed by reason of the correspondence and conformitie of our wittes, learning and studie, not that any such thing was purposely concluded vpon and accorded betwixt us. Neyther hath there at any time any worde or deede malitiously scaped or proceeded from me aginst your statute, albeit it may well be that my wordes might be wrongfully and malitiously reported to the Kinges Maiestie.

Sir Richard Rich, will you now stand before us and relate, upon your oath, the substance of your communication with Sir Thomas More in his cell? *(He does so.)*

Thomas More: In good faithe, master Riche, I am soryer for your periurye then for my own perill. And yow shall vnderstand that neyther I, nor no man else to my knowledge, ever tooke you to be a man of such creditt as in any matter of impourtance I, or any other, would at anye tyme vouchsaf to communicate with you. And I, as you knowe, of no small while haue bine acquainted with yow and your conuersacion, who haue knowen you from your youth hitherto. For we long dwelled both in one parishe together, where, as your self can tell (I am sorry you compell me so to say) you were esteemed very light of your tongue, a greate dicer, and of no comendable fame. And so in your house at the temple, wheare hath bine your cheif bringing vppe were you likewise accompted.

Can it therefore seeme likely vnto your honorable Lordshipps that I wold, in so weyghty a cause, so unadvisedly overshoote my self as to trust master Rich, a man of me alwaies reputed for one of so litle truth, as your lordshipps haue heard, so farre aboue my souereigne Lord the kinge, or any of his noble Councellours, that I wold vnto him vtter the secreates of my consciens towchinge the Kings supremacye, the speciall pointe and only marke at my handes so longe sought for: A thinge which I neuer wold, after the statute thereof made, reveale either to the kings highnes himself, or to any of his honorable councellours, as it is not vnknowne to your honors, at sundry seuerall times sent from his graces owne person vnto the Tower vnto me for none other purpose? Can this in your iudgments, my lordes, seeme likely to be true? And yet, if I had done so indeed, my Lords, as master Rich hath sworne, being it was spoken but in familiar secreate talk, nothing affirminge, and only in puttinge of cases without other displeasaunt circumstances, it cannot justly be taken to be spoken maliciouslye. And where there is no malice, there can be no offence.

Sir Richard Rich: May it be caused that Sir Richard Southwell and Master Palmer, who were in the chamber with Sir Thomas More and myself, may be sworn what words passed between us?

It shall be so caused.

Master Palmer: I was so buysye about the trussinge uppe of Sir Thomas Moores books in a sack, that I took no heed of their talk.

Sir Richard Southwell: Because I was apointed only to looke vnto the conveyaunce of his bookes, I gave no ear unto them.

Then will I charge this jury to return a true verdict. I ask you, good sirs, to determine whether Sir Thomas More did converse with Sir Richard Rich in the manner alleged? *(The jury retire for fifteen minutes.)* You do so find him guilty? Then I will proceed in judgment against the prisoner.

Thomas More: My Lord, when I was toward the Lawe, the maner in suche case was to aske the prisoner before Iudgment, why Iudgement should not be geuen agaynste him.

Sir Thomas Audley: What, then, are you able to say to the contrary?

Thomas More: Seeing that I see ye are determined to condemne me (God knoweth howe) I will nowe in discharge of my conscience speake my minde plainlye and freely touching my Inditment and your Statute withall. Forasmuch as, my Lorde, this Indictment is grounded vppon an acte of parliamente directly repugnant to the lawes of god and his holy churche, the supreeme gouerment of which, or of any parte whereof, may no temporall prince presume by any lawe to take vppon him, as rightfully belonging to the See of Rome, a spirituall preheminence by the mouth of our Sauiour hymself, personally present vppon the earth, only to St Peter and his successors, Byshopps of the same See, by speciall prerogative graunted; It is therefore in lawe amongest Christen men insufficient to charge any Christen man. This Realme, being but one member and smale parte of the Church, might not make a particuler lawe disagreable with the generall lawe of Christes vniuersall Catholike Churche. No more then the city of London, being but one poore member in respect of the whole realme, might make a lawe against an acte of parliament to bind the whole realme. No more might this realme of England refuse obediens to the Sea of Roome then might a child refuse obediens to his owne naturall father.

Duke of Norfolk: We nowe plainely see that ye are malitiously bent.

Thomas More: Nay, nay, very and pure necessitie, for the discharge of my conscience, enforceth me to speake so muche. Wherein I call and appeale to God, whose onely sight pearceth into the very depth of mans heart, to be my witnes. Howbeit, it is not for this supremacie so much that ye seeke my bloud, as for that I would not condiscende to the marriage.

Sir Thomas Audley: My Lord Fitzjames, how do you find the case?

Lord Fitzjames: My lords all, by St Julian, I must needs confes that if thacte of parliament be not vnlawfull, then is not the Indictment in my conscience insufficient.

Sir Thomas Audley: Loe, my Lordes, loe, you heare what my lord chief Iustice saith. You are judged to be guilty, Sir Thomas More. Do you have anythinge els to alleage for your defence? We will grant your favourable audience.

Thomas More: More haue I not to say, my Lordes, but that like as the blessed Apostle St Pawle, as we read in thactes of the Apostles, was present, and consented to the death of St Stephen, and kepte their clothes that stoned him to deathe, and yeat be they nowe both twayne holy Sainctes in heaven, and shall continue there frendes for euer, So I verily truste, and shall therefore hartelye pray, that thoughe your Lordshippes haue nowe here in the earthe bine Judges to my condemnacion, we may yeat hearafter in heaven meerily all meete together, to our euerlasting saluacion and thus I desire Almighty God to preserue and defende the kinges Maiestie, and to send him good counsaile.

Sir Thomas More, you are to be drawn on a hurdle through the City of London to Tyburn, there to be hanged till you be half dead, after that cut down yet alive, your bowels to be taken out of your body and burned before you, your privy parts cut off, your head cut off, your body to be divided in four parts, and your head and body to be set at such places as the King shall assign.[1]

XXXIII

The King is Good unto Me

IT is one of the most celebrated trials in English history. At first he had stood before his accusers, like Jesus, but weariness and debility mastered him before the end of the proceedings; he told one of his household that the preliminary reading of the indictment was so long that he could not properly follow its third count. He had not been given any advance warning of the case against him, although he must have anticipated its main thrust; in treason trials the accused man had no 'rights' in the contemporary sense. There was no presumption of innocence, and the prisoner was given no opportunity to call witnesses in his defence; as the testimony of Rich suggests, the rules of evidence were by no means strict. There is no reason to believe that the jury of twelve men, listening to his testimony in Westminster Hall, were overtly persuaded to find the case against More proven; but if they had declared him innocent, they might themselves have been imprisoned or even attainted. It was not a trial which More could have won.

He made his case skilfully, however, and his penultimate speech 'in arrest of judgment' was a masterpiece of legal tact and nicety. His argument was that if a parliamentary statute offends against the law of God it is 'insufficient', and cannot be imposed upon any Christian subject. The court disagreed with him, implicitly asserting English law over canon law. As for the charge of treason itself More had argued, again skilfully, that there had been no 'malicious' intent in his conversation with Richard Rich. The court and jury disagreed, on the presumption that malice was implied in any denial of the king's supremacy – or, more particularly, in More's refusal to swear the oath to that effect. There has been some controversy over the fact that Sir Richard Southwell and Mr Palmer declined to corroborate

Rich's testimony concerning the conversation in More's cell, but their silence did not seem to affect the jury's decision.

More's own silence is more interesting. He maintained that it was not of a 'corrupt' or 'perverse' nature; he also applied the commanding argument that human law could not judge what Thomas Aquinas called '*interioribus motibus*' and Christopher St German described as 'inward things'. This concerned the law of God and was, in human terms, essentially a matter of conscience. More put the case that 'in thinges touching conscience, euery true and good subiect is more bounde to haue respect to his saide conscience and to his soule than to any other thing in all the world beside'. More was engaged in a particularly difficult and subtle testing of human, as opposed to divine, law, with all the resources of his legal experience being deployed to justify his beleaguered position. His contemporaries believed that he was acting obsessively or irrationally, but he believed himself to be acting legally – in the fullest possible meaning of that term. It has often been surmised that the trial of More represents the defeat of the individual conscience by the forces of the emerging nation-state, but that is profoundly to misunderstand his position. Conscience was not for More simply or necessarily an individual matter; as Lord Chancellor he had been charged with the application of conscience to law, but upon general and traditional principles. At his trial he was affirming the primacy of law itself, as it had always been understood. He asserted the laws of God and of reason, as they had been inherited, and he simply did not believe that the English parliament could repeal the ordinances of a thousand years. It is significant that he was found to be guilty because of that conversation with Rich in which he 'put the case'. He was in that sense condemned for acting like a lawyer and, at the trial itself, he was also convicted for maintaining traditional law. He embodied law all his life, and he died for it.

He is reported to have remained impassive and composed during these proceedings, his visage showing signs of weariness but not of fear; like the early Christian martyrs who 'gazed steadfastly' at their accusers,[1] More was imperturbable. He had prepared himself for the ordeal, after all, when in his prison writing he had meditated upon the strength and humility of Christ before his Passion. By his unwavering firmness More embodied the principle of law which he wished to uphold. He spoke out after the verdict had been given against him, because at that moment his fate was determined; he could not be accused of inviting death by his own words. There was nothing tragic about his situation, as many have supposed, and indeed for More all worked towards what was for him the happiest outcome. It might even be described as a form of Socratic comedy in which the outcast is the one who remains most faithful to himself and to his principles. He rose above those who were about to kill him – it is worth noting that he spoke of 'your law' and 'your statute' – by remaining true to his divinely ordained conscience.

After the sentence had been pronounced against him he was led away from the bar of the King's Bench and escorted from Westminster Hall. The constable of the Tower, Sir William Kingston, was in charge of the guard which accompanied the prisoner from Westminster Stairs towards the Tower; the swift tides made it impossible to cross beneath London Bridge and instead the armed party disembarked from the barge at Old Swan Stairs. Here William Kingston began to cry as he took his leave of him, but More comforted him by saying, 'Good Master Kingston, trouble not yourself but be of good cheer; for I will pray for you, and my good Lady your wife, that we may meet in heaven together, where we shall be merry for ever and ever.' Kingston reported this to More's son-in-law a little while after, and added, 'In good faith, Master Roper, I was ashamed at myself that, at my departing from your father, I found my heart so feeble, and his so strong, that he was fain to comfort me which should rather have comforted him.'[2] More was taken up Old Swan Lane and then turned right into Thames Street, which would lead him back to the Tower; he was walking, according to report, in a coarse woollen gown.

His children were waiting for him close by the Tower itself. John More knelt down in the street, and, weeping, asked for his father's blessing. Margaret Roper also knelt upon the ground and received his blessing but then a few moments later, in the words of her husband, 'hasting towards him and, without consideration or care of herself, pressing in among the midst of the throng and company of the guard, that with halberds and bills [swords] went round about him, hastily ran to him and there openly, in the sight of them all, embraced him, took him about the neck, and kissed him'.[3] It was later reported, by Cresacre More, that those around him 'smelt a most odoriferus smell to come from him'.[4] He blessed Margaret again and comforted her; she started to walk away but then 'having respect neither to herself nor to the press of the people and multitude

390

that were there about him, suddenly turned back again, ran to him as before, took him about the neck, and divers times together most lovingly kissed him'.[5] William Roper adds that, among the large crowd assembled to see the famous prisoner, many then began 'for very sorrow thereof to mourn and weep'. Eventually More was escorted back to his cell. It has been suggested that, as a condemned man, he would have been consigned to the dungeons, which dated back to the earliest building of the Tower. It is much more likely, however, that he returned to the prison chamber which had now become so familiar to him.

For the last six days of his life he prayed and fasted. The stories of that short period are generally of an apocryphal or hagiographical nature, but some of them have the advantage of emphasising More's wit even in extremity. A barber was sent to cut More's beard and hair, but the prisoner is supposed to have declined his service by saying 'The king has taken out a suit on my head and until the matter is resolved I shall spend no further cost upon it.' One anecdote, in particular, is characteristic of More. He showed a visitor the urine in his chamber pot and, examining it, declared, 'For anything that I can perceive, this patient is not so sick that he may do well, if it be not the king's pleasure he should die.'[6] There is certainly no reason to doubt that he retained his humour until the end; he had conquered all the temptations of the world and may have surprised even himself by his own lack of fear.

In his cell he had no proper writing materials, but he had been given an 'algorism stone' or slate upon which he could write; this had probably been brought to him by Dorothy Colley, Margaret Roper's servant, who had been granted permission to visit him each day. At some point he composed a final prayer which is likely to have been copied down by Margaret at a later date; in this last devotion he laments his sinful life 'euen from my very childhed'[7] and aspires to being with God 'not for thauoiding of the calamyties of this wretched world' as 'for a very loue to the'.[8] He had been condemned on Thursday, and on Monday he was visited by his wife; the nature of their last conversation upon earth is not known, although its tenor may perhaps be guessed from More's usual attempts at comfort and consolation. He gave into Alice More's keeping his hair shirt and scourge, as well as the algorism stone, for which he had no further need. He also composed a letter with a piece of charcoal; it was addressed to Margaret, but within it he blessed his family and exhorted them to pray for his soul. This final epistle is unfinished; the likeliest explanation must be that Dame Alice, having been granted the customary right of visiting the condemned man, was asked to leave before the letter could be completed.

It is not at all clear when More learned that his sentence had been commuted from disembowelment to beheading; the king was graciously pleased to grant this last favour because of More's long service at court, and the decision may have afforded some natural human relief to More. This can only be surmised, however, as it is at least possible that he had set his mind and soul even beyond the worst pains of this world. He still did not know what day had been appointed for his death but in his letter he had told his daughter he wished to die on that following day, Tuesday, because of its coincidence with the vigil of the translation of the relics of St Thomas Becket. In this, at least, he was granted his wish. On the dawn of the following morning he was visited in his prison chamber by Sir Thomas Pope, a representative of the king's council, who informed him that he must die at nine o'clock of that day.

Thomas More: Master Pope, for your good tidings I heartily thank you. I have always been much bounden to the king's highness for the benefits and honours that he hath still from time to time most bountifully heaped upon me. And yet more bound am I to his grace for putting me into this place, where I have had convenient time and space to have remembrance of my end. And so help me God, most of all, Master Pope, am I bound to his highness that it pleases him so shortly to rid me out of the miseries of this wretched world. And therefore will I not fail earnestly to pray for his grace, both here and also in another world.

Sir Thomas Pope: The king's pleasure is further, that at your execution you shall not use many words.

Thomas More: Master Pope, you do well to give me warning of his grace's pleasure, for otherwise I had purposed at that time somewhat to have spoken, but of no matter wherewith his grace, or any other, should have had cause to be offended. Nevertheless, whatsoever I intended, I am readily obediently to conform myself to his grace's commandments.[9]

Sir Thomas Pope, More's 'singular friend', then broke down and wept before leaving the cell. Yet perhaps most poignant, in retrospect, is the readiness and willingness of More to 'conform' himself to the demands of the king. He remained a model of obedience; both in his life and at his death, he carried out the duties allotted to him with every possible care.

He dressed in the finest clothes left to him, but then Sir Edmund Walsingham warned him that after his death they would be given to a 'javel' or rogue of an executioner. 'What Master Lieutenant,' More is reported to have answered, 'shall I accompt him a javel that shall do me this day so singular a benefit?' He was persuaded to change into a plainer gown, but insisted upon sending his executioner a golden coin. A little before nine o'clock, he left his cell and passed under the Middle Tower in his journey of two hundred yards to Tower Hill. His face was now gaunt from debility or sickness, and his beard unkempt; the haggard and unshaven prisoner held before him a roughly made cross which had been painted red as an emblem of Christ's passion. Yet there was another form of symbolism that would not have escaped More, or any spectator aware of well ordered imagery: the prisoner wore a coarse gown of servitude, but he carried the red cross of knighthood. He was going to that place where the hierarchies of the world would be transcended. He was about to die only a mile from his birthplace in Milk Street, but now he was leaving London for eternity.

A large crowd had assembled to watch this death, and More's earliest biographers record some of the remarks of those who taunted or questioned him. Certain of these shouted words were also reported by one contemporary witness, but at this late date they cannot be verified. They serve, however, to emphasise the noise and tumult which would have accompanied More's short pilgrimage to the scaffold. One called out that, when Lord Chancellor, he had been unjust to her. 'Woman,' he replied, 'I remember well the whole matter. If now I were to give sentence again, I assure thee, I would not alter it.' Someone offered him a cup of wine as he made his way, but he declined to drink from it saying 'My master had vinegar and gall, not wine, given him to drink.'[10] A woman shouted out that he still had 'evidences' of her which she required. 'Good woman,' he is supposed to have answered, 'have patience a little while, for the king is good unto me that even within this half hour he will discharge me of all my business and help thee himself.'[11] Yet no doubt most of the crowd said nothing and stared upon the scene with no particular emotion except that, perhaps, which More described in his history of Richard III. 'And so they said that these matters bee Kynges games, as it were stage playes, and for the more part plaied vpon scafoldes.

In which pore men be but ye lokers on. And thei that wise be, will medle no farther.'[12]

When More had left the jurisdiction of the Tower he was given to one of the sheriffs of London, Humphrey Monmouth, who escorted his prisoner to the steps of the scaffold. Monmouth was one of those 'newe men' who had been interrogated and confined in the Tower by More himself. So the world had turned. More's family had not been given permission to witness the execution and he was, in everything other than the literal sense, alone. He had sought solitude, whether in the Charterhouse or in his private chapel, and his death was a mirror of his life. Yet he had always subdued his sense of self to the demands and rituals of the public world, and this final journey to his execution was as much part of his duty as his acceptance of high office. He went to a death determined by the law he had served, thus signifying his final obeisance to those forces which had shaped and determined his life. Yet, in this very last act, he had also transcended them. Those twin poles of his life, public service and private spirituality, were finally put aside when his soul left his body.

The steps of the scaffold were not firm and one of the officers present steadied him as he climbed to the block. 'When I come down again,' More is supposed to have said, 'let me shift for myself as well as I can.' His words to those assembled have been variously reported but it is known that, according to the king's will, he spoke only briefly. He asked the crowd 'to bear witness with him that he should now there suffer death in and for the faith of the Holy Catholic Church', according to William Roper; but a contemporary account suggests that 'Only he asked the bystanders to pray for him in this world, and he would pray for them elsewhere. He then begged them earnestly to pray for the King, that it might please God to give him good counsel, protesting that he died the King's good servant but God's first.'[13] He knelt down before the block and recited the words of the psalm which begins 'Have mercy upon me, O God, according to thy loving kindness'.

Then he rose and, according to custom, the executioner now knelt to beg his pardon and his blessing; characteristically the 'headsman' wore a close-fitting robe of scarlet wool, with a mask and 'horn shaped hat'[14] of the same vivid colour. More kissed him, and is reported to have said, 'Thou wilt give me this day a greater benefit than ever any mortal man can be able to give me. Pluck up thy spirits, man, and be not afraid to do thine office. My neck is very short: take heed, therefore, thou strike not awry for saving of thine honesty.'[15] These last words are not necessarily apocryphal, since More spoke loudly enough that those around him might hear what he said; his sense of drama did not desert him, indeed his journey to Tower Hill resembles that of a performer in a mystery play who walks across the plateau to another scaffold. Edward Hall was one of the under-sheriffs of the City in this year and, in his *Chronicles*, he adds the incident in which Thomas More asked the executioner not to sever his beard; if Hall was present on this occasion, as seems likely, then we may consider this to be an authentic detail. Hall's concluding remark, 'thus with a mock he ended his life', may not, however, fully comprehend More's irony in the face of death.

More knelt down and the executioner offered to bind his eyes; but he refused and covered his face with a linen cloth he had carried with him. Then he lay down with his neck upon the block, his arms stretched out before him. He was killed with one stroke of the axe and, when the head had fallen into the straw, the executioner picked it up and displayed it to the crowds with the shout 'Behold the head of a traitor!' The corpse was taken to the church of St Peter ad Vincula within the Tower, where, in the presence of some of the family, it was interred. His head was boiled, impaled upon a pole and raised above London Bridge. So ended the life of Thomas More, one of the few Londoners upon whom sainthood has been conferred and the first English layman to be beatified as a martyr.

Source Notes

Bibliography

The place of publication is London, unless otherwise stated.

Works of Thomas More

Life of Pico della Mirandola (printed by John Rastell, n.d.)
The works of Sir Thomas More, Knyght, sometyme Lorde Chancellor of England, wrytten by him in the Englysh tonge, William Rastell (ed.) (1557)
The English Works of Sir Thomas More, W. E. Campbell (ed.) (1931)
The Utopia of Sir Thomas More, J. H. Lupton (ed.) (Oxford, 1895)
Utopia, G. M. Logan, R. M. Adams and Clarence H. Miller (eds) (Cambridge, 1995)
The Correspondence of Sir Thomas More, E. F. Rogers (ed.) (Princeton University Press, 1947)
The Yale Edition of the Complete Works of St. Thomas More (New Haven and London)
  Vol. 2, *The History of King Richard III*, Richard S. Sylvester (ed.), 1963
  Vol. 3, Part 1, *Translations of Lucian*, Craig R. Thompson (ed.), 1984
  Vol. 3, Part 2, *Latin Poems*, Clarence H. Miller, Leicester Bradner, Craig A. Lynch and Revilo P. Oliver (eds), 1984
  Vol. 4, *Utopia*, Edward Surtz, SJ, and J. H. Hexter (eds), 1965
  Vol. 5, Parts 1 and 2, *Responsio ad Lutherum*, John M. Headley (ed.) and Sister Scholastica Manderville (trans.), 1969
  Vol. 6, Parts 1 and 2, *A Dialogue Concerning Heresies*, Thomas M. C. Lawler, Germain Marc'hadour and Richard C. Marius (eds), 1981
  Vol. 7, *Letter to Bugenhagen; Supplication of Souls; Letter Against Frith*, Frank Manley, Germain Marc'hadour, Richard C. Marius and Clarence H. Miller (eds), 1990
  Vol. 8, Parts 1, 2 and 3, *The Confutation of Tyndale's Answer*, Louis A. Schuster, Richard C. Marius, James P. Lusardi and Richard J. Schoeck (eds), 1973
  Vol. 9, *The Apology*, J. B. Trapp (ed.), 1979
  Vol. 10, *The Debellation of Salem and Bizance*, John Guy, Ralph Keen, Clarence H. Miller and Ruth McGugan (eds), 1987
  Vol. 11, *The Answer to a Poisoned Book*, S. M. Foley and Clarence H. Miller (eds), 1985
  Vol. 12, *A Dialogue of Comfort Against Tribulation*, Louis L. Martz and Frank Manley (eds), 1976
  Vol. 13, *Treatise on the Passion; Treatise on the Blessed Body; Instructions and Prayers*, Garry E. Haupt (ed.), 1976

Bibliography

Vol. 14, Parts 1 and 2, *De Tristitia Christi*, Clarence H. Miller (ed. and trans.), 1976
Vol. 15, *Letter to Martin Dorp*; *Letter to the University of Oxford*; *Letter to Edward Lee*; *Letter to a Monk*; with a new translation of *Historica Richardi Tertii*, Daniel Kinney (ed.), 1986

Secondary Works

Ackroyd, Peter, *Blake* (1995)
Adair, J., *The Pilgrims Way: Shrines and Saints in Britain and Ireland* (1978)
Adams, Robert P., *The Better Part of Valor: More, Erasmus, Colet and Vives on Humanism, War and Peace, 1496–1535* (Seattle, 1962)
Albin, H. O. (ed.), *Thomas More and Canterbury* (Bath, 1994)
Alexander, J. J. G., and Gibson, M. T., *Medieval Learning and Literature: Essays Presented to Richard William Hunt* (Oxford, 1976)
Alexander, M. V-C., *The First of the Tudors: A Study of Henry VII and his Reign* (1981)
Allen, P. S., *The Age of Erasmus* (Oxford, 1914)
Ames, Russell A., *Citizen More and his Utopia* (Princeton, 1949)
Amiot, F., *The History of the Mass* (1959)
Anderson, J. H., *Bibliographical Truth* (New Haven and London, 1984)
Anderson, M. D., *Drama and Imagery in English Medieval Churches* (Cambridge, 1963)
Anglo, Sydney, *Spectacle, Pageantry and Early Tudor Policy* (Oxford, 1969)
Anon., *Certaine Questions by way of a conference betwixt a Chauncelor and a Kinswoman of his Concerning Churching of Women* (1601)
Aquinas, Thomas, *Summa Theologiae*, trans. J. J. Cunningham (1975)
Summa Contra Gentiles. In Five Volumes, ed. A. C. Pegis (1975)
Archer, J. M., *Sovereignty and Intelligence* (Stanford, 1993)
Aristotle, *Meteorologica*, trans. H. D. P. Lee (1952)
Asch, R. G. and Birke, A. M. (eds), *Princes, Patronage and the Nobility: The Court at the Beginning of the Modern Age, c.1450–1650* (1991)
Atkins, J. H. W., *English Literary Criticism: The Renascence* (1947)
Aubrey, J., *Brief Lives*, ed. A. Clark (Oxford, 1898)
Augustine, Saint, *City of God*, trans. H. Betterson (Harmondsworth, 1972)
Axton, R. and Happe, P. (eds), *The Plays of John Heywood* (Woodbridge, 1991)
Bacon, F., *History of the Reign of King Henry the Seventh*, ed. R. Lockyer (1971)
The Advancement of Learning. Two or more works (1900)
Baker, J. H. (ed.), *The Reports of John Spelman*, 2 vols (1977)
Ball, W. *Lincoln's Inn* (1947)
Barron, C. M. and Sutton, A. F. (eds), *Medieval London Widows, 1300–1500* (1994)
Basset, B., *Born for Friendship* (1965)
Baumer, F. L., *The Early Tudor Theory of Kingship* (New Haven, 1940)
Beard, C. A., *The Office of the Justice of the Peace in England* (New York, 1904)
Beck, W., *Sir Thomas More* (1862)
Bell, D. C., *Notices of the Historic Persons Buried in the Chapel of Saint Peter ad Vincula* (1877)
Belloc, H., *How the Reformation Happened* (1928)
Bennet, H. S., *English Books and Readers* (Cambridge, 1969)
Bergenroth, G. A. (ed.), *Calender of Letters, Despatches and State Papers, Relating to Negotiations Between England and Spain*, 2 vols (1862)
Bindoff, S. J. (ed.), *The House of Commons 1509–1558* (1982)
Blake, N. F., *Caxton and his World* (1969)
Bland, C. R., *The Teaching of Grammar in Late Medieval England* (East Lansing, 1991)
Blatcher, M., *The Court of King's Bench* (1978)

Blench, J. W., *Preaching in England in the Late Fifteenth and Sixteenth Centuries* (Oxford, 1964)

Block, J. S., *Factional Politics and the English Reformation* (Woodbridge, 1993)

Boswell, J. C., *Sir Thomas More in the English Renaissance: An Annotated Catalogue* (New York, 1994)

Bourne-Jones, D., *Merrily to Meet: A Poetic Study of Sir Thomas More, 1478–1535* (Eastbourne, 1987)

Boutrais, C., *The Monastery of the Grand Chartreuse* (1983)

Bowker, M., *The Henrician Reformation: The Diocese of Lincoln under John Longland* (Cambridge, 1981)

Bradshaw, B. and Duffy, E. (eds), *Fisher: Humanism, Reform and Reformation* (Cambridge, 1989)

Brand, J., *Observations on Popular Antiquities* (revised edition, 1813)

Brant, S. (ed.), *The Ship of Fools*, trans. Alexander Barclay (Edinburgh, 1874, reprint of the 1509 Pynson edition)

Bridgett, T. E., *Life and Writings of Sir Thomas More* (1891)

Brigden, Susan, *London and the Reformation* (Oxford, 1989)

Brockwell, M., *Catalogue of the Nostell Collection* (1915)

Brook, R., *The Story of Eltham Palace* (1960)

Brooks, P. N. (ed.), *Reformation Principle and Practice* (1980)

Brown, Peter, *Augustine of Hippo* (1967)

Brown, R. (ed. and trans.), *Four Years at the Court of Henry VIII: A Selection of the Despatches by the Venetian Ambassador Sebastian Giustinian, 1515–1519*, 2 vols (1854)

Burke, P., *The Renaissance Sense of the Past* (1969)
Popular Culture in Early Modern Europe (1978)

Burrows, M., *Collectanea* (Oxford, 1890)

Butterfield, H., *The Origins of Modern Science* (new edition, 1957)

Butterworth, C. and Chester, A., *George Joye* (Philadelphia, 1962)

Byron, B., *Loyalty in the Spirituality of Saint Thomas More* (Nieuwkoop, 1971)

Cam, H. M. (ed.), *Selected Historical Essays of F. W. Maitland* (Cambridge, 1957)

Camm, Bede, *Courtier, Monk and Martyr: The Life and Sufferings of Sebastian Newdigate* (1901)

Campbell, W. E., *Erasmus, Tyndale and More* (1949)

Carpenter, N. C., *Music in the Medieval and Renaissance Universities* (Norman, Oklahoma, 1958)

Casady, E., *Henry Howard, Earl of Surrey* (New York, 1938)

Castiglione, Baldassare, *The Book of the Courtier*, trans. with an introduction by G. Bull (Harmondsworth, 1967)

Cave-Browne, J., *Lambeth Palace and its Associations* (Edinburgh and London, 1882)

Cavendish, George, *The Life and Death of Cardinal Wolsey*. In *Two Early Tudor Lives*, ed. R. S. Sylvester and D. P. Harding (New Haven and London, 1962)

Cawley, A., C., *Everyman and Medieval Miracle Plays* (1993)

Cecil, A., *A Portrait of Thomas More: Scholar, Statesman, Saint* (1937)

Chambers, R. W., *The Place of Saint Thomas More in English Literature and History* (1937)
The Saga and the Myth of Sir Thomas More (1927)
Thomas More (London and Toronto, 1935)

Chambers, R. W. (ed.), *A Fifteenth Century Courtesy Book* (1914)

Chaney, E. and Mack, P. (eds), *England and the Continental Renaissance* (Woodbridge, 1990)

Charlton, K., *Education in Renaissance England* (1965)

Chaucer, Geoffrey, *The Canterbury Tales*, ed. A. C. Cawley (1989)

Chauncey, M. (Dom), *The History of the Sufferings of Eighteen Carthusians in England*, translated from the Latin (1890)

Clark, F. L., *William Warham: Archbishop of Canterbury, 1504–1532* (Oxford, 1993)

Clebsch, W. A., *England's Earliest Protestants, 1520–35* (New Haven and London, 1964)

Cobban, A. B., *The Medieval English Universities: Oxford and Cambridge to 1500* (Aldershot, 1988)

Coleman, C. and Starkey, David (eds), *Revolution Reassessed* (Oxford, 1986)

Coleman, J., *English Literature in History, 1350–1400: Medieval Readers and Writers* (1981)

Corbett, J. A., *The Papacy: A Brief History* (Princeton, 1956)

Coulton, G. G., *Art and the Reformation* (Oxford, 1928)

Craig, H., *English Religious Drama of the Middle Ages* (Oxford, 1955)

Croll, M. W., *Style, Rhetoric and Rhythm* (Princeton, 1966)

Cross, C., *Church and People 1450–1660* (Hassocks, 1976)

Daniell, David, *William Tyndale* (New Haven and London, 1994)

Davies, R., *Chelsea Old Church* (1904)

Davies, R. T., *Medieval English Lyrics* (1963)

de la Bère, R. J., *John Heywood: Entertainer* (1937)

Delany, S., *Medieval Literary Politics* (Manchester, 1990)

Doe, N., *Fundamental Authority in Late Medieval Law* (Cambridge, 1990)

Doernberg, E., *Henry VIII and Luther* (1961)

Duffy, E., *The Stripping of the Altars* (New Haven and London, 1992)

Dugmore, C. W., *The Mass and the English Reformers* (1958)

Dust, P. C., *Three Renaissance Pacifists* (New York, 1988)

Dyer, C., *Standards of Living in the Later Middle Ages* (Cambridge, 1989)

Einstein, L. N., *The Italian Renaissance in England* (New York, 1899)

Elton, G. R., *England Under the Tudors* (1955)
  'The Body of the Whole Realm' (Charlottesville, 1969)
  Policy and Police (1972)
  Reform and Renewal (Cambridge, 1973)
  Studies in Tudor and Stuart Politics and Government (1974)
  Reform and Reformation: England 1509–1558 (1977)

Emden, A. B., *An Oxford Hall in Medieval Times: Being the Early History of Saint Edmund Hall* (Oxford, 1927)

Erasmus, Desiderius, *Pilgrimages* (1849)
  Letters, trans. and ed. F. M. Nichols, 3 vols (1901–18)
  Erasmi Epistolae, Opus Epistolarum des Erasmi Roterodami, ed. P. S. Allen, 10 vols (Oxford, 1910)
  Praise of Folly, trans. John Wilson, 1668 (Oxford, 1913)
  Colloquies, trans. Roger L'Estrange (1923)
  The Education of a Christian Prince, trans. Lester K. Born (New York, 1936)
  Adages, ed. M. M. Phillips (Cambridge, 1964)

Erikson, Erik H., *Young Man Luther: A Study in Psychoanalysis and History* (1959)

Farrow, J., *The Story of Thomas More* (1956)

Fisher, J. D., *Christian Initiation: Baptism in the Medieval West* (1965)

Fishwick, H. (ed.), *Pleadings and Depositions in the Court of the Duchy of Lancaster* (Manchester, 1896)

Fleisher, M., *Radical Reform and Political Persuasion in the Life and Writings of Thomas More* (Geneva, 1973)

Flower, B. O., *The Century of Sir Thomas More* (Boston, 1896)

Fortescue, Sir J. and Chrimes, S. B. (eds), *De Laudibus Legum Angliae* (Cambridge, 1942)

Foss, E., *Judges of England* (1848–64)

Foster, G. J., *The Doctors' Commons* (1868)

Fox, A., *Thomas More: History and Providence* (Oxford, 1982)
  Politics and Literature in the Reigns of Henry VII & Henry VIII (Oxford, 1989)

Fox, A. and Guy, J., *Reassessing the Henrician Age* (Oxford, 1986)

Foxe, John, *The Acts and Monuments of John Foxe*, ed. G. Townsend and S. R. Cattley, 4 vols, 1837–41

French, Peter, *John Dee: The World of an Elizabethan Magus* (1972)

Furnivall, F. J. (ed.), *The Babees Book ... The Bokes of Nurture* (1868)

Gairdner, J., *Letters and Papers of the Reign of Henry VIII*, vols 1–5 (1880)

Gairdner, J. (ed.), *The Historical Collections of a Citizen of London* (1876)

Gardiner, H. C., *Mysteries End: An Investigation of the Last Days of the Medieval Religious Stage* (New Haven, 1946)

Gasquet, F. A., *The Eve of the Reformation* (1900)

Gee, J. A., *The Life and Works of Thomas Lupset* (New Haven, 1928)

Gest, J. M., *The Image of the Lawyer in Literature* (1913)

Gilkes, R. K., *The Tudor Parliament* (1969)

Glasser, William, *Reality Therapy* (1965)

Gleason, John B., *John Colet* (1989)

Gleason, J. H., *Justices of the Peace in Elizabethan England* (Oxford, 1969)

Gogan, Brian, *The Common Corps of Christendom: Ecclesiological Themes in the Writings of Sir Thomas More* (Leiden, 1962)

Gordon Duff, E., *Fifteenth Century Books* (Oxford, 1917)

Grant, A., *Henry VII* (1985)

Green, D. H., *Irony in the Medieval Romance* (Cambridge, 1979)

Greenblatt, S., *Renaissance Self-fashioning* (Chicago, 1980)

Guy, John A., *The Cardinal's Court: The Impact of Thomas Wolsey in the Star Chamber* (Hassocks, 1977)
  The Public Career of Sir Thomas More (Brighton, 1980)
  Tudor England (Oxford, 1988)

Gwyn, Peter, *The King's Cardinal: The Rise and Fall of Thomas Wolsey* (1990)

Haigh, Christopher, *English Reformations: Religion, Politics and Society under the Tudors* (Oxford, 1993)

Haigh, Christopher (ed.), *The English Reformation Revised* (Cambridge, 1987)

Halkin, L. C., *Erasmus* (Oxford, 1987)

Hall, E., *Chronicle*, ed. Charles Whibley (1548)

Hamilton, W. D. (ed.), *A Chronicle of England During the Reigns of the Tudors by Charles Wriothesley*, 2 vols (1875)

Hanham, A., *Richard III and his Early Historians, 1482–1535* (Oxford, 1975)

Harbison, E. H., *The Christian Scholar in the Age of the Reformation* (New York, 1956)

Hardison, O. B., *Christian Rite and Christian Drama in the Middle Ages* (Baltimore, 1965)

Hardison, O. B., Jnr., *The Enduring Monument: A Study of the Idea of Praise in Renaissance Literary Theory and Practice* (Chapel Hill, North Carolina, 1962)

Harper-Bill, C. (ed.), *The Register of John Morton, Archbishop of Canterbury, 1486–1500*, 2 vols (York, 1987 and 1990)

Harpsfield, N., *The Life and Death of Thomas More*, ed. E. V. Hitchcock (1932)

Harrington, W., *Commendacions of Matrymony* (1538)

Harrison, F. L., *Medieval Music* (1958)

Haughton, R., *The Young Thomas More* (1966)

Hawking, Stephen, *A Brief History of Time* (1988)

Hay, D., *Polydore Vergil: Renaissance Historian and Man of Letters* (Oxford, 1952)

Hay, M., *Westminster Hall and the Medieval Kings* (1995)

Hazlitt, W. C. (ed.), *One Hundred Merry Tales* (1887)

Hendricks, L., *The London Charterhouse* (1889)

Hennessy, J. P., *The Portrait in the Renaissance* (1963)

Hexter, J. H., *Reappraisals in History* (1961)
    The Vision of Politics on the Eve of the Reformation (New York, 1973)

Hilderbrand, H. J., *Erasmus and his Age* (1970)

Hill, D., *Hans Holbein* (1959)

Hilton, Walter, *The Scale of Perfection*, ed. E. Underhill (1923)
    Minor Works, ed. D. Jones (1929)

Hogrefe, P., *The Sir Thomas More Circle* (Urbana, 1959)

Holdsworth, Sir William, *A History of English Law (Vol. 2)* (1936)

Hollander, A. E. J. and Kellaway, W. (eds), *Studies in London History presented to Philip Jones* (1969)

Hollis, Christopher, *Sir Thomas More* (1936)

Home, Gordon, *Medieval London* (1927)

Hook, W. F., *Books of the Lives of the Archbishops of Canterbury* (1867)

Hope, W. H. Saint-John, *The History of the London Charterhouse from its Foundation until the Suppression of the Monastery* (1925)

Horrox, R., *Richard III: A Study of Service* (Cambridge, 1989)

Hudson, H. H., *The Epigram in the English Renaissance* (Princeton, 1947)

Hurst, G., *A Short History of Lincoln's Inn* (1946)

Hutton, R., *The Rise and Fall of Merry England* (Oxford, 1994)

Hutton, W. H., *Sir Thomas More* (1900)

Huizinga, J., *The Waning of the Middle Ages* (1924)
    Erasmus of Rotterdam (1952)

Hyll, Thomas, *A Brief and Most Pleasant Epitome of the Whole Art of Phisiognomie* (1556)

Hyma, A., *The Christian Renaissance* (New York and London, 1965)

Imray, J., *The Charity of Richard Whittington* (1968)
    The Mercers' Hall (1991)

Ives, E. W., *Faction in Tudor England* (1979)
    The Common Lawyers of Pre-reformation England (Cambridge, 1983)
    Anne Boleyn (Oxford, 1986)

Jacob, E. F., *The Fifteenth Century* (Manchester, 1930)

Jane, S., *John Colet and Marsilio Ficino* (Oxford, 1963)

Johnson, S., *A Dictionary of the English Language*, ed. R. G. Latham (1870)

Jowitt, E. and Walsh, C. (eds), *Jowitt's Dictionary of English Law. Vol. II* (1977)

Kautsky, Karl, *Thomas More and his Utopia* (1927)

Keen, M., *English Society in the Later Middle Ages 1348–1500* (1990)

Kelly, H. A., *The Matrimonial Trials of Henry VIII* (Stanford, 1976)

Kempis, Thomas à, *The Imitation of Christ*, trans. and ed. C. Bigg (1898)

Kenny, Anthony, *Thomas More* (Oxford, 1983)

Kierkegaard, S., *Fear and Trembling*, trans. W. Lowrie (Princeton, 1954)
    The Concept of Irony (1966)

Kingsford, C. L., *Prejudice & Promise in Fifteenth-Century England* (Oxford, 1925)

Kingsford, H. S., *Illustrations of Occasional Offices of the Church in the Middle Ages. From Contemporary Sources* (1921)

Kinney, A. F., *Rhetoric and Poetic in Thomas More's Utopia* (Malibu, 1979)

Knight, Sir William Stanford (ed.), *An exposition of the King's Prerogative, collected out of the great Abridgement of Justice Fitzherbert, and other old writers of the Laws of England* (1607)

Knowles, D., *The Religious Orders of England*, 3 vols (Cambridge, 1948–59)

Knowles, D. and Grimes, W. F., *Charterhouse* (1954)

Knox, D. B., *The Doctrine of the Faith in the Reign of Henry VIII* (1961)

Kristeller, P. O., *Eight Philosophers of the Italian Renaissance* (1965)

Lamond, E. S. (ed.), *A Discourse on the Common Weal of England*, by W.S., c.1548 (Cambridge, 1893)

Lane Fox, Robin, *Pagans and Christians* (Harmondsworth, 1986)

Langdon, H., *Holbein* (Oxford, 1976)

Langland, William, *Piers the Plowman*, ed. W. W. Skeat (Oxford, 1869)

Leclerq, J., *The Love of Learning and the Desire for God*, 2nd revised edition (1978)

Lee, S., *Great Englishmen of the Sixteenth Century* (1904)

Le Goff, J., *The Medieval Imagination* (Chicago and London, 1988)

Lehmberg, S. E., *The Reformation Parliament* (Cambridge, 1970)

Lewis, C. S., *English Literature in the Sixteenth Century* (Oxford, 1954)

Lewis, L. (ed.), *Symbols and Sentiments: Cross-cultural Studies in Symbolism* (1977)

Lloyd, C. and Thurley, S., *Henry VIII: Images of a Tudor King* (Oxford, 1990)

Lloyd-Jones, H. *et al.* (ed.), *History and Imagination: Essays in Honour of H. R. Trevor-Roper* (1981)

Loades, David, *The Tudor Court* (1986)

Logan, G. M., *The Meaning of More's 'Utopia'* (Princeton, 1983)

Luther, M., *Selections and Extracts*, ed. E. G. Rupp and B. Drewery (1970)

Lyell, L. and Watney, F. D. (eds), *Acts of Court of the Mercers' Company* (Cambridge, 1936)

Lyte, H. C. M., *A History of the University of Oxford from the Earliest Times to the Year 1530* (1886)

MacConica, J. K., *English Humanists and Reformation Politics under Henry VIII and Edward VI* (Oxford, 1965)

MacCulloch, Diarmaid, *Thomas Cranmer* (New Haven and London, 1996)

Machiavelli, N., *The Prince*, Everyman edition, ed. B. Penman (1981)

Mack, P., *Renaissance Argument* (Leiden, 1993)

Mackie, J. D., *The Earlier Tudors, 1485–1558* (Oxford, 1994)

Macnamara, F. (ed.), *The Miscellaneous Writings of Henry VIII* (Waltham, St Lawrence, 1924)

Maddison, F., Pelling, M., and Webster, C. (eds), *Essays on the Life & Work of Thomas Linacre* (Oxford, 1977)

Manning, A., *The Household of Sir Thomas More* (London, 1851)

Marc'hadour, Abbé Germain, *The Bible in the Works of Saint Thomas More* (Nieuwkoop, 1969)

Sir Thomas More, Knight (Melbourne, 1979)

Marius, Richard, *Luther* (1975)

Thomas More (New York, 1984)

Marshall, Peter, *The Catholic Priesthood and the English Reformation* (Oxford, 1994)

Martindale, A., *Gothic Art* (New York, 1967)

Martz, L., *Thomas More: The Search for the Inner Man* (1990)

Martz, L. and Sylvester, R. S. (eds), *Thomas More's Prayer Book* (New Haven and London, 1969)

Maskell, W. (ed.), *Monumenta Ritualia Ecclesiae Anglicanae* (1846)

Mason, A. J., *Lectures on Colet, Fisher & More* (1895)

Mason, H. A., *Humanism and Poetry in the Early Tudor Period* (1959)

Matthew, M., Sister, *Saint Thomas More* (1951)

Mattingly, G., *Renaissance Diplomacy* (1955)

Mayer, T. F., *Thomas Starkey and the Commonweal* (Cambridge, 1989)

Maynard, T., *Humanist and Hero: Life of Sir Thomas More* (New York, 1947)

Medcalf, Stephen (ed.), *The Later Middle Ages* (1981)

Merriman, R. B. (ed.), *Life and Letters of Thomas Cromwell*, 2 vols (Oxford, 1902)

Miller, Helen, *Henry VIII and the English Nobility* (Oxford, 1986)

Momsen, W. J., Alter, P., and Scribner, R. W., *The Urban Classes, the Nobility and the Reformation* (Stuttgart, 1979)

Moore, M. J. (ed.), *Quincentennial Essays on Saint Thomas More* (Boone, North Carolina, 1978)

Moorman, J. R. H., *A History of the Church of England* (1953)

More, Cresacre, *The Life and Death of Sir Thomas Moore* (1631)

Morison, S., *The Likeness of Thomas More* (1963)

Mozley, T., *Henry VII, Prince Arthur and Cardinal Morton* (1878)

Muir, Kenneth, *Life and Letters of Thomas Wyatt* (Liverpool, 1963)

Neame, Alan, *The Holy Maid of Kent* (1971)

Nelson, A. H., *The English Medieval Stage* (Chicago and London, 1974)

The Plays of Henry Medwall (Cambridge, 1980)

Newell, V., *His Own Good Daughter* (New York, 1961)

Nichols, F. M., *The Hall of Lawford Hall* (1891)

Nichols, J. G. (ed.), *The Chronicles of Calais in the Reigns of Henry VII and Henry VIII to the year 1540* (1846)

Nicolas, N. (ed.), *Privy Purse Expenses of Elizabeth of York* (1830)

Norbrook, D., *Politics and Poetry in the English Renaissance* (1984)

Norrington, Ruth, *In the Shadow of a Saint: Lady Alice More* (Waddesdon, 1983)

O'Neil, F. W. (ed.), *The Golden Legend. The Lives of the Saints*, originally trans. by William Caxton from Jacobus (Cambridge, 1914)

Oberman, H. A., *The Harvest of Medieval Theology* (Cambridge, Mass., 1963)

Forerunners of the Reformation (1967)

Masters of the Reformation (Cambridge, 1981)

Oberman, H. A. and Trinkaus, C. (eds), *The Pursuit of Holiness* (Leiden, 1974)

Olin, J. C. (ed.), *Interpreting Thomas More's Utopia* (New York, 1989)

Oman, Sir C., *A History of the Art of War in the Sixteenth Century* (1937)

Ong, Walter J., *Ramus: Method and the Decay of Dialogue* (Cambridge, Mass., 1958)

Rhetoric, Romance and Technology (1971)

Orme, Nicholas, *English Schools in the Middle Ages* (1973)

Ormrod, W. M., *The Reign of Edward III* (New Haven and London, 1990)

Osler, W., *Thomas Linacre* (Cambridge, 1908)

Owst, G. R., *Literature and the Pulpit in Medieval England* (Cambridge, 1933)

Pace, R., *De Fructu qui ex Doctrina Percipitur*, ed. and trans. F. Manley and R. S. Sylvester (New York, 1967)

Panofsky, E., *Gothic Architecture and Scholasticism* (New York, 1957)

Pantin, W. A., *Canterbury College Oxford*, 4 vols (Oxford, 1947)

Pantin, W. A. (ed.), *A Medieval Collection of Latin and English Proverbs and Riddles, from the John Rylands Latin MS. 394* (Manchester, 1930)

Pattison, B., *Music and Poetry of the English Renaissance* (1948)

Paul, J. E., *Catherine of Aragon and Her Friends* (1966)

Paul, L. A., *Sir Thomas More* (1953)

Pendrill, C., *Old Parish Life in London* (Oxford, 1937)

Petrarch, *The Triumphs of Petrarch*, trans. Henry Parker, Lord Morley, 1544 (reprinted, 1887)

I trionfi di Francesco Petrarca, ed. C. Pasqualigo (Venezia, 1874)

Pickthorn, K., *Early Tudor Government*, 2 vols (Cambridge, 1934)

Pineas, R., *Thomas More and Tudor Polemics* (1968)

Bibliography

Plato, *The Parmenides of Plato*, ed. Mary Louise Gill and P. Ryan (Indianapolis, 1996)

Pocock, J. A., *The Machiavellian Moment: Florentine Political Thought and the Atlantic Republican Tradition* (Princeton, 1975)

Pohl, F. J., *Amerigo Vespucci: Pilot Major* (New York, 1945)

Pollard, A. F., *The Reign of Henry VII from Contemporary Sources* (1913) *Wolsey*, intro.
> by G. R. Elton (1965)

Potter, R., *English Morality Plays* (1975)

Prosser, E., *Drama and Religion in the English Mystery Plays* (Stanford, 1961)

Rabelais, F., *Gargantua & Pantagruel*, trans. J. M. Cohen (Harmondsworth, 1955)

Rashdall, H., Powicke, F. M. and Emden, A. B., *The Universities of Europe in the Middle Ages* (Oxford, 1987)

Rastell, John, *Verse Life of Thomas Becket* (1520)
The Four Elements, ed. R. Coleman (Cambridge, 1971)

Rawlings, J., *A History of the Origins and the Doctrines of Baptism and the Eucharist* (1863)

Reed, A. W., *Early Tudor Drama* (1926)

Reynolds, E. E., *Saint John Fisher* (1955)
The Trial of Saint Thomas More (1964)
Sir Thomas More (1965)
Thomas More and Erasmus (1965)
The Field is Won: The Life and Death of St Thomas More (1968)

Reynolds, E. E. and O'Sullivan, D., *Thomas More's London* (1980)

Ridley, Jasper, *The Statesman and the Fanatic: Thomas Wolsey and Thomas More* (1982)

Ro: Ba., *The Lyfe of Syr Thomas More Sometyme Lord Chancellor of England*, ed. E. V. Hitchcock and P. G. Hallet (1950)

Rogers, K., *Old Cheapside and Poultry* (1931)

Rogers, N., *England in the Fifteenth Century* (Stamford, 1994)

Rope, H. E. G., *Fisher and More* (1935)

Roper, William, *The Life of Sir Thomas More*, ed. S. W. Singer (1822)
The Lyfe of Sir Thomas Moore, Knight, ed. Elsie V. Hitchcock, Early English Text Society Edition (1935)
The Life of Thomas More. In Two Early Tudor Lives, ed. R. S. Sylvester and D. P. Harding (New Haven and London, 1962)

Roskell, J. S., *The Commons and Their Speakers in the English Parliaments* (Manchester, 1965)

Ross, C., *Patronage, Pedigree and Power in Late Medieval England* (Gloucester, 1979)
Richard III (1981)

Rosser, G., *Medieval Westminster 1200–1540* (Oxford, 1989)

Roston, M., *Biblical Drama in England* (1968)

Routh, E. M. G., *Sir Thomas More and his Friends: 1477–1535* (1934)

Rubin, M., *Corpus Christi: The Eucharist in Late Medieval Culture* (Cambridge, 1991)

Rupp, G., *Thomas More* (1978)

Russell, B., *A History of Western Philosophy* (New York, 1945)

Samman, N., *The Henrician Court during Cardinal Wolsey's Ascendancy* (unpublished thesis, University of Wales, November 1988)

Sargeant, Daniel, *Thomas More* (1934)

Scarisbrick, J. J., *Henry VIII* (1976)
The Reformation and the English People (Oxford, 1984)

Scattergood, V. G., *Politics and Poetry in the Fifteenth Century* (1971)

Schoeck, R. J., *Erasmus of Europe. The Making of a Humanist, 1467–1500*, vol. 1 (Edinburgh, 1990); *The Prince of Humanists, 1501–1536*, vol. 2 (Edinburgh, 1993)
Erasmus grandescens (Nieuwkoop, 1988)

Bibliography

Schofield, J., *Medieval London Houses* (New Haven and London, 1994)

Seebohm, F., *The Oxford Reformers* (1867)

Seigel, J. C., *Rhetoric and Philosophy in Renaissance Humanism* (Princeton, 1968)

Seton-Watson, R. W. (ed.), *Tudor Studies Presented to Pollard* (1924)

Shakespeare, William, *The Complete Works*, ed. Stanley Wells and Gary Taylor (Oxford, 1986)

Shebbeare, C. E., *Sir Thomas More* (1930)

Sheridan, R. and Ross, A., *Grotesques and Gargoyles: Paganism in the Medieval Church* (Newton Abbot, 1975)

Sidney, P., *The Defense of Poetry* (1787)

Simmons, T. F. (ed.), *Lay Folks Mass Book* (1879)

Singleton, C., *Dante: The Divine Comedy. Vol. II, The Inferno, Commentary* (1971)

Skelton, J., *The Complete Poems*, ed. P. Henderson (1931)

Slavin, A. J. (ed.), *Humanism, Reform and the Reformation in England* (New York, 1969)

Smith, C., *Medieval Law Teachers and Writers, Civilian and Canonist* (Ottawa, 1975)

Smith, H. M., *Pre-reformation England* (1938)

Smith, Lucy T. (ed.), *The Itinerary of John Leyland in or about the years 1535–1543* (1907-10)

Smith, R. L., *John Fisher and Thomas More: Two English Saints* (1935)

Sneyd, C. A. (ed.), *A Relation of the Island of England* (1847)

Somerville, R., *The Duchy of Lancaster* (1946)

Squibb, G. D., *The High Court of Chivalry* (Oxford, 1959)

Stanier, R. S., *History of Magdalen College School* (Oxford, 1940)

Stapleton, T., *Life of Sir Thomas More By Thomas Stapleton*, ed. E. E. Reynolds (1966)

Starkey, David, *The Reign of Henry VIII* (1985)

  Henry VIII: A European Court in England (1991)

Starnes, Colin, *The New Republic* (Waterloo, Ontario, 1990)

Stevens, John, *Music and Poetry in the Early Tudor Court* (1961)

Stewart, Agnes M., *Margaret Roper or the Chancellor and his Daughter* (1875)

  The Life and Letters of Sir Thomas More (1876)

Stobbart, Lorraine, *Utopia: Fact or Fiction?* (Stroud, 1992)

Stow, J., *A Survey of London* (revised edn, 1602), ed. H. Morley (1912)

Streitberger, W. R., *Court Revels* (Toronto and London, 1994)

Strickland, A., *Lives of the Queens of England* (1840–48)

Strong, R., *Holbein and Henry VIII* (1967)

Struever, N. S., *The Language of History in the Renaissance* (Princeton, 1970)

Sturge, C., *Cuthbert Tunstall* (1938)

Sullivan, F. and M. P., *Moreana: Materials of the Study of Saint Thomas More*, 3 vols (Los Angeles, 1985)

Surtz, Edward L., *The Works and Days of John Fisher* (Cambridge, Mass., 1967)

Swanson, R. N., *Church and Society in Late Medieval England* (Oxford, 1989)

Sylvester, R. S. (ed.), *Saint Thomas More: Action and Contemplation* (New Haven and London, 1972)

Sylvester, R. S. and Marc'hadour, G. P. (eds), *Essential Articles for the Study of Thomas More* (Hamden, Conn., 1977)

Taylor, F. and Roskell, J. S., *Gesta Henrici Quinti. The Deeds of Henry the Fifth* (Oxford, 1975)

Teetgen, A. B., *The Footsteps of Thomas More* (London and Edinburgh, 1930)

Thomas, A. H. and Thomley, I. D. (eds), *The Great Chronicle of London* (1938)

Thomas, Keith, *Religion and the Decline of Magic* (1971)

  Rule and Misrule in the Schools of Early Modern England (Reading, 1976)

Bibliography

Thomas More College, *Thomas More Quincentenial Conference* (Covington, Kentucky, 1978)

Thompson, Craig R., *The Translation of Lucian by Erasmus and Saint Thomas More* (New York, 1940)

Universities in Tudor England (Washington, 1959)

Thompson, E. M., *The Carthusian Order in England* (1930)

Thompson, J. A. F., *Towns and Townspeople* (Gloucester, 1988)

Thompson, P., *Sir Thomas Wyatt and his Background* (1964)

Thrupp, S. L., *The Merchant Class of Medieval London* (Chicago, 1948)

Thurston, H. and Attwater, D., *Butler's Lives of the Saints* (1956)

Tracy, J. D., *Erasmus: The Growth of a Mind* (Geneva, 1972)

Trapp, J. B., *Erasmus, Colet and More: The Early Tudor Humanists and their Books* (1991)

Trapp, J. B. and Herbrüggen, H. S., '*The King's Good Servant*' (1977)

Ullmann, W., *Medieval Political Thought* (Harmondsworth, 1979)

Unwin, G., *The Gilds and the Companies of London*, 2nd edn (1925)

Vergil, Polydore, *The Anglica Historia*, ed. D. Hay (1950)

Vespucci, A., *The First Four Voyages of Vespucci*, trans. M.K. (1885)

The Letters of Amerigo Vespucci, trans. C.R. (1894)

Visser, F. T., *A Syntax of the English Language of Saint Thomas More* (Louvain, 1946)

Walker, G., *John Skelton and the Politics of the 1520s* (Cambridge, 1988)

Walter, J. W., *Sir Thomas More: His Life and Times* (1840)

Walters, H. B., *London Churches at the Reformation* (1939)

Warren, F. (ed.), *Sarum Missal* (1911)

Watney, John, *The Hospital of Saint Thomas of Acon* (1892)

An Account of the Mistery of Mercers of the City of London (1914)

Wegg, J., *Richard Pace: Tudor Diplomatist* (1932)

Weiss, R., *Humanism in England during the Fifteenth Century* (Oxford, 1941)

Welsford, E. E. H., *The Fool: His Social and Literary History* (1935)

Whiting, R., *The Blind Devotion of the People* (Cambridge, 1989)

Whittington, Robert, *Vulgaria* (1521)

Wickham, G., *The Medieval Theatre* (1974)

Williams, C. H., *England under the Tudors* (1925)

Williams, P., *The Tudor Regime* (Oxford, 1979)

Willow, M. E., *The English Poems of Saint Thomas More* (Nieuwkoop, 1974)

Wilson, D., *England in the Age of Thomas More* (1978)

Wilson, K. J., *Incomplete Fictions: The Formation of English Renaissance Dialogue* (Washington, 1985)

Woltman, A., *Holbein and his Time* (1872)

Woodhouse, J., *Castiglione* (Edinburgh, 1978)

Woodhouse, R. I., *The Life of Archbishop Morton* (1895)

Wornum, R., *Some Account of the Life and Works of Hans Holbein* (1867)

Wortley, B. A. (ed.), *The Spirit of the Common Law: A Representative Collection of the Papers of Richard O'Sullivan* (Tenbury Wells, 1965)

Wrench, M., *The Story of Thomas More* (1961)

Wyatt, Sir Thomas, *Complete Poems*, ed. R. Rebolz (1978)

Collected Poems, ed. Joost Daalder (1975)

Zeeveld, W. G., *Foundations of Tudor Policy* (Cambridge, Mass., 1948)

Bibliography

Articles

The most important source of information remains *Moreana* (Angers, 1963–), the periodical devoted to More studies. Other articles of particular relevance are listed below.

Allen, P. R., 'Utopia and European Humanism', *Renaissance Studies*, 9 and 10 (New York, 1962–3)

Bossy, J., 'The Mass as a Social Institution', *Past and Present* (1983)

Brann, E. V., '"An Exquisite Platform": Utopia', *Interpretation* (Nieuwkoop, 1972)

Brown, B. K., 'Sir Thomas More, Lawyer', *Fordham Law Review* (New York, November 1931)

Carpenter, C. Nan, 'St Thomas More and Music: The Epigrams', *Renaissance Quarterly*, 30 (New York, 1977)

Cassier, E., 'Pico Della Mirandola', *Journal of the History of Ideas*, 46 (Lancaster, Pennsylvannia, 1985)

Crewe, J. V., 'The Encomium Moriae of William Roper', *English Literary History*, 55, 2 (Baltimore, 1988)

Crosset, J. 'More and Seneca', *Philological Quarterly*, 40, 4 (Iowa, October 1961)

Crossland, J., 'Lucian in the Middle Ages', *Modern Language Review*, 25 (Cambridge, 1930)

Delcourt, J., 'Saint Thomas More and France, *Traditio*, 5 (New York, 1947)
'Some Aspects of Thomas More's English', in *Essays and Studies*, 21 (Oxford, 1935)

Derrett, J., 'Thomas More and the Legislation of the Corporation of London', *Guildhall Miscellany* (1963)

Gee, J. A., 'The Second Edition of Utopia. Paris 1517', *The Yale University Library Gazette*, 7, 4 (Yale, April 1933)

Gordon, W. M., 'The Monastic Achievement and More's Utopia', *Mediéval et Humanistic*, New Series, no. 9 (Cambridge, 1979)

Harper-Bill, C., 'Archbishop John Morton and the Province of Canterbury. 1486–1500', *The Journal of Ecclesiastical History*, 29, 1 (January 1978)

Hastings, M., 'The Ancestry of Sir Thomas More', *Guildhall Miscellany* (1961)

Hexter, J. H., 'The Loom of Language and the Fabric of Imperatives: The case of Il Principe and Utopia', *The American Historical Review*, 69, 4 (New York, July 1964)

Jones, M., 'Ritual, Drama and the Social Body in the Late Medieval English Town', *Past and Present*, 98 (1983)

Kelly, D. R. 'The Conscience of "The King's Good Servant"', *Thought*, 52 (New York, 1977)
'Legal Humanism and the Sense of History', *Studies in the Renaissance*, vol. 13 (New York, 1966)

Kinney, D., 'More's Letter to Dorp: Remapping the Trivium', *Renaissance Quarterly*, 24, 2 (New York, 1981)

Lehmberg, S. E., 'Sir Thomas More's Life of Pico Della Mirandola', *Studies in the Renaissance* (New York, 1956)

Marsh, T. N., 'Humour and Invective in Early Tudor Polemic', *Rice Institute Pamphlets*, 44 (Houston, 1957)

Martz, L., 'Thomas More: The Sacramental Life', *Thought* (New York, 1977)

Miles, L., 'The Literary Artistry of Thomas More: The Dialogue of Comfort', *Studies in English Literature*, 6, 1 (Nieuwkoop, 1966)
'With a Coal? The Composition of Thomas More's Dialogue of Comfort', *Philological Quarterly*, 45, 2 (Iowa, April 1966)

Nagal, A. F., 'Lies and the Lamentable Inane: Contradiction in More's Utopia', *Renaissance Quarterly*, 26 (New York, 1973)

Nelson, William, 'The Teaching of English in Tudor Grammar Schools', *Studies in Philology*, 49, 2 (North Carolina, April 1952)

Pineas, R., 'Thomas More's Use of Humour as a Weapon of Religious Controversy', *Studies in Philology*, 58, 2, part 1 (North Carolina, April 1961)

'Thomas More's Use of Dialogue as a Weapon of Religious Controversy', *Studies in the Renaissance*, vol. 2 (New York, 1960)

Ramsay, G. D., 'A Saint in the City: Thomas More at the Mercers' Hall in London', *English Historical Review*, 97, 1 (1982)

Reed, A. W., 'John Clement and his Books', *The Library*, 4th series, 6 (1926)

Scarisbrick, J. J., 'Thomas More: The King's Good Servant', *Thought* (New York, 1977)

Schoeck, R. J., 'The Place of Sir Thomas More in Legal History and Tradition: Some Notes and Observations', *The American Journal of Jurisprudence*, 23 (Notre-Dame, 1978)

'Sir Thomas More and Lincoln's Inn Revels', *Philological Quarterly*, 24 (Iowa, October 1950)

Starkey, David, 'Court, Council and Nobility in Tudor England', in *Princes, Patronage and Nobility*, ed. R. G. Asch and A. M. Birke (London, 1991)

'Communications: A Reply', *The Historical Journal*, 31, 4 (London, 1988)

Strayer, J. R. and Queller, D. G., 'Studia Gratiana. XV', *Essays on Medieval Law* (Bologna, 1972)

Surtz, E., 'St Thomas More and his Utopian Embassy of 1515', *The Catholic Historical Review*, 34, 3 (Washington, D.C., 1953)

Sutton, A., 'Order and Fashion in Clothes: The King, his Household and the City of London at the End of the 15th Century', *Textile History*, 22, 2 (Autumn 1991)

Thompson, E., 'The Humanism of More Reappraised', *Thought* (New York, 1977)

Weisinger, H., 'Ideas of History During the Renaissance', *Journal of the History of Ideas* (Lancaster, Pennsylvania, 1985)

Notes

I: This Dark World

1 Hilton, *Scale of Perfection*, 251
2 Fisher, 161
3 Lane Fox, 435
4 Yale, vol. 13, *Treatise on the Passion*, 42
5 Quoted in Keith Thomas, *Religion and the Decline of Magic*, 69

II: Pretty Plays of Childhood

1 Thrupp, 144
2 Stow, 284
3 E. E. Reynolds, 'More, Coverdale and Cromwell', *Moreana*, vol. 3(10), 77
4 Bridgett, 6
5 There is another Thomas Graunger, merchant and later alderman, who is likely to have been Thomas More's uncle.
6 Quoted in Starkey, 'Court, Council and Nobility in Tudor England', 191
7 *Pico della Mirandola*, 4
8 Reynolds, *The Field is Won*, 18
9 Sutton, 'Order and Fashion in Clothes', 263
10 Sullivan, vol. 3, 315
11 Yale, vol. 3 (2), 254
12 *The English Works of Sir Thomas More*, 165
13 Yale, vol. 6, 313
14 E. E. Reynolds, 'Relict of Sir John', *Moreana*, vol. 5 (19–20), 25
15 Thrupp, 134
16 Ibid., 136
17 Yale, vol. 8, 492
18 Yale, vol. 12, 159

19 Yale, vol. 6, 94
20 Yale, vol. 11, 208
21 Quoted in Orme, 138
22 Quoted in de la Bère, 68
23 Yale, vol. 12, 114
24 Ibid., 116–17
25 Ibid., 115
26 Quoted in Thrupp, 202
27 Sneyd, 20–2
28 Ibid., 21
29 Ibid., 22
30 Ibid., 42

III: St Anthony's Pigs

1 Yale, vol. 12, 46
2 Quoted in Orme, 119
3 Pendrill, 4–6
4 Stow, 259
5 Ibid., 194
6 Chaucer, 376
7 Roper, ed. Singer, 3
8 Quoted in William Nelson, 'The Teaching of English in Tudor Grammar Schools', 124–5
9 Ibid., 124
10 Quoted in Wegg, 129
11 Chaucer, 376
12 Quoted in Pattison, 10
13 Translated in Wegg, 104
14 Yale, vol. 11, 159
15 Taken from Pantin, *Latin and English Proverbs and Riddles*, 14–23
16 Quoted in Carole Weinberg, 'Thomas More and the Use of English in Early Tudor Education', *Moreana*, vol. 15 (59–60), 24
17 William Nelson, 'Teaching of English', 134
18 Yale, vol. 8, 468
19 Quoted in Stanier, 41
20 Langland, 44
21 Erikson, 75
22 Quoted in Orme, 140
23 Ibid., 129
24 Quoted in R. L. de Molen, 'Pueri Christi Imitatio: The Festival of the Boy-Bishop in Tudor England', *Moreana*, vol. 12 (45), 20
25 Cresacre More, 18
26 Stow, 101
27 Ibid.

28 Ibid., 195
29 Ibid.
30 Yale, vol. 11, 12
31 Ibid., 99
32 Yale, vol. 5, 60
33 Yale, vol. 11, 177

IV: Cough Not, Nor Spit

1 Sneyd, 25
2 Quoted in Stevens, 318
3 Sneyd, 98
4 Ibid., 100
5 Ibid., 101
6 Quoted in Wegg, 5
7 Roper, ed. Hitchcock, 5
8 Furnivall, 134
9 Chambers, *A Fifteenth Century Courtesy Book*, 15
10 Quoted in Walter, 4
11 Johnson
12 Harper-Bill, *The Register of John Morton*, 10, 20 and 65
13 Foss, 66
14 Bacon, *History of the Reign of King Henry the Seventh*, 199–200
15 Quoted in Mozley, 13
16 Yale, vol. 4, 60
17 Yale, vol. 2, 91
18 Roper, ed. Hitchcock, 5
19 Ibid.
20 *Fulgens and Lucrece*, lines 1057 and 1217, quoted in A. H. Nelson, *The Plays of Henry Medwall*
21 Cresacre More, 20

V: Set on His Book

1 Quoted in Lyte, 180
2 Pantin, *Canterbury College Oxford*, vol. 4, 145
3 Quoted in Howard Baker, 'Thomas More at Oxford', *Moreana*, vol. 11 (43–4), 7–8
4 Yale, vol. 6, 132
5 Trapp and Herbruggen, 52
6 Yale, vol. 8, 197
7 Yale, vol. 7, *Letter Against Frith*, 251
8 Yale, vol. 11, 208, 215 and 212
9 Yale, vol. 9, 67
10 Cresacre More, 9
11 Sullivan, vol. 3, 148

12 Yale, vol. 8, 447
13 Cresacre More, 9
14 Erasmus, *Epistolae*, vol. 2, 328
15 Quoted in Campbell, 100
16 Yale, vol. 15, *Letter to Martin Dorp*, 28
17 Ibid., 36
18 *To the Nobility of the German Nation*, in Luther, *Selections*, 46
19 White, Michael, and Gribbin, John, *Stephen Hawking: A Life in Science* (1992), 290
20 Ibid., 252
21 Hawking, 175
22 Stubbs, quoted in Holdsworth, 129
23 Erasmus, *Praise of Folly*, 116
24 Quoted in Ong, *Ramus*, 56
25 Yale, vol. 15, *Letter to Martin Dorp*, 28 and 30
26 Quoted in J. Derrett, 'The Trial of Sir Thomas More', in Sylvester and Marc'hadour, 72
27 Quoted in Ro: Ba., 73
28 Quoted in Rashdall, Powicke and Emden, vol. 3, 414
29 Thrupp, 142
30 Pantin, *Canterbury College Oxford*, vol. 4, 228
31 Chaucer, *General Prologue*, lines 289–90
32 Quoted in Cobban, 373
33 Erasmus, *Epistolae*, vol. 4, 16
34 *The Correspondence of Sir Thomas More*, 3
35 Erasmus, *Epistolae*, vol. 4, 21
36 *The English Works of Sir Thomas More*, ciii–civ
37 Ibid.
38 Quoted in Willow, 18
39 Quoted in A. H. Nelson, *The English Medieval Stage*, 174
40 Quoted in Potter, 44
41 Quoted in Cawley, xviii
42 Quoted in Anglo, 67
43 Quoted in Home, 14

VI: Duty is the Love of Law

1 Erasmus, *Epistolae*, vol. 4, 17
2 Quoted in Thrupp, 318
3 Ives, *The Common Lawyers*, 7
4 Erasmus, *Epistolae*, vol. 1, 460

5 Roper, ed. Hitchcock, 51
6 Quoted in Holdsworth, 498
7 Ibid., 494
8 Quoted in Ives, *The Common Lawyers*, 156 and 170
9 Stapleton, 14
10 Quoted in Holdsworth, 512
11 Ibid., 550–1
12 Ibid.
13 Ibid., 552
14 Quoted in D. R. Kelly, 'The Conscience of "The King's Good Servant"', 294
15 Yale, vol. 10, 37
16 Roper, ed. Sylvester and Harding, 221
17 Ives, *The Common Lawyers*, 37
18 Ibid.
19 Quoted in Foss, 114
20 Quoted in D. R. Kelly, 'The Conscience of "The King's Good Servant"', 294
21 Quoted in R. J. Schoeck, 'More, Sallust and Fortune', *Moreana*, vol. 17 (65–6), 108
22 Quoted in D. R. Kelly, 'The Conscience of "The King's Good Servant"', 64
23 Quoted in Pickthorn, vol. 1, 135
24 Quoted in John Headley, 'More Against Luther: On Laws and Magistrates', *Moreana*, vol. 4 (15–16), 215–16
25 Yale, vol. 5, 280

VII: Most Holy Father

1 Quoted in Sneyd, 77
2 John B. Gleason, 28
3 Cresacre More, 21
4 Yale, vol. 7, *Supplication of Souls*, 200
5 *The Correspondence of Sir Thomas More*, 545
6 Ibid., 150
7 Yale, vol. 6, 86 and 92
8 Yale, vol. 4, 216
9 Yale, vol. 15, *Letter to a Monk*, 212
10 Quoted in Roper, ed. Hitchcock, 87
11 Yale, vol. 8, 1011
12 Quoted in Charles Baudelaire, *Selected Writings on Art and Literature* (1972), 191
13 Ralph Keen and Daniel Kinney, 'Thomas More and the Classics',

Moreana, vol. 22 (86), 154 and 151
14 1 Kings 15:22
15 Yale, vol. 3 (2), 276
16 Erasmus, *Epistolae*, vol. 4, 17
17 Yale, vol. 3 (2), 278
18 Stapleton, 8
19 Cresacre More, 27
20 Quoted in Stevens, 240

VIII: We Talk of Letters

1 Yale, vol. 3 (2), 294
2 Erasmus, *Epistolae*, vol. 1, 274
3 *The Correspondence of Sir Thomas
   More*, 9
4 Erasmus, *Epistolae*, vol. 2, 331
5 Quoted in Maddison, Pelling and
   Webster, xxv
6 Yale, vol. 12, 121
7 Quoted in Maddison, Pelling and
   Webster, xvii
8 All quotations from Erasmus,
   Colloquies, trans. Roger L'Estrange
9 Ibid., 57–8
10 Ibid., 135
11 Erasmus, *Epistolae*, vol. 2, 34
12 Stapleton, 11
13 Romans 3:28
14 Quoted in Jane, 49
15 D. Wilson, 2
16 Quoted in Brooks, 10
17 Erasmus, *Letters*, vol. 1, 26
18 Ibid., 20
19 Quoted in Halkin, 5
20 Ibid., 6
21 Erasmus, *Epistolae*, vol. 4, 14
22 Quoted by Halkin, 47
23 Yale, vol. 8, 177
24 Translated by Halkin, 26
25 Erasmus, *Epistolae*, vol. 1, 266
26 I am indebted for this suggestion to
   Dr David Starkey

IX: If You Want to Laugh

1 Erasmus, *Epistolae*, vol. 1, 296
2 Yale, vol. 15, *Letter to the University
   of Oxford*, 132
3 Ibid., 136
4 Erasmus, *Adages*, 183
5 Boswell, 52
6 Yale, vol. 3 (2), 252

7 Ibid., 202
8 Boswell, 153
9 Ibid.
10 Erasmus, *Epistolae*, vol. 1, 425
11 Erasmus, *Epistolae*, vol. 2, 483
12 Yale, vol. 3 (2), 166
13 Thomas à Kempis, 243

X: The Wine of Angels

1 Roper, ed. Hitchcock, 6
2 Cresacre More, 29
3 Erasmus, *Epistolae*, vol. 3, 17
4 Stow, 392
5 Ibid., 391
6 Yale, vol. 4, 232
7 Boutrais, 19
8 Chauncey, 40
9 Ibid., 44
10 Ibid., 45
11 Yale, vol. 8, 37
12 Thomas à Kempis, 212
13 Ibid., 287
14 Ibid., 90
15 Ibid., 249
16 Yale, vol. 4, 98
17 Erasmus, *Epistolae*, vol. 4, 18
18 Augustine, 213
19 Yale, vol. 15, *Letter to a Monk*, 302
20 Hilton, *Scale of Perfection*, 95
21 Hilton, *Minor Works*, 19
22 Ibid., 28
23 *The Correspondence of Sir Thomas
   More*, 4
24 Augustine, 761
25 Ibid., 597
26 *Pico della Mirandola*, 15, 16 and 24
27 Cresacre More, 32–2
28 *Pico della Mirandola*, 11
29 Ibid.
30 Ibid., 53
31 *The works of Sir Thomas More*, ed.
   Rastell
32 Quoted by Cassier, 'Pico Della
   Mirandola', 38
33 Yale, vol. 9, 159
34 *The Correspondence of Sir Thomas
   More*, 523
35 Willow, 22; Ames, 184
36 *The works of Sir Thomas More*, ed.
   Rastell
37 *The Correspondence of Sir Thomas*

More, 4
38 *The works of Sir Thomas More*, ed. Rastell
39 Roper, ed. Sylvester and Harding, 199
40 *The Correspondence of Sir Thomas More*, 7
41 Ibid.

XI: Holy, Holy, Holy!

1 Brigden, 11
2 Yale, vol. 6, 148
3 Quoted in Marshall, 42
4 Ibid., 36
5 Yale, vol. 8, 603
6 Yale, vol. 13, *Treatise on the Passion*, 143
7 Yale, vol. 9, 51
8 Quoted in Sneyd, 23
9 Surtz, *John Fisher*, 13
10 Stow, 126–7

XII: Craft of the City

1 Roper, ed. Sylvester and Harding, 199
2 Yale, vol. 3 (2), 192
3 Ibid., 186
4 Erasmus, *Epistolae*, vol. 6, 18
5 Erasmus, *Epistolae*, vol. 1, 458
6 *The Merry Wives of Windsor*, III, 3, 67–8
7 Blench, 125
8 Stow, 255–6
9 Reed, 'John Clement and his Books'
10 Quoted in Harrison, 198
11 Erasmus, *Epistolae*, vol. 1, 422
12 Ibid., 421
13 Lucy Smith, 106–7
14 Yale, vol. 15, *Letter to a Monk*, 286
15 Ibid.
16 Ibid., 288
17 Duffy, 68
18 Quoted in *Medieval English Theatre*, no. 1 (1979), 9
19 Quoted in Roston, 25
20 Quoted in Ames, 184
21 Quoted in Watney, *Account of the Mistery of Mercers*, 53
22 Lane Fox, 84
23 Unwin, 103
24 Watney, *The Hospital of Saint Thomas of Acon*, 77

25 This, and other citations from the Mercer records, are to be found in *Acts of Court of the Mercers' Company*, ed. Lyell and Watney, 329–35
26 Erasmus, *Epistolae*, vol. 1, 462

XIII: Milk and Honey

1 Hall, 422
2 Duffy, 'The Spirituality of John Fisher', in Bradshaw and Duffy, 212
3 Hall, 507
4 Erasmus, *Epistolae*, vol. 1, 450
5 Castiglione, 299
6 Hall, 503
7 Yale, vol. 3 (2), 104
8 Ibid., 106
9 Ibid.
10 Erasmus, *Epistolae*, vol. 1, 460
11 Erasmus, *Praise of Folly*, 4
12 John B. Gleason, 233
13 Ibid., 221
14 *The Correspondence of Sir Thomas More*, 15
15 Ibid.
16 Quoted in French, 53
17 Erasmus, *Epistolae*, vol. 4, 517–18
18 Skelton, 294
19 Ibid., 293
20 John B. Gleason, 226
21 Ibid., 232
22 Seebohm, 162
23 Ibid., 163
24 Ibid., 170
25 Owst, 244
26 Ibid., 246
27 Sylvester and Marc'hadour, 610
28 Ames, 214
29 Roskell, 295
30 *The English Works of Sir Thomas More*, 94
31 Yale, vol. 5, 474
32 Erasmus, *Epistolae*, vol. 4, 20
33 Roper, ed. Hitchcock, 9

XIV: A Jolly Master-woman

1 Quoted in *The English Works of Sir Thomas More*, vol. 2, 1
2 Thomas Bailey, quoted in Sullivan, vol. 1, 40
3 Quoted in Stewart, *The Life and*

Letters of Sir Thomas More, 21
4 Yale, vol. 8, 605
5 Ibid.
6 Quoted in Stewart, *The Life and Letters of Sir Thomas More*, 272
7 Yale, vol. 12, 220
8 Cresacre More, 127
9 Yale, vol. 12, 169
10 Ibid.
11 Ibid., 277
12 Ibid., 118
13 For this and other information about Alice More, I am indebted to the pioneering research within Ruth Norrington's *In the Shadow of a Saint: Lady Alice More*
14 Erasmus, *Epistolae*, vol. 1, 476
15 Erasmus, *Epistolae*, vol. 4, 19
16 Ibid.
17 Erasmus, *Epistolae*, vol. 1, 19
18 Norrington, 138–9
19 Yale, vol. 11, 217
20 Yale, vol. 12, 169
21 Yale, vol. 13, *Treatise on the Passion*, 8
22 Yale, vol. 9, 83
23 Letter to Cranevelt, quoted in *Moreana*, vol. 31 (117), 37
24 Erasmus, *Epistolae*, vol. 2, 421
25 Owst, 388
26 Yale, vol. 5, 212
27 Quoted in Bernard Fish, 'English Spiritual Writers', in Sylvester and Marc'hadour, 519
28 Augustine, 873
29 R. Brown, vol. 2, 72
30 *The Utopia of Sir Thomas More*, 230
31 *The Correspondence of Sir Thomas More*, 121
32 Clarence H. Miller, 'Thomas More's Letters to Frans van Cranevelt', *Moreana*, vol. 31 (120), 25
33 Carole Weinberg, 'Thomas More and the Use of English in Early Tudor Education', *Moreana*, vol. 15 (59–60), 26
34 Erasmus, *Epistolae*, vol. 4, 577
35 *The Correspondence of Sir Thomas More*, 122
36 Kenny, 18
37 Erasmus, *Epistolae*, vol. 4, 578
38 Yale, vol. 3 (2), 280

XV: Kings' Games

1 Erasmus, *Epistolae*, vol. 1, 488
2 Ames, 186
3 Ibid., 215
4 Ibid., 187
5 Cresacre More, 50
6 Quoted in Roskell, 325
7 Quoted in Baker, vol. 2, 80
8 Yale, vol. 4, 38
9 Yale, vol. 3 (1), 100
10 Yale, vol. 9, 223–4
11 Foxe, vol. 4, 199
12 Ibid.
13 Yale, vol. 6, 318
14 Ibid., 320
15 Ibid., 321
16 Ibid., 323
17 Ibid.
18 Yale, vol. 9, 126
19 Yale, vol. 15, *Letter to Martin Dorp*, 12
20 Quoted in Adams, 61
21 Yale, vol. 3 (2), 256
22 Ibid., 286
23 Ibid., 600
24 Ibid., 290
25 Yale, vol. 2, 7
26 Ibid., 8
27 Ibid., 44
28 Quoted in Caxton's preface to Higden's *Chronicle*, 1482
29 Yale, vol. 2, 8
30 Ibid., 52
31 Ibid., 54
32 Peter Brown, 311
33 Quoted in R. E. Reiter, 'On the Genre of Thomas More's *Richard III*', *Moreana*, vol. 7 (25), 7
34 Ibid., 30
35 Yale, vol. 2, 81
36 Ibid., 56
37 Ibid., 55
38 I am indebted for this information to Mr Nicholas Barker
39 Yale, vol. 2, 47
40 *Richard III*, III, 4, 31–2

XVI: The Best Condition of a Society

1 Quoted in Surtz, 'St Thomas More', 278
2 *The Correspondence of Sir Thomas More*, 20–1
3 Ibid.
4 Quoted in David Waters, *The Art of Navigation in Elizabethan and Early Stuart Times* (1958), 13
5 Yale, vol. 12, 301
6 Quoted in Ramsay, 'A Saint in the City', 287
7 Erasmus, *The Education of a Christian Prince*, 215
8 Erasmus, *Epistolae*, vol. 2, 93
9 *The Correspondence of Sir Thomas More*, 20–1
10 Quoted by Chambers, *Thomas More*, 119
11 Yale, vol. 4, 44
12 Wegg, 68
13 Surtz, 'St Thomas More', 293
14 Yale, vol. 4, 52
15 Ibid., 102
16 Acts 4:32
17 Plato, *Republic*, ed. J. Burnet, 592
18 Yale, vol. 4, 112
19 Starnes, 9
20 Yale, vol. 8 (1), 938
21 See Pohl
22 Yale, vol. 4, 50
23 Ibid., 150
24 Coleridge, *The Rime of the Ancient Mariner*, lines 587 and 569
25 Quoted in A. F. Kinney, 2
26 Yale, vol. 4, 195
27 Cresacre More, 235
28 Erasmus, *Epistolae*, vol. 4, 21
29 See Klibansky, R. (ed.), *Plato's Parmenides in the Middle Ages and the Renaissance* (1943), 313ff
30 Introduction by Mary Louise Gill to Plato, *Parmenides*, 104 and 81

XVII: Wholly a Courtier

1 Erasmus, *Epistolae*, vol. 2, 200
2 Yale, vol. 3 (2), 270
3 Cavendish, 25
4 Skelton, 320 and 312

5 R. Brown, vol. 1, 110
6 Ibid., 111
7 Ibid., 267–8
8 Watney, *The Hospital of Saint Thomas of Acon*, 97
9 Ibid., 98
10 Yale, vol. 12, 213
11 Erasmus, *Epistolae*, vol. 2, 331
12 Stow, 422
13 I am indebted for this information to Dr David Starkey, particularly his 'Court, Council and Nobility in Tudor England' and 'Communications: A Reply'
14 J. A. Guy, 'The Privy Council: Revolution or Evolution?', in Coleman and Starkey, 66
15 Erasmus, *Epistolae*, vol. 2, 317
16 Ibid., 430
17 *The Correspondence of Sir Thomas More*, 86
18 Erasmus, *Epistolae*, vol. 2, 504
19 Watney, *The Hospital of Saint Thomas of Acon*, 87
20 Erasmus, *Epistolae*, vol. 2, 414
21 Ibid., 259
22 Hamilton, vol. 1, 10–11
23 Erasmus, *Epistolae*, vol. 3, 46
24 R. Brown, vol. 2, 113
25 Quoted in C. H. Williams, 217
26 Vergil, Book XXIV, 9
27 Pickthorn, vol. 2, 38
28 Ibid., 40
29 Quoted in Brigden, 130
30 Boswell, 285
31 Shakespeare, 891–2
32 R. Brown, vol. 2, 75
33 Ibid.
34 Ramsay, 286
35 *The Correspondence of Sir Thomas More*, 101–10
36 I am indebted for this insight to Trapp, 68
37 Yale, vol. 3 (2), 300
38 Ibid., 298
39 Erikson, 215
40 Quoted in Luther, 19ff.
41 Sullivan, vol. 2, 251
42 Erasmus, *Epistolae*, vol. 3, 286

43 I am indebted for this information to the researches of Dr David Starkey
44 Erasmus, *Epistolae*, vol. 3, 111
45 Yale, vol. 8, 591
46 Starkey, 'Court, Council and Nobility', 183
47 Ibid.
48 Wegg, 130
49 Ibid., 130-1
50 Erasmus, *Praise of Folly*, 142

XVIII: He Sat upon a Throne of Gold

1 R. Brown, vol. 1, 85-6
2 Ibid., 91
3 Roper, ed. Sylvester and Harding, 209
4 *The Correspondence of Sir Thomas More*, 111
5 R. Brown, vol. 2, 312
6 Hall, vol. 1, 319
7 Quoted in Anglo, 108
8 Quoted by Schoeck in Sylvester, 36
9 Roper, ed. Sylvester and Harding, 221
10 Cavendish, 184
11 Ibid., 183
12 I am indebted for this information to the researches of Dr David Starkey
13 Horrox, 255
14 John Husee quoted in Miller, 79
15 Erasmus, *Praise of Folly*, 141
16 Quoted in Ives, *Faction in Tudor England*, 3
17 Quoted in Ives, *Anne Boleyn*, 25
18 Castiglione, 35-6
19 Roper, ed. Sylvester and Harding, 201-2
20 Ibid.
21 Yale, vol. 7, *Letter Against Frith*, 111-12
22 Yale, vol. 12, 220
23 Castiglione, 178
24 Gairdner, *Letters and Papers*, vol. 3, 2636
25 Castiglione, 138
26 Wyatt, *Collected Poems*, 101-2
27 Ibid., 21
28 *The English Works of Sir Thomas More*, 84
29 Ibid.
30 Ibid., 87

XIX: My Poor Mind

1 Yale, vol. 12, 169
2 *The Correspondence of Sir Thomas More*, 371
3 Ibid., 287 and 285
4 Ibid., 157
5 Ibid., 160
6 Ibid., 142
7 Ibid., 393
8 Ibid., 278
9 Ibid., 299
10 Ibid., 366
11 Ibid., 280
12 Ibid., 281
13 Ibid., 158
14 Ibid., 289
15 Ibid., 285
16 Ibid., 312-14
17 Ibid., 253
18 R. Brown, vol. 2, 215-16
19 Quoted in Gwyn, 415
20 Guy, *The Cardinal's Court*, 44
21 Yale, vol. 9, 104
22 Erasmus, *Epistolae*, vol. 3, 547
23 Yale, vol. 15, *Letter to the University of Oxford*, 138
24 Ibid., 145
25 Erasmus, *Epistolae*, vol. 3, 547
26 Yale, vol. 15, *Letter to a Monk*, 270
27 Ibid., 294 and 302
28 Yale, vol. 3 (2), 494
29 Ibid., 648
30 Ibid., 644
31 Ibid., 628
32 Yale, vol. 8, 191
33 Quoted in de la Bère, 23-4
34 Ibid., 21
35 Ibid., 26
36 Quoted in Axton and Happe, 124
37 Ibid., 76

XX: Eques auratus

1 Quoted in H. Meulon, 'Une Intaille Antique', *Moreana*, vol. 3 (10), 7
2 I am indebted for the details here to Sydney Anglo's account in *Spectacle, Pageantry and Early Tudor Policy*
3 Ibid., 140
4 Ibid., 146
5 Ibid., 154
6 Quoted in G. R. Elton, 'Thomas More,

Councillor', in Sylvester, *Saint Thomas More*, 121

7 Yale, vol. 15, Introduction to *Letter to Martin Dorp*, xxxvi
8 Quoted in Yale, vol. 5, 799. A footnote in a commentary by J. M. Headley
9 Yale, vol. 3 (2), 186
10 Quoted in H. Schulte-Herbrüggen, 'Three Additions to Thomas More's Correspondence', *Moreana*, vol. 20 (79–80), 37
11 Quoted in Routh, 108
12 Quoted in *Moreana*, vol. 20 (79–80), 38
13 Chaucer, *General Prologue*, line 46
14 *The English Works of Sir Thomas More*, 73
15 Ibid., 86
16 Ibid.
17 Yale, vol. 2, 76
18 Quoted in Ames, 56
19 Quoted in G. R. Elton, 'Thomas More, Councillor', in Sylvester, *Saint Thomas More*, 104
20 *The Correspondence of Sir Thomas More*, 248
21 Quoted in Routh, 112–13
22 Yale, vol. 12, 88
23 Yale, vol. 8, 900
24 Ibid., 815
25 Ibid., 816
26 Quoted in Bridgett, 190
27 Ro: Ba., 110
28 Hamilton, 13
29 Ames, 56
30 Chambers, *Thomas More*, 198

XXI: I Am Like Ripe Shit

1 Quoted in Erikson, 87
2 Quoted in Ackroyd, 149
3 Quoted in Erikson, 140
4 Quoted in Gwyn, 481
5 Quoted in Scarisbrick, *Henry VIII*, 112
6 Roper, ed. Sylvester and Harding, 235
7 Macnamara, 29
8 Quoted in Yale, vol. 5, 310
9 Francis Atterbury, quoted in Sullivan, vol. 1, 33
10 Ibid.
11 Quoted in Yale, vol. 5, 770

12 Ibid., 482, 484, 514 and 516
13 Ibid., 2
14 Quoted in Luther, 150
15 Yale, vol. 5, 118
16 Luther, 572
17 Yale, vol. 5, 50
18 Yale, vol. 166
19 Ibid., 130 and 332
20 Quoted in Erikson, 200
21 Ibid., 238
22 Yale, vol. 5, 418
23 Erikson, 198
24 Yale, vol. 5, 430
25 Harpsfield, 86
26 Ibid., 87
27 *The English Works of Sir Thomas More*, 72
28 Quoted in Owst, 534
29 *The English Works of Sir Thomas More*, 77
30 Ibid., 76
31 Ibid., 84
32 Ibid., 90
33 Ibid., 85–6
34 Yale, vol. 5, 438
35 Yale, vol. 9, 133
36 Quoted in *The English Works of Sir Thomas More*, 97
37 Yale, vol. 14, 127
38 From Rastell, *The Four Elements*
39 Quoted in W. H. Hutton, 45
40 Erikson, 245

XXII: Long Persuading and Privy Labouring

1 Roper, ed. Sylvester and Harding, 204
2 Ibid., 205
3 Quoted in Ridley, 144
4 Quoted in Pickthorn, vol. 2, 60, n. 3
5 Ibid., 62
6 Roper, ed. Sylvester and Harding, 206
7 Ibid., 207
8 C. H. Williams, 141
9 Ibid.
10 Ibid.
11 Roskell, 329
12 Ibid., 330
13 Merriman, vol. 1, 313
14 Roper, ed. Sylvester and Harding, 207
15 Foss, 212
16 *The Correspondence of Sir Thomas*

More, 278

17 G. Marc'hadour, '1966 remembers 1466', *Moreana*, vol. 3 (12), 108
18 Stow, 186
19 Yale, vol. 2, 44
20 *The Correspondence of Sir Thomas More*, 307
21 Roper, ed. Hitchcock, 22
22 Erasmus, *Epistolae*, vol. 4, 267
23 Quoted in Guy, *The Cardinal's Court*, 45
24 Miller, 20
25 Bridgett, 178
26 Quoted in Pickthorn, vol. 2, 19
27 Erasmus, *Epistolae*, vol. 5, 576
28 *The Correspondence of Sir Thomas More*, 289
29 Ibid., 300
30 Ibid., 294
31 Ibid.
32 Ibid., 518
33 Ibid.
34 Ibid., 300
35 Clarence H. Miller, 'Thomas More's Letters to Frans van Cranevelt', *Moreana*, vol. 31 (120), 36
36 Quoted in Chambers, *Thomas More*, 210
37 Quoted in Somerville, 7–8
38 Gwyn, 195
39 Fishwick, 174
40 Ibid., 138
41 Ibid., 145
42 Quoted in Margaret Hastings, 'Sir Thomas More: Maker of English Law?', in Sylvester and Marc'hadour, 113
43 Guy, *Public Career*, 29
44 Hastings, in Sylvester and Marc'hadour, 110
45 Reed, *Early Tudor Drama*, 172
46 Quoted in Pineas, *Thomas More and Tudor Polemics*, 29
47 Quoted in Sturge, 132
48 Yale, vol. 7, *Letter to Bugenhagen*, 40
49 Ibid., 22
50 Ibid., 74
51 Hazlitt, 71
52 Ibid., 66
53 Ibid., 75
54 Ibid., 80
55 Ibid., 75

XXIII: Thy Foolish Face

1 Erasmus, *Epistolae*, vol. 6, 443
2 R. A. Sisson, 'The Treasures of Time', Chelsea Old Church pamphlet, 1968
3 Kenny, 44
4 Thomas à Kempis, 78
5 Yale, vol. 12, 164
6 Ibid., 165
7 Matthew 10:36
8 Quoted in Hollis, 48
9 Ibid.
10 Harpsfield, 68
11 Yale, vol. 12, 187
12 Cresacre More, 42
13 Sylvester and Marc'hadour, 518
14 Ibid., 519
15 *The Correspondence of Sir Thomas More*, 422
16 Ibid., 423
17 Ibid.
18 Ibid.
19 Pollard, in Sylvester and Marc'hadour, 424
20 Ibid.
21 Quoted by Frank Carpinelli in Moore, 8
22 Baker, vol. 1, 56
23 Ro: Ba., 129
24 Ibid.
25 Cresacre More, 50
26 Ibid., 124
27 Quoted in Chambers, *Thomas More*, 183
28 Cresacre More, 43
29 Yale, vol. 12, 182
30 Ro: Ba., 55
31 Welsford, 167
32 1 Corinthians 3:19
33 Yale, vol. 15, *Letter to a Monk*, 289
34 Quoted in Walter, 372
35 Quoted in Welsford, 398
36 Erasmus, *Colloquies*, 78
37 Yale, vol. 11, 206
38 Yale, vol. 8, 127

XXIV: You Are but One Man

1 Scarisbrick, *Henry VIII*, 156
2 Stapleton, 71
3 Erasmus, *Epistolae*, vol. 4, 14
4 Sullivan, vol. 3, 19
5 Erasmus, *Epistolae*, vol. 4, 14

6 *De Arte Amandi*, line 513
7 Hyll
8 Cavendish, 48
9 Mattingly, 37
10 Yale, vol. 6, 221
11 *The Correspondence of Sir Thomas More*, 493
12 Ibid., 494
13 Leviticus 18:16
14 Leviticus 20:21
15 *The Correspondence of Sir Thomas More*, 494
16 Ibid., 495
17 Roper, ed. Sylvester and Harding, 210
18 C. H. Williams, 121
19 *The Correspondence of Sir Thomas More*, 498
20 Ibid.
21 Ibid., 524–5
22 Ibid., 498
23 Ibid., 499
24 Guy, *Public Career*, 206
25 Cavendish, 83
26 Quoted in H. A. Kelly, 81
27 Ibid., 82
28 Quoted in Bridgett, 202
29 *The Correspondence of Sir Thomas More*, 409–13
30 Yale, vol. 6, 120
31 Quoted in Adams, 293

18 Ibid., 130
19 Ibid., 331
20 Ibid., 228
21 Ibid., 143–4
22 Ibid., 149
23 Ibid., 153
24 Yale, vol. 8, 67
25 Yale, vol. 6, 296–7
26 Ibid., 378
27 Yale, vol. 10, 108
28 Yale, vol. 6, 548
29 Ibid., 24
30 Ibid., 409
31 Yale, vol. 7, *Supplication of Souls*, 415
32 Ibid., 440
33 Ibid.
34 Quoted in Daniell, 242
35 Yale, vol. 7, *Supplication of Souls*, 111
36 Ibid., 224
37 See Le Goff, 87ff.
38 Yale, vol. 7, *Supplication of Souls*, 189
39 Peter Brown, 240
40 Daniell, 224
41 Yale, vol. 7, *Supplication of Souls*, 137
42 Ibid., 167
43 Ibid., 203

XXV: Foolish Frantic Books

1 Yale, vol. 8, 1166
2 Yale, vol. 6, 34
3 Ibid., 269
4 Ibid., 328
5 *The Correspondence of Sir Thomas More*, 374
6 Yale, vol. 8, 1175
7 Guy, *Public Career*, 13
8 Yale, vol. 8, 5–6
9 Ibid., 1139
10 Yale, vol. 10, 40
11 Yale, vol. 8, 1011
12 Yale, vol. 6, 193
13 Ibid., 25
14 Ibid., 35
15 Ibid., 38
16 Ibid., 192
17 Ibid., 213, 325, 333, 366, 72–3

XXVI: We Poor Worldly Men of Middle Earth

1 Cavendish, 102
2 Ibid., 183
3 Hamilton, vol. 1, 16
4 Harpsfield, 48
5 Stapleton, 21
6 Yale, vol. 10, xxiv
7 Ibid., 328
8 Whittington
9 *The Correspondence of Sir Thomas More*, 495
10 Ibid.
11 Chambers, *Thomas More*, 231
12 Erasmus, *Epistolae*, vol. 8, 294
13 Yale, vol. 12, 29
14 Quoted in Lehmberg, *The Reformation Parliament*, 79
15 Yale, vol. 9, 49
16 Guy, *Public Career*, 115

17 F. E. Zapatka, 'Thomas More and Thomas Darcy', *Moreana*, vol. 18 (71–2), 9
18 Guy, *The Cardinal's Court*, 100
19 Miller, 111
20 Yale, vol. 5, 278
21 Quoted in Spelman, ed. Baker, vol. 2, 39
22 Ibid.
23 Roper, ed. Sylvester and Harding, 222
24 Quoted in Spelman, ed. Baker, vol. 2, 43
25 Yale, vol. 8, 912
26 Baker, vol. 2, 199
27 Cresacre More, 218
28 Roper, ed. Hitchcock, 40–1
29 Cresacre More, 233–4
30 Ibid., 220
31 Yale, vol. 9, 119
32 Ibid., 117
33 Ibid., 118
34 Ibid.
35 Ibid.
36 Ibid.
37 Sylvester and Marc'hadour, 81
38 Yale, vol. 8, 14
39 Ibid., 15–16
40 Ibid., 16–17
41 Quoted in Brigden, 180
42 Yale, vol. 8, 876
43 Ibid., 897–903
44 Ibid., 897
45 Ibid., 876
46 Ibid., 1529
47 Quoted in Elton, *Policy and Police*, 219
48 Yale, vol. 8, 814–15
49 Foxe, vol. 4, 621
50 Yale, vol. 8, 23
51 Yale, vol. 6, 409
52 Ibid.
53 Guy, *Tudor England*, 26
54 Yale, vol. 8, 590
55 Yale, vol. 9, 113
56 Foxe, vol. 4, 485
57 Campbell, 200
58 Ibid.
59 Yale, vol. 8, 18
60 Ibid., 20
61 Ibid., 21
62 Ibid., 22
63 Ibid., 1046
64 Ibid., 11
65 Ibid., 710
66 Hamilton, vol. 1, 17
67 Quoted in Ridley, 257–8
68 Yale, vol. 8, 139
69 Ibid., 135
70 Ibid., 327
71 Ibid., 169
72 *An Answer to Sir Thomas More's Dialogue*, ed. H. Walter (Cambridge, 1850), 151
73 *The Supper of the Lord*, ed. H. Walter (Cambridge, 1850), 231
74 Yale, vol. 9, 5
75 Ibid.
76 Ibid., 10
77 Yale, vol. 8, 399
78 Ibid., 912
79 Ibid., 741
80 Ibid., 742
81 Ibid., 121
82 Ibid., 338
83 Ibid., 48
84 Ibid., 51
85 Ibid., 271
86 Ibid., 479
87 Cresacre More, 224
88 Roper, ed. Sylvester and Harding, 221
89 Erasmus, *Epistolae*, vol. 10, 261
90 Ibid.
91 Hastings, 'The Ancestry of Sir Thomas More', 101
92 Yale, vol. 8, 389

XXVII: Infinite Clamour

1 *The Correspondence of Sir Thomas More*, 489
2 Ibid.
3 Yale, vol. 12, 161
4 H. A. Kelly, 176
5 Scarisbrick, *Henry VIII*, 259
6 Bergenroth, vol. 2, 727
7 Ibid.
8 Quoted in Gwyn, 626
9 Cavendish, 108
10 Ibid.
11 Scarisbrick, 'Thomas More: The King's Good Servant', 259
12 Quoted in J. A. Guy, 'Thomas More

and Christopher St Germain: The Battle of the Books', *Moreana*, vol. 21 (83–4), 9
13 Ives, *Anne Boleyn*, 336
14 Quoted in Neame, 137
15 Quoted in Bridgett, 234
16 Quoted in Guy, *Public Career*, 160
17 Ibid., 157
18 Quoted in Edward Surtz, 'Henry VIII's great matter in Italy', *Moreana*, vol. 13 (52), 61
19 Guy, *Public Career*, 157
20 Ibid.
21 Ibid., 158
22 Chambers, *Thomas More*, 388
23 Bergenroth, vol. 1, 114
24 Ibid.
25 Ives, *Anne Boleyn*, 168
26 Lehmberg, 138
27 Ibid.
28 Fox, *Thomas More*, 188
29 Ives, *Anne Boleyn*, 190
30 Neame, 156
31 Ibid.
32 Ibid., 157
33 MacConica, 129
34 Guy, *Public Career*, 198–9
35 Ibid.
36 Ibid., 199
37 Haigh, *English Reformations*, 113
38 Quoted in Lehmberg, 150
39 Quoted in Bridgett, 235
40 Bergenroth, vol. 1, 446
41 Yale, vol. 8, 36
42 Yale, vol. 9, 145

XXVIII: All the Beasts of the Woods

1 Cresacre More, 244–5
2 Maynard, 186
3 Roper, ed. Hitchcock, 54–5
4 Yale, vol. 3 (2), 302
5 Roper, ed. Sylvester and Harding, 227
6 Erasmus, *Epistolae*, vol. 10, 32
7 Yale, vol. 9, 47
8 Ibid., 47–8
9 Ro: Ba., 269
10 Yale, vol. 9, 123
11 Ibid., 121
12 Ibid., 122

13 Yale, vol. 7, *Letter Against Frith*, 234
14 Yale, vol. 9, 123
15 Yale, vol. 7, *Letter Against Frith*, 233
16 Yale, vol. 9, 158
17 Ibid.
18 Ibid., 51
19 Yale, vol. 9, 70
20 Brigden, 208
21 H. A. Kelly, 195
22 Quoted in Thomas, *Religion and the Decline of Magic*, 472–7
23 Ibid., 472
24 Quoted in Neame, 74
25 Ibid., 115
26 Ibid., 253
27 Bergenroth, vol. 2, 1153
28 Quoted in Neame, 174
29 *The Correspondence of Sir Thomas More*, 482–3
30 Ibid., 481
31 Ibid., 482
32 Guy, *The Cardinal's Court*, 133
33 Bindoff, 11
34 Guy, *The Cardinal's Court*, 134
35 Hamilton, vol. 1, 17
36 Neame, 200
37 *The Correspondence of Sir Thomas More*, 483
38 Reynolds, *The Trial of Saint Thomas More*, 49
39 Ives, *Anne Boleyn*, 217
40 Roper, ed. Sylvester and Harding, 229–30
41 *The Correspondence of Sir Thomas More*, 484
42 Ibid., 485
43 Ibid.
44 Neame, 207
45 *The Correspondence of Sir Thomas More*, 465
46 Ibid., 466
47 Neame, 204
48 Ibid.
49 Merriman, 361
50 *The Correspondence of Sir Thomas More*, 486
51 Quoted by Brigden, 212
52 Quoted in Fox and Guy, 116
53 *The Correspondence of Sir Thomas More*, 546

54 Yale, vol. 12, 107
55 Ibid., 108

XXIX: The Wrath of the King Means Death

1 Stapleton, 159
2 Yale, vol. 10, 15
3 Ibid., 16
4 Ibid., 187
5 Yale, vol. 11, 4
6 Ibid., 5
7 Ibid., 60
8 Ibid., 159–60, 175
9 Bergenroth, vol. 2, 1153
10 *The Correspondence of Sir Thomas More*, 486
11 Scarisbrick, *Henry VIII*, 323
12 *The Correspondence of Sir Thomas More*, 469
13 Ibid., 468
14 Bridgett, 322
15 *The Correspondence of Sir Thomas More*, 470
16 Ibid., 480
17 Ibid.
18 Ibid., 488
19 Ibid.
20 Neame, 315
21 *The Correspondence of Sir Thomas More*, 497
22 Ibid., 489
23 Ibid., 492
24 Ibid., 491
25 Ibid., 492
26 Ibid.
27 Roper, ed. Sylvester and Harding, 233
28 Ibid., 234
29 Ibid.
30 Ibid.
31 Ibid.
32 Ibid., 235
33 Ibid., 235–6
34 Quoted in Neame, 317
35 Roper, ed. Sylvester and Harding, 236
36 Ibid., 237
37 Ibid., 236
38 Ibid., 237
39 Reynolds, *The Trial of Saint Thomas More*, 40
40 Quoted in MacCulloch, 142
41 Ibid., 116
42 Yale, vol. 13, *Treatise on the Passion*, 70
43 Ibid., 75
44 Ibid., 119
45 Ibid., 36
46 Ibid., 173
47 Ibid., 174
48 Ibid., 177

XXX: The Weeping Time

1 Roper, ed. Sylvester and Harding, 241
2 Ibid., 238
3 Ibid.
4 *The Correspondence of Sir Thomas More*, 502
5 Ibid., 521
6 Ibid., 503
7 Ibid.
8 Ibid., 504
9 Ibid.
10 Ibid., 504–5
11 Ibid., 505
12 Ibid.
13 Ibid., 507
14 Roper, ed. Sylvester and Harding, 240
15 Quoted in Reynolds, *The Field is Won*, 300
16 Roper, ed. Sylvester and Harding, 239
17 Quoted in Stewart, *The Life and Letters of Sir Thomas More*, 219
18 Roper, ed. Sylvester and Harding, 239
19 Ro: Ba., 119
20 Ibid.
21 Ibid.
22 I am indebted for this information to Sonja Johnston of the Tower of London.
23 Yale, vol. 12, 277
24 *The Correspondence of Sir Thomas More*, 507
25 Yale, vol. 12, 6
26 *The Correspondence of Sir Thomas More*, 527
27 Ibid., 549
28 Ibid., 516

29 Ibid., 542
30 Hamilton, vol. 1, 24
31 Neame, 335–6
32 Ibid., 338
33 *The Correspondence of Sir Thomas More*, 543
34 Ibid., 531
35 Kempis, 78, 127, 223, 302
36 Yale, vol. 12, 124
37 Ibid., 125
38 Ibid., 127
39 Ibid., 101
40 Ibid., 228
41 Ibid., 200–1
42 Ibid., 318
43 Ibid., 85
44 Ibid., 86
45 Ibid., 11
46 Ibid., 273
47 Ibid., 271
48 Ibid., 311
49 *The Correspondence of Sir Thomas More*, 508
50 Yale, vol. 12, 42
51 *The Correspondence of Sir Thomas More*, 515
52 Ibid., 516
53 Ibid., 514
54 Roper, ed. Sylvester and Harding, 239
55 Ibid.
56 Ibid., 243
57 Yale, vol. 12, 219–20
58 Ibid., 277
59 Roper, ed. Sylvester and Harding, 244
60 *Hamlet*, II, 1, 65
61 *The Correspondence of Sir Thomas More*, 512
62 Ibid.
63 Ibid., 513
64 Ibid., 515
65 Ibid., 532
66 Ibid., 514
67 Ibid., 529
68 Ibid.
69 Hamilton, vol. 1, 25
70 *The Correspondence of Sir Thomas More*, 548
71 Ibid., 548

72 Ibid., 540
73 Ibid., 549
74 Ibid., 550
75 Yale, vol. 14, 301
76 Ibid., 417
77 Ibid., 249
78 Ibid., 55
79 *The Correspondence of Sir Thomas More*, 557
80 Yale, vol. 13, *Treatise on the Blessed Body*, 201
81 Walters, 329–31
82 Ibid., 605

XXXI: Peck of Troubles

1 Hendricks, 141
2 Ibid., 147
3 *The Correspondence of Sir Thomas More*, 552
4 Ibid.
5 Ibid.
6 Ibid., 553
7 Ibid., 555
8 Roper, ed. Sylvester and Harding, 242
9 Quoted in Walter, 234
10 *The Correspondence of Sir Thomas More*, 550
11 Ibid., 557
12 Ibid., 559
13 Quoted by Reynolds, *The Trial of Saint Thomas More*, 98
14 Ibid., 166–7
15 Ro: Ba., 119
16 Quoted in Surtz, 30
17 Manuscript Room of the British Library, M.S., Titus B.I.f.475r

XXXII: Call Forth Sir Thomas More

1 The proceedings of Thomas More's trial have been collated from the following sources: Roper, ed. Sylvester and Harding; Reynolds, *The Trial of Saint Thomas More*; Derrett, 'The Trial of Thomas More', in *Guildhall Miscellany*; Chambers, *Thomas More*

XXXIII: The King is Good Unto Me

1 Quoted in Lane Fox, 422
2 Roper, ed. Sylvester and Harding, 251
3 Ibid.
4 Cresacre More, 343
5 Ibid., 251–2
6 Ro: Ba., 120
7 Yale, vol. 13, *Instructions and Prayers*, 228
8 Ibid., 230
9 Roper, ed. Sylvester and Harding, 252–3
10 Chambers, *Thomas More*, 348
11 Reynolds, *The Trial of Saint Thomas More*, 155
12 Yale, vol. 2, 81
13 Chambers, *Thomas More*, 349
14 H. V. Morton, *In Search of London* (1951), 68
15 Stapleton, 189

Index

Index